Michael Amoah is a Visiting Fellow at the Firoz Lalji Centre for Africa, Institute of Global Affairs, The London School of Economics and Political Science. He is the author of *Nationalism, Globalization and Africa*; *A Decade of Ghana* and *Reconstructing the Nation in Africa* (I.B.Tauris).

'Michael Amoah's new book is a significant interrogation of Pan-Africanism in an era where the forces of nationalism and globalism compete and ruin the prospects of stability, progress and unity. In a series of case studies, Amoah lets us know that no romanticism will save Pan-Africanism; nor will elite and long-lasting presidentialisms; but that the very idea of Pan-Africanism must take into account corruptions within and competitive forces without.'

– **Stephen Chan OBE, Professor of International Relations, SOAS University of London**

'Michael Amoah takes a dispassionate look at approaches to political problems adopted by African states, under the auspices of the African Union. His discussion of what he calls "the new pan-Africanism" emphasizes its pragmatic qualities – romantic notions of the first generation of African leaders have been largely set aside. He is particularly interested on how notions of the nation state relate to institutions of global governance, and the ways which sitting heads of state manipulate constitutions to remain in power. Where international pressures are applied by other African states, they are limited in scope, and are likely to be compromised by the fact that the heads of state of the countries involved are also doing all they can not to be removed from office. Amoah's clearly written book is a good antidote for overblown claims about the emergence of African developmental states or a continent-wide "renaissance". It is a timely and sobering read.'

– **Tim Allen, Professor of Development Anthropology, London School of Economics**

'The book sets a scene for an important discussion on a much-needed alteration of political infrastructure of the African continent.'

– **Thembisa Fakude, Researcher, Research Centre, Al Jazeera Center for Studies**

THE NEW PAN-AFRICANISM

Globalism and the Nation State in Africa

MICHAEL AMOAH

Published in 2019 by
I.B.Tauris & Co. Ltd
London • New York
www.ibtauris.com

Copyright © 2019 Michael Amoah

ISBN (HB): 978 1 78453 331 1
ISBN (PB): 978 1 83860 049 5
eISBN: 978 1 83860 048 8
ePDF: 978 1 83860 051 8

A full CIP record for this book is available from the British Library
A full CIP record is available from the Library of Congress

Library of Congress Catalog Card Number: available

Typeset in Garamond Three by OKS Prepress Services, Chennai, India
Printed and bound in Great Britain

CONTENTS

LIST OF MAPS

PREFACE

Nationalism is an expression of one's identity. Every individual has an identity; it is impossible not to have one. Each individual is also a citizen of the globe irrespective of their identity. Also, they interact with others or refuse to interact based on that identity, perceived or real. A state of belonging is therefore a universal attribute. Global society is politically arranged in the form of national identities, hence the most pervasive identity document being the passport. Consequently, the global citizen's endeavour to have nationality is as persistent as the justification for the continuity of the nation state in the era of globalism and globalization. There will always be inter-national relations, and, with that, the politics of nation-groups or supranationalism, hence the unending discussion on the continuity or viability of the nation state in a globalized web of dependencies and interdependencies. Herewith, so long as country-specific institutional maladies, such as the global financial downturn generated by Wall Street, can generate a globalized domino effect, each country's matter is necessarily everyone's matter on the globe. Therefore, it is incumbent on institutions of global governance not to ignore individual nation state problems as if they were separate from global ones. To that effect, the age-old United Nations Security Council (UNSC) as an institution of global governance attends to almost every conflict across the globe regardless of the cause – and increasingly so in an era of heightened globalism, conflicts and interconnected impacts.

The central theme of this book is how extended periods of rule by particular African heads of state have either precipitated or contributed to conflict or political crisis in their respective countries, generating attention and resolutions from the international institutions of global governance. The New Pan-Africanism is Africa's answer to the systems and institutions of global governance when it comes to handling African crises, which for a working definition, could be put simply as pragmatic doses of case-by-case solutions to real-time African problems, taking into account the live geopolitical issues, the wider context of international politics and lessons from the historical context. The issue of heads of state prolonging their presidencies by constitutional manoeuvres, elections or other means is a major cause of conflict on the African continent. What currently prevents the African Union (AU) from dealing with the problem is that a large number of African heads of state are themselves guilty, and do not want to tackle the issue head-on.

This book examines the evolution of the New Pan-Africanism by exploring a number of key cases. The discussion of the New Pan-Africanism, in the context of international politics and institutions of global governance, tests the viability of the nation state in a globalized world, addressing conflict situations in Africa that are nationalized and globalized at the same time. It also explores what has been Africa's response to each political crisis within the context of international politics, in other words, what amounts to the New Pan-Africanism.

While the New Pan-Africanism may have begun with the launch of the AU in July 2002, it is the period from the last quarter of 2010 to the present day that forms the time frame for the eight selected case studies in this book. The international response to Côte d'Ivoire's general elections in October–November 2010 (discussed at length in chapter 5 of my *Nationalism, Globalization, and Africa* (2011)) and the 2011 Libyan Civil War that erupted during the Arab Spring both generated peculiar dilemmas which have contributed to shaping the New Pan-Africanism.

Each country case study in this book revolves around a chosen presidential personality who has governed over a period of at least two presidential terms and intended to extend or has already extended their presidency, and the political crisis generated as a consequence. Hence the narrative in each case begins with a snapshot or concise summary of the state of nationalism in that country; followed by the political context prior to the ascent of the chosen presidential personality under discussion; followed by what ensued in their tenure that generated the political crisis or conflict; followed by what ensued during and/or after the crisis, plus how the New Pan-Africanism has unfolded in each case, or what Africa is doing to fix or resolve the crisis. Each case study includes analyses of the international political economy and the accompanying security challenges. The background to the newest African country, South Sudan, prior to its secession from Sudan and independence on 9 July 2011, has been treated in Amoah (2011, pp. 47–61) and is therefore not repeated in this book.

Chapter 1 is the introduction and Chapter 10 presents my conclusions, with the eight alphabetically ordered case studies in between. Chapter 1 sets the tone by discussing 19 examples of African heads of state who exceeded the maximum presidential terms set at the time they first took office, and how they managed to do so. Chapter 10 gives the gist of where the AU is, in terms of capability to handle political crises or conflict, plus a mention of exemplary success stories so far, and recommendations as to what the AU may wish to do to defuse the ticking time bombs.

As to the choreography, it has to be said that, wherever possible, Africa's response to the systems and institutions of global governance, and even to Africa's local institutions, regarding conflict situations, does not follow a particular script. Rather, Africa has responded on a case-by-case basis in whatever manner is deemed convenient or practicable in the circumstances, taking into account the context while making use of the measures and provisions on offer from the institutions of global governance, and balancing assistance with whatever leverage Africa can exert against the peculiarities on the ground, bearing in mind that some political actors and situations are amenable while others are recalcitrant, depending on the peculiarity of the network among the presidential club. Even where there are established principles and procedures to follow within the AU, the sub-regional presidential kingpins still make the ultimate decisions, as seen in East Africa in particular. For example, anything to do with Burundi or South Sudan which come under the auspices of the East African Community (EAC) would have President Museveni of Uganda pulling the strings.

The case may be different in the Economic Community of West African States (ECOWAS) sub-region, where Burkina Faso and Mali are located and where the ordinary populace have played proactive key roles in the process of resolving their presidential conflicts, regardless of the culpability of France in generating the problem. Ghana and Gambia do not have case study chapters in this book, but the Gambian presidential election held on 1 December 2016 ousted the incumbent Yahya Jammeh who had been head of state for 22 years. Although Jammeh wanted to challenge the result in accordance with Article 49 of the Gambian Constitution, ECOWAS resisted him and forced him to relinquish power and leave for exile in Equatorial Guinea, paving the way for Adama Barrow the opposition leader to become president. The Ghanaian presidential election on 7 December 2016 was beautifully held, and saw the incumbent replaced by the opposition candidate Nana Akufo-Addo without sub-regional intervention. The 2017 Liberian elections also saw a peaceful outcome and the first democratic handover in 73 years since independence in 1847.

The Central African Republic, which sits within the Economic Community of Central African States (ECCAS), has had a similar experience of ordinary citizens responding positively to conflict resolution measures alongside the UN and other international organizations. In the case of Mali, the French intervention of January 2013 was an extremely useful game-changer that opened up the playing field for subsequent due process to restore the country to constitutional and democratic order, even if securing the lives and economic interests of the few thousand French nationals residing in Bamako formed one of the key motivations for the French intervention.

In Libya, however, it is quite clear that the US and its North Atlantic Treaty Organization (NATO) allies pulled the strings for Muammar al-Gaddafi's removal. This is an example of Western imperial powers at work, although Africa does not dance to their tune when it comes to resolving African problems. In this particular case, the Western powers forged a UNSC resolution under false pretences to impose a no-fly zone on Libya in order to facilitate the overthrow of Gaddafi, thereby triggering the post-Gaddafi political instability that created a haven for: (a) the subsequent Islamic State of Iraq and the Levant (ISIL) occupation of Libya from May 2015, as well as; (b) the top migratory route to Europe via the Mediterranean from the Middle East, Eritrea, Somalia, West Africa, the Sahel and the Sahara itself. Subsequently, the Western powers have had to offer overt support to the renegade Libyan general Khalifa Hafter, so as to use him to fight ISIL and related Islamist forces in Libya, seeing that Hafter is also against Islamists. Consequently, they have had to deploy secret service agents and French special forces to Libya, in order to fight ISIL, as well as engage in other unconventional military overtures, while the rowing continued between the relevant EU member states and the relevant AU member states about migratory policy across the Mediterranean, with the International Organization for Migration and other related policy organizations or civil society organizations grappling with just how to formulate the migration policy, let alone implement it.

Much further down the line, when NATO forces were still struggling to maintain security in Libya, and it was clear the Libyan interim Government of National Unity (GNA) was struggling to hold on to even the little power base that it had assumed by the beach, the AU began to look at what steps Africa should take to resolve the Libyan crises generated by Western forces. It commenced with a high-level meeting of African heads of state in Congo-Brazzaville on 27 January 2017 to deal with the issue.

Rationalization of ethnonanationalism (RoE) or rationalized ethnonationalism – a form of political behaviour whereby citizens demonstrate ethnonationalism as the most rational way of rendering their civic loyalties to the state, with the firm conviction that, for their own purposes, voting along the lines of ethnonational identity is in the best interests of the state, given the realities of the overall political context – can be found in a number of cases, such as Burundi and Rwanda where the phenomenon was imposed or served on citizens by the state apparatus. On the other hand, in the Democratic Republic of the Congo (DRC), citizens broadly resolved not to acquiesce in this game. In Burkina Faso, civil society and citizens in Ouagadougou overtly and outrightly rejected the phenomenon by their populist march against parliament on 30 October 2014, while in Gabon the opposition torched the chamber of parliament after the Ministry of Interior announced the incumbent Ali Bongo as winner of the presidential election held on 27 August 2016.

As regards political economy, each subregional block on the continent has their own ongoing arrangements, and this has been the case for a notable while. However, interregional economic cooperation advanced to a new level on 21 March 2018 when 53 out of the 55 nation states or member economies of the African Union signed the agreement in Kigali which established the African Continental Free Trade Area (AfCFTA). This is the biggest trade agreement since the formation of the World Trade Organization in 1995. The AfCFTA is aimed to create a single market for goods, services and movement of people across the African continent.

I am very grateful for the help and support that I received from the staff of I.B. Tauris (now Bloomsbury), particularly Joanna Godfrey, Sophie Campbell, Olivia Dellow, Tia Ali, Sylvia Dell'Amore, the marketing team, the graphic and cover designers, all those who worked behind the scenes, and of course Lester Crook.

I would like to acknowledge the Firoz Lalji Centre for Africa at the London School of Economics and the Centre for Public Authority and International Development (ESRC grant number ES/P008038/1) for hosting me as a Visiting Fellow while I completed the book.

CHAPTER 1

INTRODUCTION

Theorizing on nationalism is now a well-trodden path. In the preface to my first book on nationalism,[1] I state that:

> The study of nationalism has burgeoned in the last twenty-five years during which theorizing has improved not least because of increasing awareness and debate about the phenomenon and its recurrences, but also because the dynamic has challenged scholars to revisit their perspectives. The variety of uncertainties in this process include to what extent the theories are applicable outside of the time and place which have most influenced the theorizing – eighteenth century Europe; and also what the nationalism should be long after national self determination has been achieved, particularly in multinational states where a heterogeneity of national groups share similar citizenship.[2]

The points highlighted above were comprehensively, yet succinctly, addressed in chapter 1 ('Theorizing on Nationalism') of my second book on nationalism in 2011.[3] I therefore do not intend to rehash the old debates, but rather to bring out new or emerging themes, which also relate directly to current affairs. Furthermore, I intend to be more policy-orientated in order that theorizing can have practical relevance or due application to reality.

It has always been obvious that the course of nationalism in any country is heavily influenced by the agenda of the leadership. This has remained the case in the postmodern era of the nation state, in that the course of nationalism is directly influenced by the head of state at any particular time, for the simple reason that nationalism is predominantly elite-driven, with the masses just tagging along.

Whatever course nationalism is charting or would chart in any country on the African continent at this point in the evolution of history, it has become increasingly common for the driver of nationalism also to be the most serious challenge to the ensuing nationalism and its progress, directly through extensions of presidential term limits by heads of state who deem themselves as destined to rule for as long as it takes them to address some strategic politics that they feel destined to resolve, or have calculated for themselves to resolve.

The extensions to the presidential limits (or prolonged presidencies) and their usual concomitants of electoral disputes, are in themselves causes of conflicts that pose a major challenge to African politics, global governance, the global security space, as well as the global policy space on democratic governance in the current milieu of globalism and globalization. With regard to Africa, the institutions of global governance on global security, such as the UNSC; the African Union Peace and Security Council (AU-PSC) that is the UNSC's peer-related regional body; relevant sub-regional bodies such as the Intergovernmental Authority on Development (IGAD), the Economic Community of West African States (ECOWAS), the East African Community (EAC), the Southern African Development Community (SADC), the Economic Community of Central African States (ECCAS), Community of Sahel-Saharan States (CEN-SAD), Union du Maghreb Arabe (UMA), Common Market for Eastern and Southern Africa (COMESA); plus NATO, which is the UNSC's peer-related regional body for the West, happen to be the institutions that get involved with these conflicts arising from prolonged presidencies and their concomitants.

Within the global policy space on democratic politics and the presidential system of government vis-à-vis the arena of global governance and the global security space, in a milieu where agents of insecurity, conflict and terrorism such as Boko Haram, Al Shabaab, Al Qaeda, the Islamic State (IS) movement and similar organs are international bodies with a globalized modus operandi, we are fast approaching the point in the history of the human race where each country's matter is everyone's matter. The New Pan-Africanism as a theme runs through this book against the context of the nation state in an arena of globalism, and, in the process, tests both the validity and the viability of the nation state by examining conflict situations in Africa that are nationalized and globalized at the same time, and what became Africa's response to the systems and institutions of global governance, and the ensuing mechanisms for resolving the conflict(s).

The Presidential System of Government and Extensions to Term Limits

Although the majority of countries across the globe that practise the presidential system of government adopt the policy of two maximum terms for their presidents, this has become a mere rule of thumb, or good practice at best. In reality, the merits or demerits of any term limits, and the potential for additions or extensions, vary from case to case. In the absence of a universal or global policy, the increasing number of cases across the African continent of presidents staying as long as they possibly can, heaps both pressure and ridicule on the serious business of constitution-making, as well as the trickier business of its enforcement over the long term, where policy planning and game planning converge. As a universal set of rules is impossible or rather impracticable to agree to across the global policy space, the stage has long been set for the political game of extensions to evolve and chart its own course, and it appears that the busiest theatre has been the African continent.

There are more than 80 countries in the world that implement the system of two-term presidencies, whereas only 12 countries have the one-term presidential system.[4] It is fair to say that a stipulated limit to the number of presidential terms is common to the presidential system, rather than the parliamentary system whereby heads of government or prime ministers are limited by the length of period that parliament has confidence in them, hence the vote of no confidence or snap elections to dispose of a leader or rejuvenate their tenure, respectively. Suffice to say that a semi-presidential system would have both president and prime minister, for example France, Tunisia, Algeria, Côte d'Ivoire, Burkina Faso, Mali, Senegal and the DRC.

The evolution or natural history of the two-term limit policy is simply that, once upon a time, a leader governed so well that it behoved

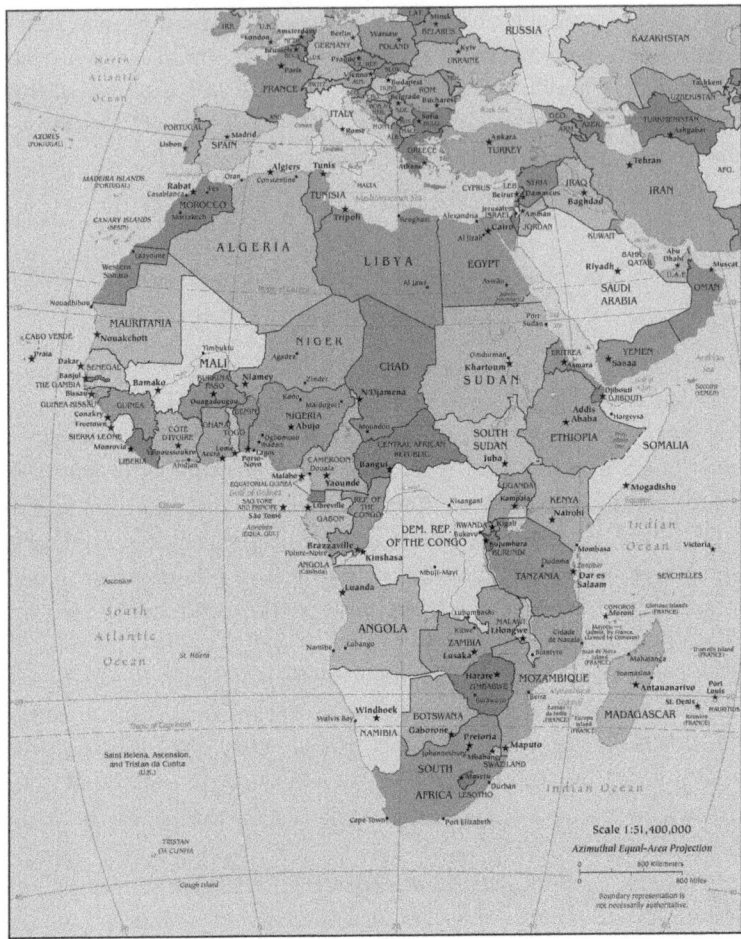

Map 1 Political Map of Africa.

their subjects to request or campaign for them to be retained, or, on the other hand, a leader sought for another consecutive opportunity in order to make good a poor performance in a first term, in order to complete unfinished business, or in order to improve on a previous exceptional performance, etc. The case made for the additional term has varied from country to country according to context, often with sophisticated and well-calculated constitutional processes to back the presidential aims of the incumbent.

As far as policy is debatable, and without universal global stipulations other than good practice guides, the merits or demerits of extending the limits to presidential terms impinge on what each constitution would aim to justify for the context of each country. In this regard, the scheming to fiddle with constitutions so as to extend presidential term limits for various reasons has increased on the African continent, with several examples itemized in this chapter, in alphabetical order: Algeria, Angola, Burkina Faso, Burundi, Cameroon, Chad, Congo-Brazzaville, the DRC, Egypt, Equatorial Guinea, Gabon, Guinea, Nigeria, Rwanda, Senegal, Togo, Tunisia, Uganda and Zimbabwe.

Institutions of global governance, such as the UNSC and the AU-PSC, and their sub-regional partners are striving to keep pace or step in to deal with situations ranging from escalations of violence to violations of human rights and crimes against humanity. The wide selection of varied attempts to extend presidential term limits across the African continent are set out briefly in the following paragraphs, as a tone-setter for the more selected and in-depth case studies to follow in the next chapters of this book.

Algeria

Abdelaziz Bouteflika became president in 1999 after President General Liamine Zéroual stepped down. Bouteflika stood as an independent candidate with a lot of military support behind him, and won an overall 74 per cent of the vote. In 2004, he was re-elected for a second five-year term, with 85 per cent of the votes cast. However, before his second term of office was due to end in 2009, Bouteflika managed to rally his Council of Ministers who proposed on 3 November 2008 a constitutional revision to remove the presidential term limit of five years that was renewable only once.[5] The proposed amendment was subsequently endorsed by the Algerian People's National Assembly on 12 November 2008, and allowed Bouteflika to run for a third term in 2009 as an independent candidate just like previously. Results of the presidential election that took place on 9 April 2009 gave him a third five-year term. On 17 April 2014, Bouteflika stood for a fourth term, in an election that generated only a 45-per cent voter turn-out.[6] As at October 2018, the 81 year old Bouteflika was poised for a fifth term election in April 2019 despite the serious illness from a stroke he suffered five years ago, and the resounding calls from across the political spectrum for him to step down. During his presidential career, he has been chair of the Organisation of African Unity (OAU) from 10 July 1999 to 12 July 2000, and brokered the Algiers Peace Agreement signed on 12 December 2000 to end the war between Ethiopia and Eritrea. He was also elected to serve as president of the 29th Session of the UN General Assembly.

Angola

José Eduardo dos Santos was president for 38 years from 1979 to 2017. Following the passing of President Agostino Neto on 10 September 1979, dos Santos was elected as president of the People's Movement for the Liberation of Angola (MPLA), the ruling party in a one-party state established by Neto. The civil war had already begun in 1975, hence dos Santos would carry on as president of the one-party state until the first real multi-party elections of 29–30 September 1992, which pitted the MPLA led by dos Santos against the National Union for the Total Integration of Angola (UNITA) led by Jonas Savimbi; the result was (49.57 per cent versus 40.07 per cent) in favour of dos Santos, however the civil war continued until the passing of Savimbi in February 2002 became a game-changer. Although dos Santos announced in 2001 that he would step down at the next election, he was re-elected as leader of the MPLA in December 2003, after which there were no presidential elections even though there were further announcements for such in 2006, 2007 and 2009. However, the MPLA's landslide victory in the 2008 legislative elections (191 out of 220 seats) led the way to a new constitution in 2010 which legislated that the leader of the party with the most parliamentary seats assumed the presidency. This has been the narrative ever since, because in the 2012 general elections the MPLA won 175 seats out of the 220 in the National Assembly.[7] In December 2016, President dos Santos announced that he would not run again for the presidency. The MPLA's key decision-making body endorsed the party's vice president at the time, João Lourenço, who also happened to be Angola's defence minister, as the standard-bearer to succeed President dos Santos.[8] As per the 2010 constitution, the MPLA won the August 2017 legislative elections with 150 seats, hence João Lourenço assumed the office of the president, and was sworn in on 26 September 2017.

Burkina Faso

Blaise Compaoré was head of state for 27 years, but had to flee on 31 October 2014 as citizens had marched on to the presidential palace to demand his resignation the previous day. He had been the head of state since 15 October 1987, when he overthrew President Thomas Sankara. He organized elections in 1991 for a seven-year term and was re-elected in 1998. In 2000, Parliament revised the presidential term from seven to five years. Article 37 of the Burkinabe Constitution states that the president is 're-eligible one time',[9] hence Compaoré's bid to run in 2005 was challenged by opposition candidates. But the Burkinabe Constitutional Court ruled that the new five-year and two-term restriction should not apply to Compaoré until after 2005,[10] thus paving the way for him to run in 2005 and to win. He was re-elected in 2010,[11] after which one would have thought that he should be prepared to hang up his boots. But he wanted to remain in power instead, and on 30 October 2014 the National Assembly was to debate the constitutional amendment that would have allowed him to do so. It appears that he had misjudged the political climate; the citizens thought they had had enough of him, and staged an unarmed uprising to disrupt parliament and burn down the facilities; 24 protesters died in the process. On 31 October 2014, Compaoré was rescued by French special forces and flown to neighbouring Côte d'Ivoire. In an election that took place on 29 November 2015, both Compaoré and his Congress for Democracy and Progress (CDP) party were banned from competing. He was OAU chair from 8 June 1998 to 12 July 1999. Compaoré would later be tried along with 34 of his ex-government ministers for the deaths of the 24 protesters.[12]

Burundi

Pierre Nkurunziza has been president since 2005. He was re-elected in 2010 for a second and final five-year term. In 2015, he refused to step down, organized rigged elections and remained as president. Nkurunziza's beef is that he was not elected by universal adult suffrage in his first term of office from 2005 to 2010, and therefore his first term of office does not count as a term, so he deserved to run for another term from 2015 to 2020. Although Article 96 of the amended constitution of 2005 states that the president 'is elected by universal direct suffrage for a mandate of five years renewable one time',[13] the Arusha Peace and Reconciliation Agreement for Burundi, which brought Nkurunziza into the presidency, stated in Article 7 (3)[14] that any president shall do a maximum of two terms, and also set very strict guidelines in Article 7 (1) (c)[15] that 'For the first election, to be held during the transition period, the President shall be indirectly elected as specified in Article 20 (10) [...] by the National Assembly and Senate';[16] in other words by a parliamentary electoral college. If Nkurunziza accepted his election to the presidency by the parliamentary Electoral College in 2005, then he should abide by the rules that the first election was to be by an electoral college as stipulated (and not by universal adult suffrage) and that he would serve a maximum of two terms including the first indirectly elected term. Therefore, he should not turn around and say that the first election was indirect – that is a non-starter. It must be noted that the Arusha Agreement was written in blood (the blood of the Burundian genocide) and incorporated with a special Protocol V guaranteeing the implementation of the Agreement. It was considered a betrayal of trust of the political system in Burundi for Nkurunziza to even moot the idea of attempting a third term, and subsequently forcing it on Burundians.

It must also be noted that, at the signing of the 2000 Arusha Agreement, Nkurunziza's Hutu CNDD-FDD party only existed in the form of the CNDD – Conseil National pour la Défense de la Démocratie or National Council for the Defence of Democracy – as the political wing of a rebel organization headed by Hutu intellectuals, and therefore the CNDD signatory to the 2000 Arusha Agreement was Professor André Nkundikije.[17] The fighting wing of the CNDD rebel group, known as Forces for the Defence of Democracy (FDD), remained in the bush (outside of the Arusha process), where Nkurunziza later assumed its leadership. The political and military wings of the CNDD-FDD remained conveniently 'separate' for a while, until 2003 when the CNDD-FDD as a joint enterprise signed the 2000 Arusha Agreement. Subsequently, even though Nkrunziza became party to the process of drafting the 2005 constitution, he was not really committed to the bedrock 2000 Arusha Agreement. Nkurunziza has since remained ideologically distant from the 2000 Arusha Agreement and would seek to undermine it at any opportunity, as he does not see it as something he signed up to originally. The CNDD-FDD registered as a political party in January 2005, with Nkurunziza now in full control of the whole outfit.

In April 2015, Nkurunziza announced he would seek a third term as president, and as the candidate for his (CNDD-FDD) party. Subsequently, on 5 May 2015, the Burundian Constitutional Court ruled that Nkurunziza could seek a third term. Violence erupted soon after the April 2015 announcement, and sporadic violence has ensued ever since. There was an unsuccessful coup on 13 May 2015 when Nkurunziza attended an African leaders' summit in Tanzania. The presidential elections took place on 21 July 2015, and he won with 69.41 per cent of the votes cast, though the voter participation rate was as low as 30 per cent. He was sworn in as president on 20 August 2015.

Over 1,000 people have died since the April 2015 announcement of Nkurunziza's intention to seek a third term. The AU threatened to send 5,000 peacekeepers to Burundi without the consent of the Burundian Government,[18] to protect civilians and prevent further human rights abuses and a potential genocide, as well as keep the peace in order to create the political space for further dialogue between government and opposition. This was the first time in history that the AU sought to invade a country without national consent, even if President Nkurunziza objected to this on 19 December 2015. The UN Human Rights Council (UNHRC) investigated human rights violations, and on 20 September 2016 the Office of the High Commissioner for Human Rights (OHCHR) published its Report of the UN Independent Investigation on Burundi (UNIIB). Subsequently, in August 2017, the UNHRC also published its report on the Commission of Inquiry on Burundi that was created on 30 September 2016. The debates on Burundi have continued at the UN Security Council.

On 17 May 2018, Burundi successfully conducted a constitutional referendum which removed one of two existing vice presidential roles and replaced it with that of a prime minister. The new constitution also restricted the presidential term to a maximum of two, but revised the term from five to seven years, and to commence from 2020, allowing Nkurunziza to be eligible to stand if he wished, and thereby creating the potential for him to remain as president until 2034. On 7 June 2018, Nkurunziza made a surprise announcement to step down at the 2020 elections, however, judging by the subregional style from President Museveni of Uganda who once indicated he did not want to be a future presidential candidate but turned round and said 'the people don't want me to leave', only time would tell whether Nkurunziza could abide by his announcement.

Cameroon

Paul Biya has been president since 6 November 1982. He became the sole candidate within a single-party system of governance, and he conducted and won elections in 1984 and 1988. Multi-party politics was grudgingly introduced in 1990; as the political landscape was heavily tilted in his favour, he won the first multi-party election in 1992, and subsequent ones in 1997 and 2004. A new and amended constitution in 1996 (from the 1972 constitution) ushered in the 1997 election and gave him a new presidential lease with a longer seven-year term renewable just once.[19] This election did not allow an independent electoral commission and was boycotted by the opposition parties.[20] Having won the 2004 election, one would have thought that Paul Biya should be ready to step aside in 2011 (that would have been 29 years as president). Not so. In December 2006, he created a new electoral body, Elections Cameroon (ELECAM) — 10 of whose 12 board members were from his own Cameroon People's Democratic Movement (CDPM) party. He then went on to get the puppet National Assembly to endorse the removal of constitutional limits to his presidency altogether in April 2008,[21] so that he could remain president for life. He won the 9 October 2011 presidential elections with 68.68 per cent of the vote.[22] The October 2018 presidential election would have Biya as the leading candidate and outright winner, to grant him another term to last until 2025. Biya won this election by 71.28 per cent of the vote. He was OAU chair from 8 July 1996 to 2 June 1997.

Chad

Idriss Deby has been president of Chad since 1990. He came to power by ousting President Hissène Habré in 1990, and ruled by charter until 1996, when a referendum introduced a new constitution and presidential elections, which he won. He was re-elected in 2001 for another five-year term. A constitutional referendum in 2005 abolished term limits to the presidency, and allowed him to run in 2006 and 2011. Article 61 of the Chadian constitution simply states: 'The President is elected for a mandate of five years by universal direct suffrage. It is re-eligible.'[23] He became chair of the AU from 30 January 2016 to 30 January 2017.

Congo-Brazzaville

Denis Sassou Nguesso's 'second coming' as president occurred in October 1997. He had earlier been president for 14 years during a single-party rule from 1979 to 1992. After his return to power in 1997, he won the 2002 multi-party elections. Despite having clocked up so many years as president, the January 2002 constitutional referendum gave him a new presidential lease of a seven-year term renewable once. With that, he won the 10 March 2002 presidential election comfortably, as well as the next one on 12 July 2009[24] with a 78.61-per cent win,[25] which should have taken him up to 2016. However, in 2015, Nguesso and his Congolese Labour Party (PCT) proposed constitutional revisions which quite clearly were designed to keep Nguesso in power. Among other things, the package of revisions sought: (a) for three consecutive presidential terms; (b) to get rid of the 70 years age limit which had appeared in the 2002 constitution just to eliminate Nguesso's ageing political opponents at that time, but did not now suit Nguesso, who was 72 at the time of the amendment; and (c) to reintroduce the role of a prime minister as head of government that was scrapped in the 2002 referendum just to enhance Nguesso's executive powers. With the significantly diminished stature of opposition politics on the Congolese political landscape, the proposed amendments passed through the National Assembly with ease and a referendum was scheduled for 25 October 2015. Opposition protests on 20 to 21 October 2015 were too little too late, and the results of the referendum a few days later were a resounding 92.96 per cent for the new constitution. Nguesso was chair of the OAU from 28 July 1986 to 27 July 1987 and became chair of the AU from 24 January 2006 to 24 January 2007.

Democratic Republic of the Congo

Joseph Kabila took office in January 2001, ten days after the assassination of his father Laurent-Désiré Kabila. He was elected as president in 2006 and re-elected in 2011. His second term expired on 19 December 2016 and elections should have been held in November 2016, but the government could not hold this election, citing lack of funding as the principal reason. The Constitutional Court ruled that in the absence of the election, the incumbent remains in office until further notice, according to Article 70 of the constitution. Therefore, although Kabila had not officially announced his intention to run for a third term in 2016, every suspicious move in that direction generated violent opposition. For example, there were violent protests on 19 January 2015 following the announcement of proposed legislation for a new census prior to the forthcoming 2016 elections, as this had potential to defer the election well beyond 2016. The proposed legislation was then rejected by parliament. Subsequently, the decentralization of the country into 26 provinces instead of the existing 11 raised further suspicion that Kabila had a third-term agenda. Eventually, the election was deferred to April 2019 as the ideal time to hold it, in agreement with technical and international experts.

As a strategy to move political opponents out of the way, the government jailed one formidable opposition candidate, Moise Katumbe, in June 2016, using allegations over a real estate dispute. In the same month, the broad spectrum of key opposition forces, led by three main opposition figures Moise Katumbi, Vital Kamerhe and Etienne Tshisekedi, formed a new platform or coalition known as 'Rassemblement' (translated as rally or gathering), which was adamant that Kabila must leave office at the end of his second term on 19 December 2016. Subsequently, Etienne Tshisekedi of the Union for Democracy and Social Progress (UDPS) returned to the country on 27 July 2016, from Belgium where he was receiving medical treatment. Tshisekedi began leading protests, holding campaign rallies and stirring up a firm opposition against Kabila, insisting that he hand over power at the end of his second term in December 2016.

The national dialogue that was principally to avert the looming crises at the end of Kabila's second term in December 2016 commenced on 1 September 2016 without the participation of the Rassemblement, which had laid down its preconditions for participating as:

- freeing political prisoners;
- lifting the ban on several TV stations; and
- resignation of the AU-appointed facilitator, Edem Kodjo.[26]

The dialogue was attended by the Pope's representative in the DRC, and of course Maman Sidikou, the representative of the UN

Stabilization Mission (MONUSCO). However, the talks were suspended after violent scuffles broke out between supporters of rival opposition parties. Four options emerged from this particular dialogue, none of which included holding the elections before the end of 2016, or Kabila not being a candidate in the impending election. The options were:

- Organize the election as soon as possible, which also meant that new voters could not be registered, and millions of eligible voters would not be able to vote;
- Enlist some of the eligible new voters, which would still disenfranchise some citizens, and the partial selection would be problematic;
- Enlist all 45 million eligible voters; however, the exercise to update the voter registration would take 10 to 16 months to complete, and would surely postpone the election timetable beyond 2016, or even 2017;
- Lucien Bussa, spokesperson of the Rassemblement, which refused to participate in the dialogue, and who was sceptical of the above options, announced that if the elections must be postponed, then so be it, but Joseph Kabila should leave power by 19 December 2016, and the country had four months (from September to December 2016) to work out another option.[27]

Nevertheless, Kabila made clear his determination to remain in office beyond December 2016, by appointing an interim 'coalition' cabinet headed by a new prime minister, Samy Badibanga, who was not part of the Rassemblement, although this appointment was rejected by the UDPS, leading to Badibanga's resignation on 6 April 2017. Kabila then appointed Bruno Tshibala (also not of the Rassemblement) as the new prime minister. On 9 July 2017 the Electoral Commission announced that the presidential elections, then scheduled for December 2017, could not be held,[28] thereby reiterating the 17 October 2016 ruling by the Constitutional Court that Joseph Kabila could only leave office when there was a replacement, and reopening the agonizing conundrum of whether Kabila really intended to leave power. On 5 November 2017, the Electoral Commission reversed the technically ideal date of April 2019 to hold the election for the politically expedient date of 23

December 2018 in order to lessen the increasing agitation and unrest. Provisional results for the presidential election were scheduled to be announced on 30 December 2018, definitive results on 9 January 2019, and the next president was to take office on 12 January 2019.

Egypt

Hosni Mubarak was president from 1987 to 2011. He became president on 14 October 1981, eight days after the assassination of President Anwar Sadat, in which he had no part, and to whom he was vice president from 1975. He was re-elected unopposed in 1993 and 1999, because of a restriction in the Egyptian Constitution that allowed for Parliament to simply endorse the incumbent who nominates himself. Mubarak himself proposed constitutional amendments in February 2005 that allowed multiple candidacy in presidential elections, and which were passed.[29] Subsequently, Gamal Mubarak, his son, was widely tipped to become president. However, on 11 February 2011, in the course of the Arab Spring, Vice President Omar Suleiman announced on state television the resignation of Hosni Mubarak. The latter was chair of the OAU from 24 July 1989 to 9 July 1990, and from 28 June 1993 to 13 June 1994.

Equatorial Guinea

Teodoro Obiang Nguema Mbasoko became head of state on 3 August 1979, when he overthrew his uncle President Francisco Macias Nguema. Obiang, as he is popularly known, has been head of state ever since, spanning 40 years to date. He was elected president in 1982 for a seven-year term and re-elected in 1989, both times as the only candidate. When other parties and candidates were allowed into the fray in 1992, he was re-elected in 1996 and 2002, and subsequently re-elected in 2009, yet he officially indicated that he wanted another seven years; on 10 November 2015, he announced on state radio that he had won the support of the ruling Democratic Party of Equatorial Guinea (PDGE) to run for a third mandate in 2016.[30] This came as no surprise because in a televised interview with CNN presenter Christian Amanpour on 5 October 2012, Obiang said that 'the people have to amend the laws in order to confirm that the president cannot continue, because the law is not retroactive.'[31] The PDGE won 99 of 100 parliamentary seats in the last 2008 general elections, and Obiang won 97 per cent of the vote in the 2009 presidential elections.

All constitutional revisions to suit him have passed with ease, as there has been very little opposition to his tenure of office or his party since he became head of state. The process leading to the 2011 constitution was railroaded by Obiang. He had a meeting with political parties on 24 March 2011 to call for a constitutional review and subsequently issued decree number 84/2011[32] on 9 May 2011 to establish a 31-member National Committee tasked with reviewing the 1995 constitution, only to follow up just three days later with his own guidelines on how this should be done. The committee submitted its report on 30 May 2011, and the PDGE-dominated House of Representatives approved it on 15 July 2011, paving the way for a national referendum. Despite a protest letter published on 21 July 2011 by the opposition Convergencia para la Democracia Social de Guinea Ecuatorial (CPDS) party to warn of the fraudulent process, Obiang signed another decree, 139/2011,[33] on 14 October 2011 that set 13 November 2011 as the referendum date. He further appointed his son Teodoro Nguema as the national director of his PDGE party campaign. An eleventh-hour joint statement by Human Rights Watch and Equatorial Guinea Justice to denounce the reform process fell on deaf ears, and the referendum took place as planned. Three days afterwards, the government announced 97.7-per cent voter approval and a 91-per cent voter turnout for the referendum.[34] This successful referendum also established the post of vice president who automatically assumed power if the president died in office. The current vice president is the son of the president. Obiang was chair of the AU from 31 January 2011 to 29 January 2012.

Gabon

The Bongo dynasty has presided over Gabon since 1967. Ali Bongo Ondimba became president on 30 August 2009 after his father, Omar Bongo Ondimba, died on 8 June 2009. President Omar Bongo had been head of state since 1967 and died in the 42nd year of his presidency. From 2 December 1967, when he became president, the country was a one-party state, until the first multi-party elections, in 1993, confirmed him and his Gabonese Democratic Party (PDG) in power with a presidential vote of 51.4 per cent for a five-year term. He was re-elected in 1998, and in 2001, before his second term ended in 2003, he began a constitutional process that resulted in a successful 2003 referendum which granted him unlimited terms of the presidency. He therefore remained in the presidential seat until his passing in 2009.[35] He was the chair of the OAU from 2 July 1977 to 18 July 1978.

After Omar Bongo's passing, his son Ali Bongo became head of the ruling PDG, stood for the presidential elections of August 2009 which generated highly questionable results, and was declared winner by the establishment. The credibility of the 2009 presidential election was so dubious that in January 2011 (some two years into Ali Bongo's presidency) Andre Mba Obame, the independent opposition candidate in that election, formed the National Union Party, declared himself President of Gabon and announced a parallel cabinet of 19 ministers, who later would have to seek refuge at the UN compound in the Gabonese capital Libreville.

The subsequent presidential elections on 27 August 2016 also attracted allegations of fraud, including a ridiculous voter turnout of 99.93 per cent in the Haut Ogooue province that happened to be the stronghold of the Bongo family. The electoral result was officially contested by the opposition leader, Jean Ping, who also happened to be Ali Bongo's brother-in-law. The opposition appeal against the electoral result was submitted to a constitutional court chaired by Marie-Madeleine Mborantsuo, a long-time mistress of former president Omar Bongo. The Constitutional Court managed to whittle down Bongo's winning votes in Haut Ogooue but also announced examples of polling results with 100-per cent voter turnout for Ping in the second district of Libreville that was Ping's stronghold, and summarily cancelled the results of 21 polling stations in Libreville. These statistical gymnastics resulted in Ali Bongo winning the election with 50.66 per cent of the vote versus Ping's 47.24 per cent. The AU observers claimed to be part of the review process but it is not clear what influence they were allowed to exert in the crucial aspects of rectifying anomalies observed during the count. Ballot papers had been burned, hence the tally count could not be disproved even if it had been falsified. The EU electoral observer mission asserted that they were restricted in some crucial aspects of the recount procedures and vehemently proclaimed that the constitutional court 'had been unable to satisfactorily rectify anomalies observed during the count'.[36] In other words, the election was rigged.

Guinea

When Guinea gained independence on 2 October 1958, Ahmed Sekou Toure became the nationalist president through leadership of the Democratic Party of Guinea (PDG) which he subsequently declared as the only legal party, and governed until 26 March 1984. Colonel Lansana Conté took advantage of Sekou Toure's interim replacement by Prime Minister Louis Lansana Beavogui, and before the former president's Democratic Party of Guinea (PDG) could elect a new leader, or the nation itself could conduct new elections for a new president, staged a coup d'état (with Diarra Traore) and seized power from Beavogui. Lansana Conté's junta ruled until the multi-party elections in 1993, which he won, becoming president for a five-year term. He was re-elected in 1998, and before his second term ended in 2003, he organized a referendum in November 2001 that amended the constitution to remove presidential term limits, while anachronistically extending the presidential term to seven years. Even during a protracted illness, he won the December 2003 elections hands-down, as they were boycotted by the opposition. With no limits or potential challenges to his presidency, he comfortably managed to hang on to power for another five years, despite his illness, until he died on 22 December 2008.[37]

Nigeria

Olusegun Obasanjo was president from 28 May 1999 to 29 May 2007, during which period he served two four-year terms. He attempted to change the constitution to allow him to stay longer, but the bill that contained the proposed clauses to revise the constitution was thrown out in a senate debate that was televised live on 16 May 2006.[38] He was chair of the AU from 6 July 2004 to 24 January 2006.

Rwanda

Paul Kagame has been president since 2000 when he was elected by government ministers and the National Assembly to replace Pasteur Bizimungu, who resigned in March 2000. Winning the 25 August 2003 multiple candidate election with a 95.1-per cent vote ushered him into the first seven-year term of his presidency, which was renewable just once, according to Article 101 of the 2010 constitution amended from the 2003 original constitutional document. Subsequently, he won the 2010 multi-party elections with 93.08 per cent of the vote. He was supposed to hand over in 2017; however, he instituted parliamentary procedures that set in motion a constitutional amendment to allow him beyond 2017. Following the 28–29 October 2015 debates in parliament, both the lower and upper houses voted massively in support of a constitutional draft that would potentially keep him in the presidency until 2034. The revised constitution granted a further one-term extension exclusively to Kagame's current term, after which the constitutional clock resets to two maximum five-year terms for whoever else takes over from that point, with Kagame not disqualified from competing. As the exclusive extension for Kagame's third term takes him to 2024, a further two five-year terms can proceed to 2034.

The 26 May 2003 referendum revised the transitional version of the 1991 constitution. From when the new 2003 Rwandan Constitution came into effect on 4 June 2003, it took on a variety of ad-hoc amendments through to 2010. The process for the major revisions to the 2010 Rwandan Constitution kicked off with a petition for constitutional changes based on Article 2 of the constitution, plus Article 193 that was wrongfully invoked by the government. The petition generated 3,784,686 signatures from Rwandans. What is in dispute is whether the petition could ask for changes to accommodate further presidential terms over and above the two maximum terms stipulated in Article 101 of the constitution, in other words whether Article 193 could be invoked in this instance. This was challenged in court by the Democratic Green Party of Rwanda (DGPR) on the basis that Article 193 only allows the duration of the presidential term (and not the number of terms) to be amended by a referendum. The term could be shortened or lengthened but not multiplied. Article 193 of the 2003 Rwandan Constitution states:

> The power to initiate amendment of the Constitution shall be vested concurrently in the President of the Republic upon the proposal of the Cabinet and each Chamber of Parliament upon a resolution passed by a two-thirds (2/3) majority vote of its members. The passage of a constitutional amendment requires a three-quarters (3/4) majority vote of the members of each chamber

of Parliament. However, if the constitutional amendment concerns the **term** of the President of the Republic or the system of democratic government based on political pluralism, or the constitutional regime established by this Constitution especially the republican form of the government or national sovereignty, the amendment must be passed by referendum, after adoption by each Chamber of Parliament. No amendment to this Article shall be permitted.[39]

The Rwandan Supreme Court dismissed the DGPR application on 8 October 2015 and:

> held that there was nothing in the Constitution that prohibited the amendment of article 101 [...] The Court questioned the wisdom of a people binding themselves and future generations in perpetuity without the flexibility to bring the law or the constitution in line with changed beliefs and circumstances.[40]

The court however did not set out what were the changed beliefs and circumstances at this stage of Rwanda's progress that should warrant an amendment to Article 193 when such an amendment was forbidden by the 2010 constitution. It is interesting to note that when Article 193 of the 2010 constitution reappears in the 2015 constitution as Article 175, the word 'term' is replaced by the phrase 'term of office', which means the latter could now be multiplied whereas the former could only be shortened or lengthened. This should be seen as an attempt to address the wrongful invocation of Article 193 of the 2010 constitution in the first place, and cover up for the past.

Subsequently, both chambers of parliament debated on 28–29 October 2015 and voted massively in support of the constitutional draft that could potentially keep Kagame in the presidency until 2034. The new draft has granted a further one-term extension exclusively to Kagame's current seven-year term, after which the constitutional clock resets to two maximum five-year terms for whoever else takes over from that point, with Kagame again not disqualified from competing. As the exclusive extension for Kagame's third term takes him to 2024, a further two five-year terms could proceed to 2034. Consequently, the result of the constitutional referendum to amend the presidential term that took place on 18 December 2015 was a resounding 98.3 per cent in favour, as well as for the voter turnout.

We should examine why the Supreme Court judges and parliamentarians so unflinchingly supported this constitutional referendum. Quite apart from reverence for Paul Kagame (or fear of him as the case may be), among the constitutional revisions voted for by this referendum, the term of service for senators, the president and vice president of the Supreme Court has also changed from an eight-year non-renewable to a five-year renewable term. Furthermore, the senators, president and vice president of the Supreme Court 'in office at the time of commencement of the revised constitution shall continue the term of office for which they have been elected or appointed'.[41] Quite clearly, there was a lot in it for the senators and the Supreme Court judges, because the revised constitution would commence from 2024 or seven years from 2017, and these public servants knew which side their bread was buttered. They would surely behave themselves because whoever survived to 2024, or came in from 2024, could retain their positions until 2034. It also becomes clear that President Kagame would have a conniving judicial and legislative infrastructure in place to support his rulership for life. We are talking about a titanic government machinery, in place to govern comfortably unchallenged for a considerable period of time without opposition – a sure recipe for corruption and whatever else imaginable. On 4 August 2017, Kagame was elected with 98.79 per cent of votes cast in the presidential ballot.

There is some strange nationalism demonstrating itself in Rwanda, and Kagame's looming profile is at the centre of it. At one point, he was head of military intelligence in the Ugandan Army while working for Museveni, the seasoned guerrilla specialist. He subsequently worked his way to become Rwanda's vice president and minister of defence. A spymaster who is now the chief executive is a tough adversary. After all, this is the man who makes sure that even his opponents under security protection in foreign countries do not escape his vengeance. It is true that Kagame holds sway and is very much revered in Rwanda, yet to scheme in advance, or galvanize 3.7 million signatures just for a petition that was to become the foundation for launching the most impossible constitutional revisions, suggests that friends, Rwandans and countrymen are behind him. He has both the backing and the determination to pursue his unfinished business, in the same way that President Museveni says that if there were term limits, he would not have obtained the 20 years he needed to get Joseph Kony and the Lord's Resistance Army (LRA) out of Uganda.[42]

Senegal

Abdoulaye Wade was president from 2000 to 2012, during which period he served two six-year terms. On 27 January 2012, the Constitutional Court ruled that Wade could run for a third term. However, Wade lost in the run-off elections held on 25 March 2012.[43] In contrast to the trend on the African continent (except in Burkina Faso during the time of Blaise Compaoré in 2000 and in Rwanda during 2015), on 20 March 2016 Senegal voted in a constitutional referendum, instigated by Maki Sall, to reduce the term of office from seven to five years.

Togo

Faurre Gnassingbe is the son of former President Gnassingbe Eyadema, who was president of Togo from 1967 to 2005, and who clocked up 38 years in the role, to become the longest-serving president at the time of his passing. In 2005, Faurre was illegitimately sworn in as president by the National Assembly even though the existing constitution required the president of the National Assembly to assume the vacancy.[44] Faurre would later be nominated anachronistically as head of his father's Rally of the Togolese People (RPT) party on 25 February 2005, and subsequently as presidential candidate. He won the 2005, 2010 and 2015 elections,[45] the last of which gave him a controversial third term. Article 59 of the current constitution of Togo simply states that 'he is reeligible',[46] therefore Faurre Gnassinbge could potentially be president for life, just like his father. During the latter half of 2017, a spate of angry mass protests erupted about the illegitimacy of Gnassingbe's presidency, and moved him to direct his cabinet on 5 September 2017 to approve plans to amend Article 59 to reintroduce a two-term limit that should commence from the next elections in 2020, as well as other elections-related portions of the constitution. However, protesters were adamant that the two-term limits should be applied retroactively, and that Gnassingbe should not be in office in the first place. The rampant protests continued well into 2018, hence ECOWAS mandated a team of heads of state chaired by the President of Ghana to mediate between Gnassingbe's government and the opposition parties, over the constitutional reforms. In September 2018, the electoral commission announced that local elections and a constitutional referendum would take place on 16 December 2018 without specifying what reforms would be on the ballot. However, in addition to the retroactive stipulation of the two-term presidential limit effective from 2015 (which made Faurre Gnassingbe ineligible to be presidential candidate in 2020), protesters called for the re-instating of the two-round voting system, instead of the one-round system inherited from France (and generally practiced by francophone African countries) which allows the incumbent or any candidate to win by the most marginal of votes and by the least voter turn out imaginable.

Tunisia

Zine El Abidine Ben Ali became president on 7 November 1987 by ousting President Habib Bourguiba. Subsequently, he conducted elections in 1989, which he won, giving him a five-year term. He was re-elected in 1994 and again in 1999. A constitutional referendum in 2002 pushed through a revision to allow unlimited terms for the presidency while increasing the age limit from 70 to 75.[47] He was therefore re-elected in 2004 and finally on 25 October 2009[48] until his fifth term of office was interrupted on 14 January 2011 by the Arab Spring. He was OAU chair from 13 June 1994 to 26 June 1995.

Uganda

Yoweri Museveni has been president since January 1986. He was re-elected in March 2001 for another five-year term and subsequently in February 2006. In his first 20 years as president, he governed with a single party, until the ban on multi-party politics was lifted after the July 2005 referendum which gave him a new lease that washed 20 years under the bridge. Limits to presidential term limits were also removed by parliament in 2005, as it was quite clear Museveni would win the impending elections. Hence he won the first multi-party elections of February 2006 and assumed a third term of office; he was further re-elected with 68.38 per cent of the vote in February 2011.[49] Museveni and his National Resistance Movement (NRM) party do not believe in having term limits, and opined that the consistency of his leadership has been necessary to deal with long-term problems such as getting rid of the LRA and its rebel leader Joseph Kony, which took some 20 years to accomplish.[50] When Museveni hit 74 years in 2018, he successfully removed the constitutional age limit of 75 set out in Article 102 (b) of the constitution in order to carry on as president for life. Oppositionists in Uganda face constant intimidation, and Kizza Besigye, the opposition leader, has been arrested and beaten many times, as happened in the 20 February 2016 presidential election process that maintained Museveni in power with a 60.75-per cent win. On 4 October 2017, a Museveni loyalist introduced a bill in parliament to remove the constitutional age cap, and on 20 December 2017, members of parliament voted 315–62 in favour of the amendment that would allow Museveni to stand for the presidential elections in 2021. He was chair of the OAU from 8 July 1990 to 3 July 1991.

Zimbabwe

Robert Mugabe became president on 22 December 1987 and remained so until 2017, simply because his Zimbabwe African National Union–Patriotic Front (ZANU–PF) is too mighty to be unseated from government. He led the party from 1975, became prime minister of the nation in 1980 and governed by a one-party state until the first genuinely multi-party elections in March 2008, when Morgan Tsvangirai, the opposition candidate and head of the Movement for Democratic Change–Tsvangirai (MDC-T), defeated Mugabe in a first round result (47.8 per cent versus 43.3 per cent) but did not reach the absolute winning threshold. In the political chaos of the aftermath, the Global Political Agreement, or power-sharing deal that was tediously brokered between the two sides also failed to work in practice.[51]

The political landscape of Zimbabwe is heavily skewed on behalf of ZANU–PF. In the last disputed election of 2013, Mugabe won with 61 per cent of the vote to assume his seventh presidential term of office. Mugabe prided himself on the achievement of being in the presidential seat for so long that he had seen off many a British prime minister, the latest being David Cameron who shortened his tenure by a political miscalculation in gambling on a referendum on whether the United Kingdom should leave or remain in the European Union. The following scornful quote is attributed to Mugabe, after Cameron's loss of the Brexit referendum:

> The colonials are reaping what they deserve now; for the Lord is not a God of injustice. For as they have wrongly and unjustly divided Africa and raped our natural resources; so would God divide their households. Today, fantastic stupidity is when an idiot cynically calls for an unnecessary referendum in furtherance of his personal ambition and not only lose the vote, but end up disuniting the country, partially unbundle the European Union, make the world's financial markets lose $2 trillion in a few hours, as well as lose his job to boot. What do I know [...] I was here when he came to office; I am still here as he shamefully leaves office.[52]

Mugabe was OAU chair from 2 June 1997 to 9 June 1998 and AU chair from 30 January 2015 to 30 January 2016. In December 2014, he verbally dismissed First Vice President Joice Mujuru for allegedly plotting to kill him, obviously without recourse to the tortuous dismissal procedures set out in Section 97 of the 2013 Zimbabwe Constitution. On 6 November 2017, he repeated the verbal dismissal act, this time against Emmerson Mnangagwa who was Mujuru's replacement as first vice president, using a similar trumped-up charge that Mnangagwa was making enquiries from spiritual sources about the timing of Mugabe's death. This upset the military, who launched Operation Restore Legacy on 13 November 2017 which placed Mugabe under house arrest on 15 November, and during which he was cautioned to resign in accordance with Section 96 of the constitution, or face impeachment under Section 97, which he had refused to follow in the previous dismissals of his deputies. Mugabe resisted for a few days and eventually resigned just when the impeachment process had begun on 21 November 2017.

Conclusion

Although the two-term maximum limit in the presidential system is the most common practice in the global policy space, it serves merely as a rule of thumb, as there is no binding global policy to enforce adherence, and the merits or demerits vary from country to country according to context. The serious business of constitution-making can be rendered somewhat ridiculous if constitutional courts do not exercise political independence when making judgements in a terrain heavily skewed towards incumbents who are surreptitiously breathing down their necks, especially where the proposed revisions were originally sponsored by the incumbent, and equally where judges are corrupt or susceptible to corruption. The existing conundrum makes it awkward for the AU-PSC, UNSC, IGAD or other relevant bodies to navigate a way forward when most of the existing heads of state have themselves served as chair(s) of the AU at one point or another.

As presidential peers would always have reservations about refereeing, repudiating or sanctioning each other (even from the position of the AU chair), perhaps an experimental way forward might be to obtain consensus from the current heads of government, to erect a superstructure body over and above themselves, with mandatory powers to deal with presidential terms of office.

CHAPTER 2

BURKINA FASO

Nationalism in Burkina Faso has yielded a shining example of a popular revolt that deposed a sitting president (Blaise Compaoré) who wanted to govern forever, as well as of a regular army that stood up to the nonsense of a presidential guard whose existence was not provided for in the constitution, both instances playing a strategic role in the process that restored the country to democratic governance. The country's pedigree of changing government by popular revolt dates back to the immediate post-independence period, and runs through its modern history. When the process of popular revolt repeated itself in October 2014, the New Pan-Africanism kicked in to restore the country to normalcy and democracy.

What Existed before Blaise Compaoré

On 5 August 1960, Burkina Faso attained full independence from France as The Republic of Upper Volta, the country's name when it was a self-governing French colony from 1958. At independence, the country's first president was Maurice Yaméogo, who was also the leader of the Voltaic Democratic Union (UDV). The 1960 constitution provided for presidential and parliamentary elections for five-year terms. However, just like his contemporaries who pursued the politics of one-party systems within their newly formed independent states, such as Kwame Nkrumah of Ghana, Sekou-Toure of Guinea, Omar Bongo of Gabon, Modibo Keita of Mali, Jomo Kenyatta of Kenya and Julius Nyerere of Tanzania, Yaméogo banned all political parties other than his UDV. Just

Map 2 Map of Burkina Faso.

like Nkrumah, Yaméogo's government lasted until 1966, when he was deposed by the military, and his tenure as president was characterized by mass demonstrations involving students, workers and the labour unions which happened to be the most efficient civil society organization at the time. This process of popular revolt forced the hand of the military, who effected Yaméogo's resignation on 3 January 1966, after which Colonel Sangoulé Lamizana emerged from among his military colleagues as Yaméogo's replacement.

Lamizana headed a transitional military government which suspended Yaméogo's one-party constitution, and supervised a process to ratify a new constitution on 14 June 1970, as well as conducting elections that transformed Lamizana into an elected president, although the UDV (which was not deposed when Yaméogo was deposed) became the majority party in the new National Assembly. As if the appetite for over-staying was already apparent, Lamizana managed to stay on as head of state to oversee two further constitutions, one of which guaranteed him a transitional period of four years, and a subsequent one which guaranteed his running as presidential incumbent for an election which he won in 1978. He then suffered the same fate as his predecessor, running into problems with civil society and the labour unions, and was overthrown by Colonel Zaya Yerbo's military coup on 25 September 1979.

Colonel Yerbo equally faced off with the labour unions, and was taken out by the same conniving sword of the military, in a coup d'état led by Major Dr Jean-Baptiste Ouédraogo on 7 November 1982. Ouédraogo formed, and governed with, the Council of Popular Salvation (CSP) which attempted to take the country back to the one-party days, even though he tried to camouflage his motives by preaching constitutionalism and democracy at the same time. Hence a faction of cadres emerged among the military, and was championed by Captain Thomas Sankara, who had been appointed prime minister in January 1983. This faction thought that the country deserved better or should at least progress, not retrogress, even if Sankara was also ideologically to the left on the political spectrum. The internal political struggle that ensued, plus Sankara's leftist rhetoric, led to his arrest, followed by efforts to effect his release that were directed by Captain Blaise Compaoré. The Sankara release effort resulted in yet another military coup d'état on 4 August 1983 which brought Sankara to power as head of state.

Thomas Sankara was very charismatic, as was his contemporary Flight Lieutenant Jerry John Rawlings, in next-door Ghana, who had emerged as a military head of state from a coup that was also staged to effect his release. The two became friends, and Sankara's government began to implement a series of revolutionary programmes. The Sankara revolution ignited a process of nationalism consonant with his charisma and style, and as a result the country's name was changed from Upper Volta to Burkina Faso (meaning 'land of the upright people') on 4 August 1984. In the same vein, Sankara's government formed the National Council for the Revolution (CNR) and established Committees for the Defence of the Revolution (CDRs) as grassroots cell groups to implement the CNR's revolutionary programmes, in the same period as CDRs were operating in Ghana under Jerry Rawlings. The two West African heads of state seemed to have taken their cue from the Green Book authored by President Muammar al-Gaddafi of Libya, another charismatic African leader at the time. In support of a fellow head of state's revolutionary zeal, and in honour of the Burkinabe revolution, Jerry Rawlings named Redemption Circle in Accra as Thomas Sankara Circle.

In Burkina Faso, the Pioneers of the Revolution became the youth version of the CDR to indoctrinate the younger generation. Also, the government commissioned and equipped CDR members to expose anti-revolutionary personalities and sentiments, in a move that was not universally welcomed. On 15 October 1987, Sankara and 12 others died in a coup d'état, staged by Blaise Compaoré the former colleague of Sankara who put Sankara in power in 1983. Blaise Compaoré became Burkina Faso's president until October 2014. The extent of Sankara's charisma and revered popularity led some ardent CDR members to resist the army for some period well after the coup that toppled him, until the resistance died away when Sankara's death became public.

What Occurred during Blaise Compaoré's Rule

Blaise Compaoré was head of state for 27 years, from 15 October 1987 when he overthrew President Thomas Sankara, until he was forced to flee the presidency on 31 October 2014, when, in a popular revolt, civil society and ordinary citizens marched to the presidential palace and demanded his resignation. In that period, Compaoré began to tilt towards France and served the interests of the former colonial master, which probably explains why Compaoré (unlike his predecessors) survived for so long despite his lacklustre tenure during which Burkina Faso deteriorated. Obviously, Compaoré had to offer a difference from Sankara to justify his coup, and he realized that Sankara's revolutionary actions had undermined relations with old colonial France and neighbouring Côte d'Ivoire, another former French colony. Subsequently, Compaoré's inherent philosophy and modus operandi was to negate Sankara's anti-Western policies and get close to Western institutions such as the International Monetary Fund (IMF). Compaoré became a faithful tool of France in West African politics in the negotiating roles which he played in several West African disputes, including the 2010–11 Ivorian crisis, the Inter-Togolese Dialogue and the 2012 Malian crisis. Compaoré was chair of the Organisation of African Unity (OAU) from 8 June 1998 to 12 July 1999.

Reforms introduced by Compaoré in 1990 led to a new constitution, plus elections in 1991 in which he was elected for a seven-year term, after which he was re-elected in 1998. In 2000, the Burkinabe parliament revised the presidential term from seven to five years. Article

37 of the Burkinabe constitution states that the president is 're-eligible one time',[1] hence Compaoré's bid to run in 2005 was challenged by opposition candidates. But the Burkinabe Constitutional Court ruled that the new five-year and two-term restriction should not apply to Compaoré until after 2005,[2] and paved the way for him to run and win in 2005. Compaoré was re-elected in 2010,[3] after which, one would have thought that he should be prepared to hang up his boots. Instead, he wanted to remain in power for much longer.

Typical of the Burkinabe modern history of agitations and strikes, labour unions and civil society led protests against Compaoré's attempt to perpetuate his rule after so many years. On 30 October 2014, the National Assembly was to debate the constitutional amendment that would have allowed Compaoré to do just that. It appears that Compaoré had misjudged the political climate; citizens thought they had had enough of him, and staged a popular unarmed revolt to disrupt parliament and burn down the legislative complex. The next target was the presidential palace. However, on 31 October 2014, Compaoré was rescued by French special forces and flown to neighbouring Côte d'Ivoire, according to France24 English as confirmed by Al Jazeera English.[4] He has since taken up Ivorian nationality, perhaps to place a stumbling block in the way of Burkinabe authorities in case of potential future confrontation. On 28 April 2016, the Ivorian Supreme Court cancelled the arrest warrants of Blaise Compaoré and Guillaume Soro issued by the Burkinabe military, on the grounds of procedural defects. However, the warrants could be reissued if the procedural corrections were made.

What Transpired after Blaise Compaoré – the New Pan-Africanism

Following Compaoré's resignation and departure, General Honore Traore, the army chief, announced that he had taken charge as head of state, only to be overridden the next day by Lieutenant Colonel Isaac Zida who was Compaoré's bodyguard or head of the Regiment of Presidential Security (RSP), also known as the presidential guard. Once again, and typical of Burkinabe modern history, another transitional government was put in place by Colonel Zida, in which he became both prime minister and defence minister, two strategic positions that gave him the strategic influence needed to preserve the existence of the unconstitutional presidential guard. Compaoré's UN ambassador, Michel Kafando, was made transitional president in this new arrangement which put the country back on a normal footing and paved the way for presidential and parliamentary elections in which neither Kafando, Zida nor Compaoré could stand as candidates. Compaoré's CDP party was outlawed altogether.

African regional authorities, as well as the wider international community, expressed their clear dissatisfaction with the ongoing developments, and the AU denounced the transition. On 2 November 2014, Dr Ibn Chambas, head of the United Nations Office for West Africa (UNOWA), and Kadré Désiré Ouédraogo, president of the ECOWAS Commission, visited Ouagadougou and held a cordial meeting with Colonel Zida and his colleagues. However, the next day, the AU's Peace and Security Council (AU-PSC) issued an ultimatum to Zida and the military to hand over power to civilians, presumably parliament, in accordance with Article 43 of the constitution that provided for the senate president to take charge when a president resigned.[5]

It was reported on 8 November 2014[6] that a meeting of military leaders, civil society and opposition party leaders lasted only 30 minutes because the participating parties could not agree on a timetable. On 10 November 2014, AU Chair Mohamed Ould Abdel Aziz visited Colonel Zida in Burkina Faso and emphasized that it was not sanctions the AU preferred to impose on the interim Burkinabe leadership, and the country for that matter, but rather a plan for a civilian handover within the stipulated two-week ultimatum issued by the AU on 3 November 2014, hence Burkinabes should work towards that end. Suffice to say that a proposed new constitution that was yet to be agreed by parties was mentioned to the AU chair at this visit, but he was not impressed by it. In that same month (November 2014), a high court judge, who was reportedly reluctant to say whether he supported the constitutional change to remove presidential term limits in the last days of Compaoré, was murdered and dropped by the roadside; his stance was taken to have been oppositional, and therefore he had been silenced by the much-feared presidential guard.[7] The political situation remained unsettled, and Colonel Zida's subsequent announcement that constitutional order had been restored did nothing to restore normalcy to the uncertain political, social and economic state of affairs generated by the existence of the Zida junta.

At the helm of government, an uneasy calm reigned concerning weightier matters; a report had been submitted to the cabinet which among other things recommended the dissolution of the presidential guard, an idea mooted by Colonel Zida in the past, and which was now regarded as traitorous, especially as Zida was now prime minister. Not surprisingly, on 17 September 2015, Interim President Kafando and his transitional government were removed through a coup plot staged by the presidential guard and led by General Gilbert Diendéré who announced himself as chair of a new National Council for Democracy (NCD) government. In the process, Kafando and Prime Minister Zida were placed under house arrest. This latest coup proved to be rather unpopular, because it purposed to jettison progress towards the imminent elections to restore the country to democratic governance. The disqualification of Compaoré's CDP party from competing in the imminent election was an issue that had forced the hand of Gilbert Diendéré, a key ally of the exiled Compaoré, to thwart the process towards the elections scheduled for 11 October 2015.

The Diendéré coup generated a flurry of diplomatic activity, first with the AU suspending the country and the coup plotters, followed by ECOWAS issuing its usual empty rants. On 18 September 2015, Dr Ibn Chambas scrambled the chair of ECOWAS, President Macky Sall of Senegal, and President Boni Yayi of Benin to accompany him to see Gilbert Diendéré. All that the trio managed to achieve was the release of Kafando (but not Zida), and to put forward a rather feeble proposal for Kafando to resume the interim presidency and oversee the conduct of elections now rescheduled for November 2015. The mediation efforts that began on 18 September 2015 ran through to 20 September, when President Boni Yayi announced that Kafando was reinstated, but without Gilbert Diendéré and the NCD junta relinquishing power until after the elections. Quite clearly, the NCD wished to influence the election for the exiled Compaoré. Zida remained under house arrest, and public protest was banned.

To confuse matters further, on 21 September 2015, some opposition leaders complained that they were not shown the content of the so-called deal mediated by Ibn Chambas, Macky Sall and Boni Yayi to reinstall Kafando and allow pro-Compaoré parties to feature in the forthcoming elections, even if former president Blaise Compaoré and Mrs Fatoumata Diallo Diendéré (an MP in the deposed Compaoré CDP party and wife of coup leader Gilbert Diendéré) would be banned from contesting. The regular army were also opposed to point number five of this 13-point deal that granted amnesty to Gilbert Diendéré and his NCD junta. It also did not help matters that France, the former colonial master, was trying to railroad this deal process from behind the scenes, and wanted the deal announced to ECOWAS on 22 September 2015, hence the French overtures were firmly opposed by Interim President Kafando, as well as by civil society. In all of this, the unclear whereabouts of Colonel Zida posed more questions than answers to the jigsaw.

Meanwhile, the Speaker of Parliament suddenly rediscovered his constitutional rights and began making noises that he was now in charge, and furthermore that the presidential guard was now dissolved, in what looked like an attempt to invoke Article 106 of the Burkinabe constitution, which states:

> The Parliament meets of plain right in the case of [a] state of siege, if it is not in session. The state of siege can only be extended more than fifteen days with the authorization of the Parliament. The declaration of war and the sending of military contingents or observers abroad are authorized by the Parliament.[8]

Incidentally, the regular army had no principal base in the capital, Ouagadougou, but had moved towards the capital on 22 September 2015 as a warning gesture to the presidential guard. ECOWAS convened an emergency summit in Abuja and agreed to send five presidents to Ouagadougou the next day to negotiate a truce with a five-point plan or agreement. Michel Kafando was reinstalled by the presidential guard on 23 September 2015; however, with the RSP still in barracks (and not disbanded), there was effectively no political solution in sight. Meanwhile, on 26 September 2015, the state prosecutor froze the financial and property assets of Gilbert Diendéré, Compaoré's CDP party and operatives, plus three other parties linked to Compaoré. Also, the state prosecutor sacked the Minister for National Security and created a commission to investigate and establish those responsible for the coup led by Gilbert Diendéré. As at 28 September 2015, Diendéré and his NCD coup plotters were still refusing to disarm, and the public, which was banned from protesting, complained of being terrorized by the RSP. The recalcitrance exhibited by the presidential guard persuaded the regular army to re-enact the popular revolt that toppled Compaoré, and move headlong against Diendéré and the presidential guard. After all, the defence of the realm was the constitutional right of the regular army and not the RSP (which had always been a presidential token and had no place within the constitution). Furthermore, the Speaker of Parliament had spoken.

Hence the regular army issued an ultimatum to the RSP to surrender. But as the latter would not, the army duly surrounded the RSP and moved in to disarm and capture them on 29 September 2015. Some 300 (out of 1,200) RSP troops surrendered at a camp in Ouagadougou without a fight, while others managed to disappear; Gilbert Diendéré had taken refuge in the Vatican diplomatic compound. Djibrile Bassole, former foreign minister in the Compaoré government, was arrested for supporting Gilbert Diendéré's NCD junta; Bassole had already been banned from participating in the upcoming elections. The airport closed on 29 September 2015, by which date 11 people had been killed and 271 injured in clashes between the RSP and protesters. It was reported on 16 October 2015 that Gilbert Diendéré had been charged with crimes against humanity, among others. Also, Djibrile Bassole, the former foreign and security minister (also a former joint UN–AU mediator in Sudan's Darfur conflict), was formally charged with supporting Gilbert Diendéré's coup.

In the election that finally took place on 29 November 2015, Roch Marc Christian Kaboré of the People's Movement for Progress (MPP) party won in the first round of voting by 53.5 per cent against Zephirin Diabré of the Union for Progress and Reform (UPC) party who won 29.7 per cent. President Kabore was sworn in on 29 December 2015.

Under Compaoré's pro-Western regime, Burkina Faso became host to US and French military installations, including drone bases, to monitor and combat jihadist forces in the Sahelian and West African sub-region. In retaliation, gunmen attacked the luxury Splendid Hotel in Ouagadougu, which was very popular with foreign diplomats, on 15 January 2016, killing at least 29 people.[9] Burkinabe security forces together with French special forces stormed the hotel to kick out the attackers, of whom four died, including two females. Al Qaeda in the Islamic Maghreb (AQIM) claimed responsibility for this attack, in which the death toll went up to 32, with 33 wounded. President Modibo Keita of Mali and President Boni Yayi of Benin visited Ouagadougou on 17 January 2016 to form a joint alliance with Burkina Faso to tackle the threat of terrorism in the Sahelian and West African sub-regions.[10]

International Political Economy

Burkina Faso is handicapped by being landlocked and dependent on the existing export/import infrastructure of the surrounding developing countries. Although it happens to be the fourth-largest gold producer in Africa (after South Africa, Mali and Ghana), just like neighbouring Mali, it can only boast of gold and cotton as its chief exports, even though both commodities suffer from high-risk world market fluctuations. The other minerals are manganese, tin ore, iron, copper and phosphates. The country's Sahelian climate and vegetation have dictated low-return economic activities such as low-tech rearing of livestock, and cultivating peanuts, shea nuts, millet, sorghum, maize and rice. Hence the real GDP growth rates of 3.9 per cent in 2015, 5.9 per cent in 2016, 6.4 per cent estimated for 2017 and 6.0 per cent forecasted for 2018, 2019 and 2020 respectively[11] do not really translate to much economic substance, and the country has to rely on substantial foreign aid. The periodic bouts of violence, political instability and the current insecurity from the threat of terrorism have also not helped. The economic cost of violence in 2016 alone, which amounted to $1,837,000,000 in purchasing power parity (PPP) terms,[12] had somehow reduced to $724,500,000 in 2017.[13] Underdevelopment has been an obvious characteristic, and the country has been among the bottom eight countries on the Human Development Index (HDI) since the 2010 Human Development Report (HDR). It would take sustained development under good governance and peaceful conditions over a considerable period of time for there to be significant change.

Below is a snapshot of Burkina Faso's governance performance on the Ibrahim Index on African Governance (IIAG):

- In the 2010 index, Burkina Faso ranked 18th overall, with a score of 53.29 per cent;
- In the 2011 index,[14] Burkina Faso ranked 19th overall, with a score of 55 per cent;

- In the 2012 index, Burkina Faso ranked 18th overall, with a score of 55 per cent;
- In the 2013 index, Burkina Faso ranked 23rd overall, with a score of 53 per cent;
- In the 2014 index, Burkina Faso ranked 21st overall, with a score of 53.3 per cent;
- In the 2015 index, Burkina Faso ranked 22nd overall, with a score of 52.2 per cent;[15]
- In the 2016 index,[16] Burkina Faso ranked 23rd overall, with a score of 51.8 per cent, which signified a 1 per cent comparative improvement over the decade trend index of 2006–15;
  - ✔ 24th in Safety and Rule of Law with a score of 57 per cent, which signified a − 4.6-per cent comparative downward spiral in the decade trend index of 2006–15, and, worse still, 34th in the personal safety sub-category or a − 17.9-per cent comparative downward spiral in the decade index; 25th in the national security sub-category or a − 4.1-per cent comparative downward spiral in the decade index; 13th in the accountability sub-category or a mere 0.3-per cent improvement in the decade trend index; and 27th in the rule of law sub-category or a 3.4-per cent comparative improvement in the decade trend index;
  - ✔ 22nd in Participation and Human Rights with a score of 57.6 per cent which signified a 1.5-per cent positive change in the comparative decade index 2006–15; 27th in the participation sub-category or a − 3.9-per cent comparative deterioration in the decade trend index; 9th in the rights sub-category or a comparative positive change of 7.8 per cent in the decade index; and 30th in the gender sub-category or a comparative positive change of just 0.7 per cent in the decade trend index;
  - ✔ 27th in Sustainable Economic Opportunity with a score of 44.8 per cent or just a 0.3-per cent rise in the comparative trend index 2006–15; 42nd in the infrastructure sub-category or a − 2.3-per cent downward spiral in the comparative decade index; a − 29.4 per cent deterioration in electricity supply over the decade; 12th in the public management sub-category or a − 1.1-per cent comparative deterioration over the decade; 24th in the business environment sub-category, signifying just a 0.3-per cent improvement in the comparative decade index;

a − 6.7 indicator drop in employment creation over the decade; 17th in the rural sector sub-category or a positive change of 4.3 per cent on the comparative decade index;

✔ 41st in Human Development with a score of 47.8 per cent or a 6.7-per cent positive change in the comparative decade trend index; 48th in the education sub-category or a 7.3-per cent improvement in the comparative decade index; 39th in the health sub-category or a 10.4-per cent comparative improvement over the decade; 30th in the welfare sub-category or a mere 2.5-per cent improvement in the comparative index over the decade; and a 2.6 indicator improvement in poverty reduction pertaining to the living standards of the poor, comparatively over the decade 2006–15.[17]

- In the 2017 index,[18] Burkina Faso ranked 21st overall with a score of 53.7 per cent, which signified a 1.1-per cent comparative aggregate improvement over the ten-year period from 2007 to 2016, and 0.3 per cent over the five-year period from 2012 to 2016; improved from 24th to 18th in Safety and Rule of Law over the 2007–16 decade; improved comparatively from 22nd to 21st in Participation and Human Rights over the decade; improved comparatively from 27th to 23rd in Sustainable Economic Opportunity; and improved from 41st to 40th in Human Development;[19]

- In the 2018 index,[20] Burkina Faso ranked 16th overall (with Lesotho) with a score of 57.1 per cent, which signified a 4.8 per cent comparative aggregate improvement over the ten-year period from 2008 to 2017; but deteriorated from 18th to 23rd in Safety and Rule of Law over the 2008–17 decade; improved remarkably from 21st to 10th in Participation and Human Rights over the decade; improved significantly from 23rd to 18th in Sustainable Economic Opportunity; and improved outstandingly from 40th to 19th in Human Development. The index identified Burkina Faso as 'one of only two countries (with Senegal) that has improved its health score every year over the past decade'.[21]

Burkina Faso's performance on the Global Peace Index (GPI) is as follows:

- In the 2010 GPI, Burkina Faso ranked 57th out of 149 countries – scoring 1.852;

- In the 2011 GPI, Burkina Faso ranked 51st out of 153 countries – scoring 1.832;
- In the 2012 GPI, Burkina Faso ranked 56th out of 159 countries – scoring 1.881;
- In the 2013 GPI, Burkina Faso ranked 87th out of 162 countries – scoring 2.064;
- In the 2014 GPI, Burkina Faso ranked 78th out of 162 countries – scoring 1.998;
- In the 2015 GPI, Burkina Faso ranked 83rd out of 162 countries – scoring 1.994;[22]
- In the 2016 GPI, Burkina Faso ranked 88th out of 163 countries – scoring 2.063.[23] This score points to a worsened performance, 'as insecurity and crime levels deteriorated as a result of the turbulent political transition following the ousting of the country's long-time president in late 2014';[24]
- In the 2017 GPI, Burkina Faso ranked 91st out of 163 independent states and territories globally – scoring 2.07.[25] From a regional perspective, the country ranked 19th out of 44 countries in sub-Saharan Africa;[26]
- In the related Positive Peace Index of 2017, Burkina Faso ranked 102nd among 163 independent states and territories, with a score of 3.37.[27] Positive Peace is 'defined as the attitudes, institutions and structures that create and sustain peaceful societies [...] creating an optimum environment in which human potential can flourish';[28]
- In the 2018 GPI, Burkina Faso improved and ranked 80th out of 163 independent states and territories globally – scoring 2.029, and also ranked 16th among the 44 Sub-Saharan African countries featured in the index.[29]

For the obvious reasons already discussed, Burkina Faso has maintained rank among the bottom countries in development. Below is Burkina Faso's performance on the United Nations Development Programme (UNDP)'s Human Development Index (HDI):

- In the 2010 HDI, it ranked 161st out of 169 countries in the 2010 HDR;
- In the 2011 HDI, it ranked 181st out of 187 countries in the 2011 HDR;

- In the 2012 HDI, it ranked 181st out of 187 countries in the 2012 HDR;
- In the 2013 HDI, it ranked 183rd out of 186 countries in the 2013 HDR;
- In the 2014 HDI, it ranked 181st out of 187 countries in the 2014 HDR;
- In the 2015 HDI, it ranked 183rd out of 188 countries in the 2015 HDR;[30]
- In the 2016 HDI, it ranked 185th out of 188 countries in the 2016 HDR;[31]
- In the new style and more comprehensive 2018 Human Development Indices and Indicators (HDII) Statistical Update which covers human development progress over the period 1990 to 2017, Burkina Faso ranked 183rd out of 189 countries.[32]

Corruption has also been a key issue, especially during the period of Blaise Compaoré. Here are Burkina Faso's rankings on the Corruption Perceptions Index (CPI):

- In 2010, the country ranked 98th out of 178 positions, scoring just 3.1 (with Egypt and Mexico);
- In 2011, the country ranked 100th out of 182 positions, scoring just 3.0 (with Argentina, Benin, Djibouti, Gabon, Indonesia, Madagascar, Malawi, Mexico, Sao Tome and Principe, Suriname and Tanzania);
- In 2012, it ranked 83rd out of 174 positions, scoring a meagre 3.8 (with El Salvador, Jamaica, Panama and Peru);
- In 2013, it ranked 83rd out of 175 positions, scoring just 3.8 (with El Salvador, Jamaica, Liberia, Mongolia, Peru, Trinidad and Tobago and Zambia);
- In 2014 it ranked 85th out of 174 positions, scoring just 38 (with India, Jamaica, Peru, the Philippines, Sri Lanka, Thailand, Trinidad and Tobago and Zambia);
- In 2015, it ranked 76th out of 167 country positions, scoring just 38 (with Bosnia and Herzegovina, Brazil, India, Thailand, Tunisia and Zambia);[33]
- In 2016, it ranked 72nd out of the 176 countries and territories, scoring 42 (with Serbia and the Solomon Islands).[34]

- In 2017, it ranked 74th out of 180 countries and territories globally, scoring 42 (with Lesotho and Tunisia),[35] and tenth among 49 Sub-Saharan countries featured in the index.[36]

Security Challenges

Although Burkina Faso has historically been among the worst performers on the HDI (among the bottom eight countries since the 2010 HDR), security is now at the forefront of national concerns, especially since 2012 when the existence of foreign military facilities to combat jihadist forces, including the US drone base at Ouagadougou airport, became public. It is clear that the country's rankings on the GPI began to deteriorate significantly from this point in the 2013 GPI, as was confirmed by the report that 'Burkina Faso suffered the third largest deterioration',[37] and this was compounded by local riots and anti-government protests that formed the systematic build-up of public agitation against the Blaise Compaoré establishment, for a variety of reasons, not least the high levels of corruption also confirmed by the Compaoré regime's performance on the CPI, plus the foreign military presence and its concomitant perception of foreign endorsement of the corrupt regime. Ordinary citizens have always wondered what was in it for them, especially if the foreign military presence would expose them to systematic attacks from terrorists, as had been the experience of neighbouring Sahelian countries that contributed to the anti-jihadist coalition. Their worries were not unfounded, as became clear from subsequent attacks.

The Ouagadougou Splendid Hotel, which is very popular with foreign diplomats, was attacked in January 2016 by AQIM gunmen,[38] who killed 30 people. Also, on 16 December 2016, 12 soldiers were killed in an attack on the Nassoumbo army base in the north of the country, when a group of 40 unidentified heavily armed fighters stormed the barracks in the morning and set fire to tents and military vehicles. The attack was targeted at the army's special anti-terrorist group at this army base, who have direct responsibility for countering armed groups in neighbouring Mali, and adjunct responsibility for monitoring the long desert border between Mali and Burkina Faso which is a potential hotbed transit point for jihadists and other militants.[39] Press statements issued after each attack by President Kabore blamed the attacks on terrorists,[40] as was the case when the Aziz Istanbul café, close to the Splendid in Ouagadougou and also popular with foreigners, was similarly attacked by jihadists on 13 August 2017, with 20 customers and two of the attackers being killed.[41]

Below are Burkina Faso's ratings on the Global Terrorism Index (GTI), which lists rankings in reverse order in contrast to most other indexes. For example, Iraq was at the top of the 2015 GTI:

- In the 2015 GTI, Burkina Faso ranked 107th among 162 countries that featured on the index, with a score of 0.305;[42]
- In the 2016 GTI, the country deteriorated to 63rd among 163 countries that featured on the index, with a score of 2.623,[43] and received its first AQIM-related attack;[44]
- In the 2017 GTI, Burkina Faso deteriorated further to 43rd among 163 countries that featured on the index, with a score of 4.52,[45] and is now firmly listed among countries with ISIL affiliates or networks.[46]

Burkina Faso now bears the brunt of jihadist wrath for its part in hosting a major US drone base to fight the Sahelian Islamist threat. Relatively ill-equipped to engage terrorism, Burkinabe territory easily became a 'free zone' for terrorist habitation, as Islamists chose northern Burkina Faso to establish a terrorist front, thereby disrupting normal life and economic activity. The state's incapacity to handle the jihadist hub paved the way for the Ansarul Islam (Defenders of Islam) movement to emerge as an umbrella AQIM affiliate for the area, under the leadership of the radical imam Ibrahim Malam Dicko, who hails from the Burkinabe northern city of Djibo, and fought alongside the Movement for the Oneness and Jihad in West Africa (MUJWA/MUJAO) in Mali, where he was jailed briefly in 2013. Dicko is now on the state's anti-terrorism priority list. To stem the trend of terrorism, Burkina Faso has considered a tactical withdrawal of its contingents deployed in peacekeeping missions abroad (mainly Sudan and Mali) to reassign them against the jihadist threat in northern Burkina. The country would also benefit from the multinational G5 Sahelian West African force[47] of which Burkina Faso is a member.

However, terrorist attacks surged in the north and east of the country as a result of the pressure on jihadist insurgents in Mali and Niger. On 11 August 2018, five policemen and a sixth individual were killed by a bomb and gun attack near the Boungou gold mine. On 28 August, at least seven Burkinabe security personnel were killed when their vehicle was hit by a roadside bomb en route to Pama where a police station had come under attack. On 5 September 2018, two Burkinabe soldiers were killed and five others injured in a roadside bomb attack in Kabonga in the Kompienga province where nine civilians were also killed in twin attacks on 15 September. On 26 September, at least eight Burkinabe security forces in a convoy were killed when their vehicle drove over a home-made mine planted near Baraboulé in the north, close to the border with Mali. On 5 October 2018, six police officers were killed when their convoy was ambushed by an improvised explosive device in the northern town of Solle near the border with Mali.[48]

From August 2016, the World Health Organization (WHO) began reporting an outbreak of dengue fever in Ouagadougou, the Sahel Region in the north of Burkina Faso, and the Hauts Bassins region in the west of the country; over 1,000 cases were diagnosed. As health workers were more used to looking out for malaria rather than dengue, a need arose to strengthen the capacity to diagnose dengue at an early stage.[49] At least 20 people died in the outbreak, which seemed more widespread in at least 12 districts of Ouagadougou.[50] In January 2017, prevention teams took to the streets of Ouagadougou to highlight awareness of the disease by alerting residents as to what symptoms to look out for.[51]

On 27 April 2017, Mathieu Ouedraogo, president of the Ouagadougou High Court, adjourned to 4 May the trial of Blaise Compaoré and his cabinet for their alleged role in the killing of 24 protesters during the October 2014 popular uprising that toppled him.[52] Numerous protesters who demanded immediate justice demonstrated against the adjournment.[53] A closely watched resumptive trial on 15 May 2017 was also adjourned for a month because Compaoré's defence lawyers launched an appeal that he would not get a fair hearing, and questioned the format of the hearing.[54]

CHAPTER 3

BURUNDI

Burundian nationalism has assumed the complexity of a president pursuing a strategic line of political action to balance geopolitics in the sub-regional context of Hutus versus Tutsis (a set of twins separated by a border demarcation imposed at independence) in order to avoid another genocide among the two identity groups, even if it also constituted a war between the aspirations of President Pierre Nkurunziza (the first president since the 2000 Arusha Peace and Reconciliation Agreement for Burundi that brokered the transition to a fresh start in Burundian politics) and any remainder of the Burundian population who disagreed with his strategic political aspirations. Whether this strategic line of action, or form of nationalism, resulted in loss of lives is immaterial to Nkurunziza, whose Hutu-motivated aim amounted to remaining president as long as the Tutsi president of next-door Rwanda, Paul Kagame, also remained as president. In this case a form of rationalized ethnonationalism[1] was imposed on Burundi, and forced upon the people, even if the political process was railroaded so that the July 2015 presidential elections rubber-stamped an end result that was dictated from the beginning by Nkurunziza's decision to run for a third consecutive term, for the strategic political or geopolitical reasons already outlined.

The politics of Burundi and Rwanda have been intertwined ever since the Belgian colonial masters pitched the two identity groups of Hutu and Tutsi against each other in a single geographical area, until the unbearable rivalry split into the independence of Burundi and Rwanda at the same time, yet with each country populated by Hutus and Tutsis in equal measure; 84 per cent Hutu, 14 per cent Tutsi and 1 per cent Twa/Pygmies, whether in Burundi or Rwanda. Consequently, the tussle between the two identity groups has continued in each country, with a different see-saw effect for each, where Hutus dominated the leadership of Rwanda until Tutsis assumed supremacy with President Paul Kagame, and where Tutsis dominated the leadership of Burundi until Hutus emerged supreme with President Pierre Nkurunziza. Hence Nkurunziza believed that he should be president for long enough to redress the *longue durée* of Tutsi heads of state in Burundi, if not to surpass it altogether; and there was no way of gauging when enough would be enough for him, except by himself. Consequently, before Nkurunziza's third term expired in 2020, he effected a constitutional revision that could keep him in the presidency for as long as Kagame remained president in Rwanda until 2034, even if Nkurunziza announced that he would step down in 2020.

It would seem that Nkurunziza had unfinished business to complete and needed a lot of time to do so, just like Paul Kagame, as well as Yoweri Museveni of Uganda, who says that it took 20 years to get the LRA and Joseph Kony out of Uganda, and that imposing limits on his presidential terms would not have allowed him to deal with the LRA.[2] The LRA still survive in Central Africa, and it was reported on 3 March 2016 that in 2015 alone, they abducted 217 people in the Central African Republic (CAR), of whom 54 were children.[3] Obviously, someone else could have completed the job of annihilating the LRA in Uganda, but Museveni has deemed himself as the one destined to undertake this particular task.

As a nation, Burundi had to grapple or put up with Nkurunziza, as awkward and uncomfortable as this was for at least half of Burundians. Both Nkurunziza and Kagame had suffered from the previous genocides in each country, and harboured pertinent reasons for their intense aspirations and entrenched positions. Nkurunziza's father, Eustache Ngabisha, who was previously a Burundian parliamentarian, was killed during the Tutsi-led (Micombero) Burundian Genocide of 1972 when he was governor. Likewise, Kagame led the Rwandan Patriotic Front (RPF) from 1991 that waged a guerrilla war against the Rwandan Army until the Arusha Accords were signed in August 1993, and has remained the RPF's leader after the accords; Kagame is therefore regarded as the one who successfully fought the Hutu government-backed militias, notably the Interahamwe and Impuzamugambi, to end the Hutu-led Rwandan Genocide of 1994.

Map 3   Map of Burundi.

What Existed before Pierre Nkurunziza

Burundi is a very small, landlocked country surrounded by Rwanda, Tanzania, the DRC and Lake Tanganyika in the Great Lakes Region of Africa. It is bordered clockwise by Rwanda to the north, Tanzania to the east and south, and the DRC to the west. Burundians are mainly Hutus (84 per cent) and Tutsis (14 per cent) and up to 1 per cent are Twa/ Pygmies. Burundi was a monarchical kingdom led by Tutsi kings for some 200 years before its territory was colonized by Germany at the beginning of the twentieth century, thereafter, on 20 October 1924, becoming a League of Nations territory under Belgian mandate after World War I, and automatically a United Nations Trust Territory under Belgian administration after World War II. Together with Rwanda, the territory became known as Ruanda-Urundi under the broader Belgian colonial empire, which was very good at playing off Hutus against Tutsis as a divide-and-rule colonial tactic.[4]

Hence the Rwandan Revolution of 1959 to 1961 between Hutus and Tutsis precipitated a move by Burundians to separate from Rwanda. The Tutsi-dominated Union for National Progress (UPRONA)[5] was born out of this process and won the first multi-party elections of 8 September 1961, with Prince Louis Rwagasore as leader. As Rwagasore was assassinated a few weeks later on 13 October 1961, his father Mwami Mwambutsa IV, pioneer of the move for independence as well as ruler of the existing monarchical Burundi Kingdom, pressed on with the anticolonial nationalism and gained independence for Burundi on 1 July 1962. Burundi therefore became a constitutional monarchy at independence and was accepted into the United Nations as such, on 18 September 1962.

The Hutu–Tutsi rivalries of the colonial period, which developed into the political lynchings of the post-independence era, meant that the one-party state which emerged from the first republic of 1966 became an instrument of state terror, and a sponsor of ethnic cleansing, leading to civil war and genocide in the 1970s, which appeared to simmer down but was rekindled in the 1990s. The many years of painstaking negotiations that followed, with regional and other diplomatic interventions, culminated in the 2000 Arusha Peace and Reconciliation Agreement for Burundi, which strategically guided a transition back to multi-party democracy to balance the vitriolic political landscape. The second interregnum did not last for long, and it does not take too long for the embers to flare up if the fires are stoked well enough. A decision by the Hutu Pierre Nkurunziza to run for a third and excessive term as president and leader of the National Council for the Defence of Democracy–Forces for the Defence of Democracy (CNDD-FDD) political party unravelled the hard-won 2000 agreement and plunged the country back in time.

The colonial Hutu-versus-Tutsi rivalry was replayed in the tit-for-tat post-independence era. Pierre Ngendandumwe, a Hutu whom King

Mwambutsa IV appointed prime minister in 1963, was assassinated on 15 January 1965 by a (Rwandan) Tutsi. The May 1965 parliamentary elections brought more Hutus into parliament, who perhaps felt that a Hutu ought to become prime minister, but the King appointed a Tutsi instead. Soon afterwards, Gervais Nyangoma, a Hutu, launched a coup and ousted King Mwambutsa IV, only for his son, Prince Atare V, to reclaim the throne. But Antoine Serkwavu, the Hutu head of police, in 1965 championed Tutsi massacres. Hence Michel Micombero, a Tutsi defence minister, launched a coup d'état and became prime minister on 11 July 1966, as well as president on 28 November 1966 when he deposed King Atare and abolished the monarchy altogether. Under Micombero, some 5,000 Hutus were initially purged from the military ranks.

The concerned and broader multi-state Hutu population in the sub-region staged an uprising in 1972, but this was forcefully crushed by the Tutsi-dominated military led by Micombero, during which an estimated 80,000 to 210,000 died. In 1976, Micombero was overthrown by his deputy chief of staff, Jean-Baptiste Bagaza, a relative, who became president on 10 November 1976. In the course of Bagaza's administration, the 1981 constitution maintained the one-party state governance established by Micombero's dictatorship, and Bagaza's further election in 1984 entrenched the suppressions and repressions even further, until he was overthrown by Pierre Buyoya, also a Tutsi, in 1987.

Buyoya proved to be a moderate Tutsi and reformist who brought in a new constitution which attempted a multi-party, ethnically even government, and duly handed over to a Hutu president, Melchior Ndadaye, chosen at the ballot box in June 1993. Unfortunately, Ndadaye was also assassinated just three months into his presidency. Speaker of Parliament Sylvestre Ntibantunganya assumed state leadership with a coalition government, but could not stop the civil war that had already erupted months before his parliamentary leadership from December 1993 and subsequent presidency from April 1994 to July 1996.

Buyoya therefore staged a comeback by a military-backed coup d'état against Ntibantunganya on 25 July 1996, and in due course appointed Domitien Ndayizeye, a Hutu, as his vice president, in order to get back on track with his inclusive government agenda. Buyoya and Ndayizeye saw to the brokering of the 2000 Agreement, which became the Bible for restoring political sanity to Burundi. Ndayizeye would later become president from 30 April 2004 until 26 August 2005 when the Hutu

Pierre Nkurunziza became president – elected by a parliamentary college as stipulated by the 2000 Arusha Agreement.

What has Transpired under Pierre Nkurunziza

The 2000 Arusha Agreement stipulated comprehensive checks and balances built into the road map ahead, which should be strictly adhered to. For example, it stated in two separate places that:

> For a period to be determined by the Senate, not more than 50 per cent of the national defence force shall be drawn from any one ethnic group, in view of the need to achieve ethnic balance and to prevent acts of genocide and *coups d'état* [...] only the president may authorize the employment of the defence and security forces.[6]

In that same spirit, the 2000 Agreement consequently stated that:

> Not more than 50 per cent of the members of the national police shall be drawn from any one particular ethnic group, with a view to achieving the necessary balances and preventing acts of genocide or of *coup d'état*.[7]

The above principles were duly transferred into Article 257 of Burundi's 2005 constitution, for the precise purposes of 'taking into account the necessity to assure the ethnic equilibrium and to prevent the acts of genocide and the coups d'état'.[8]

The 2000 Arusha Agreement also stipulated that the president should be assisted by two vice presidents belonging to different ethnic groups and political parties, regardless of the ethnicity of the president,[9] in line with Article 1(4) in Chapter I of Protocol II of the Agreement, which states:

> The Government of Burundi shall be so structured as to ensure that all Burundians are represented in and by it; that there is equal opportunity to serve in it; that all citizens have access to government services; and that the decisions and actions of government enjoy the widest possible level of support.[10]

In the spirit of the above principle, there was to be positive discrimination across the board in order to promote the numerically and politically disadvantaged Twa group and correct the inherent imbalances in the system.[11]

The key principle of two ethnically and politically different vice presidents became fully enshrined in Article 92 of the existing 2005 constitution that also stipulated in Article 96 a maximum two-term limit for the president. The 2000 Agreement and the 2005 constitution acted like the Old and New Testament of the Bible, each reinforcing the other; the 2000 Agreement established the modalities for the 2000–5 transitional government and the drafting of the 2005 post-transitional national constitution. In addition to running for a third presidential term, other potential reforms sought by Nkurunziza included an agenda to remove the safeguards of having two deputy presidents (one Hutu and the other Tutsi) and preferring just one prime minister instead.

Also to be noted in Articles 129, 143 and 164 of the 2005 constitution is that, whereas the government, Senate and public institutions such as the civil service were open to all ethnic groups, a maximum 60:40 ratio was enshrined for Hutus versus Tutsis (even if Tutsis amounted to no more than 15 per cent of the Burundian population). Hence the government at any time should include at most 60 per cent Hutu ministers and vice-ministers and at most 40 per cent Tutsi ministers and vice-ministers. The ethnic representation in the public enterprises should be 60 per cent at most for the Hutu and 40 per cent at most for the Tutsi. The Senate or National Assembly should be composed of at least 100 deputies in proportions of 60 per cent Hutu and 40 per cent Tutsi. A 30-per cent representation for women was stipulated across the board, whatever the compositions might be at any time.[12]

In the light of the 2000 Agreement that was written in the blood of the previous genocides, plus the 2005 constitution, red flags were raised and alarm bells kept ringing in direct response to President Nkurunziza's April 2015 announcement that he would seek a third term in office as the candidate for his CNDD-FDD party. After all, his quest to maintain a Hutu presidency so as to balance the Tutsi-dominated political history was also achievable by grooming a Hutu successor for his incumbent CNDD-FDD that had, and continues to have, the political advantage. The Tutsi-led UPRONA party, of independence fame, is very much diminished and Gerard Nduwayo, its candidate, could only muster 2.14 per cent of the July 2015 presidential vote. The opposition leader Agathon Rwasa, who is leader of the Independents of Hope party and the closest contender to Nkurunziza, won just 18.99 per cent of the July 2015 presidential vote. The opposition was evidently already so disadvantaged within the Burundian political space that there was no question about the superiority of the incumbent CNDD-FDD party and the assured victory of their candidate.

Nkurunziza's current behaviour and motivation must be carefully sourced and explained. At the signing of the 2000 Arusha Agreement, Nkurunziza's Hutu CNDD-FDD party only existed in the form of the CNDD – Conseil National pour la Défense de la Démocratie or National Council for the Defence of Democracy – as the political wing of a rebel organization headed by Hutu intellectuals. Hence the CNDD signatory to the 2000 Agreement was Professor André Nkundikije.[13] The fighting wing of the CNDD rebel group, known as Forces for the Defence of Democracy (FDD), comprised the troops that remained in the bush, outside of the Arusha process and later to be led by Nkurunziza. He has therefore remained ideologically distant from the 2000 Arusha Agreement and would seek to undermine it at any opportunity, as he could not see it as something he signed up to originally. The political and military wings of the CNDD-FDD remained considerably so up to a point, and the CNDD-FDD as a joint enterprise conveniently signed the 2000 Arusha Agreement in 2003, when it was already in place. Subsequently, even though Nkrunziza became party to the process of drafting the 2005 constitution, he was not really committed to the bedrock 2000 Arusha Agreement. The CNDD-FDD registered as a political party in January 2005, with Nkurunziza in full control of both the military and political enterprise.

Quite clearly, Nkurunziza had always wanted to remain in power himself, in order to carry out his personal agenda of maintaining the Hutu grip on Burundian politics, and furthermore preventing any potential for his replacement to seek redress for the atrocities and corruption of his presidency, especially during his second (2010–15) term. His blatant contravention of both the 2000 Agreement and the 2005 constitution created room for the rejuvenation of the Hutu–Tutsi rivalry that was subsiding in the second interregnum. It should be noted that the Tutsi presidency of Paul Kagame next door in Rwanda posited a strong factor in the shadowy mind of Nkurunziza, judging from the inseparable political histories of the two countries, and obviously Nkurunziza had read the game in advance that Kagame would remain as president of Rwanda for a long time to come, because the Rwandan petition, carefully devised by Kagame to formulate a national opinion in support of his third presidential term, had already garnered some 3.7 million signatures.

The Burundian presidential elections were held on 21 July 2015, with Nkurunziza winning by 69.41 per cent of the votes cast, though with voter participation rates as low as 30 per cent. Judging from the political history of Burundi so far discussed, and as already indicated at the beginning of this chapter, a form of rationalized ethnonationalism was imposed at this presidential election. As defined:

> Rationalized ethnonationalism is an observed electoral behaviour whereby ethnonationalism synchronizes with patriotism; whereby citizens demonstrate ethnonationalism as the most rational way of rendering their civic loyalties to the state; with the firm conviction that, for their own purposes, voting along the lines of ethnonational identity is in the best interests of the state, given the realities of the overall political context.[14]

In this case, the presidential elections resulted in a win for the Hutu Nkurunziza. He was sworn in on 20 August 2015. The senate elections took place on 24 July 2015, just three days after the presidential elections. The parliamentary election had already been held on 26 June 2015, with the opposition boycotting it. Equally, the Rwandan referendum to keep Kagame in the presidency was held on 18 December 2015, resulting in 98.3 per cent approval and the potential for Kagame to remain president until 2034.

Pierre Nkurunziza was therefore president since 2005 and was re-elected as president in 2010 for a second and supposedly final five-year term. In 2015, he refused to step down and rigged the elections to remain as president. Pierre Nkurunziza's beef was that he was not elected by universal adult suffrage in his first (2005–10) term of office, and therefore that period should not count, so he deserved to run for another term from 2015 to 2020. Although Article 96 of the amended constitution of 2005 states that the president 'is elected by universal direct suffrage for a mandate of five years renewable one time',[15] the

2000 Agreement which brought Nkurunziza into the presidency, stated in Article 7 (3)[16] that any president shall do a maximum of two terms, and also set very strict guidelines in Article 7 (1) (c)[17] that 'For the first election, to be held during the transition period, the President shall be indirectly elected as specified in Article 20 (10) [...] by the National Assembly and Senate sitting together by a majority of two-thirds of the votes',[18] in other words by a parliamentary electoral college. If Nkurunziza accepted the election by the parliamentary Electoral College into the presidency in 2005, then he should have abided by the rules that the first election was via the Electoral College as stipulated (and not by universal adult suffrage) and that he would serve a maximum of two terms including the first term when he was indirectly elected via the Electoral College. Therefore, he could not now turn around and say that the first election was indirect – that argument is complete nonsense. It must be noted that the 2000 Agreement incorporates a special Protocol V guaranteeing the implementation of the Agreement. It was therefore regarded as a betrayal of trust in Burundian politics for Nkurunziza to attempt a third term and force it on Burundians.

Violence erupted soon after Nkurunziza's April 2015 announcement that he would seek a third term as president, and sporadic violence continued. On 5 May 2015, the Burundian Constitutional Court ruled that Nkurunziza could run for a third term even though Sylvere Nimpagaritse, the vice president of the Constitutional Court, had fled to Rwanda the day before the announcement, claiming that he could not sanction a third presidential term against his conscience. That said, most of the judges were of the opinion that the president's third term bid was really unconstitutional, but they could not be seen to challenge that officially.

Subsequently on 13 May 2015, Major General Godefroid Niyombare, who was head of the Burundi Intelligence Service but had been dismissed by Nkurunziza in February 2015, took advantage of Nkurunziza's absence to attend a summit in Tanzania, and announced from four private or independent radio stations that he had dismissed Nkurunziza. But this coup was unsuccessful, principally because even though the rebel group had captured Bujumbura International Airport and the president could not land there, forces loyal to the president were in control of the state Radio-Télévision Nationale du Burundi (RTNB) station. In the modern era of multimedia, it is impossible to take over a country just by radio announcements from subsidiary stations. Indeed the presidency had already tweeted against the coup attempt. Niyombare announced the following day that his coup had failed, especially as Nkurunziza managed to sneak into the country by land and made a national broadcast from his hometown. All other private broadcasting facilities were later burnt down by the police. Niyombare escaped but former defence minister Cyril Ndayikuye was arrested. It appears that Niyombare is Hutu, hence it would look like the coup was not ethnically motivated, or rather was ethnically motivated by Hutus so as not to look bad because of the president's prolonged stay in office. Niyombare went on to lead the rebel Forebu group.[19]

What Continued with Pierre Nkurunziza and the New Pan-Africanism

On 13 May 2015, the EAC convened a special meeting in Dar es Salaam to deal with the Burundian political crisis; Nkurunziza had to be there, but the attempted coup in his absence failed. Of the eight heads of state who were co-signatories to the 2000 Arusha Agreement for Burundi,[20] only two (Yoweri Museveni of Uganda and Paul Kagame of Rwanda) were alive and in post when this EAC meeting was convened. Museveni attended but left early; unsurprisingly, Kagame did not attend, although he sent a representative. In the circumstances, all the EAC could be heard stating was to formally condemn the coup as unconstitutional and ask for the restoration of constitutional order, even though they might have been happy about a coup to depose Nkurunziza who was also present at the meeting. Equally, the condemnation sounded funny because there was no 'right' constitution to revert to, as the revised 2005 version was in dispute and was the cause of the trouble in the first place, which was the reason the EAC had convened. The EAC leaders reconvened on 31 May 2015 and 30 July 2015.

The following chronology of events should give some idea of the systematic deterioration of security in Burundi, and the escalation of violence since the 2015 political crisis that began with Nkurunziza's first public announcement that he would run for a third presidential term:

- The Nbonerakure, a youth militia loyal to the president, has been acting with impunity as the regime's enforcer.

- On 29 May 2015, the vice president of the Electoral Commission, Spes Caritas Ndironkeye, became the second of the five-member body to flee the country; she fled with her daughter.[21]
- In the first week of June 2015, there was widespread national and international condemnation that the Electoral Commission was not ready to undertake a credible election, among other things. International observers had made clear they would not attend to the election, and Belgium announced it would not offer its financial aid previously promised for the election.
- On 24 June 2015, Vice President Gervais Rufykiri announced on television that he could not support Nkurunziza's third term, which he viewed as unconstitutional, and departed from the country the next day into exile in Belgium. He was implicated by the government to have been involved in the failed coup attempt on 13 May 2015.[22]
- On 28 June 2015, the day before the parliamentary election, Pie Ntavyohanyuma, the Speaker of Parliament, followed suit and also fled to Belgium, where he stated on France24 English television that the election would not be free and fair.[23]
- On 18 July 2015, the African Union Commission (AUC) reiterated its readiness to immediately deploy human rights observers and military experts to Burundi, as part of the follow-up and implementation of the relevant decisions of the AU-PSC.
- On 30 July 2015, the EAC convened a third emergency meeting, recommended that Burundi postpone the scheduled upcoming elections and appointed President Museveni of Uganda to mediate between the government and opposition, because the government had failed to accept two UN negotiators.
- Also on 30 July 2015, the main opposition leader Agathon Rwasa was elected as the deputy head of parliament.
- On 2 August 2015, Lt General Adolphe Nshimirimana, the chief presidential security aide, was assassinated by gunmen in military fatigues who used a vehicle with sub-machine guns and rocket launchers.
- On 8 September 2015, opposition spokesman Patrice Gahungu was shot dead.
- On 11 September 2015, the military chief was attacked.
- On 5 November 2015, a prominent opposition leader and civil rights defender was found dead.

- As the tit-for-tat continued and government had no handle on how to stop it, the government issued a directive for all civilians in Bujumbura to hand over, or turn in, their private weapons by 8 November 2015.
- To complete the above directive, on 9 November 2015, the president ordered government forces to use all means necessary to collect 'illegal' weapons. In response, gunmen rounded up and killed nine people allied to government, including one UN official, in a bar. The government therefore ordered the military to comb that particular opposition area related to the incident from door to door, and two people were killed in the process. As part of this deadly crackdown on opposition members, Reverien Ndikuriyo, the president of the Senate, threatened to: 'pulverize regime opponents who don't surrender their arms'. He went on to say that 'Today the police shoot in the legs [. . .] but when the day comes that we tell them to go to "work", do not come crying to us [. . .]'[24]
- The UN High Commissioner for Human Rights Zeid Ra'ad Al Hussein, briefed at the UNSC that the President of the Burundian Senate had ordered local authorities to 'identify elements which are not in order' and report them to the police for them to be dealt with, plus the senate president's instructions calling on the police to 'get ready to finish the work'. The Human Rights Commissioner highlighted that the official inflammatory rhetoric aimed at targeting people from a perceived affiliation could take on an ethnic dimension, and was similar to what had been used in the Rwandan genocide 20 years before. A draft UNSC resolution was passed – in response to the hate speech – calling for options to be presented within 15 days or Burundi could face a UN contingent in Burundi. Burundian foreign minister Alain Nyamitwe responded to the UNSC debate via videolink that 'Burundi is not in flames. There are certain criminal acts attempting to attract the attention of the international community. But they have been reined in.'[25]
- On 12 November 2015, Resolution 2248 (2015) was adopted by the UNSC at its 7557th meeting. The resolution requested 'the Secretary-General to update the Security Council within 15 days, including by presenting options on the future presence of the United Nations in Burundi, and then regularly on the situation in Burundi, in particular on security, human rights violations, and incitement to violence or hatred against different groups in Burundian society'.[26]

- On 14 November 2015, it was reported on Al Jazeera English television that the European Union (EU) were evacuating their staff from Burundi.
- On 23 November, the UN confirmed that the US White House had issued an executive order signed by Barack Obama, to impose sanctions on four individuals: the Minister for Public Security, the Deputy Director-General of Police, the former Head of Intelligence and the former Head of Defence, all accused of preparing a failed coup. All four would have their assets frozen in the US, meaning they would not have access to any money they might be holding in US bank accounts, and would not be allowed to travel to the US. The White House kept open the possibility of adding to the sanctions and/or increasing the list of sanctioned Burundians. The text of the statement said Burundi was 'on the precipice' of genocide, but the White House restrained itself from using the word 'genocide'.
- The Burundian Government responded to the UN sanctions by suspending the licences of ten non-governmental organizations (NGOs), for allegedly playing a role in the failed coup against Nkurunziza back in May 2015.
- On 7 February 2016, four people were killed in a grenade attack in a bar in Bujumbura.[27]
- On 15 February 2016, two attackers from a drive-by vehicle threw a grenade at the Ngagara military base, killing a child and wounding his father as they came out of a hairdressing salon; one other person was wounded.[28] In a separate drive-by incident on the same day, three men on a motorbike hurled grenades at targets in Bujumbura, wounding at least a dozen people.[29]
- On 24 April 2016, Martin Nivyabandi, the minister for human rights, survived a grenade attack as he was coming out of a church service.[30]
- The next day, on 25 April 2016, General Althanase Kararuza, the security adviser to the vice president, was shot dead in his car, together with his wife, while dropping off his daughter at school; the daughter was injured in the attack.[31]
- On 14 June 2016, some 230 students in a secondary school in Ruyigi province were sent home from sitting an examination for defacing a photograph of the president in textbooks with scribbles and other markings. The teachers claimed that pupils refused to yield up the culprits. Dozens of schools had also reported similar graffiti cases,

because earlier in the month police had clashed with students in Muramvya after some young people were arrested for drawing on portraits of Nkurunziza.[32]

- Also on 14 June 2016, at the president's hometown in Ngozi, a grenade exploded in the hands of a soldier, killing the soldier and two civilians and wounding several others. The soldier was preparing to launch an attack and had removed the pin from one of two grenades. The explosion occurred at a parking lot by the school, at around 7.30 a.m., when the school children were getting ready to salute the national flag.[33]
- On 13 July 2016, Hasfa Mossi, an MP in the East African Parliament, was gunned down in Bujumbura.[34]

Over 1,000 people have died since Nkurunziza's April 2015 announcement that he would seek a third term. A series of UNSC debates had already ensued that led to Resolution 2248 (2015). In December 2015, the AU announced that investigators were looking into Burundi's crises, amidst reports of extensive abuses, with communities in Bujumbura still reeling from violent incidents on 11 December 2015 that had left 87 dead when three military bases were attacked by unknown gunmen. Eyewitnesses accused the police of rounding up and executing dozens of young people in retaliation, as bodies of children and youths lay dead on the streets. The sight of dead bodies became a regular feature on the streets of Bujumbura, and the UNSC feared this escalation could lead to civil war.

It was reported on 15 December 2015[35] that the Burundian Government had accused opposition groups of the attacks on the three military sites, and had summarily executed civilians in return. John Gin, the operations director of the UN Office for the Coordination of Humanitarian Affairs (UNOCHA), made a televised statement that the Burundian Government was acting out a military solution to a political problem, and that the government was at odds with OCHA. Meanwhile OHCHR resolved to discuss a resolution to send UN investigators to Burundi to probe abuses. The AU also threatened to send 5,000 peacekeepers to Burundi without the consent of the Burundian government, on the basis of Article 4h of the Constitutive Act,[36] in order to protect civilians and avoid further human rights abuses or a potential genocide, as well as create the political space for further dialogue between government and opposition. This was the first time that the AU sought to invade a country without national consent. President Nkurunziza objected to it on 19 December 2015.

On 22 January 2016, Amnesty International published the awaited special report on the events of 11 December 2015 that involved an armed rebellion of opposition citizens attacking three military installations in Bujumbura: (a) Base Camp in the Musaga neighbourhood south of the city; (b) Ngagara Camp in the north of the city; and (c) the Higher Military Training Academy or ISCAM – Institut Supérieur des Cadres Militaires. The report cited mass retaliatory killings of innocent civilians in opposition neighbourhoods and their bodies buried in mass graves principally in Kanyosha cemetery, and elsewhere,[37] including five burial sites in undisclosed locations on the outskirts of Bujumbura, of which Amnesty International had released images in satellite photographs, plus witness statements to back them up.[38] The UN also investigated reports of mass graves.

At the 26th Ordinary Session of the Assembly of the AU (Summit) held on 30–31 January 2016, which was preceded by the 29 January New Partnership for Africa's Development (NEPAD) Heads of State and Government Orientation Committee (HSGOC) briefing, Africa's political instability, terrorism and top security challenges featured prominently, with security in Burundi appearing at the top of the agenda because of the ongoing unrest. On the table was a proposed vote on the AU-PSC draft resolution to deploy AU peacekeepers to Burundi. Within the context of the Burundian administration's vehement opposition to the resolution, which was seen by Burundi as an 'invasion clause', was the fact that this would require a two-thirds majority vote of the heads of state to pass. However, Burundian foreign minister Alain Nyamitwe was already confident that this could not be attained, nor indeed was it, not least because most of the African heads of state were themselves long-term presidents. There were some 20 countries whose leaders had exceeded their terms of office or who had abolished constitutional limits to presidential terms in their respective countries. Even the AU chair, Idriss Deby, who supervised the vote on Burundi, had abolished those limits in 2005 and had already been in power for 26 consecutive years in Chad; his predecessor as AU chair, Robert Mugabe, had been in power for 29 years in Zimbabwe; and Teodoro Obiang, who had then been in power for

37 years in Equatorial Guinea, was among Mugabe's predecessors as AU chair.

The theme of the summit was '2016: African Year of Human Rights with a particular focus on the Rights of Women', quite appropriately for Burundi, and also given other human rights abuses by UN peacekeepers in the CAR and the DRC and by Boko Haram in Nigeria. The UNHRC reports on Burundi stated that 3,496 people had been arrested since April 2015, of whom 452 were arbitrarily arrested in November 2015 alone, and that arbitrary arrests from opposition neighbourhoods had now become a regular occurrence.[39] The summit resolved to send a delegation to discuss with the Burundian administration. Quite clearly, the AU-PSC had already shifted into overdrive on this particular issue, and was hoping that Nkurunziza would be the one to bend over backwards and acquiesce to foreign peacekeepers. The AU-PSC seemed oblivious of the fact that Nkurunziza was so determined to stay the course, and potentially plan for an even longer period in office, precisely because he wanted to be president long enough to redress the previous *longue durée* of Tutsi heads of state in Burundi, if not surpass that record altogether, and for as long as the Tutsi Paul Kagame remained president in next-door Rwanda.

Moreover, Nkurunziza was not amused that while he risked his security to attend the special meeting convened by the EAC in Dar es Salaam on 13 May 2015 to thrash out the Burundian crisis, a coup was staged in Burundi to overthrow him. Nkurunziza would therefore seek firm and unbreakable assurances, when the AU or UN made any overtures to send peacekeepers to Burundi, that foreign troops on Burundian soil would not be there to overthrow him, and those assurances would have to be mutually agreed in clear and unmistakable military terms. Granted that the UNHRC for that matter was the global face for championing the cause of addressing the escalation of human rights abuses in Burundi, it was daring for opposition rebels to be invading military installations at their own peril, as occurred on 11 December 2015, when the Burundian Government retaliation resulted in 87 deaths.

On 4 February 2016, it was reported[40] that a confidential UN report had accused the Rwandan military of recruiting and training Burundian refugees so that they could join an insurgency against Burundian president Pierre Nkurunziza. At least 400 recruits were under the instruction of Rwandan military personnel for this task.[41] The confidential report also revealed attempts to get arms to Burundian rebels by smuggling weapons from the DRC through Rwanda. Congolese authorities reportedly arrested Rwandan and Congolese civilians and two Congolese officers on smuggling charges at the end of 2015. As it turned out, the Burundian authorities also sent out agents and militias to hunt down these trained refugees sheltering in the Ndutu displaced camp in Tanzania, and abduct or kill them. Over 200,000 Burundians had been displaced since Nkurunziza's attempt to secure a third term, and about half of them were sheltering in refugee camps in neighbouring Tanzania.[42]

On 22 February 2016, UN Secretary-General Ban Ki-moon paid an official visit to Burundi to lend international support to the political dialogue between the government and all opposing sides in the Burundian crisis.[43] This was on the invitation of President Nkurunziza who had lodged an official request for the UN to assist with the talks in order to reconcile the country. As a gesture of good faith, the government announced plans to release 2,000 prisoners and 1,200 detainees. But the opposition parties, who also met with the UN Secretary-General, expressed their scepticism about Nkurunziza's motives for reconciliation. Nkurunziza used the occasion to complain to the UN about Rwandan interference in Burundian affairs, including Rwandan assistance with the opposition protests.[44] Nkurunziza's gestures appeared to be aimed at scoring political points ahead of schedule, because prior to Ban Ki-moon's visit, the AU had already decided at the summit on 31 January 2016 to send a high-level delegation to hold reconciliation and inclusiveness consultations with the government of Burundi and other Burundian stakeholders on 25–26 February 2016. The delegation, led by Jacob Zuma of South Africa, included President Macky Sall of Senegal representing ECOWAS, President Ali Bongo Ondimba of Gabon representing the Economic Community of Central African States (ECCAS)/CEMAC, the presidents of Ethiopia and Mauritania.

A key issue at the January 2016 AU summit was whether Nkurunziza would allow 5,000 AU peacekeepers into Burundi. Whether Nkurunziza had received sufficient reassurances from the UN through Ki-moon's visit, plus further reassurances from the revived AU-led diplomacy between the opposing sides of the Burundian crisis, that a peacekeeping force would not undermine his government, became somewhat inconsequential at this stage because, as one diplomat put it: 'The issue of deploying a peacekeeping force in Burundi is not on the agenda.'[45] The remaining key issue therefore was whether the continued presidency of Nkurunziza was now practically no longer in dispute (from the opposition), as that was the trigger point for the crisis in the first place. It therefore became an open question how to put up with Nkurunziza's continued presidency and how all sides could live in peace. Obviously, the Rwandan interferences in Burundian affairs and their assistance to the Burundian opposition and riots in Burundi had not helped the AU cause, and once that had been exposed and dealt with, the open question of whether the Burundian opposition could swallow the bitter pill of comporting themselves and putting up with Nkurunziza had to be addressed.

A significant opportunity to address this question presented itself at the 21–24 May 2016 Inter-Burundi Dialogue (IBD) held in Arusha, Tanzania, under the auspices of the EAC. The event was chaired by the former Tanzanian president Benjamin Mkapa, acting in the form of chief mediator and facilitator for the IBD which involved all political parties, civil society organizations (CSOs) including women and youth groups, plus prominent political actors within and outside of Burundi. But, the opposition groups presented themselves as a coalition known as the Conseil National pour le respect de l'Accord d'Arusha pour la Paix et la Réconciliation au Burundi et de l'Etat de droit (Le CNARED) – translated as National Council for Compliance with the Arusha Agreement for Peace and Reconciliation in Burundi and the Rule of Law. Le CNARED was disqualified from participating because it was not officially recognized or registered in Burundi as a political party and had already been blacklisted by the Burundian authorities as politically responsible for the abortive May 2015 coup attempt, among other things. Just why the opposition groups failed to represent themselves as individual parties at the IBD is difficult to explain, because they could just as well have aired or tabled their views and held inter-group caucuses at this dialogue summit, and their activities would have been equally valid and officially recognized without the CNARED tag. However, the role of the Women Network for Peace and Dialogue funded by the UN Peacebuilding Fund rose to prominence at this dialogue event. The network consisting of some 534 women mediators across 129 municipalities in 17 Burundian provinces had been established since January 2015 and had already addressed over 5,000 local conflicts and initiated dialogues with political actors, other CSOs and the security forces.[46]

The subsequent dialogue talks held under the auspices of the EAC from 12 to 14 July 2016 were boycotted by the Burundian Government's representatives, owing to their displeasure at the presence of the previous invitees to the talks, whom they deemed to be affiliated with terror organizations.[47]

On 7 October 2016, Burundi announced plans to withdraw from the International Criminal Court (ICC) in order to avoid a dossier of charges systematically compiled by the UNHRC and the ICC from March 2016, and the threat of imminent preliminary investigations – possibly leading to prosecutions – of allegations of crimes against humanity including murder, torture, rape and forced disappearances, in which some six members of the Nkurunziza regime including General Allain-Guillaume Bunyoni, the minister of public security, were implicated.[48] Burundi said the ICC was violating the rights of Africa. Leaving the ICC meant that Burundi would no longer be bound by the 1998 Rome statute that established the ICC, would refuse to cooperate with the investigations and would not be liable for non-cooperation. The ICC began to operate in July 2002 and had a membership of 124 states as at October 2016. Subsequently on 18 October 2016, President Nkurunziza signed the decree for Burundi to quit the ICC. This example was followed three days afterwards by the South African Government, which also threatened to quit the ICC, because of the ICC's pursuit of South Africa for ignoring a provisional high court order to arrest and detain Sudanese president Omar Hasan al-Bashir when he visited South Africa in March 2015 for the AU summit. Burundi also made clear on 8 December 2016[49] that it would punish the 25 Burundian peacekeepers identified by the UN and accused of sexual abuse and exploitation in the CAR during 2014 and 2015,[50] if the cases were proven.

Also, on 16 January 2017, Burundi began the withdrawal of up to 5,500 soldiers from AMISOM, as a result of a dispute with the EU over paying troop salaries worth $5.3 million per month directly to the troops rather than to the Burundian state, against which the EU had imposed sanctions for the ongoing political crises generated by Nkurunziza's third term in office. Up to 12 months of salaries had accrued unpaid, which was quite a sensitive matter because the Burundian troops were crucial to the survival and success of AMISOM going forward to dealing with Al Shabaab.[51] However, the issue was resolved through discussions at the 649th meeting of the AU-PSC on 16 January 2017, and the consequent intercession of AU Commissioner for Peace and Security Smail Chergui with the EU authorities. Subsequently, normal troop rotations resumed, and on 14 February 2017 a new rotating-in battle group from the 40th Battalion of the Burundi National Defence Force (BNDF) arrived in Mogadishu to replace soldiers from the 34th battalion who were rotating out.[52]

International Political Economy

Burundi has consistently been among the bottom 13 countries on the Human Development Index (HDI) over a period of eight consecutive years since the 2010 Human Development Report (HDR). Under-development is a key characteristic, and the country is handicapped by being landlocked and having to depend on the existing export/import infrastructure of poor surrounding countries. The country specializes in low-return export commodities such as tea, coffee and sugar for its chief exports, and has an unimpressive real GDP growth record of − 3.9 per cent in 2015, − 0.6 per cent in 2016, 0.5 per cent estimated for 2017, and forecasts of 1.9 per cent, 2.3 per cent and 2.5 per cent for 2018, 2019 and 2020 respectively,[53] in part due to the political crisis and violence that arose from Nkurunziza's April 2015 announcement that he would run for a third term. The economic cost of violence in 2016 alone which amounted to $1,045,000,000 in purchasing power parity (PPP) terms,[54] became $1,116,100,000 in 2017.[55]

The country relied heavily on foreign aid, mostly from countries that expressed disapproval of Nkrunziza's politics; it will be recalled that potential international partners, financiers and election observers, including Belgium, expressed misgivings and withdrew from the electoral process in 2015. However, a budget announcement made on 13 December 2017 by Finance Minister Donatien Ndihokubwayo stated that the economy was forecast to grow by 3.5 per cent in 2017 and up to 3.8 per cent in 2018, owing to a gradual economic recovery, with spending set to rise by 5 per cent from 1.32 trillion francs in 2017 to 1.38 trillion francs ($789.98 million) in 2018. The spending would be primarily on defence, energy, agriculture and infrastructure projects. Judging from the finance minister's assertion that 81 per cent of the budget would be sourced internally, it has to be assumed that the government income would come from domestic tax collection and modest revenues from tea and coffee exports. The budget deficit was also forecast to drop from 1.74 billion francs in 2017 to 1.64 billion in 2018. However, the IMF counter-forecast against the budget was for 0-per cent growth in 2017 and 0.1 per cent in 2018.[56]

Historically, the country has not been that peaceful, as shown by its turbulent political background, and its rankings on the global annual peace index since 2010. Repercussions from the pressures of the political violence, ethnic and security conflicts brewed in the Burundian pot have combined to render the economy moribund and without further cash for crucial imports such as fuel. Petrol rationing became official from 16 May 2017 at the price of 2,200 Burundian francs per litre; however, black market prices soared to 6,000 francs.[57]

Here is a snapshot of Burundi's performance on the Ibrahim Index on African Governance (IIAG):

- In the 2010 index, Burundi ranked 32nd overall, with a score of 45.77 per cent;
- In the 2011 index,[58] Burundi ranked 37th overall, with a score of 45 per cent;
- In the 2012 index, Burundi ranked 37th overall, with a score of 45 per cent;
- In the 2013 index, Burundi ranked 40th overall, with a score of 43.8 per cent;
- In the 2014 index, Burundi ranked 38th overall, with a score of 45.3 per cent;
- In the 2015 index, Burundi ranked 38th overall, with a score of 45.8 per cent;[59]
- In the 2016 index, Burundi ranked 43rd overall, with a score of 41.9 per cent, which signified a 2.1-per cent comparative downward spiral in the decade trend index of 2006–15;
  - ✔ 48th in Safety and Rule of Law, with a score of 32.6 per cent, which signified a − 13.6-per cent downward spiral in the decade comparative trend index of 2006–15, and, worse still, 47th in the personal safety sub-category or a − 21.1-per cent downward

spiral in the decade comparative index; 49th in the national security sub-category or a -7.4-per cent downward spiral in the decade comparative index; 42nd in the accountability sub-category or a -3.8-per cent comparative deterioration in the decade trend index; and 47th in the rule of law sub-category or a -21.9-per cent comparative deterioration in the decade trend index;

✓ 35th in Participation and Human Rights with a score of 44 per cent which signified a -0.3-per cent deterioration in the comparative decade index 2006–15; 40th in the participation sub-category or a huge -13.1-per cent comparative deterioration in the decade trend index; 46th in the rights sub-category or a significant deterioration of -13.6 per cent in the decade index; and a surprise 6th in the gender sub-category or a comparative improvement of 22.7 per cent in the decade trend index;

✓ 37th in Sustainable Economic Opportunity with a score of 35.4 per cent, or a mere 0.3-per cent rise in the comparative trend index 2006–15; 37th in the infrastructure sub-category or a 2.7-per cent improvement in the decade comparative index; a 6.8-point improvement in electricity supply over the decade; 40th in the public management sub-category, or a 1.8-per cent comparative improvement over the decade; 39th in the business environment sub-category, signifying a 5.1-per cent deterioration in the comparative decade index; an improvement of 3.2 on the employment creation indicator over the decade; 40th in the rural sector sub-category or an improvement of 2.1 per cent on the decade comparative index;

✓ 24th in Human Development with a score of 55.7 per cent or a 5.3-per cent improvement in the decade comparative trends index; 28th in the education sub-category or a 5.6-per cent improvement in the comparative decade index; 12th in the health sub-category or a mere 0.4-per cent comparative improvement over the decade; 33rd in the welfare sub-category or a 9.8-per cent improvement in the comparative index over the decade; and a -5.8 indicator deterioration in poverty reduction pertaining to the living standards of the poor over the decade, comparatively across the 54 countries in Africa.[60]

- In the 2017 index,[61] Burundi ranked 44th overall with a score of 39.9 per cent, which signified a − 6.5-per cent comparative aggregate deterioration over the ten-year period from 2007 to 2016, and − 6 per cent over the five-year period from 2012 to 2016; dropped down from 48th to 49th in Safety and Rule of Law over the 2007–16 decade; deteriorated comparatively from 35th to 38th in Participation and Human Rights over the decade; deteriorated from 37th to 39th in Sustainable Economic Opportunity; and deteriorated from 24th to 26th in Human Development;[62]
- In the 2018 index, Burundi ranked 43rd overall with a score of 39.8, which signified a − 5 per cent comparative aggregate deterioration over the ten-year period from 2008 to 2017; returned to 48th in Safety and Rule of Law over the 2008–2017 decade; worsened from 38th to 40th in Participation and Human Rights over the decade; returned to 37th in Sustainable Economic Opportunity; and improved slightly from 26th to 23rd in Human Development. The index highlighted Burundi as a country 'where freedom of expression has fallen by − 25.0 points' in the five-year period from 2013 to 2017.[63]

Burundi's performance on the Global Peace Index (GPI) is as follows:

- In the 2010 GPI, Burundi ranked 131st out of 149 countries − scoring 2.577;
- In the 2011 GPI, Burundi ranked 132nd out of 153 countries − scoring 2.532;
- In the 2012 GPI, Burundi ranked 138th out of 159 countries − scoring 2.524;
- In the 2013 GPI, Burundi ranked 144th out of 162 countries − scoring 2.593;
- In the 2014 GPI, Burundi ranked 130th out of 162 countries − scoring 2.418;
- In the 2015 GPI, Burundi ranked 130th out of 162 countries − scoring 2.323;[64]
- In the 2016 GPI, Burundi ranked 138th out of 163 countries − scoring 2.500[65] − and placed itself firmly among the countries with the worst deteriorations;[66]
- In the 2017 GPI, Burundi ranked 141st out of 163 independent states and territories − scoring 2.641[67] to register further deteriorations in

internal conflict and violent demonstrations.[68] Even from a regional perspective, Burundi ranked 39th out of 44 countries in sub-Saharan Africa within the index;[69] in the related Positive Peace Index of 2017, Burundi ranked 138th among 163 independent states and territories, with a score of 3.82;[70]

- In the 2018 GPI, Burundi improved to rank 134th out of 163 independent states and territories globally – scoring 2.488, and ranked 35th among the 44 Sub-Sarahan African countries featured in the index.[71]

Below is Burundi's performance on the UNDP's Human Development Index (HDI):

- In the 2010 HDI, it ranked 166th out of 169 countries in the 2010 HDR;
- In the 2011 HDI, it ranked 185th out of 187 countries in the 2011 HDR;
- In the 2012 HDI, it ranked 180th out of 187 countries in the 2012 HDR;
- In the 2013 HDI, it ranked 178th out of 187 countries in the 2013 HDR;
- In the 2014 HDI, it ranked 180th out of 187 countries in the 2014 HDR;
- In the 2015 HDI, it ranked 184th out of 188 countries in the 2015 HDR;[72]
- In the 2016 HDI, it maintained status at 184th out of 188 countries in the HDR;[73]
- In the 2018 Human Development Indices and Indicators (HDII) Statistical Update, it ranked 185th out of 189 countries.[74]

Burundi has consistently ranked among the bottom 20 on the Corruption Perceptions Index (CPI) over the last seven consecutive years:

- In 2010, it ranked 170th out of a total 178 positions with a score of just 1.8 on the scale of 0–10;
- In 2011, it ranked 172nd out of 182 positions, scoring just 1.9 (with Equatorial Guinea and Venezuela);

- In 2012, it ranked 165th out of 174 positions, scoring just 1.9 (with Chad, Haiti and Venezuela);
- in 2013, it ranked 157th out of 175 positions, scoring just 2.1 (with Zimbabwe and Myanmar);
- in 2014, it ranked 159th out of 174 positions, scoring just 2.0 (with Syria);
- in 2015, it ranked 150th out of 167 country positions, scoring just 21 (with Cambodia and Zimbabwe);[75]
- in 2016, it ranked 159th out of 176 countries and territories, scoring 20 (with the CAR, Chad, Haiti and Congo-Brazzaville).[76]
- in 2017, it ranked 157th out of 180 countries and territories globally, scoring 22 (with Zimbabwe, Haiti and Uzbekistan),[77] and 38th (with Zimbabwe) among 49 Sub-Sarahan African countries featured in the index.[78]

Security Challenges

In the sub-category of national security under Safety and Rule of Law in the 2017 IIAG, the index states that:

> Burundi is the most deteriorated country over the decade (-34.7) as well as over the last five years (-38.7). The country shows the largest annual average decline on the continent in the last five years (-9.68), almost tripling its annual pace of deterioration compared with the decade's (annual average decline of -3.86).[79]

The country also registered the largest decline in freedom of expression in the index.[80] Burundi has not had an easy modern history from the impact of the two genocides of 1972 and 1994 in the Great Lakes Region of Africa, and has been dealing with the repercussions systematically; the country has peculiar problems of its own. In this regard, it appears that the gains Burundi had made in less-turbulent periods, such as 'a lower number of refugees and displaced persons',[81] had been erased and worsened by the political crisis that erupted with Nkurunziza's third presidential bid from April 2015. It is already known that the country has had to deal with 'a rise in the number of external and internal conflicts fought due to involvement in fighting Al-Shabaab in Somalia';[82] however, what also became more pertinent was whether and how to host AU peacekeepers (and perhaps UN peacekeepers), and if so under what arrangements. A more sinister and continuous threat would continue to be how to deal with Rwandan interference. Among other things, this relates directly to the geopolitical point made in this book – the chief reason why Nkurunziza defiantly imposed himself as president of Burundi during the third-term bid.

Below are Burundi's ratings on the Global Terrorism Index (GTI), which lists rankings in reverse order in contrast to most other indexes. For example, Iraq was at the top of the 2015 GTI:

- In the 2015 GTI, Burundi ranked 55th among 162 countries that featured in the index, with a score of 3.342;[83]
- In the 2016 GTI, the country deteriorated to 31st among 163 countries that featured in the index, with a score of 5.417,[84] except that neither ISIL nor its affiliates were responsible for the notable increase in the GTI scores;[85]
- In the 2017 GTI, the country deteriorated further to 28th among 163 countries that featured in the index, with a score of 5.637.[86]

It is curious that Israeli prime minister Benjamin Netanyahu missed out Burundi from his famous July 2016 foreign policy trip to the EAC countries, at which sub-regional security concerns and new security challenges, particularly in agriculture, were top of the agenda, at a time when Israel was launching a £13-million aid package for Africa.[87] There was obvious potential for Burundi to have gained from this China-style Israeli government trip to Africa with as many as 80 businessmen among the entourage, and from the developing security architecture that was on the table, even if Burundi was not facing the same security pressures as the other EAC countries in terms of fighting Al-Shabaab or Islamist forces. Given that about 25 per cent of Israel's arms exports are to African countries,[88] and constituted a potential source of the arms proliferation in Burundi, the blatant exclusion of Burundi from this trip raised very curious questions.

On 30 July 2016, over 1,000 citizens staged government-backed protests in Bujumbura, a day after sections 13 and 14 of the French-drafted UNSC Resolution 2303 (2016) authorized the deployment of a UN police force to the country. The text of the resolution read as follows:

13. *Requests* the Secretary-General to establish a United Nations police officers component in Burundi for an initial period of one year to monitor the security situation and to support OHCHR in monitoring human rights violations and abuses, under the authority of the Office of the Special Adviser for Conflict Prevention, including in Burundi, in coordination with the AU human rights observers and military experts in Burundi, in accordance with their respective mandates;

14. *Authorizes* a ceiling of 228 United Nations individual police officers for the United Nations police component as referred to in paragraph 13 of this resolution, headed by a United Nations senior police adviser, to be deployed in Bujumbura and throughout Burundi, and *requests* the Secretary-General to ensure their progressive deployment.[89]

The Burundian authorities, who had earlier hinted they would accept no more than 50 police officers, rejected the resolution outright on 2 August 2016.

On 20 September 2016, OHCHR published its Report of the UN Independent Investigation on Burundi (UNIIB)[90] which verified at least 564 executions in Burundi since April 2015 when Nkurunziza announced his controversial third term bid. The Burundian Government denied that it ever kept a death list of people to be eliminated, rejected the allegations of torture and murder in the report, which it labelled as politically motivated, and sent a 40-page rebuttal to the UN Human Rights Commissioner.[91]

Following the announcement of Burundi's withdrawal from the ICC on 18 October 2016, the government withdrew the licences or permits of at least nine human rights groups and NGOs, on the grounds that they had tarnished the country's image. Among the groups targeted was the Association for the Protection of Human Rights and Detained Persons (APRODH), founded by Pierre Claver Mbonimpa, who survived an assassination attempt in 2015 and fled Burundi for Europe.[92] This revised the civil society landscape of the country, in that it reduced the level of vigilance against government abuse.

On the night of 28 November 2016, top government spokesman and senior communications officer William Nyamitwe, who is the brother of Foreign Minister Alaim Aimé Nyamitwe, narrowly escaped an assassination attempt, only sustaining minor wounds in an attack in the Kajaga district of West Bujumbura by assailants with guns and grenades, as he returned to his home in Bujumbura. One of his two personal bodyguards, who was a police officer, was killed in the incident, and the other was seriously injured.[93] In a statement issued at a press conference by police spokesperson Pierre Nkurukiye, the government blamed Rwandan influence for the attack, and alleged the assailants to be Kigali-based Burundians who had in the past killed high-ranking policemen and soldiers using a similar modus operandi. President Nkurunziza's right-hand man General Adolf was killed in August 2015.[94] On 26 November 2016, the government organized a massive demonstration against a UN report warning against potential genocide brewing in Burundi, to buttress its official refusal of two days earlier to cooperate with the UN enquiry into human rights abuses.[95]

On 1 January 2017, a gunman shot dead Emmanuel Niyonkuru, the minister for environment and water, on his way home. He was the first senior government figure to be hit since April 2015 when Pierre Nkrunziza announced his decision to run for a third term as president. Four people arrested for questioning included the owner of a bar the minister regularly visited, the two security personnel guarding his home on the day, and a woman who was with the minister when he was killed.[96] Unfazed by the intimidating posture of the ruling regime, the opposition continued to attack at every opportunity. On 17 May 2017, a grenade hurled into a house by an unidentified man claimed the lives of three members of the Mbonerakure (the youth wing of the ruling CNDD-FDD,) in revenge for the group's notorious rapes and lynchings across the country.[97]

Reverting to the ethnic-based, vitriolic political lynchings of the immediate post-independence era, the Nkurunziza regime intensified its cleansing of the Burundian Army of its Tutsi elements, as alleged by the International Federation of Human Rights (FIDH).[98] The systematic ridding of strategic Tutsis from the army confirms the author's view that the Nkurunziza regime existed to perpetuate Hutu supremacy in Burundi so long as Kagame the Tutsi remained president of next-door Rwanda.

Regardless of Burundi's exit from the ICC announced in October 2016, as a result of UNHRC Resolution 33/24 adopted on 30 September 2016 to create the Commission of Inquiry on Burundi, and the state's subsequent non-cooperation with investigations into human rights violations and abuses committed in Burundi since 2015, the UNHRC followed through with the inquiry and published its report in August 2017. The UNHRC report confirmed crimes against humanity, from 'the persistence of extrajudicial executions, arbitrary arrests and detentions, enforced disappearances, torture and cruel, inhuman or degrading treatment and sexual violence in Burundi since April 2015',[99] and among other things pointed the finger at members of the National Intelligence Service, the police, the army and the Imbonerakure. The report concluded that

> without a real willingness on the part of the Burundian authorities to combat impunity and guarantee the independence of the judiciary, the perpetrators of these crimes will remain unpunished. The Commission therefore requests the International Criminal Court to initiate, as soon as possible, an investigation into the situation in Burundi since April 2015.[100]

A year after Burundi announced that it was quitting the ICC, it exited the ICC on 26 October 2017, and subsequently rejected its calls to allow in prosecutors to further investigate war crimes allegedly committed by the government of Burundi and allied groups against political foes between April 2015 and October 2017 while Burundi was a member of the ICC.

For a while therefore, security in Burundi remained unassured, and at the same time a 'no go' area for the international community, so that a canopy was created under which one could not apportion certainty or blame on anything that happened to ally or foe. Meanwhile, the authorities successfully conducted a constitutional referendum on 17 May 2018, which removed one of the two vice presidential roles and replaced it with that of a prime minister. The new constitution also restricted the presidential term to a maximum of two, but revised the term from five to seven years, commencing from 2020. This effectively granted Nkurunziza the eligibility to stand as a presidential candidate if he so wished, and created the potential for him to remain as president until 2034. Whether he would carry on or step down remained an open question until 2020.

CHAPTER 4

CENTRAL AFRICAN REPUBLIC

The question of nationalism in the Central African Republic (CAR) has become one of how the country's leadership can reconcile the essential differences between the Seleka and anti-Balaka identities that have clashed on a variety of issues, including the Muslim Seleka having been widely disenfranchized from the salaried regular army and left to their own devices as rebel groups occupying large swathes of territory not under state security. With or without former president François Bozizé, the political storm has intermittently brewed and calmed down, whereby the current leadership now has to successfully integrate the Seleka into the regular army, which is the perennial and thorny issue that unseated Bozizé, and which Michel Djotodia, who replaced Bozizé, could also not successfully grasp even if that was his main reason for unseating Bozizé. This issue remained on the political table into the elections that brought in President Faustin-Archange Touadéra.

What Existed before François Bozizé

In 1957, the Movement for the Social Evolution of Black Africa (MESAN) established by Barthélémy Boganda won an unquestionable majority of votes, as well as every legislative seat, in the Ubangi-Shari territorial assembly election; this led to Boganda's election as president of the Grand Council of French Equatorial Africa and vice-president of the Ubangi-Shari Government Council. Boganda went on to declare the establishment of the CAR and served as the country's first prime minister. MESAN continued to exist, even if in a limited role.

Boganda died in a plane crash on 29 March 1959, after which his cousin David Dacko became leader of MESAN, as well as the country's first president when the CAR gained political independence from France in 1960. There were some political casualties under Dacko, such as the former prime minister and co-founder (with Pierre Maleombho) of the Mouvement d'Évolution Démocratique de l'Afrique Centrale (MEDAC), Abel Goumba, who fled into exile in France. In November 1962, Dacko declared MESAN as the official party of the CAR, as was typical of contemporary African heads of state who also championed one-party systems in the 1960s, such as Kwame Nkrumah of Ghana, Sekou-Toure of Guinea, Omar Bongo of Gabon, Modibo Keita of Mali, Jomo Kenyatta of Kenya and Julius Nyerere of Tanzania. Life and politics carried on until 31 December 1965, when Dacko was overthrown by Colonel Jean-Bédel Bokassa.

As head of state, Bokassa immediately suspended the constitution, dissolved parliament and reconfigured the political space over a period of seven years, after which he declared himself president for life and emperor of the Central African Empire – the new name he gave to the country on 4 December 1976. As events unfolded, France managed to get rid of Emperor Bokassa in September 1979 and brought back David Dacko, as well as the previous name of the country – Central African Republic. However, Dacko was overthrown on 1 September 1981 by General André-Dieudonné Kolingba, who also suspended the constitution and ruled with a military junta until 1985. A nationwide referendum in 1986 ushered in a new constitution, following which Kolingba set up his Rassemblement Démocratique Centrafricain (RDC) party, and imitated some of his contemporaries across the African continent, by disallowing his top political opponents (Abel Goumba and Ange-Félix Patassé) from participating in the parliamentary elections held in 1987 and 1988.

However, Kolingba proceeded to lose the 1993 presidential run-off elections to his much-feared rivals Patassé (who won with 53 per cent) and Goumba (45.6 per cent). Patassé's party was the Mouvement pour la Libération du Peuple Centrafricain (MLPC) or Movement for the Liberation of the Central African People. In the political turbulence that followed, the country received another constitution in 1994, experienced three mutinies against Patassé in 1996–7 and witnessed the deployment of the United Nations Mission in the Central African Republic

Map 4 Map of the Central African Republic.

(MINURCA) in 1998 under UNSC Resolution 1159. There was a mini-revival of Kolingba's political fortunes when his RDC party won 20 out of 109 seats in the 1998 parliamentary elections. But Patassé won the 1999 presidential elections, and with the help of some Congolese and Libyan mercenaries survived the coup of 28 May 2001 in which two of his top military chiefs (Abel Abrou and General François N'Djadder Bedaya) were killed. After this, Patassé became openly vengeful, murderous and dictatorial. During this particular period, his regime was assisted by the Mouvement de Libération du Congo (MLC), a private militia under the command of Jean-Pierre Bemba Gombo who was later convicted by the ICC in 2016 for crimes against humanity and war crimes including crimes of sexual violence committed by his troops while they fought for the Patassé regime,[1] but subsequently acquitted by the ICC's Appeal's Chamber on 8 June 2018.[2] Amidst the unfolding political turmoil, François Bozizé came into focus as a serial coup plotter who then fled to Chad (with government troops) and made a dramatic comeback in March 2003 when Patassé was out of the country. Subsequently, forces loyal to Patassé, and no doubt to other incipient interests, began to take shape in the unlegislated thick forests of the CAR, where they blatantly prepared to haunt the Bozizé establishment.

What Occurred under François Bozizé

François Bozizé also suspended the constitution, but adopted a slightly modified approach by forming an inclusive multi-party cabinet for his government, with Abel Goumba as vice president, and a National Transition Council to see to the drafting of a new constitution. But rebellion was easy to brew in the undisciplined and insecure political pot of the post-independence CAR. Hence in 2004, rebel forces mobilized against Bozizé and the National Transition Council, in what became known as the Bush War of the Central African Republic. The Bozizé presidential election victory of May 2005 (which naturally excluded former president Patassé from participating) simply spiced up the toxic political brew, and spurred on fighting between government soldiers and rebels, which carried on well into 2006. Subsequently, Bozizé secured French military assistance in November 2006 to deal with the effective rebel occupation of the CAR's northern towns. Bozizé went on to win a much-maligned election in 2011, but again, his tenure of office was anything but peaceful, and even more chaotic than ever before.

It is difficult to pin down just what inspired Bozizé's opponents to fight him, apart from sheer disgust at the ousting of Patassé, and perhaps other belligerent interests, because judging from its post-independence history, the CAR was never an easy country to govern under any circumstances. Moreover, it would appear that the religious divide among citizens had not been that apparent or pertinent in the country's previous evolution. However, starting with the Syrte Agreement of February 2007 and the Birao Peace Agreement of April 2007 which set out a raft of measures such as:

- cessation of hostilities between the Democratic Front of the Central African Republic (FDPC) fighters and government forces;
- billeting FPCA fighters and integrating them with the Central African Armed Forces (FACA);
- liberating political prisoners;
- integrating the FDPC into government;

- granting amnesty to the Union of Democratic Forces for Unity (UFDR) and recognizing it as a political party;
- integrating UFDR fighters also into the FACA

an impression emerges that the religious divide was a pivot all along or was shaping up to that, especially as several other smaller groups did not sign these agreement(s), while even the Convention of Patriots for Justice and Peace (CPJP), a major group, did not budge until 25 August 2012, when it signed a peace agreement with the Bozizé apparatus.

The religious element evolved and emerged as a single or coherent Seleka movement consisting of three major groups, namely the Patriotic Convention for Saving the Country (CPSK), the CPJP and the UFDR (and other insignificant groups alongside the broader Muslim religious movement), together led by Michel Djotodia who ignored the 25 August 2012 agreement and went on to take towns and villages in the northern and central parts of the country. Hence the Muslim Seleka rebel group became the umbrella body for the coalition of the CPSK–CPJP–UFDR Muslim militias, plus the FDPC and, more recently, the new Alliance for Revival and Rebuilding (A2R). The Seleka forced Bozizé into signing a 'power-sharing' deal or Comprehensive Peace Agreement on 11 January 2013 which Bozizé lacked the political will to keep. Bozizé, now old and sloppy, was overthrown just two months later.

I was interviewed live on Al Jazeera English television within minutes of the coup that overthrew Bozizé on 24 March 2013,[3] and which occurred amidst widespread looting, raping and gunfire. Shops, schools and offices were shut for a while until the dust settled days later; telephone lines had been cut in the process. The Seleka rebels had been marching towards Bangui for several months, and only halted their advance in January 2013 after the peace deal was signed with Bozizé in Libreville. However, Bozizé reneged on fulfilling the deal.[4] Hence the rebels resumed their advance towards the capital during the week of the coup and finally took control of the presidential palace. President Bozizé was not there, as he had already fled to the DRC.

The rebels announced that they would conduct elections. Arda Hakuma, the Seleka chief of staff, complained of how they had negotiated with Bozizé some ten different times and had become fed up with his intransigence, even by 2007. The rebels said Bozizé was ruling the country as a dictator, hence they had taken up arms to fight for the rights of the people. Among other things, the unfulfilled deal with Bozizé included the integration of Seleka rebels into the regular army, and the departure of Ugandan troops, and particularly South African troops that were there ostensibly to protect the interests of South African mining concerns.

What Transpired after François Bozizé – the New Pan-Africanism

The Seleka coup was led by Michel Djotodia who became head of state on 24 March 2013. Nicolas Tiengaye became his prime minister. In the Djotodia–Tiengaye period, the Seleka government was unable to reintegrate into the already sidelined army, even though that was a major pretext for their coup. It emerged in the Seleka's view that the regular army was dominated by the Christian 'anti-Balaka' militia, in a country that is deemed to be mostly Christian. Anti-Balaka reprisals against Muslims multiplied and intensified. On 18 April 2013, the sub-regional Economic Community of Central African States (ECCAS) held a summit in Ndjamena, Chad, to work out a road map to resolve the crisis in the CAR. Meanwhile, internal displacement of persons increased rapidly as a result of the internecine battles that raged between the Seleka and anti-Balaka. Human rights abuses by indigenous troops, as well as foreign peacekeepers, became a hallmark. On 31 May 2013, former president Bozizé was indicted for crimes against humanity and incitement of genocide.

Prior to Bozize's indictment, a CAR Contact Group set up under the auspices of President Denis Sassou Nguesso of Congo-Brazzaville (and his foreign minister) funded immediate intervention, including the facilitation of talks between all conflicting parties. The first meeting of the CAR Contact Group in Brazzaville on 3 May 2013 appealed to participants to make individual and collective contributions to restore full constitutional order to the CAR. On 19 July 2013, the AU-PSC set out what amounted to a follow-up strategy on the Appeal of Brazzaville, to pursue a transformation of the existing ECCAS-led Mission for the Consolidation of Peace in the CAR (MICOPAX) into an AU-led International Support Mission to the CAR (MISCA) out of the AU's Multinational Force of Central Africa (FOMAC) that comprised soldiers from Congo-Brazzaville, Cameroon, Gabon and Chad. The MISCA was to be supported by the 2,000 French special forces already stationed in Bangui.

The CAR Contact Group's second meeting, chaired by Congo-Brazzaville in Addis Ababa on 28 July 2013, pursued the transformation agenda from MICOPAX to MISCA with a concept of operations which emerged at the third meeting of the CAR Contact Group held on 1 August 2013:

- the protection of civilians and restoration of public order;
- the stabilization and restoration of government;
- the reform and restructuring of the defence and security sector; and
- the creation of conditions for humanitarian assistance.

On 19 August 2013, the AU-PSC and an international team of experts were in Bangui to assess the logistical and other needs of MISCA. They met with President Djotodia on 28 August 2013 to determine the precise additional capacity needed and the best means for mobilization. The AU-PSC then issued a press statement on 30 August to highlight the consultations between AU military advisers, civilian experts and the ECCAS general secretariat, on the modalities and calendar of the MICOPAX transition to MISCA. The efforts of the CAR Contact Group under the leadership of Congo-Brazzaville, including the facilitation of talks between the conflicting sides, resulted in the signing of a peace deal on 23 July 2014.

While all of the above transpired, there was another international effort to compose a wider international peacekeeping force to be brought under a UN umbrella. Prime Minister Tiengaye had already approached the UNSC for direct assistance as far back as May 2013 prior to the formal indictment of former president Bozizé. Following a February 2014 announcement by UN chief Ban Ki-moon, 3,000 UN troops were scrambled to go and augment the military effort in the CAR. On 10 April 2014, the existing MISCA arrangement transitioned into the UN Multidimensional Integrated Stabilization Mission in the Central African Republic (MINUSCA) set up under Chapter VII of the UN Charter, to resume operations and protect civilians in the CAR, even if MINUSCA only became operational much later on 14 September 2014, with 10,000 army personnel and 1,820 police personnel. At a later stage, a Senegalese

Quick Reaction Force (QRF) was positioned in Bangui, to bolster MINUSCA forces.

In the course of time, President Djotodia was still touting for a census of all disarmed militias and a process of organized recruitment into a regular republican army, although this was perhaps too wishful, too late, because in September 2013 he had to officially disband the Seleka and leave them to their own devices in their accustomed rebellious and unaccountable existence. The Seleka government came under international pressure from the UN and France, the colonial master, to step aside and allow in a more inclusive transitional government to be led by Catherine Samba-Panza. On 11 January 2014, President Djotodia and Prime Minister Tiengaye resigned at the regional summit in Ndjamena, Chad. Barely two weeks afterwards on 23 January 2014, Catherine Samba-Panza was elected as interim president by the National Transitional Council, although she and her entire cabinet would resign again on 6 August 2014 to pave the way for a unity government. The head of parliament delayed naming the cabinet for days, as renewed clashes broke out between local militias and the international peacekeepers. When the cabinet was eventually announced at the beginning of September 2014, the Seleka rebels ousted and disowned those of their members who had been grafted into the newly formed unity government of Catherine Samba-Panza.

The Seleka appear to have a broad resource base, for example, lumberjacks have been accused of financing them. The watchdog NGO Global Witness has linked the logging company SEFCA, which employs some 1,300 local people, to the funding of local Seleka militias. Global Witness therefore called on buyers to think twice about purchasing CAR timber, but at the same time, the watchdog's campaign infuriated the state which relies on the logging sector for much-needed money to return stability to the country. According to Ibrahim Fakhoury, the assistant director-general of SEFCA, from January 2015 when the Global Witness campaign began, timber piled up at the local holding centre because up to 40 per cent of timber orders had been cancelled in SEFCA's Mamberri concession following the Global Witness report; in other words, SEFCA sales amounted to 60 per cent. The logging towns survive on their income from the forestry businesses, and taxes paid would finance water wells and health centres, among other amenities. Hence both locals and government exports suffer if the logging industry is hampered, one of the adverse effects being unemployment. The government therefore challenged the Global Witness report, with an investigation of its own, with the aim of presenting an alternative report to the European Union in August 2015.

Against this political background, the ICC opened a second investigation during September 2014, into crimes against humanity: murder, rape and recruitment of child soldiers in the CAR in the preceding two years. Human rights abuses kept rearing their ugly head, and it became clear to the ICC and the international community that the UN was not doing enough to prosecute the rape and killing allegations levelled against UN troops in the CAR, even though Amnesty International had confirmed the claims. The UN later resolved to follow through with a thorough investigation. On 12 August 2015, Boubacar Gaye, the head of MINUSCA, resigned at the request of Ban Ki-moon over the numerous allegations of sexual misconduct and killing by UN forces in the CAR. General Gaye, who appeared to have been made a scapegoat, stated that he was a symbol of the UN's institutional responsibility, but also said ultimate disciplinary action lay with member states; MINUSCA receives troop contributions from at least 37 countries.

The saga of human rights abuses by international peacekeepers continued to play out in the news, as France24 reported more details on 19 August 2015; three Congolese soldiers of MINUSCA had raped three young girls (one of whom was a minor) in Bambari, while in a separate incident, MINUSCA peacekeepers killed a father and son, then raped a 12-year-old. UN procedures indicated that the culprits would be handed over to their respective countries, and if after ten days they had not taken action, the UN would step in with their own action. An independent report commissioned by Ban Ki-moon said the UN 'failed to act on gross institutional failures [. . .] instead of following on the allegations of child rape, the claims went from desk to desk, inbox to inbox across multiple UN offices, with no one willing to take responsibility'[5] when French troops in the CAR working under a UN mandate were accused of raping six young boys. The chair of the UN report, Marie Deschamps, said 'the lack of co-ordination leaves most victims unattended and vulnerable.'[6] Those implicated in the report and subsequently questioned were Boubacar Gaye, Ban Ki-moon's former chief of staff in New York, as well as the serving UN High Commissioner of Human Rights in Geneva.

The report recommended that such things be seen as human rights violations and not just 'misconduct' by peacekeepers.[7]

The saga of reports continued on a higher note, because on 9 January 2016 there were further reports of peacekeeper abuse of young girls (which occurred at the same time as the cases with the boys reported earlier) that were similarly ignored by UN officials. On 29 January 2016, new allegations of sexual abuse of girls by European soldiers surfaced, and some alleged victims identified French and Georgian troops as their abusers, in cases that involved minors aged between 7 and 16,[8] Rupert Colville, the UNHRC spokesperson, said in a press statement:

> These are of course extremely serious accusations and it is crucial these cases are thoroughly and urgently investigated. We are heartened that the initial response we've received from the countries concerned, as well as the European Union, do show that they take these terrible allegations very seriously. We will continue to closely follow up on these cases and any others which emerge, as the UN team on the ground continues its investigations.[9]

The cases involved European contingencies; in particular a boy of seven and a girl of eight said they had been sexually abused by French soldiers in 2014. Further allegations against EU troops who were in the CAR for about a year in 2014 came from four teenage girls, three of whom identified Georgian troops and episodes in a camp for displaced people outside the capital, Bangui. Five new allegations of sexual abuse at the hands of UN peacekeepers also came to light, dating back to 2014, and involving peacekeepers from Morocco, Nigeria, Bangladesh and the DRC, plus a UN police officer from Senegal.[10]

On 4 February 2016, it was further reported[11] that MINUSCA had been hit by another round of sex allegations involving 120 Congolese peacekeepers who were stationed in Bambari from 17 September to 14 December 2015; these peacekeepers had now been confined to barracks and were due to be sent home; the allegations against them, which were now being investigated, included seven separate sex abuse claims that encompassed 29 cases of sexual exploitation, assault and rape of minors by the Congolese troops at the UN peacekeeping post in Bambari which was just opposite an old cotton mill now serving as a displaced persons camp. The responsibility for disciplining peacekeepers rested with their respective countries; however, financial sanctions could be imposed against countries that failed to investigate reported allegations of sexual abuse.[12]

A fresh round of allegations soon followed at the end of March 2016, about sexual abuse incidents in 2015 involving minors; some UN peacekeepers were implicated, together with French special forces serving under Operation Sangaris which was not under UN command. France promised to investigate and deal with it.[13]

Meanwhile clashes raged on after the coup in March 2013. The following selection of events offers some indication of their intensity and consistency:

- It was reported on 9 October 2014 that seven people including one Pakistani peacekeeper were killed, and seven others were injured, as fresh violence broke out in Bangui – the first since MINUSCA took over peacekeeping from the AU. The peacekeepers were ambushed by rebel militias in the PK5 area of Bangui, which is a Muslim enclave. The clashes continued for several days until 15 October 2014. A further two civilians were killed and six Pakistani peacekeepers were injured on 11 October 2014.
- A report by Human Rights Watch, published on 22 December 2014, stated that UN peacekeepers 'block Moslems from fleeing abroad or provide no assistance when they try to leave'.[14]
- On 26 September 2015, some 21 people were reportedly killed and another 100 injured in an outbreak of violence in which Muslims attacked a mainly Christian neighbourhood after a Muslim taxi driver was killed in Bangui. The chaos carried on for three days on the streets of Bangui, accompanied by deadly violence. About 500 prison inmates escaped on 29 September 2015.[15] Also on this day, three people died and several hundred were injured as the main streets in the country were closed by UN peacekeeping barricades and troops who opened fire and dispersed several hundred protesters approaching the presidential palace. The inter-religious nature of these clashes was due to the fact that a taxi driver had been murdered in the PK5 neighbourhood which is predominantly Muslim and a regular flashpoint for the Christian and Muslim communities.[16] As protesters targeted international NGOs and demanded that Catherine Samba-Panza stand down, she sacrificed delivering her

speech at the UN General Assembly and made her way back to attend to the security situation in the country. The overnight curfew was not being respected and there was looting of shops at night and in broad daylight, even though the country was supposed to hold elections in three weeks' time.

- On 30 September 2015, both the CAR defence and security ministers were dismissed in a cabinet reshuffle, amidst heavy gunfire that was heard in several districts of Bangui.
- On 18 May 2016, a staff member of the international medical humanitarian organization Doctors Without Borders/Médecins Sans Frontières (MSF) was shot and killed during an ambush on two MSF vehicles.[17]
- Following more than a dozen attacks against aid workers in May 2016, MINUSCA and the UN Office for the Coordination of Humanitarian Affairs (OCHA) reported on 17 June 2016 a spate of attacks and reprisals in the Ngaoundaye area between groups backed by Christian militias and herders supported by Muslim fighters. Several people were killed and injured, and thousands forced out of their homes to seek refuge in neighbouring Chad and Cameroon, as their houses had been burned and looted. OCHA's assessment was that the increasing insecurity was hampering humanitarian efforts and making the work of humanitarian actors even more challenging.[18] Reports of renewed clashes between armed groups continued.[19]

On 8 December 2015, the Constitutional Court rejected former president Bozize's application (plus 14 other applications) to participate in the elections scheduled for 27 December 2015. On 18 December 2015, the AUC Chairperson approved the deployment of AU Short-Term Observers (STOs) for the 2015 general elections. The AU Electoral Observation Mission (AUEOM) was led by Souleymane Ndene Ndiaye, former prime minister of the Republic of Senegal. The presidential and parliamentary elections were postponed from 27 December to 30 December to reflect the provision in the existing constitution that elections should be held only on Sundays. The 2004 constitutional referendum had changed the constitution from a presidential to a semi-presidential system, with a maximum two-term presidential limit, which was approved by 91.37 per cent of voters on a 77.1-per cent turnout. The Transitional Council had already decided, on 30 August 2015, that a constitutional referendum should be held in 2015, before the general elections. Hence the referendum originally scheduled for 5 October 2015 was held on 13–14 December 2015. The referendum retained the semi-presidential system but created a senate and a national election authority, and allowed for government to inform parliament prior to signing any mineral contracts or concessions; it was approved by 93 per cent of voters.

However, the constitutional referendum was marred by violent clashes in which up to five people were killed by gun and rocket fire, while some 20 others were wounded, in the Bolondom Muslim (PK5) district of Bangui. General Bala Keita of MINUSCA noted that despite the presence of 12,000 UN peacekeepers, large swathes of the country remained out of bounds and under the control of rebel chiefs or bandits. It was therefore not a surprise that in the weeks prior to the election, Noureddine Adam, a deputy commander of Seleka, who also doubles as head of the Popular Front for the Renaissance of Central Africa (FPRC), declared the Logone region in the country's north-east as autonomous, and threatened to ban elections in Logone. The state took a position that the autonomy would be treated as a declaration of war. After days of talks brokered by the Organisation of the Islamic Conference (OIC), Adam announced on 23 December 2015 that he would no longer oppose the elections, and that he regretted calling for a partition of the country.

The 30 December 2015 elections for president and 141 parliamentarians, which had already been delayed for the fifth time, had to take place even if the authorities were not completely ready. There were logistical teething problems. On Christmas Day 2015, a mountain of election materials were still waiting to be flown by helicopter from Bangui airport to the provinces, to be subsequently transported by off-road vehicles on bad roads to some 4,000 polling stations across the country; smaller packages were to be distributed by motor cycles. Election staff were not well trained and did not know what to do on election day about the logistics of verifying votes and getting sealed ballot boxes back to either the provincial headquarters or Bangui after the ballot was over. One of the leading candidates, Anicet Dologuele, publicly stated that he was backed by the ousted and exiled Bozizé. It was intriguing to note that some 460,000 people had left the country since the 2013 coup that ousted Bozizé, and another 470,000 were internally displaced and were hosted in camps within the CAR; one wondered what to make of the voter turnout data. Even more worrying was the speculation that some 75 per cent of current CAR occupants were either not citizens or were not from Central Africa.[20]

On 29 January 2016, opposition protesters called for the cancellation of the presidential election results, saying that the vote was plagued with irregularities and should be annulled by the Constitutional Court. They may have hoped that the same court that had ruled the previous week that the parliamentary elections held on the same day as the presidential election should be re-run would pay heed to their protest. However, the presidential run-off scheduled for 14 February went ahead, irrespective of the fact that the two run-off candidates were not of Seleka background even if this was not intentional. These contestants had competed legitimately to become run-off candidates. Hence the critical issue of integrating the Muslim Seleka into the regular army (the thorny and perennial issue that unseated former president Bozizé, and which also defeated President Djotodia who replaced him) remained on the political table as a key election issue, among the related issue of establishing state control over the rebel-ridden and unlegislated north-east controlled by Seleka elements. The country was awash with dangerous weapons, and according to Human Rights Watch (HRW), a grenade was cheaper than a can of coke in the CAR.[21] Anicet Georges Dologuelé, who publicly declared his alliance with Bozizé, lost the run-off ballot to Faustin-Archange Touadéra who won 63 per cent of the vote.

The lack of state control over large expanses of land has benefited not just rebel militias in the country, but also Joseph Kony's Lord's Resistance Army (LRA). It was reported on 3 March 2016 that the LRA had abducted 217 people in the CAR during 2016 alone, of whom 54 were children.[22] Also, out of 12,000 child soldiers recruited in the CAR during the conflict between 2012 and 2014, the United Nations Children's Fund (UNICEF) says 6,000 still need to be demobilized. Hence a UNICEF-funded NGO known as CARITAS had undertaken to help the adolescent soldiers to rebuild their lives and reintegrate into society, whether by going back to school and/or training in a variety of suitable vocations of their choice such as tailoring, carpentry and vehicle maintenance. The UNICEF/CARITAS centre is in Boali, about 100 km from Bangui, and was a stronghold of the armed anti-Balaka faction.[23]

On 17 November 2016, some 80 countries and international agencies at the Brussels donor conference pledged €2.6 billion in aid over the next four years for the CAR.[24]

International Political Economy

The CAR has consistently been among the bottom ten countries on the Human Development Index (HDI) over a period of eight consecutive years from the 2010 Human Development Report (HDR). Despite its rich mineral and other natural resources, underdevelopment has been a key characteristic, and the country is further handicapped by being landlocked and dependent on the existing export/import infrastructure of equally poor or relatively less poor surrounding countries. That said, the country has enviable resources such as uranium, gold, diamonds, crude oil and timber, but the obvious governance deficit and history of conflict has not allowed development to take place. Data limitations have prevented the forecasting of GDP components, [25] however, since 2014 when the semblance of a relatively stable government began to emerge, real GDP growth has improved and was forecasted by the IMF to hit 4.7 per cent in 2017 if the 'ongoing government dialogue with armed groups helps to reduce violence'.[26] The economic cost of violence in 2016 alone, which amounted to $1,012,000,000 in purchasing power parity (PPP) terms,[27] increased to $1,215,900,000 in 2017,[28] and the CAR became sixth among the ten most affected countries in the world with respect to the economic costs of violence.[29]

Here is a snapshot of the CAR's performance on the Ibrahim Index on African Governance (IIAG):

- In the 2010 index, the CAR ranked 47th overall, with a score of 34.34 per cent;
- In the 2011 index,[30] the CAR ranked 49th overall, with a score of 33 per cent;
- In the 2012 index, the CAR ranked 48th overall, with a score of 34 per cent;
- In the 2013 index, the CAR ranked 49th overall, with a score of 32.7 per cent;
- In the 2014 index, the CAR ranked 51st overall, with a score of 24.8 per cent;

- In the 2015 index, the CAR ranked 42nd overall, with a score of 24.9 per cent.[31]
- In the 2016 index, the CAR ranked 57th overall, with a score of 25.7 per cent, which constituted a negative 4.9-per cent drop in comparative improvement over the decade trend index of 2006–15;
  - ✔ 52nd in Safety and Rule of Law with a score of 15.7 per cent, which constituted a − 16.2-per cent comparative downward spiral in the decade trend index of 2006–15; 52nd again in the personal safety sub-category which constituted a − 29.6-per cent comparative downward spiral in the decade index; 52nd again in the national security sub-category or a − 23.7-per cent comparative downward spiral in the decade index; 48th in the accountability sub-category or a − 1.8-per cent drop in the decade comparative trend index; and 51st in the rule of law sub-category or a − 9.9-per cent drop in comparative performance in the decade trend index;
  - ✔ 37th in Participation and Human Rights with a score of 38.8 per cent which signified a − 1.1-per cent drop in comparative performance on the decade trend index 2006–15; 34th in the participation sub-category or a − 1.2-per cent comparative deterioration in the decade trend index; 41st in the rights sub-category which constituted a − 5.2-per cent comparative drop in the decade trend index; and 32nd in the gender sub-category which constituted a comparative positive change of 3.3 per cent in the decade trend index;
  - ✔ 51st in Sustainable Economic Opportunity, with a score of 21.6 per cent which constituted a 1-per cent drop in the comparative trend index 2006–15; 53rd in the infrastructure sub-category or a − 2.1-per cent downward spiral in the comparative decade index; 47th in the public management sub-category or a − 8.8-per cent comparative deterioration over the decade; 44th in the business environment sub-category which constituted a mere 1.1-per cent improvement in the comparative decade index; and 50th in the rural sector sub-category which constituted a 6-per cent comparative positive change in the decade index;
  - ✔ 52nd in Human Development with a score of 26.8 per cent, which constituted a − 1.2-per cent comparative drop in the decade trend index; 52nd in the education sub-category which constituted a − 0.2-per cent comparative drop in the decade index; 53rd in the

health sub-category which constituted a −0.4-per cent comparative drop over the decade; and 52nd in the welfare sub-category which constituted a −3.1-per cent comparative drop in the index over the decade.[32]

- In the 2017 index,[33] the CAR ranked 51st overall with a score of 30.5 per cent, which signified a −1.3-per cent comparative aggregate deterioration over the ten-year period from 2007 to 2016, and −3.9-per cent over the five-year period from 2012 to 2016; improved slightly from 52nd to 51st in Safety and Rule of Law over the 2007−16 decade; deteriorated comparatively from 37th to 39th in Participation and Human Rights over the decade; improved from 51st to 47th in Sustainable Economic Opportunity; and maintained position at 52nd in Human Development;[34]

- In the 2018 index, Central African Republic ranked 50th overall with a score of 29.5, which signified a −2.5 per cent comparative aggregate deterioration over the ten year period from 2008 to 2017; improved from 51st to 49th in Safety and Rule of Law; improved from 39th to 36th in Participation and Human Rights over the decade; worsened from 47th to 49th in Sustainable Economic Opportunity; and maintained position at 52nd in Human Development.[35]

The CAR's performance on the Global Peace Index (GPI) has been as follows:

- In the 2010 GPI, the CAR ranked 136th out of 149 countries – scoring 2.753;
- In the 2011 GPI, the CAR ranked 144th out of 153 countries – scoring 2.869;
- In the 2012 GPI, the CAR ranked 151st out of 159 countries – scoring 2.872;
- In the 2013 index, the CAR ranked 153rd out of 162 countries – scoring 3.031;
- In the 2014 GPI, the CAR ranked 156th out of 162 countries – scoring 3.331;
- In the 2015 GPI, the CAR ranked 158th out of 162 countries – scoring 3.332;[36]

- In the 2016 GPI, the CAR ranked 157th out of 163 countries – scoring 3.354;[37] and indeed contributed to the overall deterioration of the index's global average score, even if the CAR's political instability lessened after holding the December 2015 elections;[38]
- In the 2017 GPI, the CAR ranked 155th out of 163 independent states and territories – scoring 3.213.[39] Despite the slight improvement, the country still ranked 42nd out of 44 among sub-Saharan African countries within the index;[40]
- In the related Positive Peace Index of 2017, the CAR ranked 162nd among 163 independent states and territories, with a score of 4.39;[41]
- In the 2018 GPI, the CAR ranked 155th out of 163 independent states and territories globally – scoring 3.236, and 41st among the 44 Sub-Saharan Afrian countries featured in the index. More seriously, the CAR became listed among the five least peaceful countries in the world, according to the 2018 index.[42]

Below is the CAR's performance on the UNDP's Human Development Index (HDI):

- In the 2010 HDI, it ranked 159th out of 169 countries in the 2010 HDR;
- In the 2011 HDI, it ranked 179th out of 187 countries in the 2011 HDR;
- In the 2012 HDI, it ranked 185th out of 187 countries in the 2012 HDR;
- In the 2013 HDI, it ranked 180th out of 186 countries in the 2013 HDR;
- In the 2014 HDI, it ranked 185th out of 187 countries in the 2014 HDR;
- In the 2015 HDI, it ranked 187th out of 188 countries in the 2015 HDR;[43]
- In the 2016 HDI, it got to the very bottom, 188th out of the 188 countries indexed in the 2016 HDR.[44]
- In the 2018 Human Development Indices and Indicators (HDII) Statistical Update, it escaped the bottom position by one, as 188th out of 189 countries.[45]

Below is the CAR's performance on the Corruption Perceptions Index (CPI):

- 2010 – 154th out of 178 positions, with a score of 2.1 (same as Cambodia, Comoros, Congo-Brazzaville, Guinea-Bissau, Kenya, Laos, Papua New Guinea, Russia and Tajikistan);
- 2011 – 154th out of 182 positions, with a score of 2.2 (together with Congo-Brazzaville, Côte d'Ivoire, Guinea-Bissau, Kenya, Laos, Nepal, Papua New Guinea, Paraguay and Zimbabwe);
- 2012 – 144th out of 174 positions, with a score of 26 (together with Bangladesh, Cameroon, Congo-Brazzaville, Syria and Ukraine);
- 2013 – 144th out of 175 positions, with score of 25 (same as Cameroon, Iran, Nigeria, Papua New Guinea and Ukraine);
- 2014 – 150th out of 174 positions, with a score of 24 (with Paraguay);
- 2015 – 145th out of 167 country positions, scoring just 24;[46]
- 2016 – 159th out of 176 countries and territories, scoring 20 (with Burundi, Chad, Haiti and Congo-Brazzaville).[47]
- 2017 – 156th out of 180 countries and territories globally, scoring 23,[48] and 37th among 49 Sub-Saharan African countries featured in the index.[49]

Security Challenges

The lack of government security over large areas of land, mostly thick forests, would remain a security concern for the foreseeable future, especially as the forest areas act as havens for local and foreign rebel groups, including the LRA. The perennial issue of integrating the Seleka into the regular army was already on the desk of every head of state prior to the recent elections that brought in President Faustin-Archange Touadéra.

Below are the CAR's ratings on the various terrorism indexes:

- In the 2011 Verisk Maplecroft Terrorism Index (for the 2010 period), the CAR ranked 9th among the top ten countries on the index;
  - ✔ the CAR did not feature among the top ten during the 2011 period;

- In the 2012 Global Risks Index (for the 2012 period), the CAR ranked 7th and was rated in the 'high' category;
  ✔ In the 2014 index (for the 2013 period) the CAR ranked 8th among the top ten 'extreme'-rated countries;
- In the 2015 Political Violence Index (for 2014), the CAR ranked 9th among the top ten countries rated 'extreme';
- In the 2016 Political Risk Index, the CAR was rated in the 'extreme' risk category;[50]
- In the 2015 Global Terrorism Index (GTI), which lists rankings in reverse order in contrast to other performance indexes, so that the worst-performing (in this case, Iraq) is at the top, the CAR ranked 14th among 162 countries that featured on the index, with a score of 6.721;[51]
- In the 2016 GTI, the CAR ranked 20th among 163 countries that featured on the index, with a score of 6.518,[52] having registered the fourth-largest decline in deaths from nearly 600 in the previous index to 166,[53] thanks to the work of counter-terrorist groups;[54]
- In the 2017 GTI, the CAR worsened slightly further to 19th among 163 countries that featured on the index, with a score of 6.394,[55] and was 5th among sub-Saharan colleagues within the index.[56]

Peacekeeping is MINUSCA's priority, but because of dire want and poverty, priority has had to be allocated to addressing poverty as a security challenge, which has also generated the issue of peacekeepers taking advantage of the vulnerability of citizens (particularly women and young girls) to commit abuses, itself a widespread issue under intensive investigation, and an unwanted distraction of the UN's resources away from its priority aims. Adults can barely feed themselves and their dependants, let alone afford medical treatment for anything. Nearly 2.5 million people faced hunger, according to an emergency food security assessment by the UN World Food Programme (WFP) conducted in June 2016. Alarmingly, this constituted a doubling of hungry people within the last year alone and, furthermore, almost a million people were still displaced[57] and were scared to go back to their original places of livelihood three years after the civil war broke out, despite a peace agreement being in place, and a new president having been elected in February 2016. There was a concurrent situation in South Sudan where internally displaced people were too scared to return to their places of origin and remained in UN protection sites (discussed in Chapter 9 of this book).

Some of the camps for displaced people were located in 'enemy territory', for example, the Catholic Missionary camp visited by Pope Francis on 29 November 2015 located in the notorious PK5 district which is a Muslim enclave in Bangui and still controlled by armed groups. Many other displaced Muslims in the north of the country continued to live in UN protected sites, owing to the hazards of the broad Muslim Seleka versus Christian anti-Balaka divisions across the country.

A more precarious potential for continued unrest remained with rebel factions within the broad Seleka camp. Rebel groups across the country remained armed after the civil war subsided, and although the UN saw an urgent need to disarm them, the idea was strongly opposed by the rebel groups. The task of disarming would be extremely ardous even if the rebel groups agreed to disarm, not least because of the large stretch of ungoverned territory without visible state authority, rule of law or security for citizens living in such areas; suffice to say that even Bangui and the surrounding area, which have a visible MINUSCA presence, continued to experience unrest. On 4 July 2016, UN High Commissioner for Human Rights Zeid Ra'ad Al Hussein visited Bangui and expressed grave concerns that security and human rights had begun to deteriorate and, moreover, that fighting could re-escalate.[58] On the next day, 5 July 2016, in Bambari, which hosted a UN peacekeeping post, intense fighting broke out between two rival groups of the Union for Peace in Africa, a somewhat new faction of the now fragmented Seleka coalition;[59] at least 12 people were killed and at least 14 injured.[60]

The well-armed and coordinated UPC controlled most of Bambari; however, the UN mandate is restricted to peacekeeping and excludes troubleshooting. Hence UN patrols following the attack had just to ensure that the fighting stopped and/or that peace was restored as quickly as possible. Quite clearly, the security situation had the potential to get worse, as rightly diagnosed by the UN rights chief, especially in the rural areas where conflicts between rival factions were very common.[61]

On 24 October 2016, four people were killed and several injured in violent protests in Bangui. The protesters called for MINUSCA to step up efforts or leave the country because the peacekeepers had been unable to maintain peace, and should have been doing more to combat the armed militias operating and killing people in the provinces. There were clashes between the peacekeepers and armed residents in Bangui, who had called a general strike in the capital. Protest organizer Gervais Lakosso petitioned that MINUSCA should withdraw the peacekeepers from the country over lack of performance, because they were 'doing the opposite of what they were supposed to do'.[62] However, this view was rejected by MINUSCA, principally because the national army was not yet ready to defend citizens. MINUSCA reported that on 27 October, 15 people died in clashes between former Seleka rebels and anti-Balakas, while six police officers and four civilians died in an ambush on 28 October.[63]

However, on 31 October 2016, French defence minister Jean Yves le Drian announced that France was bringing its Operation Sangaris peacekeeping mission in the CAR to a close, even in the face of ongoing further violence. He argued that the French mission had fulfilled its aims: (a) to maintain sufficient security and stability necessary for a congenial political space to conduct the presidential and parliamentary elections of January to February 2016; (b) to prevent large-scale or mass massacres and potential genocide during the conflict following the ousting of President Bozizé; and (c) to disarm ex-Seleka and anti-Balaka militias, and eventually transfer the whole peacekeeping role to MINUSCA.[64] Even though the disarmament of rebel factions was far from completed (as discussed previously), France had judged the mission as successful, and more or less completed, but would leave behind some 350 soldiers as critical back-up to MINUSCA.[65]

Just where the departure of the French mission left the capability of MINUSCA to handle the remaining challenges became open to question. In the week commencing 15 May 2017, MINUSCA reported that intense clashes between Christian and Muslim militias in the diamond-mining town of Bria resulted in at least 22 dead and some 10,000 others fleeing the town.[66] On 21 June 2017, rival armed factions signed a peace deal aimed at ending the years of bloodshed, but at least 100 were killed in Bria the very next day in renewed clashes. The escalating violence cut off humanitarian aid routes and access, while the fighters infiltrated the camps of humanitarian agencies and destroyed bridges and roads. At least 100,000 people were displaced from Bria,

Bangassou and Alindao as a result of the clashes. Later, in July 2017, a Moroccan UN soldier was killed and three others injured in Bangassou, as Christian militia attempted to seize a cathedral that sheltered hundreds of Muslims who had fled from the religious clashes that began in May 2017.[67] Furthermore, aid organizations such as the Red Cross continued to suffer a series of attacks, as six volunteer staff were killed at the organization's health centre in Gambo on 3 August 2017. This was the third murderous attack against the organization's staff in 2017.[68]

On 15 November 2017, the UNSC adopted Resolution 2387 (2017) to extend MINUSCA's mandate for another 12 months to 2018. The resolution added 900 more military personnel, bringing the authorized troop ceiling to 11,650 military personnel, 2,080 police personnel and 108 corrections officers. The UNSC further called for an enhancing of MINUSCA's personnel, mobility and data-gathering capabilities so that its resources could be optimized.

CHAPTER 5

DEMOCRATIC REPUBLIC OF THE CONGO

Nationalism in the Democratic Republic of the Congo (DRC) consists in struggling to hold together a large and unwieldy geographical territory with a busy history of sub-regional and foreign interferences, not least to exploit the mineral and human capital resource, but also to throw spanners into the work of governance for achieving that very purpose. Hence the solution for fixing this country is practically impossible for the central government alone to provide, but at the same time the opportunity for decentralization was overshadowed by the uneasy suspicion that President Joseph Kabila was scheming to remain after his two maximum presidential terms had expired. This mistrust left insufficient space for effective planning and implementation of countrywide policies for development. In an already-devastated pot of problems, the drama of government overtures vis-à-vis the second-guessing of presidential scheming and related problems has made the Congolese theatre an interesting one to watch, along with its high security risks.

What Existed before Laurent-Désiré Kabila

The DRC, known formerly as Zaire from the period 1971 to 1997, is located in the centre of Africa and is surrounded by as many as nine countries. Clockwise, it is bordered in the north by the CAR and South Sudan, and in the east by Uganda, Rwanda, Burundi and Tanzania (the countries that the former Zaire has the most intense relations with, because of the Hutu–Tutsi rival ethnicity that spans Uganda, Rwanda and Burundi). In the south, the DRC is bordered by Zambia, Angola and a bit of the Atlantic Ocean, and in the west by Congo-Brazzaville.

Located in the very heart of a naturally well-endowed African continent, the DRC projects immense wealth in natural resources, alongside an unstable political history and bad governance, and a concomitant deficient infrastructure and disorganized economy reflecting a history of colonial and external looting, which has thrown several spanners into national development and whatever else remains of the country. This combination of factors makes the country rather unwieldy to govern, not least because of the largeness of its territory, within which internal human displacements from the numerous inter-group conflicts over time are extremely difficult to handle, despite having the largest contingent of United Nations (UN) peacekeepers on its soil for the longest duration.

Perhaps the history of the exploitation of the DRC can be dated from the creation of the Congo Free State as an exploitative private venture by

Map 5 Map of Democratic Republic of the Congo.

King Leopold II of Belgium at the 1885 Berlin Conference that sponsored the partition of Africa. The railway infrastructure from the heartland capital to the coast, and millions of acres of rubber plantations for the international vehicle tyre market, were the chief exploits at the expense of the toil, sweat and tragic diseases of Congolese indigenes in the process. Subsequently, the Belgian Government resolved that the property would be better managed by the state rather than a private individual, and took it over by a parliamentary vote in Belgium on 18 October 1908. In the last days of empire, the Mouvement National Congolais (MNC) party led by Patrice Lumumba won the May 1960 local parliamentary elections, even if parliament would then elect Joseph Kasavubu of the Alliance des Bakongo (ABAKO) party as president.

Prime Minister Lumumba and President Kasavubu became the effective combination to gain independence on 30 June 1960, although a crisis soon developed between the two, leading to the sacking of the former by the latter on 5 September 1960. Joseph Mobutu the emerging army staff who effected Lumumba's arrest on 14 September 1960, took advantage of the national frailty of the moment to execute a coup against both masters (president and prime minister), and handed over to a flurry of state leaders. In the governance paralysis that followed, Mobutu emerged as army chief of staff, and subsequently executed another coup on 25 November 1965 against the establishment. When he became head of state this time, a previously ongoing constitutional referendum had already resolved to change the independence name Republic of Congo to Democratic Republic of the Congo, plus awarding other political perks, such as extreme powers to the presidency, from which Mobutu would later benefit and which he would abuse, whether or not he schemed for this prior to becoming head of state himself.

Mobutu later capitalized on the extreme powers of the presidency to run a military dictatorship, while underwriting a one-party state system of kleptocracy and bad governance to the point of the ridiculous. He changed the country's name from the Democratic Republic of the Congo to Republic of Zaire in 1971, and the name of the River Congo to the Zaire River. Meanwhile, strong US anti-communist backing for Mobutu sidelined the 1967 People's Revolutionary Party (PRP) founded by Laurent-Désiré Kabila into a Marxist-Communist existence in the South Kivu backwater of eastern Zaire, under the firm support of the People's Republic of China, as the capitalist–communist proxy battles unfolded.

Out of this woodwork, Laurent-Désiré Kabila met President Museveni of Uganda, Julius Nyerere of Tanzania and Paul Kagame, the future president of Rwanda, and waited for his presidential turn in the Congo.

What Occurred under Laurent-Désiré Kabila

What is most significant in the context of this book, and the current politics of the sub-region, is how the First Congo War of 1996–7 began. The Rwandan Genocide of 1994 and the resumption of a Kagame (Tutsi-led) administration resulted in mass migrations of Hutus into Zairean territory and the pursuit of anti-Rwandan operations by the Hutu resistance, Interahamwe, from their new bases in eastern Congo, assisted by the naïve Zairean Armed Forces (FAZ) of Mobutu at the time. This development incurred the wrath of Rwandan president Paul Kagame, who effectively led a rebellion against Mobutu, with direct assistance from the Ugandan forces of his previous boss President Museveni. Rwanda and Uganda found a faithful ally in the person of Laurent-Désiré Kabila who had returned to Zaire in October 1996 to form the Alliance of Democratic Forces for the Liberation of Congo-Zaire (ADFL). Kabila and the AFDL fought Mobutu, overran a large part of Zaire, and forced Mobutu to flee into exile on 16 May 1997. Laurent-Désiré Kabila effectively became president on 17 May 1997 but appointed James Kabarebe, a Rwandan, as his chief of staff, thereby sowing the seeds of his own downfall.

Laurent-Désiré Kabila renamed the country he inherited as the Democratic Republic of the Congo, which by this time had become so devastated and proliferated with arms, cliques and subgroups within the military fabric, that it was unwieldy to govern, let alone make sense of the economics. When Laurent-Désiré Kabila replaced Chief of Staff James Kabarebe with a native Congolese, Celestin Kifwa, on 14 July 1998, and subsequently ordered Rwandan and Ugandan forces to leave Zaire, the Second Congo War of July 1998 to July 2003 began, with Rwanda and Uganda turning around to provide backing to a new Rally for Congolese Democracy (RCD), thereby inviting neighbouring countries Angola, Namibia, Zimbabwe and even Chad and Sudan into the fray as pro-government allies. The strategic involvement of neighbouring countries continued even after Laurent-Désiré Kabila was shot on 16 January 2001 allegedly by his own bodyguard Rashidi Muzelein, and was replaced by his son Joseph Kabila eight days later.

What Transpired with Joseph Kabila – the New Pan-Africanism

Joseph Kabila reiterated the call for peace talks involving all parties and supervised by the UN. The UNSC had already passed Resolution 1291 in 2000 to deploy the UN Organization Mission in the Democratic Republic of the Congo (MONUC) from April 2000, although the peace process evolved to be so complex and prolonged that in 2010 the UNSC had to replace MONUC with the UN Stabilization Mission in the Democratic Republic of the Congo (MONUSCO).

Joseph Kabila took office in 2001, was elected as president in 2006 and re-elected in 2011. Although he never officially announced his intention to run for a third term in 2016, any suspicious move in that direction, or any move at all however unrelated, has generated violent opposition. For example, there were violent protests on 19 January 2015 following the announcement of proposed legislation for a new census prior to the forthcoming 2016 elections, as this had potential to defer the election well beyond 2016. The Senate managed to stop this proposal from being legislated, and a new version would remove the requirement to hold a census before the next elections then scheduled for November 2016.[1]

However, another significant feature in the electoral timetable was a schedule prepared by the National Independent Electoral Commission (CENI) slightly earlier on 14 January 2015, a few days prior to the announcement of the defeated proposal, that a revised voters register was necessary before an election should take place, and would require 16 months to complete the full revision exercise, which would cost some £290 million. The DRC's 2016 budget could only run to $58 million for the elections, even though potential support for the voter registration process had been promised by the US and the European Union (EU). Although the existing register that had been used for the December 2011 presidential elections included 30.7 million or 82 per cent of eligible voters, about seven million citizens within the 18–22 age bracket needed to be registered for the next elections, while some 1.6 million deceased and 300,000 duplicate voters had to be removed from the register. A revision of the voters register was indeed a must.

But, the Constitutional Court ruling in May 2016 for Joseph Kabila to remain in office beyond 2016 if the elections were not held in 2016 became a real cause for concern, especially as the government said it had no money for the electoral exercise. Also in the background was the 2015 decentralization of the country into 26 provinces instead of the previous 11, which had already raised suspicion that Kabila had a third-term agenda.[2] Although legislation for the new provinces had taken effect as far back as 18 February 2006 under Article 2 of the 2005 constitution, the timing of implementation in 2015 became highly suspicious.

At least 40 per cent of the country is Catholic, and in November 2015 the Catholic Church officially called on citizens to defy any attempt by Kabila to hold on to the presidency beyond his second term. The church's National Episcopal Conference of Congo (CENCO) issued a statement saying:

> We ask the Congolese people to prove their vigilance in the spirit of article 64 (of the constitution) [. . .] All Congolese have the duty to thwart any individual or group of individuals that takes power by force or exercises it in violation of the provisions of the present constitution.[3]

Subsequently, the opposition were not convinced that Kabila's recent calls for a national dialogue did not have a hidden agenda to amend the constitution to allow him a third term. Opposition parties wanted upfront conditions prior to engaging in the national dialogue, especially as the elections were supposed to take place in November 2016. On 23 February 2016, Ban Ki-moon paid an official visit to the DRC,[4] and among other things advised Kabila against any attempt to remain in power beyond his second term, as that would not be legitimate.[5] Despite Ki-moon's warning, there were real fears that Kabila could stay on for longer if the argument holds that the country had insufficient money to run the election, especially as the Constitutional Court issued a statement on 11 May 2016 that Kabila could stay in office if the elections occurred after November 2016. This announcement ignited nationwide protests on 26 May 2016, during which one protester and a police officer were killed.

It appears that DRC citizens were quite determined to ensure that rationalized ethnonationalism[6] was not imposed or served on them, as had occurred in Burundi and Rwanda respectively (Chapters 3 and 8 of this book) because, quite frankly, there was no case or appetite for it.

In June 2016, the broad spectrum of key opposition forces formed a new platform or coalition known as Rassemblement (translated as rally or gathering), and were quite adamant that Kabila must leave office at the end of his second term in December 2016.

It also appeared that the government was playing a game of its own, as the 'politricks' unfolded every now and then. For example, in the third week of June 2016, the price of going online skyrocketed as the cost of an internet connection more than tripled in the month of June alone. The government insisted that this was a purely commercial decision taken by private operators who said they had to hike their prices because of financial and other constraints, and that the decision on pricing was overseen by the relevant regulatory body and not by the telecommunications ministry. Critics deemed the pricing hike to be a political move aimed at limiting people's access to information, and limiting the use of the internet for potential online and social media activity that could contribute to the political opposition. Previously, the government had already shut down the internet for several weeks following riots against Kabila on 19 January 2015.[7] Conflict and rioting have become so typical of the DRC landscape that clashes could erupt from just about anything. On 17 June 2016, nine people died in clashes between government troops and former M23 rebels who were prevented from leaving the Kamina camp for demobilized rebels, based in south-eastern DRC.[8]

The AU-PSC, which was closely observing the unfolding of events, saw the national dialogue as a practical way forward and appointed the former prime minister of Togo, Edem Kodjo, to facilitate this dialogue. On 4 July 2016, the AU held the inaugural meeting of the Support Group to the AU-led Facilitation of the Congolese National Dialogue, chaired by Smail Chergui the AU commissioner for peace and security, and attended by Said Djinnit the UN special envoy for the Great Lakes; Maman Sidikou, the UN special representative for the DRC and head of MONUSCO; Koen Vervaeke, the EU managing director for Africa; Pascal Couchepin, the special envoy for the Francophonie; Dr Stergomena Lawrence Tax, the executive secretary of the Southern Africa Development Community (SADC); and Ambeyi Ligabo from the International Conference of the Great Lakes Region (ICGLR). Among other things, the meeting 'called on all stakeholders to create an environment conducive for holding the national dialogue'.[9]

Meanwhile, on 27 July 2016, Etienne Tshisekedi, the 83-year-old veteran opposition politician and leader of the Union for Democracy and Social Progress (UDPS), returned to Kinshasa after two years of medical treatment in Belgium. His homecoming, which generated a rousing hero's welcome at Kinshasa airport, coincided with the ongoing national dialogue initiated by Joseph Kabila, and therefore became an opportunity for Tshisekedi to find common ground with the Kabila government on how to hold a free and fair election amidst the problems and issues discussed above. Tshisekedi wasted no time and addressed a campaign rally organized by his party on 29 July 2016. Earlier, in June 2016, Moise Katumbe, the other opposition candidate and owner of TP Mazembe football club, had been sentenced to three years in prison over a real estate dispute, making him ineligible to stand for the 2016 election. The president of the court that sentenced him said she was under presssure from the Kabila government to remove Katumbe from the electoral equation, as he was Kabila's biggest opponent.[10]

On the same day as Tshisekedi's first rally after his homecoming, pro-government activists also staged a rally in Kinshasa stadium to show their support for the president, while the opposition maintained that the delay in setting an election date for 2016 was a deliberate strategy for Kabila to hang on to power beyond the expiry of his second term in December 2016. Tshisekedi therefore called for Kabila to step down at the end of his term. There was another public protest by opposition partners on 23 August 2016, demanding that Kabila step down before the end of 2016.

Subsequently, on 1 September 2016, the national dialogue that was held principally to avert the looming crises at the end of Kabila's second term in December 2016 commenced without the participation of the Rassemblement, which had laid down their preconditions for participating as:

- freeing political prisoners;
- lifting the ban on several TV stations; and
- resignation of the AU-appointed facilitator, Edem Kodjo.[11]

In attendance were the pope's representative in the DRC, and of course Maman Sidikou the MONUSCO representative. However, the talks were suspended due to violent scuffles breaking out between supporters of rival opposition parties. Also on the agenda of the dialogue was the situation in the eastern DRC where residents in the Kivu area had been hacked to death not long before these talks began.

One week after the national dialogue exercise, four options emerged, none of which included holding the elections before the end of 2016 as originally scheduled, or Kabila leaving office at the end of his second presidential term on 19 December 2016.

- Organize the election as soon as possible, which also meant that new voters could not be registered and millions of eligible voters would not be able to vote.
- Enlist some of the eligible new voters, which would still disenfranchise some citizens, and the partial selection would be problematic.
- Enlist all 45 million eligible voters; however, the exercise to update the voter registration would take at least ten to 16 months to complete, and would surely postpone the elections timetable beyond 2016, or even 2017.
- Presidential, legislative and provincial elections would all take place on the same day (date to be decided), under the auspices of an interim government that would be set up with opposition members to take over running the affairs of state from 20 December 2016, with Kabila still at the helm of affairs.
- The Rassemblement, which refused to participate in the dialogue, opined through their spokesperson Jean Lucien Bussa, that if the elections must be postponed, then so be it, but Joseph Kabila must leave power by 19 December 2016, and that the country had four months (from September to December 2016) to work out another option.[12]

It appeared that Kabila hinted at a possible departure and an interim government to be controlled by his party, as bait to lure the AU into officiating the dialogue. The Rassemblement were vehemently opposed to this because Kabila had not expressly announced he would step aside, let alone refuse to be a candidate for the impending election. As was also indicative, the Constitutional Court ruling that Kabila should remain as president was as curious and ridiculous as the dialogue exercise itself, and sent mixed messages. On 19 September 2016, there were further violent protests in Kinshasa that lasted at least two days. Armed troops from the Republican Guard set fire to the headquarters of the UDPS and two other parties.[13] MONUSCO reported that more than 50 people killed in the two-day unrest were shot by police and soldiers; five were killed inside the party headquarters where their bodies were found burned, as reported by survivors; the others died in the streets. An interesting element of the political dynamic revealed that the bereaved families would be relying on politicians to cover the sanitary fees of burials. The Governor of Kinshasa (a member of Kabila's party) had announced that city authorities would give $5,000 to each bereaved family. Although the political factions competed to help the bereaved, they did not prove competent in making progress to resolve the ensuing national political deadlock.[14]

In spite of the national dialogue, and in what appeared to be a sure sign that Kabila was taking the country for a perilous ride, the Constitutional Court made a ruling on 17 October 2016 that Kabila could remain in office, even in the post-December 2016 duration, while the country effected the necessary electoral preparations and the new timetable towards election in April 2018. Kabila was to govern with Vital Kamerhe, from the Union for the Congolese Nation, as prime minister. The issues about extending the election timetable were well rehearsed and understood by all political factions, so the ruling to stretch the election timetable for the practical reasons given, and in response to the Electoral Commission's request (to the Constitutional Court) for its approval, was not as controversial as the decision that Kabila could also remain in office while the new electoral timetable took effect.

This latest Constitutional Court ruling, in the aftermath of the national dialogue, was in very bad taste, to say the least, and was not unanimous. There was an ominous sign of disagreement within the Constitutional Court, which appeared to operate without a quorum in making that decision.[15] This decision was obviously unacceptable to the Rassemblement, who were poised to hit the streets with further demonstrations, oblivious of whatever agreement had been reached between the Kabila government and other minor opposition parties which participated in the national dialogue, to form an interim government to function between December 2016 and April 2018.[16] The cabinet of this interim government was sure to consist of portfolios distributed among the minor and feeble opposition parties and Kabila's cronies within the ruling party.

On 17 November, the authorities announced the outcome of a power-sharing deal with the minor oppostion parties. Samy Badibanga, a constituency member of parliament in the Kinshasa area, and previously of the UDPS, was named as prime minister in the new government, with Kabila staying put.[17] The Rassemblement were not fazed. Quite frankly, the national dialogue organized under the auspices of the AU was a wasted effort and a non-starter in the first place, as there was no guarantee that Kabila could be disallowed from being part of the state edifice after 2016. The spin from the Constitutional Court using Article 70 of the constitution[18] to browbeat citizens so that Kabila should not leave office until the installation of a newly elected president did not go down well with citizens and the Rassemblement, not least because Articles 75 and 76[19] of the same constitution allowed for Kabila to resign for the president of the Senate to oversee the interim governmental period of preparation for the impending election scheduled to occur in April 2018. This was especially so in the prevailing vitriolic climate in which there was no appetite for Kabila to remain as president longer than necessary to allow him to scheme the electoral preparation, or for him to stand as a candidate for the impending election.

Hence on 20 December 2016, there were violent opposition protests in Kinshasa and Lubumbashi. HRW and MONUSCO reported that at least 40 protesters were shot dead by police, at least 265 were injured, and some 460 including pro-democracy youths were arrested by government forces in Kinshasa, Lubumbashi and other towns.[20] HRW Central Africa Director Ida Sawyer reported a new and dangerous development: the emergence of armed vigilante groups that had taken on security responsibilities on the premise that Kabila was no longer legitimate, along with the state security establishment.[21]

Eventually, it was CENCO, which had previously invoked Article 64[22] of the constitution in November 2015 to arouse public unrest against the government, and which on 20 September 2016 had pulled out of the ill-fated AU-sponsored dialogue because of violent public unrest, that assumed the responsibility to organize another dialogue, working from a draft compromise resolution of 23 December 2016. The resolution stated that Kabila could remain in office but must leave before the end of 2017, and that during that period he would neither amend the constitution nor stand as candidate in the impending elections; Etienne Tshisekedi the head of the Rassemblement would be appointed to oversee the implementation of this deal; a prime minister would be appointed by the opposition in this interim government presided over by Kabila; and the election could also take place by December 2017. What remained unclear at this stage was whether the Rassemblement would allow the prime minister to be anyone other than Etienne Tshisekedi or at least someone from among their ranks, and why the carefully crafted election timetable stretching to April 2018 was now being brought forward to December 2017, when a key sticking point in the whole drama was for Kabila not to preside over the impending election. Obviously, an agreement could not be reached before Christmas, and the CENCO dialogue was postponed. However, there were Christmas Day killings in North Kivu related to the political impasse in far away Kinshasa.

Upon resumption after Christmas, the CENCO dialogue concluded on 31 December 2016 with a deal that was to be signed well into 2017, because several issues remained to be streamlined before serious signatures could be appended on the dotted line. The issues included sensitive conversations about the frail state of Etienne Tshisekedi, and hushed negotiations for his agile son Felix Tshisekedi to be slotted into the political fabric as prime minister while his ailing father provided an oversight and mentoring role for the transitional period. Other issues included what role there should be for the small opposition parties that had participated in the first dialogue held in October 2016 under the auspices of the AU.

However, as fate would have it, veteran Etienne Tshisekedi passed away on 1 February 2017 at the age of 84, paving the way for the hushed conversations to become public debate over his succession by Felix Tshisekedi after he had been made leader of the UDPS. An already complex political scenario now took on extra complexity, with the emergence of Felix Tshisekedi as the new leader of the opposition, and one whose leadership capabilities were an unknown quantity. Ironically, the ruling Kabila party was somewhat more comfortable with, or less apprehensive over, Felix than Etienne.

In a bizzare twist of fate, Joseph Kabila announced Bruno Tshibala as prime minister, to replace Samy Badibanga who was unacceptable to the

UDPS and resigned on 6 April 2017.[23] Being an ousted opposition figure, Tshibala's appointment was a tactical move by Kabila to frustrate the UDPS front's wish to offer their candidate Etienne Tshidekenu for the prime ministerial position. Kabila's affront against a promising and peaceful road map to the elections escalated tensions in the country, and alarmed foreign partners and observers who had multiple concerns in addition to the politics. About a week prior to Kabila's announcement, the US had already issued a travel warning to discourage visits to the DRC, after two UN researchers and their translator who were investigating mass murders in Kasai province had been murdered and buried in a shallow grave.[24] Subsequently, the EU also extended assets-freeze and travel-ban sanctions to nine more senior security officials of the DRC government, bringing the total to 16, including the current and former interior ministers and a government spokesperson. All the officials faced sanctions in connection with obstruction of the electoral process.[25]

On 9 July 2017 the Electoral Commission announced that the presidential elections to replace Joseph Kabila, scheduled for December 2017, could not be held,[26] thereby reiterating the 17 October 2016 ruling by the Constitutional Court that Kabila could only leave office when there was a replacement, and reopening the agonizing conundrum of whether Kabila really intended to leave power although his term of office had expired. On 11 October 2017, CENI announced that the presidential elections would not be held until April 2019 at the earliest, citing among other things that it needed some 504 days after the ongoing census to organize the poll; if anything, what could allow an earlier poll would be if the country accepted the use of electronic voting machines, and if the electoral law was changed.[27] The issue remained, however, that Kabila would be in power to preside over the election. Meanwhile revelations that security forces killed at least 62 people and arrested hundreds of others during protests across the country between 19 and 22 December 2016, after Kabila refused to step down at the end of his constitutionally mandated two-term limit, made both local and international news when this was published by HRW in their December 2017 report.[28]

On 5 November 2017, CENI reversed the scheduled ideal date of April 2019 to hold the election for the politically expedient date of 23 December 2018 in order to lessen the increasing agitation and unrest, especially as CENI had now contracted the use of electronic voting machines for the poll. Provisional results for the presidential election were scheduled to be announced on 30 December 2018, definitive results on 9 January 2019, and the next president was to take office on 12 January 2019. On 8 August 2018, Kabila announced Emmanuel Ramazani Shadary as his party's presidential candidate for the December 2018 elections, thereby laying to rest the thorny issue of a Kabila candidacy.

It has always been awkward for the AU to steer through moves to resolve DRC issues in the face of the influence exercised by such obvious and awkward players as Museveni of Uganda and Kagame of Rwanda. However, the AU has managed to push through what has been necessary. On 13 February 2013, the DRC government handed over 500 infantry men to join the AU-led Regional Task Force (RTF), the military component of the Regional Cooperation Initiative for the elimination of the Lord's Resistance Army (RCI-LRA).[29] It was also decided around the same time that Tanzania would provide the force commander for a New Intervention Force created under the control of the Southern Africa Development Community (SADC), and lead this mission to deal with the M23 and other rebel groups in the eastern DRC, regardless of the presence of the large MONUSCO peacekeeping contingent. The push for the intervention force to consist of at least 4,000 troops was led by Tanzania and supported by South Africa. Obviously, this was not palatable news for Rwanda and Uganda, which have historical fingers in the conflict pie in the DRC.[30]

Meanwhile, the series of trials involving various warlords, rebel leaders and even constitutional leaders continued. It was announced on 17 June 2016 that a further trial of warlord Germain Katanga, who faced ICC charges of war crimes and crimes against humanity, was set to resume in the country. The ICC gave prosecutors the green light to proceed with the domestic case against the convicted war criminal. He was sentenced to 12 years in prison by the ICC in March 2014 but finished serving a reduced sentence on 18 January 2016 after the original sentence was converted in November 2015 when he voiced regret. But the DRC authorities decided to keep him behind bars and prosecute for other cases.[31]

Also, on 21 June 2016, Jean-Pierre Bemba Gombo, one of four vice presidents in the DRC's transitional government from 17 July 2003 to December 2006, was sentenced to 18 years' imprisonment on two counts of crimes against humanity (murder and rape) and three counts of war crimes (murder, rape and pillaging), of which he was convicted on 21 March 2016. His 18-year sentence was the longest ever handed down by the ICC, and took into account crimes of sexual violence committed by the Mouvement de Libération du Congo (MLC) troops under the command of Jean-Pierre Bemba in the CAR from 26 October 2002 to 15 March 2003. Bemba's private militia had been there to assist the beleaguered President Patassé who was overthrown on 15 March 2003. This Bemba landmark case became the first instance of the ICC prosecuting sexual violence and rape as an instrument of war during conflict.[32] The victims of sexual assault included underaged girls ranging from ten to 17 years. Bemba's defence complained that the sentence was both excessive and unfair as he was not in control of soldiers on the ground, and had therefore already filed an appeal in March 2016, when the convictions became registered in the court books.[33] On 28 September 2016, Bemba was convicted, and his appeal was launched on the same day. It will be recalled from the extensive discussions in Chapter 4 of this book that the UN, human rights groups and the ICC catalogued widespread sexual assault of underaged boys and girls involving UN peacekeepers and French special forces serving under Operation Sangaris, which was not under UN command.[34] On 8 June 2018, the ICC's Appeals Chamber acquitted Bemba from war crimes and crimes against humanity.[35] Bemba was immediately nominated by his MLC as a presidential candidate for the next presidential election in DRC whenever that occurred.[36] However, on 3 September 2018, the constitutional court disqualified Bemba from the presidential race because of a conviction for witness tampering by the ICC in 2017 while on trial for the other crimes of which he had been acquitted.

It was reported on 29 September 2016 that the US Treasury had placed two close security allies of Joseph Kabila, who were accused of human rights violations, on a US sanctions blacklist. Major-General Gabriel Amisi Kumba, commander of the DRC's armed forces, was accused of repressing political demonstrations, and General John Numbi, a former inspector of the National Police, was accused of threatening to kill opposition candidates who refused to withdraw from regional elections in March 2016. The sanctions banned US companies and US individuals from doing business with the two accused. This move contributed to the broader pressure on Kabila to step down at the end of his second term. However, details of a 16 May 2017 ruling that leaked online on 6 June 2017 listed Numbi among eight senior police officers named as 'national heroes' by President Kabila.[37]

International Political Economy

The DRC has consistently been among the very bottom countries on the UNDP's Human Development Index (HDI) over a period of eight consecutive years since the 2010 Human Development Report (HDR). Despite its rich mineral and other natural resources, underdevelopment has been a key characteristic of the DRC, and the country is further handicapped by being landlocked and dependent on the existing export/import infrastructure of poor neighbouring countries. That said, the country has enviable resources such as coltan, cobalt, diamonds, copper, crude oil and timber, but the obvious governance deficit and history of conflict has not allowed development to take place despite the real GDP growth rates of 6.9 per cent in 2015, 2.4 per cent in 2016, 3.4 per cent estimated for 2017, and 3.8 per cent, 4.1 per cent and 4.4 per cent forecasted for 2018, 2019 and 2020 respectively,[38] in part reflecting the political turmoil as a result of President Kabila's recalcitrance in remaining in office at the end of his second term. The economic cost of violence in 2016 alone, which amounted to $7,688,000,000 in purchasing power parity (PPP) terms,[39] had somehow reduced to $5,512,900,000 in 2017.[40]

The 2015 political decentralization that increased the number of provinces from 11 to 26 posed economic risks for each new province. For example, it would increase transportation costs for mining companies, and would incur the risk of double taxation in mineral-rich Katanga, which has been divided into four provinces.[41] That said, Katanga also hosts many of the poorest citizens despite its vast mineral wealth. Obviously, Katanga citizens do not benefit from their natural resources; hospitals are very few and far between, and health provision is way below normal; also schools have been, and still are, severely underfunded.

The postal service, which had been dysfunctional for some 30 years, had only just resumed in the capital Kinshasa;[42] however, funding was yet to be secured to make it a national delivery service. The resumption of service only became possible after employees were forced to give up at least 18 months of backdated pay claims. The postal service is funded by the state from fees charged to telecommunications operators for the use of an undersea fibre optic cable. To ensure some level of sustainability and growth, the postal service was aiming to sign deals with the DRC's water and electricity companies;[43] presumably utility bills and related paper communications would be very reliant on post, though this has future implications for when the billing goes principally online, which seems to be the global trajectory.

Here is a snapshot of the DRC's performance on the Ibrahim Index on African Governance (IIAG):

- In the 2010 index, the DRC ranked 51st overall, with a score of 31.7 per cent;
- In the 2011 index,[44] the DRC ranked 50th overall, with a score of 32 per cent;
- In the 2012 index, the DRC ranked 51st overall, with a score of 33 per cent;
- In the 2013 index, the DRC ranked 51st overall, with a score of 31.3 per cent;
- In the 2014 index, the DRC ranked 47th overall, with a score of 34.1 per cent;
- In the 2015 index, the DRC ranked 48th overall, with a score of 33.9 per cent;[45]
- In the 2016 index, the DRC ranked 46th overall, with a score of 35.8 per cent, which signified a 2.7-per cent comparative improvement over the decade trend index of 2006–15;
  - ✔ 49th in Safety and Rule of Law with a score of 31 per cent, which constituted a 1.5-per cent comparative positive change in the decade trend index of 2006–15, yet 50th in the personal safety sub-category which constituted a −10.4-per cent comparative downward spiral in the decade index; 48th in the national security sub-category or a −2.9-per cent comparative drop in the decade index; 38th in the accountability sub-category which constituted a 13.1-per cent improvement in the decade trend index; and 44th in the rule of law sub-category which constituted a 6-per cent comparative improvement in the decade trend index;
  - ✔ 42nd in Participation and Human Rights with a score of 36.2 per cent which constituted a −0.5-per cent drop in the

comparative decade index 2006–15; 33rd in the participation sub-category which constituted a −1.6-per cent comparative deterioration in the decade trend index; 39th in the rights sub-category which constituted a −0.4-per cent comparative drop over the decade; and 42nd in the gender sub-category or a comparative positive change of just 0.6 per cent in the decade trend index;

✔ 47th in Sustainable Economic Opportunity with a score of 29 per cent which constituted a 4.4-per cent comparative rise in the decade trend index 2006–15; 51st in the infrastructure sub-category or a 3-per cent comparative rise over the decade; 36th in the public management sub-category which constituted a 9.6-per cent comparative rise over the decade; 43rd in the business environment sub-category which constituted a 2.3-per cent comparative improvement in the decade index; 47th in the rural sector sub-category which constituted a comparative positive change of 2.9 per cent in the decade index;

✔ 42nd in Human Development with a score of 47 per cent which constituted a 5.4-per cent positive change in the comparative decade trend index; 31st in the education sub-category which constituted an 8.2-per cent improvement in the comparative decade index; 43rd in the health sub-category which constituted a 1.4-per cent comparative improvement over the decade, and; 48th in the welfare sub-category which constituted a 6.6-per cent comparative improvement over the decade;[46]

- In the 2017 index,[47] the DRC ranked 48th overall with a score of 35 per cent, which signified a 0.5-per cent comparative aggregate improvement over the ten-year period from 2007 to 2016, and 0.9 per cent over the five-year period from 2012 to 2016; improved slightly from 49th to 48th in Safety and Rule of Law over the 2007–16 decade; deteriorated from 42nd to 45th in Participation and Human Rights over the decade; improved from 47th to 45th in Sustainable Economic Opportunity; and maintained position at 42nd in Human Development.[48]

- In the 2018 index, the DRC ranked 47th overall with a score of 32.1 per cent, which signified a-2.8 per cent comparative aggregate deterioration over the ten-year period from 2008 to 2017; worsened from 48th to 52nd in Safety and Rule of Law; worsened from 45th to 46th in Participation and Human Rights; improved slightly from 45th to 44th in Sustainable Economic Opportunity; and maintained 42nd position in Human Development. The index identified the DRC as among the bottom scoring countries in Transparency and Accountability.[49]

The DRC's performance on the Global Peace Index (GPI) is as follows:

- In the 2010 GPI, the DRC ranked 140th out of 149 countries – scoring 2.925;
- In the 2011 GPI, the DRC ranked 148th out of 153 countries – scoring 3.016;
- In the 2012 GPI, the DRC ranked 154th out of 159 countries – scoring 3.046;
- In the 2013 GPI, the DRC ranked 156th out of 162 countries – scoring 3.085;
- In the 2014 GPI, the DRC ranked 155th out of 162 countries – scoring 3.213;
- In the 2015 GPI, the DRC ranked 155th out of 162 countries – scoring 3.085;[50]
- In the 2016 GPI, the DRC ranked 152nd out of 163 countries – scoring 3.112,[51] and among other things, was found to be a key contributor to state failure and conflict, and a major driver of increase in refugees and internally displaced persons (IDPs);[52]
- In the 2017 GPI, the DRC ranked 153rd out of 163 independent states and territories – scoring 3.061. Put in regional perspective, the country ranked 41st among 44 sub-Saharan African countries within the index;[53]
- In the related Positive Peace Index of 2017, the DRC ranked 154th among 163 independent states and territories, with a score of 4.17;[54]
- In the 2018 GPI, the DRC ranked 156th out of 163 indpendent states and territories globally – scoring 3.251, and remained 41st among the 44 Sub-Saharan African countries featured in the index.[55]

Below is the DRC's performance on the UNDP's Human Development Index (HDI):

- In the 2010 HDI, it ranked 168th out of 169 countries in the 2010 HDR;
- In the 2011 HDI, it ranked 187th out of 187 countries in the 2011 HDR;
- In the 2012 HDI, it ranked 187th out of 187 countries in the 2012 HDR;
- In the 2013 HDI, it ranked 186th (with Niger) out of 187 countries in the 2013 HDR;
- In the 2014 HDI, it ranked 186th out of 187 countries in the 2014 HDR;
- In the 2015 HDI, it ranked 176th out of 188 countries in the 2015 HDR;[56]
- In the 2016 HDI, it maintained status at 176th out of 188 countries in 2016 HDR;[57]
- In the 2018 Human Development Indices and Indicators (HDII) Statistical Update, it maintained again the 176th rank but out of 189 countries.[58]

Below is the DRC's performance on the Corruption Perceptions Index (CPI):

- in 2010, it ranked 164th out of 178 positions, scoring 2.0 (with Guinea, Kyrgyzstan and Venezuela);
- in 2011, it ranked 168th out of 172 positions, scoring 2.0 (with Angola, Chad and Libya);
- in 2012, it ranked 160th out of 172 positions, scoring 21 (with Laos and Libya);
- in 2013, it ranked 154th out of 175 positions, scoring 22 (with Congo-Brazzaville and Tajikistan);
- in 2014, it ranked 154th out of 174 positions, scoring 22 (with Chad);
- in 2015, it ranked 147th out of 167 country positions, scoring 22 (with Chad and Myanmar);[59]
- in 2016, it ranked 156th out of 176 countries and territories, scoring 21 (with Cambodia and Uzbekistan).[60]
- in 2017, it ranked 161st out of 180 countries and territories globally, scoring 21 (with Congo-Brazzaville, Cambodia and Tajikistan),[61] and

41st (with Congo-Brazzaville) among 49 Sub-Saharan African countries featured in the index.[62]

Security Challenges

Below are the DRC's ratings in the various terrorism indexes:

- In the 2011 Verisk Maplecroft Terrorism Index (for the 2010 period), the DRC ranked 8th among the top ten countries;
  - ✔ in the 2012 index (for the 2011 period), the country ranked 6th with an 'extreme' rating;
- In the 2012 Global Risks Index (for the 2012 period), the DRC ranked 2nd with an 'extreme' rating;
  - ✔ in the 2014 index (for the 2013 period), the DRC was 2nd with an 'extreme' rating;
- In the 2016 Political Risk Index, the DRC was rated as a 'high'-risk country;[63]
- In the 2015 Global Terrorism Index (GTI), which lists rankings in reverse order in contrast to other performance indexes, so that the worst-performing (in this case, Iraq) is at the top, the DRC ranked 19th among 162 countries that featured on the index, with a score of 6.487.[64] The riots against President Kabila's scheming to remain in office beyond his second term began in earnest from January 2015;
- In the 2016 GTI, the DRC deteriorated to 17th among 163 countries that featured on the index, with a score of 6.633;[65]
- In the 2017 GTI, the DRC deteriorated further to 13th among 163 countries that featured on the index, with a score of 6.967.[66] The DRC 'rejoined the ten countries with the most deaths from terrorism for the first time since 2010 with 479 deaths' in this index,[67] and was 3rd among sub-Saharan colleagues within the index.[68]

The Hutu–Tutsi presence in the DRC vis-à-vis the sub-regional politics involving Rwanda, Burundi, Uganda and the DRC itself will remain a conundrum for the foreseeable future, and for as long as Museveni, Kagame and Nkurunziza remain presidents of their respective countries. The AU-led New Intervention Force is certainly worth keeping, not least because of the continual tensions among the multiplicity of ethnic groups who have made the Kivu area of the eastern DRC their home. It may be necessary in the near future to amend the status of the MONUSCO contingent to give it an attack role, rather than just peacekeeping, especially as armed groups take advantage of that restriction and continue to pose a threat.

On 4 June 2016, some 100 people were abducted by the LRA as child soldiers and forced to loot from their own people across two villages that were targeted in the north-eastern DRC.[69] Also in June 2016, MONUSCO peacekeepers killed seven militiamen who tried to prevent aid workers giving out food to Hutu civilians. The Governor of Kivu subsequently named Roger Kungerwa Bihango as a mediator to try and reconcile the rival ethnic communities, but this could not prevent ethnic tensions flaring up in Buleusa village in North Kivu on 19 July 2016.[70]

On 13 August 2016, scores of people were hacked to death with machetes in Beni, North Kivu, this time at the hands of the ADF rebel group that originated from Uganda, in what appeared to be a revenge massacre against peacekeeping military operations. Three days of national mourning was declared by the state.[71] The death toll had risen from 36 to 64 by the next day's count, and may have been more.[72] Over 600 people had been killed by the ADF in the Beni area since 2014.

The security situation in the eastern DRC remained in an indeterminable state of flux, as the tit-for-tat continued between MONUSCO peacekeepers and residents. A bomb attack in Goma, eastern DRC, on 8 November 2016 killed a child and injured at least 32 peacekeepers from India. The blast targeted troops who were on a morning run.[73]

There were reports of clashes between police and militias of the Bundu dia Kongo (BDK) religious sect founded by Ne Muanda Nsemi in the 1980s, as police attempted to effect the arrest of the leader.[74] Also, on 25 February 2017, the UNSC issued a press statement condemning the spate of violence in south-central Kasai province reported by MONUSCO, and called on the DRC government to investigate, and take responsibility for security in the DRC.[75]

To add to the woes of security challenges from ongoing political tensions, disaster struck at the beginning of January 2017 when torrential rains caused the Kalamu river to peak 2 m above its average level, to burst its banks and devastate entire towns and villages, especially Boma, through which the river flowed. One bridge was washed away, 50 people were confirmed dead on the day, and at least 10,000 were rendered homeless by the devastation of dwellings caused by the flash flooding. The force of the current washed dead bodies 35 km into neighbouring Angola. The ill-equipped state was slow to respond to the situation, which generated further distress and anger among citizens in an already troubled country.[76]

On 23 June 2017, the UN opened an international investigation into alleged killings, mutilations and destruction of villages in the Kasai provinces, to be led by the Geneva-based Human Rights Council which comprises 47 member countries. The consensus resolution mandated human rights chief Zeid Ra'ad Al Hussein to appoint a team of international experts to carry out an independent investigation according to international standards. The restiveness in Kasai had begun in August 2016 when the Kamwina Nsapu, consisting of Luba miltants, attacked DRC security forces, and their customary chief who headed the militia was killed by the DRC Army. In revenge, the Kamwina Nsapu militia ran riot against non-Luba tribespeople and systematically killed and buried victims in mass graves, of which 42 were discovered in April 2017 by MONUSCO and human rights workers.[77] Since August 2016, at least 3,300 have been killed and 1.3 million displaced by the violence. Furthermore, 600 schools have been attacked and destroyed (as part of abductions to recruit child soldiers) and two members of the UN Group of Experts on Congo (Zaida Catalán, a Swede, and Michael Sharp, an American) were murdered in March 2017.[78]

UNHRC investigators discovered at least 80 mass graves in the Kasai region, in connection with the ethnic violence sparked in August 2016 between the Kamwina Nsapu and the countervailing new Bana Mura militia formed in March 2017 with backing from government FARDC soldiers who fronted the militia's attacks. A health centre in Cinq where displaced persons sought refuge was attacked and 90 people were killed. According to the UNHRC, out of 251 extrajudicial killings resulting from this ethnically charged violence, the Bana Mura had been responsible for 150, Kamwina Nsapu 79 and the government forces 22.[79]

Further escalations persisted in Kivu. Heavy fighting broke out between Mai-Mai Yakutumba rebel militia and government forces at Uvira in South Kivu on the weekend of 29 September 2017, resulting in a visit from the DRC Army chief Bakavu Didier Etumba.[80] The army's rejuvenated presence in Kivu during that period coincided with a further spate of attacks from 7 October 2017, with ambushes on road users and killings of at least 30 villagers in North Kivu's Beni territory, which later evolved into assaults on two MONUSCO bases in Mamundioma where a peacekeeper was also killed. Although the DRC authorities have blamed the ADF for the attacks in Beni, independent UN experts have also pointed fingers at other militias, and the DRC Army itself.[81] On the evening of 7 December 2017, suspected ADF elements attacked a MONUSCO Company Operating Base at Force at Semuliki in Beni Territory, North Kivu. MONUSCO fought back together with FARDC government forces; however, 14 peacekeepers and 4 government soldiers were killed and 53 peacekeepers were wounded.[82] The peacekeepers who died were from Tanzania. According to reports, the UN has reduced MONUSCO's budget by 8 per cent, hence peacekeepers were at risk.[83] On 5 October 2018, four soldiers and two civilians were killed in Beni Territory by ADF militia. Also, in October 2018, at least 200,000 illegal Congolese migrants were expelled to DRC from Angola's Lunda Norte province which borders the DRC.

CHAPTER 6

LIBYA

The Libyan example is a case of the ball of international politics eluding the feet of the AU, whether because the New Pan-Africanism did not react or respond sufficiently quickly and powerfully to arrest the beginning of the end of the long-reigning head of state (Muammar al-Gaddafi), or because Africa was betrayed by a handful of states (Nigeria, South Africa and Gabon) that represented the continent at the UN Security Council (UNSC) when it really mattered. The Western powers had long had their eyes on the defiant Gaddafi, and pondered just how to unseat him, not least in order to obtain influence over Libya's oil wealth which had made Gaddafi so pompous and defiant to the West. It appeared that the domino effect of the Arab Spring, which began in Tunisia in December 2010, provided the right opportunity for Western intelligence to take advantage of the social media element which offered organization and momentum for the Arab Spring movement. Western covert efforts that outwitted the AU and destabilized the Gaddafi establishment then had to be re-invoked in an attempt to prevent the Islamic State (IS) movement from overrunning Libya in the newly created post-Gaddafi political and security vacuum. A Group of Five Sahelian states (G5) plus France joined forces to play a similar role across the Sahel region, and, perhaps more incipiently, to prevent or regulate the flow of migrants routing to Europe via Libya across the Mediterranean, which underscored the obvious point that ousting Gaddafi generated the security vacuum for the migration to thrive.

What Existed before Muammar al-Gaddafi

Libya is the fourth-largest country in Africa, with many interactive and interesting neighbours. Besides its northern border, the Mediterranean Sea, it is bordered clockwise to the east by Egypt, to the south-east corner by Sudan, to the south by Chad and Niger, and to the west by Algeria and Tunisia. Italian rule ended at the end of World War II, and Libya became an independent kingdom in 1951 under King Idris I, who was overthrown by Muammar al-Gaddafi in 1969. Gaddafi then led the Jamahirriyah, a revolution in the culture of politics, which endured for 42 years, until the Arab Spring which began in Tunisia finally unseated him in 2011. Being endowed with crude oil and having the largest proven oil reserve in Africa, and the ninth in the world, Libya has always featured in the target plans of superpowers hungry to capture the global oil market, or to subdue non-nuclear oil states with trigger-happy leaders. This, plus the loud mouth of Gaddafi, attracted sufficient attention for his downfall to be countenanced for many and various reasons.

What Occurred during the Tenure of Muammar al-Gaddafi

The Libyan version of the Arab Spring, or the Libyan Civil War of 2011, was symbolically preceded by protests in Zawiya on 8 August 2009, the sentiments of which stabilized initially, but simmered gradually in the background until it evolved into the Arab Spring season, during which a protest in Benghazi on 15 February 2011 became the re-charger or detonating event, because it degenerated into security forces firing at the protesters. This particular episode triggered local and international displeasure that seemed to have turned against the Libyan authorities, because a rebellion of a new kind kicked off, and the leaders of this rebellion, who were obviously already opposed to Gaddafi, took advantage of the ripe political season within the context of the Arab Spring and launched a National Transitional Council (NTC) on 27 February 2011; treason had declared itself. Moreover, this rebellion somehow managed to reject moves by the AU to resolve it.

Subsequently, there was widespread international condemnation of the use of deadly force against the Zawiya protests, and generally against civilians participating in the Arab Spring, which

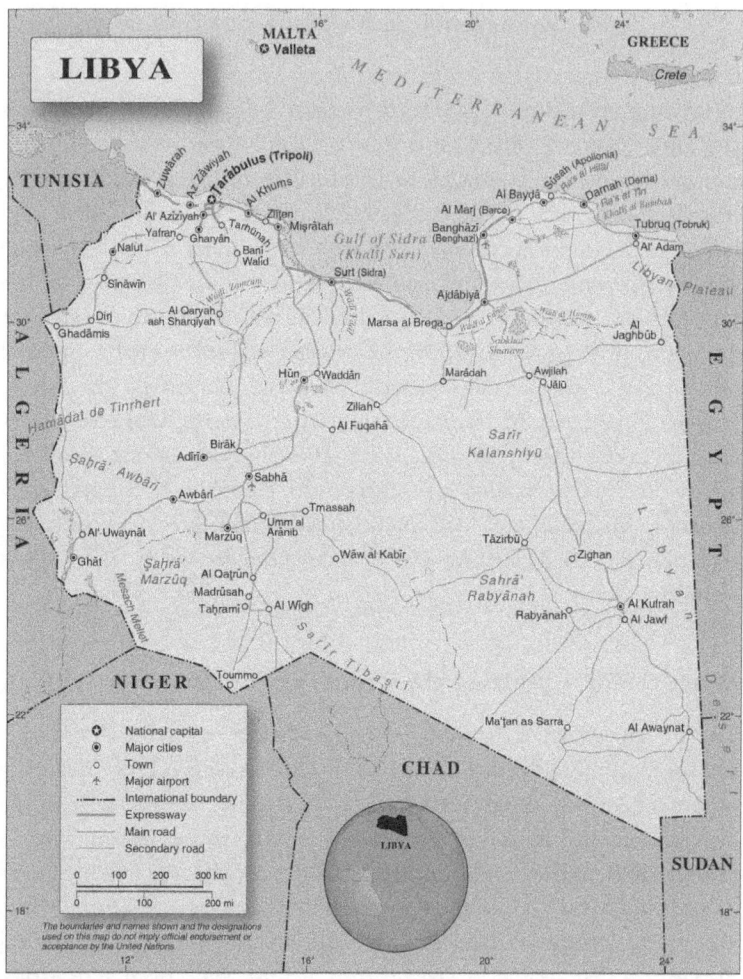

Map 6   Map of Libya.

Gaddafi ignored. Hence the UNSC passed Resolution 1970 (2011) on 26 February 2011. The resolution, drafted and sponsored by the US, France and UK, had a Chapter VII mandate under the UN Charter, and among other things, imposed a trade ban against Libya, a travel ban against selected members of the Gaddafi regime, and referred Libya to the ICC by the decision already taken to that effect on 15 February 2011.

There was further widespread condemnation from the international community of serious violations of human rights and international humanitarian law,[1] reportedly because Gaddafi had 'used warplanes, warships, tanks and artillery to seize back cities taken over by rebels'.[2] Subsequently, the 'no-fly zone' resolution was sponsored by the US, France and UK to deprive Gaddafi of the authority to fly planes in his own country, in order to curtail his flying capabilities. Resolution 1973 (2011) was passed on 10 March 2011 with ten votes in favour and five abstentions including veto-holding Russia and China, plus Germany, Brazil and India. Astonishingly, Nigeria, Gabon and South Africa, the AU representatives on the UNSC, voted in favour of the no-fly-zone resolution despite the loud intellectual noises emanating from the African background, particularly South Africa, against the resolution.

A rather belated call for the no-fly zone came from the League of Arab States (hereafter Arab League) and the Organization of the Islamic Conference (OIC) on 12 March 2011,[3] even though it was incumbent on them to cooperate with their own Arab League member states under Chapter VIII of the UN Charter,[4] and even though Syria and Algeria (both members of the Arab League, as well as the OIC) voted against the no-fly zone at the emergency meeting convened by the Arab League foreign ministers in Cairo on 12 March 2011.[5]

On 20 May 2011, President Robert Mugabe aired his sentiments from the African continent, exposing the naivety of the African vote that supported the no-fly-zone resolution, in an interview with the *New Zimbabwe* newspaper:

> Our African countries were naïve, absolutely naïve, to vote with the West when the West had its interests, you know, its own motives [...] ulterior motives [...] These motives include wanting to re-occupy our countries. They are in search of our resources, in search of political control. It's now the reversal of the freedoms that we attained through various struggles, in some cases political but in others armed struggles [...] We should by now have been very much aware that these aggressors and colonisers of yesterday had not repented, relented on their past ways of relating to us, and that they were still enemies [...] Once an enemy, once an imperialist, always an imperialist. Is it not [Kwame] Nkrumah who said an imperialist is never a good friend? He's only good

when he is dead – the only good imperialist is a dead one [. . .] We
are seeing that achievement, that status of liberating Africa, now
being reversed by the same people who colonised us yesterday, our
erstwhile colonisers. They are coming back now using our own
people and presenting to the world that it is we, the Africans, who
would want to see change, when in fact they are using that
pretence as a way of paving entry back into Africa, perhaps entry in
search of resources – oil or other forms of wealth.[6]

The no-fly zone imposed under Chapter VII of the UN Charter became
an impossible trap for Gaddafi to avoid, since in March the Gaddafi
regime campaigned back to retake lost ground and cities including
Benghazi. However, the real reason for imposing the no-fly zone was a
condition sought by Western allies, to sneak in special forces without
aerial bombardment from Gaddafi, and prepare the build-up to counter-
manage Gaddafi and oust him from power. It was a deliberate plan for
Western allies to invite themselves into the thick of things without
aerial capability from Gaddafi's air force and, once on land, subsequently
to turn the tide against Gaddafi. Resolution 1973 demanded an
immediate ceasefire, which was unrealistic in the circumstances, even
with the best will and intentions. The no-fly-zone resolution was
enforced by NATO reconnaissance flights and supported by satellite.
NATO was flying over the no-fly zone in order to monitor it, and the
most efficient means of addressing Gaddafi's contravention of the no-fly
zone was by fighter jets.

At the initial stage, using 'all necessary means' under Chapter VII
excluded foreign occupation, and meant preventing attacks against
civilians in Libya under the aegis of international responsibility to
protect (R2P). Hence within weeks after Resolution 1973, US jets and
warships were deployed to the Mediterranean. It was reported[7] that more
than 3,000 targets were struck by some 14,202 strike sorties, mostly
against Tripoli (716 sorties) and Brega (492 sorties), chiefly aimed at the
Gaddafi war apparatus, including 304 ammunition storage facilities,
100 tanks and 55 rocket launchers. Rebel fighters then gained ground as
a result of the NATO onslaught against Gaddafi, and eventually made
their way to Tripoli. As the Gaddafi apparatus was gradually diminished,
he became peripatetic and had to dodge many attempts on his life,
finally seeking refuge in his hometown of Sirte. The intelligence would

therefore lead the fighting to Sirte, where a final showdown resulted in a chance encounter and capture of Gaddafi, who was shot dead on 20 October 2011.

It is not obvious why Libya was betrayed by its two giant African compatriots (Nigeria and South Africa). As already mentioned, the rhetoric from the South African authorities supported Gaddafi, hence the South African vote at the UNSC surprised many. Furthermore, one cannot be sure if it was a previous gaffe from Gaddafi, in saying that Nigeria should be partitioned into a Muslim north and a Christian south,[8] that infuriated Nigerians or the Nigerian diplomats at the UNSC. Gabon's vote was not a surprise because Gabon has always been subservient to France, and a key instrument of French neo-colonial overtures in African diplomatic circles. That said, Mugabe made clear at a 2015 AU Summit that Africa would never agree to any future scenario where South Africa and Nigeria represented the continent as holders of permanent seats on the UNSC.[9] The background to this was the 2005 Ezulwini Consensus, which resolved that Africa should have at least two permanent seats on the UNSC with the same veto powers as those held by the US, UK, China, Russia and France, plus five non-permanent seats, in a future UNSC reform mooted to make the world body on global governance more representative of the globe.

What Transpired after Muammar al-Gaddafi

Having been wrong-footed to start with, it appeared in the immediate aftermath of Gaddafi's demise that the AU had more or less abandoned matters, leaving the local Libyans and Western allies behind the toppling of Gaddafi to get on with it and reap the oil spoils – perhaps the very motive for deposing Gaddafi in the first place. The Islamic State (IS) movement also took advantage of the security vacuum, as well as the arms pilfering and proliferation created by Gaddafi's absence, to develop their presence, and to seize any oilfield they could lay hands on, while vandalizing the oil installations in the process.

The NTC that was formed in Benghazi on 27 February 2011 attempted to assume governance of whatever was left of Libya, and conducted nationwide elections after ten months to form a parliament or legislative body they called a General National Congress (GNC), which took power from the NTC on 8 August 2011, with the principal aim of progressing Libya back into a political norm or a workable democracy with a constitution, and an 18-month deadline to achieve this. UNSC Resolution 2009 was adopted on 16 September 2011 to support the political process with the establishment of a United Nations Support Mission in Libya (UNSMIL) initially for a period of three months, which was subsequently extended by UNSC Resolution 2022 to 16 March 2012. However, on the ground, this political goal was not achieved by the 18-month deadline, hence the GNC recast or reinvented itself through another election on 25 June 2014 into a House of Representatives or Council of Deputies, that took effect from 4 August 2014, with Aguila Saleh Issa as president or chair (more or less the head of state of Libya). The turnout in June 2014 was very low: 18 per cent, compared with 60 per cent for the previous election that formed the GNC.

Unhappy with the results of the legislative elections, Islamist groups that had allied themselves into a Muslim Brotherhood under the leadership of Nouri Abusahmain invaded and took control of Tripoli, abducting and harassing political rivals. As it became unsafe to operate in Tripoli, the Council of Deputies moved to Tobruk. A complication arose when Libya's Supreme Constitutional Court, based in a Tripoli now under the control of the Muslim Brotherhood, ruled on 6 November 2014 that the elections for the Council of Deputies were unconstitutional and asked for its dissolution. The Council of Deputies resolved to remain and not dissolve. The support base for the complication became clearer when a rival New General National Congress (GNC), nicknamed the Libyan Dawn, announced itself under the leadership or presidency of Nouri Abusahmain who also happened to be president of the original GNC. Two forms of government existed in Libya from this point:

- the House of Representatives or Council of Deputies supported by the UN but now stationed in Tobruk; and
- the GNC in Benghazi.

A political solution had to be sought. As a practical way forward, on 17 December 2015, the UNSC adopted Resolution 2259 (2015) to institute the Libyan Political Agreement signed in Morocco, that created the Interim Government of National Accord (GNA), which allowed for:

- a Presidential Council of nine members;
- the existing House of Representatives or Council of Deputies to be the official legislative body;
- the formation of a State Council as the official advisory body, with 134 of its 145 members coming from the GNC, and which became led by Abdulrahman Soueihli, who was elected as its head on 6 April 2016;
- the State Council to serve as an upper chamber of parliament with the Interim GNA.

The UNSMIL base that still remained in Libya was tasked to play a key role in ensuring a safe military and civilian environment for the politics to work. On 19 January 2016, the GNA announced its cabinet of 32 ministerial appointees.

While the above process played out, the following selected chronology of events portrayed the chaotic state of affairs engendered by the ousting of Gaddafi, and the political, socio-economic and security vacuum created by his absence:

- On 11 September 2012, Islamist militants attacked the US Embassy in Benghazi and killed Ambassador Christopher Stevens, Information Management Officer Sean Smith, Glen Doherty and Tyrone Woods. A press release from the White House on 30 October 2017 stated that Mustapha al-Imam who was responsible for this attack had been captured and would face justice in the US;[10]
- On 10 August 2014, Brigadier General Mohamed Hadia al-Feitouri, a former official of the defence ministry, was killed in a drive-by shooting as he returned from Friday prayers. It was reported that he was one of the first few defectors from the regular army, and as he held a sensitive role over weapons and ammunitions, he was thought of as a valuable defector;
- On 12 August 2014, the Libyan Ministry of Interior announced that while two armed militias battled for control of Tripoli airport, the Tripoli chief of police, Colonel Mohammed Sweissi, was gunned down by masked assassins as he left a meeting in the Tajoura neighbourhood;[11]
- On 25 August 2014, it was reported by Al Jazeera English television that some 4,000 people had been rescued at sea off the Libyan coast by

the Italian Navy and Coastguard over the weekend of 22–24 August 2014, and that some 24 bodies had been washed ashore or recovered from the sea;

- It was reported[12] on 25 August 2014 that Egypt and the United Arab Emirates (UAE) had launched air strikes against Islamist targets in Libya;
- At an African security summit in Senegal on 16 December 2014, the presidents of Chad, Mali and Senegal sang from the same hymn sheet that NATO should do what was necessary to stem the flow of weapons from Libya into the sub-region, as well as end the hostilities between the two rival governments that were operating in Libya;[13]
- On 27 January 2015, at least 11 people were reportedly killed, including five foreigners and three guards, when a car bomb exploded outside Corinthia Hotel which is popular with foreigners. Explosives were also detonated in the hostage situation that arose, which lasted several hours. Leaders of the rival GNC were in the luxury hotel when the attack took place and the gunmen stormed the place. A gun battle with security forces defused the hostage situation;
- On 15 February 2015, Egyptian war planes hit Jihadi targets in Libya in retaliation for the 21 Coptic Christians killed by Islamists;[14]
- On 23–24 April 2015, the European Union convened a special meeting in Brussels about the regularity with which migrant boats were crossing the Mediterranean from Libya and docking at Italian shores. Concurrent with the EU event on 24 April, a court in Catania was to decide the fate of a 27-year-old Tunisian boat captain Mohammed Ali Malek and his mate, who had been charged by the Italian authorities with recklessly steering their boat into a rescue patrol at sea on 19 April 2015, and causing an estimated 800 people to lose their lives, with only 28 people surviving.[15] A total of 1,300 people had been killed on Mediterranean crossings to Europe in April 2015 alone, and over 1,800 had died or disappeared at sea in 2015. In 2014, 174,000 made it across the Mediterranean while another 3,200 died at sea;[16]
- On 7 January 2016, a truck loaded with explosives blew up outside a police training centre in the western town of Zliten, killing at least 65 people and injuring more than 200 others. Ambulances bussed bodies to Misrata;[17]

- It was reported[18] on 27 January 2016, that officials in Libya raised the alarm and approached the World Health Organization (WHO) to grant Libya access to extra funds by raising the country's profile into the top category for health emergencies, because the medical infrastructure and system had crumbled in the face of the political and security crises. Categorizing Libya for health emergencies would place it alongside other crisis-struck nations such as Syria, Iraq and those West African countries hit hardest by the Ebola virus. Up to 70 per cent of Libya's hospitals had been forced to shut down or were close to grinding to a halt. According to an official estimate from the Libyan health minister, almost €3 million a day was needed to buy medicines. Jaffar Hussein, the WHO representative, highlighted that the most vulnerable people (children, mothers and the old) could not afford to wait for the political situation to stabilize, but needed immediate support. The WHO representative lamented that the vulnerable were at risk of death because even the most basic headgear was not available, and hospitals were short of life-saving medicines, while health facilities were being attacked, damaged and becoming non-functional. Oil-producing Libya was a high-income or upper-middle-income country that did not normally need financial and resource assistance; however, it now had insufficient money to buy even the most basic of medicines such as insulin for people in dire need of these resources;
- A televised Human Rights Watch (HRW) report on 28 January 2016 highlighted that the breakdown in the rule of law had allowed widespread human rights abuses to take place, including violence committed by ISIL, whose strength in the country was growing, and who habitually set fire to oil terminals they did not control, as part of a diabolical campaign to weaken or even obliterate the competition against them. A further complication was the growing presence or evolution of both small and large armed groups that were taking advantage of the chaos to defend their turf. Martin Kobler, the UNSMIL envoy to Libya, noted that ISIL was growing in strength and had established its political headquarters in Sirte, and furthermore, that ISIL's version of sharia law was harsh, with regular executions and detentions for years without charge. The judicial system in Libya had collapsed in most places, and kidnapping for ransom had become another big business;

- On 7 February 2016, Dr Mohamad al-Jeddayimi, the radiologist at Al-Wehda hospital, reported that a nurse and her two-year-old son were killed in an air strike in Darna, eastern Libya. Two Mujahedeen Shura Council fighters were also killed. It is understood that air forces loyal to the anti-Islamist army chief General Khalifa Hafter, who was appointed on 2 March 2015, launched the attack to strike several homes,[19] the Faculty of Medical Technology Science in the Bab Tobruk district of Darna, and the local Al-Wehda hospital. It is also understood that the the Mujahedeen Shura Council of Darna was a coalition of Islamist militias formed to oppose the forces of the controversial General Haftar;[20]
- On 14 February 2016, a Libyan Air Force jet was shot down over the city of Benghazi as it was carrying out strikes against Islamist fighters. The pilot ejected and landed safely. This was the third Libyan jet to be downed in that season of onslaught;[21]
- On 8 September 2016, two car bombs exploded close by the foreign ministry in Tripoli and the naval base used by the 'ashore' UN-backed government in Tripoli;[22]
- On 21 November 2016, a car bomb exploded in a car park next to Al Jalaa Hospital in Benghazi, killing at least seven people, including three children, and injuring some 20 others.[23] There had been heavy fighting in Benghazi since May 2014, and although no group claimed responsibility for this bomb attack, the Benghazi Revolutionaries Shura Council (BRSC) as well as ISIL had claimed responsibility for several car bombings in the weeks leading up to the attack, which were targeted at Hafter's LNA and their supporters.[24]

Evidently, the road map towards good governance had to resume. Hence on 14 February 2016, the Presidential Council proposed a revised and reduced cabinet of 18 ministers to be approved by the Council of Deputies. The approval vote scheduled for 24 February 2016 had to be postponed because of fierce disagreements in the parliament's chamber, amidst severe fighting on the ground between the Libyan National Army (LNA) headed by General Khalifa Hafter and allied to the Tobruk government on the one side, versus rebel fighters including ISIL on the other side. Hafter's war with ISIL was largely in Benghazi, with the assistance of French special forces and intelligence units operating covertly in Libya to support the Libyan Army in its fight against ISIS and other jihadist allies that had taken advantage of the political instability in the aftermath of Gaddafi.[25] However, the French and allied soliciting of Hafter's cooperation would not be officially confirmed by the French Government at this stage.

The IS group controlled Sirte, Gaddafi's hometown, and cities in close proximity to oilfields that they had repeatedly attacked, including the coastal city of Sabratha which was a hub for migrants heading for Europe. In a broader Western effort to halt the increasing fortification of the IS group in Libya which remained geographically strategic for entry to European shores, Italy also gave permission for the US to use a Sicily airbase to launch drone operations against the IS group, while the US planned the opening of its new drone base in Agadez in Niger. French special forces already stationed in Chad and Niger had joined the Libyan national army to conduct covert operations,[26] though French involvement was still deemed as speculation at this stage.

It must be noted that Western efforts, support and prioritization in dealing with the IS group in Libya at this stage had been covert because there was as yet no UNSC resolution in place for it and time was of the essence. Moreover, China and Russia were unlikely to acquiesce in a resolution to launch a bombing campaign or a NATO-led military campaign of any sort in Libya, given how the West had gone about obtaining the no-fly-zone Resolution 1973 (2011) with the ulterior motive of destabilizing Gaddafi and ousting him from power, by using the R2P excuse of protecting Libyan citizens from Gaddafi's onslaught. It therefore remained to be seen how veto-holding China and Russia would or could respond to any potential attempt to obtain a resolution, should the Libyan Government in Tobruk specifically request support from the international community. Article 55 of the UN Charter could be invoked to cover a variety of concerns ranging from living standards to human rights in this case:

> With a view to the creation of conditions of stability and well-being which are necessary for peaceful and friendly relations among nations based on respect for the principle of equal rights and self-determination of peoples, the United Nations shall promote:
> a. higher standards of living, full employment, and conditions of economic and social progress and development;

b. solutions of international economic, social, health, and related problems; and international cultural and educational cooperation; and

c. universal respect for, and observance of, human rights and fundamental freedoms for all without distinction as to race, sex, language, or religion[27]

Once Article 55 of the UN Charter was successfully invoked to concoct a resolution, any reservations from Russia or China would be inconsequential, because from that point, Western forces, and indeed any country at all, could unilaterally cooperate with the UN to carry out that resolution on the basis of Article 56 of the UN Charter, which states that:

All Members pledge themselves to take joint and separate action in cooperation with the Organization for the achievement of the purposes set forth in Article 55.[28]

The diplomatic push for a resolution on the ground carried on nevertheless, even if Martin Kobler, the UNSMIL envoy, admitted on 2 March 2016 that he still had not managed to convince the two political sides in Libya to go the way of peace. He expressed his concern that military processes (involving varous combinations of forces and militias allied to one or other side of the Libyan political spectrum, ISIL and their allies in the country, or allied to NATO and covert forces) were moving much faster than the political process of forming the unity government.[29] The UN's assessment of the situation was that the two rival governments (including the UN-backed administration or Council of Deputies in Tobruk that originally fled from Tripoli) existed merely on paper and were dysfunctional. They 'do not deliver services to the people. My idea of a government is that they are responsible for schools, hospitals and security for the people; they are not doing this',[30] according to Kobler.

Judging from the ensuing devastating hits by ISIL, especially at oil installations and refineries, quite clearly the UNSMIL could not guarantee a safe military and civilian environment for politics to work. Therefore, it appears that the covert intelligence operations and networks served to, among other things, deal with all forms of intimidation from ISIL and clear the path for the interim GNA to be established in Tripoli (the more traditionally recognized central seat of government) so that the GNA could begin to function properly towards national reconciliation and act like a government. The intelligence might have advised that the best way of regaining entry to Tripoli was by sea, after rival factions had prevented the GNA from flying in. Hence on 30 March 2016, Prime Minister Fayez al-Sarraj and seven members of the Presidential Council called the NGC's bluff and arrived by sea to set up a temporary seat of government at a naval base in Tripoli. Khalifa al-Ghawi, leader of the NGC, responded by referring to the Presidential Council as infiltrators, and asked for them to leave Tripoli, but was ignored.[31] A National Salvation Congress headed by Khalifa Ghweil also emerged from the woodwork as a coalition of powerful militias allied to ISIL. In the meantime, Western-backed intelligence and security networks continued to engage ISIL fighters while the political game played out on the ground. A practical outcome of this was the formation of the Petroleum Facilities Guard (PFG) to support the GNA in stopping ISIL's advances and destructive activities.

Also significant was the decision by the GNA on 16 May 2016, at an international meeting in Vienna co-chaired by Italy, Germany and the US, to seek exemptions from the UN Libya Sanctions Committee concerning the UN arms embargo on Libya, in order to obtain more arms to fight ISIS and Daesh.[32] A new joint command of military operations emerged, which in all practicality could not leave out the regular army stationed in Tobruk headed by General Khalifa Hafter that was already receiving arms from some Western-backed countries in the sub-region, so that Prime Minister al-Sarraj of the ashore GNA in Tripoli had to work with General Hafter of the Tobruk establishment. The other curiously significant outcome of the Vienna meeting was the agreement between Tripoli and Tobruk on how to handle oil sales and proceeds. The practical gestures from the Vienna meeting yielded some quick and significant gains, in that the PFG announced on 30 May 2016 that they had regained the key town of Ben Jawad from ISIL, and subsequently set their eyes on Sirte, which was ISIL's stronghold, taking control of Nawfiliyah along the way.

On 9 June 2016, the PFG and forces allied to the GNA, including militias from Misrata, entered Sirte and forced ISIL militants into a retreat, before capturing the port of Sirte the following day. The Sirte offensive continued piece by piece in the following days and weeks; ISIL fought back and bombed the Sirte hospital on 12 June 2016 using suicide bombers who entered the hospital perimeter with ambulances. The balance of power oscillated as the PFG and allied forces loyal to the GNA came under fire in the course of their advance. The battle to retake Sirte raged on for longer than expected, featuring further street-by-street incursions of assymetrical warfare and a high casualty rate, as ISIL had occupied domestic and commercial buildings en route, as well as setting up booby traps in the form of landmines and mined vehicles ready to explode, compounded by the unknown quantity of just how many ISIL fighters were engaged – the closest estimate provided by the CIA was 5,000–8,000.[33] Sirte had been under ISIL control since 2015, becoming their most important base outside Syria and Iraq. More than 300 soldiers had been killed and around 1,300 wounded since the start of the PFG offensive with Operation Al-Bunyan Al-Marsoos that was launched in Sirte on 12 May 2016. The PFG and forces allied to the GNA continued attacking ISIL positions with artillery shells and advanced further forward (with help from US air raids) toward the centre of Sirte. These systematic skirmishes continued until the first real sign of victory in taking over what appeared to be ISIL's command centre and symbolic base in Sirte, including a large conventional complex in the centre of Sirte, a hospital and the University of Sirte campus.[34]

Government forces were not operating in a political vacuum, but rather amidst ongoing civil wars across the length and breadth of the whole country over the concept of power in a post-Gaddafi state, which in itself generated sympathizers for ISIL, and made the the psychology of war a little more difficult for the government forces. The battle for hearts and minds was yet to be won across the country, and ISIL benefited a great deal from battle-tested Libyans who had fought for Gaddafi in his last days, and who knew the territory of Sirte intimately.

It would not be too long before what was already mentioned in hushed tones among analysts – illegal Western interventions in Libya or Western covert intelligence operations in Libya – became embarassing public information. On 8 July 2016, Al Jazeera English televised the story by Karim El-Bar in the *Middle East Eye* regarding leaked air traffic recordings between British, French, Italian and US pilots and ground operatives coordinating air strikes in support of General Khalifa Hafter.[35] El-Bar had previously pointed to Western-backed air operations in support of the renegade Libyan general in June 2016.[36]

The embarrassing thing about this story is that, while Western forces pretended to be fighting against ISIL in order to protect oil installations and secure an operable political space for the UN-backed GNA now based in Tripoli (as reasons for supporting Hafter and arming him to the teeth with air strikes, covert supplies and other military support), Hafter was himself very much against the UN-backed GNA in Tripoli, and had made it abundantly clear he would not work with the GNA. Moreover, Hafter's immediate interest was to carve out a clear autonomy in Eastern Libya, headquartered at Tobruk, while he was less bothered about anything that occurred outside his immediate confines. Hafter and his so-called Libyan National Army (LNA) are principally against any form of pro-Islamist militias and jihadists including ISIL. Hence it appeared that Western forces were militarily equipping the LNA, which was at odds with the GNA (and the PFG for that matter). The reality of the situation was quite absurd.

General Khalifa Hafter had duly earned his stripes in many ways. A former key ally of Gaddafi, he had helped him to seize power in 1969 but fell out with him later, and joined the uprising that eventually brought Gaddafi down in October 2011. After Gaddafi, he had successfully formed and waged a campaign to drive out ISIL elements from Benghazi, thereby aligning himself with the rival government based in Benghazi, hence his reluctance to support the GNA now based in Tripoli. But at the same time, both the UN and the West treated Hafter as an ally, and continually armed and supported him with neck-breaking and highly coordinated covert and intelligence air strikes against ISIL targets. Hafter's forces were politically at odds with jihadists and ISIL affiliates, and should automatically be aligned with the GNA and PFG allies; however, Hafter overtly undermined and spoke against the Tripoli-based GNA and even the PFG, which was doing the real fighting against ISIL in the 2016 campaign to recapture Sirte on behalf of the GNA. In short, Hafter exploited the Western fight against ISIL to strengthen his own influence in Eastern Libya and his secret agenda of ultimate autonomy short of independence.

The situation became more absurd the more it was analysed, because some of Hafter's funding came from the Libyan (GNA's) defence ministry[37] even though Hafter was destroying the GNA's military support and forces allied to the PFG, and even though the GNA thought that it had UN and Western support. Moreover, the very idea of French and Italian efforts to secure the Mediterranean refugee route to Europe was foolhardy considering that Hafter's actions undermined that process, and furthermore that he was being assisted to undermine that process by the very forces who sought his help. The analyses twisted around in circles, just as obviously as Hafter had the UN and Western forces twisted around his finger.

After this intelligence leak, the problem for the West was not so much whether it could or could not procure Article 55 of the UN Charter to obtain a UNSC resolution for its further illegal intervention in Libya, or the covert operations, intelligence flights and dropping of weapons for that matter, but rather that once again it had been exposed for engaging in what was forbidden in international law: (a) direct military interference in another country without UNSC approval; and (b) worse still, in the same country about which the West lied in order to obtain UNSC Resolution 1973 (2011) which imposed a no-fly zone against Gaddafi, the cover for Western forces operating covertly in and out of Libya.

On 20 July 2016, the Ministry of Defence in France confirmed that three French soldiers had been killed in Libya, in what became known as the first official or public admission by the French Government of their covert involvement in Libya. As mentioned previously, French Government policy supports the UN-backed GNA in Tobruk; however, the French special forces operated for the renegade General Khalifa Hafter who was a publicly declared enemy of the GNA.[38] The day after the French official announcement, there were mass public protests to denounce the French presence and operations in Libya. The UN-backed GNA based in Tripoli also denounced the French presence as a violation of Libyan sovereignty, and discredited French backing for the renegade Hafter.[39] The UN also began an investigation after 21 unidentified bodies were found in Benghazi. The bodies had gunshot wounds to the head and appeared to have been tortured. It was not clear who the deceased were or who killed them. Libya's UN envoy confirmed what appeared to be summary executions, deemed as a war crime, and demanded justice. However, it was left for Libya's chief prosecutor to open the case and conduct investigations, as the UN was not up to the job (in the case of Libya) due to the vast scale of ISIL operations.[40]

Just what was the French interest in (or Western reasons for) supporting the renegade Hafter was the subject of speculation along the following lines: the West was doing the bidding of Egypt and the UAE[41] in continuation of what began in 2014 as coordinated Egyptian and Emirati efforts against Islamist militias in Libya funded by other Middle Eastern countries, as an escalation of the regional (Middle East) power play between Islamist movements (such as ISIL) that have sought to undermine the region's old order since the start of the Arab Spring in 2011, versus opposing governments in the Middle East, and which began in 2014 with UAE pilots flying out of Egyptian air bases to conduct air strikes in Libya.[42] This continued in 2015, for example, when Egyptian war planes hit jihadi targets in Libya in mid-February in retaliation for the murder of 21 Coptic Christians by masked militants affiliated with ISIL,[43] and was followed in May 2015 by ISIL moving into Sirte to establish its Libyan stronghold there. Hence Libya became ISIL's third operational stronghold after Iraq and Syria. The admission of French special forces' involvement made by the French Ministry of Defence was just the tip of the iceberg, in that it did not say specifically why the French troops were in Libya. Egyptian air strikes against ISIS targets in Libya would be repeated in May 2017, in retaliation for the killing of 29 Coptic Christians by IS gunmen south of Cairo.[44]

On 2 August 2016, the Pentagon announced in a press conference that the US military had carried out pinpoint air strikes against ISIL positions or strongholds in and around Sirte, at the request of the GNA's Presidential Council acting in their capacity as supreme commander of the Libyan Army. This was confirmed by Prime Minister Farez al-Sarraj's announcement of direct coordination between the GNA's Supreme Council and the operation's central command, which happened to be a US Navy vessel – an amphibious warship – based in the Mediterranean. The GNA's prime minister, Farez al-Sarraj, claimed that the strikes were against selected positions in Sirte and caused grave losses in ISIL's ranks and equipment, resulting in GNA ground troops seizing control of strategic positions and advancing steadily with minimal loss of life. The air strikes followed an official request to the US alongside an existing principled agreement by the US to help the UN-recognized and Tripoli-based GNA to deal with ISIL's presence, to prevent ISIL taking advantage of the ongoing political and security chaos, and ultimately to help the GNA establish full control over Sirte and Tripoli. The Pentagon briefing made clear this campaign would continue, without US boots on the ground, until stability and security were established in Libya by the

GNA and allied forces.[45] To reiterate this, Farez al-Sarraj also stated on 10 August 2016 that the pro-GNA forces and the PFG did not need foreign troops on the ground, and that they could manage so long as they had US air cover. Hence on 10 August 2016 and subsequently, the GNA and PFG ground troops were engaged in special operations to retake the coastal city of Sirte, with support from US air strikes.

On 22 August 2016, the State Council, which is the upper chamber of parliament and the official advisory body for the GNA but based in Benghazi, with a majority (134 out of 145) of its members belonging to the GNC, cast a vote of no confidence in the Tripoli-based GNA, summarily stalling the unity process. This vote was not a surprise and was perhaps long overdue, in that Benghazi was under the thumb of the renegade General Khalifa Hafter who was at odds with the GNA, and more practically, this so-called upper chamber of parliament had not convened in eight months. In response, the Tobruk-based lower chamber of parliament, the House or Representatives or Council of Deputies, complained that they were not aware of the vote.[46]

The push to retake Sirte continued, though the PFG and allied forces also encountered heavy casualties, despite the air cover from US jets. On 28 August 2016, at least 34 fighters on the government side died, and 180 were wounded, in skirmishes to take the last areas occupied by ISIL who were defending to the last inch with suicide bombers, sniper fire and landmines.[47] According to the US Africa Command (AFRICOM), from 1 to 24 August alone, they had carried out 82 air strikes.[48] In the first week of September 2016, pro-government forces began patrolling and securing the Sirte coastline in order to prevent ISIL fighters from escaping.[49]

On 15 October 2016, the militia of the National Salvation Congress led by Khalifa Ghweil and allied to ISIL seized key offices of the Tripoli-based GNA, thereby jettisoning whatever existed of stable governance in the Libyan political space.[50] This prompted an emergency meeting in Niamey on 19 October 2016, in the form of the ninth ministerial meeting of foreign ministers of Libya's neighbours (Niger the host country, Algeria, Tunisia, Egypt, Chad, Sudan), and of course Libya, to discuss the detriorating security situation there since the demise of Muammar al-Gaddafi. The meeting was also attended by Martin Kobler, the UN Secretary-General's Special Representative to Libya; Jakaya Kikwete, the AU's Special Envoy for Libya; and Ahmed Abu Al-Gheit, the Arab League's Secretary General. This ninth meeting was in consonance with the seventh and eighth meetings of December 2015 and March 2016 in Algiers and Tunis respectively, which agreed in advance the mobilization of all necessary support for the UN-sponsored political agreement and Libya's Presidential Council, chaired by Fayez al-Sarraj, although these two penultimate meetings also objected to military interventions, local or foreign.[51]

Eventually, the GNA took over Sirte, after seizing the Jiza al-Bahrieh district which was the last hold-out of ISIL and Daesh fighters.[52] However, the country remained deeply divided, with the polarity of a GNA headquartered in Tripoli and the elected parliament or State Council headquartered in Benghazi and dominated by the GNC, with the latter refusing to recognize the former by the vote of no confidence that was cast on 22 August 2016, plus the spanner thrown in the works by Khalifa Gweil's militia seizing some key offices of the GNA on 15 October 2016.

International Political Economy

Libya's position on the UNDP's Human Development Index (HDI) plunged in 2015 when the instability and bad governance that followed the 2011 political crisis began to bite, and since the crisis, the country has consistently ranked among the bottom 14 countries on the corruption index, although Libya has enviable crude oil and natural gas reserves, as well as gypsum. Data limitations have prevented the forecasting of GDP components.[53] However, the economic cost of violence in 2016 alone, which amounted to a staggering $21,887,000,000 in purchase power parity (PPP) terms,[54] somehow reduced to $17,715,900,000 in 2017.[55]

Here is a snapshot of Libya's performance on the Ibrahim Index on African Governance (IIAG):

- In the 2010 index, Libya ranked 23rd overall, with a score of 51.45 per cent;
- In the 2011 index,[56] Libya ranked 28th overall, with a score of 50 per cent;
- In the 2012 index, Libya ranked 38th overall, with a score of 44 per cent;

- In the 2013 index, Libya ranked 38th overall, with a score of 45.3 per cent;
- In the 2014 index, Libya ranked 43rd overall, with a score of 40.9 per cent;
- In the 2015 index, Libya ranked 47th overall, with a score of 35.5 per cent;[57]
- In the 2016 index, Libya ranked 51st overall, with a score of 29 per cent, which constituted a − 18-per cent nosedive in comparative performance in the decade trend index of 2006−15;

  ✓ 51st in Safety and Rule of Law with a score of 16.3 per cent, which constituted a − 34.1-per cent comparative downward spiral in the decade trend index of 2006−15, and again 51st in the personal safety sub-category which constituted a − 44.5-per cent comparative downward spiral in the decade index; 50th in the national security sub-category which constituted a − 54.7-per cent comparative downward spiral in the decade index; 51st in the accountability sub-category which constituted a − 15.3-per cent deterioration in the decade trend index; and 52nd in the rule of law sub-category which constituted a − 22.1-per cent comparative downward performance in the decade trend index;

  ✓ 50th in Participation and Human Rights with a score of 22.5 per cent which constituted a mere 0.3-per cent positive change in the comparative decade index 2006−15; 47th in the participation sub-category which constituted a 4.4-per cent comparative positive change in the decade trend index; 49th in the rights sub-category which constituted a − 1.9-per cent comparative deterioration in the decade index; and 53rd in the gender sub-category which constituted a comparative downward trend of − 1.7 per cent in the decade trend index;

  ✓ 52nd in Sustainable Economic Opportunity with a score of just 19 per cent, which constituted a − 22.4-per cent deterioration in the comparative trend index 2006−15; 19th in the infrastructure sub-category which constituted a − 7.9-per cent downward spiral in the comparative decade index; a − 28.1-per cent deterioration in electricity supply over the decade; 53rd in the public management sub-category, which constituted a − 29.9-per cent comparative deterioration over the decade; 50th in the business environment sub-category, which constituted a − 17.6-per cent comparative downgrade in the decade index; and 53rd in the rural sector sub-category which constituted a − 34.1-per cent comparative deterioration over the decade;

🗸 19th (with Comoros) in Human Development, with a score of 58.1 per cent which constituted a − 15.7-per cent comparative deterioration in the decade trend index; an impressive 8th in the education sub-category, which constituted a − 9.7-per cent comparative deterioration in performance in the decade index; an impressive 4th in the health sub-category which constituted a − 1-per cent comparative deterioration over the decade; and; 50th in the welfare sub-category, which constituted a − 36.3-per cent comparative downward spiral in the index over the decade.[58]

- In the 2017 index,[59] Libya ranked 49th overall with a score of 33.3 per cent, which signified a − 13.3-per cent comparative aggregate deterioration over the ten-year period from 2007 to 2016, and − 11.8-per cent over the five-year period from 2012 to 2016; improved slightly from 51st to 50th in Safety and Rule of Law over the 2007−16 decade; improved comparatively from 50th to 47th in Participation and Human Rights over the decade; maintained position at 52nd in Sustainable Economic Opportunity; and improved slightly from 19th to 18th in Human Development:[60]

- In the 2018 index, Libya ranked 52nd overall with a score of 28.3 per cent, which signified a − 15.6-per cent comparative aggregate deterioration over the ten-year period from 2008 to 2017; worsened from 50th to 51st in Safety and Rule of Law; worsened from 47th to 49th in Participation and Human Rights; improved slightly from 52nd to 51st in Sustainable Economic Opportunity; and dropped significantly from 18th to 43rd in Human Development.[61]

Libya's performance on the Global Peace Index (GPI) is as follows:

- In the 2010 GPI, Libya ranked 56th out of 149 countries – scoring 1.839;
- In the 2011 GPI, Libya ranked 143rd out of 153 countries – scoring 2.816;
- In the 2012 GPI, Libya ranked 147th out of 159 countries – scoring 2.830;

- In the 2013 GPI, Libya ranked 145th out of 162 countries – scoring 2.604;
- In the 2014 GPI, Libya ranked 133rd out of 162 countries – scoring 2.453;
- In the 2015 GPI, Libya ranked 149th out of 162 countries – scoring 2.819;[62]
- In the 2016 GPI, Libya ranked 154th out of 163 countries – scoring 3.200.[63] Among other things, the situation in Libya including violent crime, instability and political terror contributed to the deterioration in the overall global average score of the 2016 index itself, in addition to Libya being a key contributor to increases in displaced populations;[64]
- In the 2017 GPI, Libya ranked 157th out of 163 independent states and territories – scoring 3.328.[65] From a regional perspective, Libya ranked 17th among the 20 countries from the Middle East and North Africa (MENA) featured within the index;[66]
- In the related Positive Peace Index of 2017, Libya ranked 139th among 163 independent states and territories, with a score of 3.84;[67]
- In the 2018 GPI, Libya ranked 157th out of 163 independent states and territories globally, with a score of 3.262, and 17th among the 20 Middle East and North Africa (MENA) countries featured in the index.[68] The 2018 report noted that average positive peace scores for Libya had been deteriorating annually since 2013, and hostility to foreigners escalated by 61.5 per cent from 2013 to 2016.[69]

Quite clearly, the big fall in peace rankings after 2010 is due to the outbreak of the 2011 civil war that toppled Gaddafi. The rankings have maintained their deteriorating levels ever since. Moreover, the 2015 GPI report stated that 'a key factor in Libya's fall in the 2015 rankings is a deterioration in its relations with neighbouring countries. Relations between the internationally recognized government in the east and Turkey, Qatar and Sudan have soured owing to their alleged material and logistical support of Islamist militias.'[70]

Listed below are Libya's rankings on the UNDP's Human Development Index (HDI):

- In the 2010 HDI, Libya ranked 53rd out of 169 countries in the 2010 Human Development Report (HDR);

- In the 2011 HDI, Libya ranked 64th out of 187 countries in the 2011 HDR;
- In the 2012 HDI, Libya ranked 50th out of 187 countries in the 2012 HDR;
- In the 2013 HDI, Libya ranked 64th out of 186 countries in the 2013 HDR;
- In the 2014 HDI, Libya ranked 55th out of 187 countries in the 2014 HDR;
- In the 2015 HDI, Libya ranked 163rd out of 188 countries in the 2015 HDR;[71]
- In the 2016 HDI, Libya ranked 102nd out of 188 countries in the 2016 HDI;[72]
- In the 2018 Human Development Indices and Indicators (HDII) Statistical Update, Libya ranked 108th out of 189 countries.[73]

Below is Libya's performance on the Corruption Perceptions Index (CPI):

- In 2010, Libya ranked 146th out of 178 positions, scoring 2.2 (with Cameroon, Côte d'Ivoire, Haiti, Iran, Nepal, Paraguay and Yemen);
- In 2011, Libya ranked 168th out of 182, scoring 2.0 (with Angola, Chad and the DRC);
- In 2012, Libya ranked 160th out of 174 positions, scoring 21 (with the DRC and Laos);
- In 2013, Libya ranked 172nd out of 175 positions, scoring 15;
- In 2014, Libya ranked 166th out of 174 positions, scoring 18 (with Eritrea and Uzbekistan);
- In 2015, Libya ranked 161st out of 167 country positions, scoring just 16 (with Iraq);[74]
- In 2016, Libya ranked 170th out of 176 countries and territories, scoring 14 (with Sudan and Yemen).[75]
- In 2017, Libya ranked 171st out of 180 countries and territories globally, scoring 17 (with Guinea-Bissau, Equatorial Guinea and North Korea),[76] and 16th out of 18 Middle East and North Africa (MENA) countries featured in the index.[77]

Libya's oil reserves of 48 billion barrels remain the largest proven in Africa to date. However, since the civil war in 2011, production has plummeted from 1.5 million barrels per day to a meagre 200,000 barrels per day. The oil ports of Ras Lanuf and Al Sidra that produced 700,000 barrels per day had to be closed following ISIL attacks in January 2016, and have not resumed production even after being rescued back from ISIL, not least because no settlement has been reached between the two rival governments: the Tripoli-based GNA and the Benghazi-based Hafter government. Although the PFG under the command of the GNA were authorized to open Ras Lanuf and Al Sidra ports in July 2016, they were later seized by the self-styled LNA under Hafter's command on 11 September 2016. Libya's National Oil Company had to be split between the two rival (GNA and LNA) governments.[78]

Security Challenges

The lack of security in Libya has been stressed throughout this discussion, and justifies the country's abysmal performance in the terror indexes of the past few years. However, the threat of IS became potent and real in a country where the previous leadership under Gaddafi was not that religious, and Gaddafi himself was not much of a Muslim as widely thought, let alone to be associated with the extremisms of Islam. Obviously, IS took advantage of the political and military vacuum created by the divided administrations (Tripoli, Tobruk, Benghazi) that govern Libya; a situation that did not generate the corporate political will and capacity to exercise sufficient security control over large swathes of desert land already difficult to inhabit under normal circumstances, except where there were oil installations to incentivize investment, habitation or essential security coverage.

The rising Islamist element in the Benghazi establishment became an obvious forerunner to the advent of IS and their allied incursions. One has to wonder whether IS operations constitute(d) a form of retribution against the conquest of the Gaddafi regime. The 2015 GPI report stated that 'a key factor in Libya's fall in the 2015 rankings is a deterioration in its relations with neighbouring countries. Relations between the internationally recognized GNA and Turkey, Qatar and Sudan have soured owing to their alleged material and logistical support of Islamist militias.'[79]

Below are Libya's rankings on the various terrorism indexes:

- In the 2014 Verisk Maplecroft Terrorism Risk Index (for the 2013 period), Libya ranked 7th among the top ten countries in the 'extreme'-rated category;
- In the 2015 Political Violence Index (for 2014), Libya ranked 10th among the top ten countries rated 'extreme';
- In the 2016 Political Risk Index, Libya was rated as an 'extreme'-risk country,[80] and the resilience of IS was noted at the centre of the growing terrorism threat;[81]
- In the 2015 Global Terrorism Index (GTI), which lists rankings in reverse order in contrast with other performance indexes, so that the worst-performing (in this case, Iraq) is at the top, Libya ranked 9th among 162 countries that featured on the index, with a score of 7.29;[82]
- In the 2016 GTI, Libya ranked 10th among 163 countries that featured on the index, with a score of 7.283.[83] This index estimated the value of the arms trade in Libya at $4 to $15 million, and that some 250,000 to 700,000 weapons from the Libyan arsenal fell into the hands of arms traffickers, and subsequently terrorist groups.[84] Also, 'The International Organization for Migration (IOM) reported that during the first three months of 2016, at least 170,000 migrants and refugees entered Europe along seaborne routes, which is more than eight times the number recorded through the first three months of 2015. In total, over one million migrants and refugees crossed the Mediterranean in 2015';[85]
- In the 2017 GTI, Libya maintained position at 10th among 163 countries that featured on the index, with a score of 7.256,[86] and was 4th among the Middle East and North Africa (MENA) group within the index.[87]

The security vacuum in Libya, coupled with Libya's strategic migration route to Europe that feeds from ongoing ravaging wars in Syria and elsewhere, would continue to enrich the criminal gangs operating the migration trips and other allied businesses. It appears that the breakdown of law and order, and with it of the Libyan judicial system itself, augured well for criminality within the context of arms proliferation in a country awash with ammunition and willing recruits. Securing a stable environment for the ashore GNA to gain a governmental foothold in Tripoli remained a huge undertaking for quite some time, if possible at all.

Libya's status as the key transit point to Europe across the Mediterranean from war-torn areas of the Middle East such as Syria and other trouble zones in Africa, such as Somalia and Nigeria, exacerbated the security issues, especially as ISIL took advantage of migrants' vulnerability to recruit them. It was reported in June 2016 that at least 5,000 Tunisians, including around 700 women, had been recruited by ISIL and other armed groups as they transited to Libya from neighbouring countries.[88] Indeed the migrant route issue and its related economy of commoditizing refugees in the process had become exacerbated beyond effective monitoring. Worst of all, it became under-reported and politically shelved or swept under the carpet to a degree, until matters took a different turn when CNN released video footage of men being sold in Libya by an auctioneer for the equivalent of $800. This sparked international outrage, and, among other things, brought to the fore what had already been documented by the International Organization for Migration (IOM) in April 2017 as slave markets that had been generated in the middle chain.

Principally, the Italian Government bribed the Libyan Coast Guard with millions of euros and new boats to enforce border controls, and also paid the police in Niger to prevent migrants from entering Libyan space, while disregarding reports that these recipient agents formed a network that rounded up migrants into camps and prisons where they were abused and sold as slaves. The Italian mafia operations benefited from the cover of EU headline pledges such as €93 million for 'improved migration management' in Libya. The EU appeared to be outsourcing its responsibilities to rogue authorities in Libya and Niger who were neither kitted nor committed to cater for refugees or treat them as human beings.[89] This was even more poignant, given that Libya under Gaddafi had not been a route haven to EU economies, and even more so that the powers that principally contributed to ousting Gaddafi appeared to be shirking responsibility for the outcome of their actions. When President Emmanuel Macron of France addressed a student audience at the University of Ouagadouou on 28 November 2017, the first thing he was asked after the speech was to account for the role of France in the ousting of Gaddafi and to what extent it relates to the refugee crises in Libya en route to the Mediterranean.

Since the the civil war began in 2011, oil production, pipelines and terminals have been at the heart of complex security manouevres by all sides in the conflict. Several oil facilities have had to be vandalized by jihadists, and others closed altogether, whether by the National Oil Company or by rogue forces of one kind or another. The ports of Ras Lanuf and Al Sidra, both in the 'oil crescent', were closed for a while following ISIL attacks in January 2016, and were reopened by the PFG on the GNA's instructions in July 2016, only to be seized by Hafter's LNA on 11 September 2016. Zuwaytina and Brega ports were also seized by the LNA the next day. Libya's National Oil Company, which managed the oil sector, was split into rival branches, one loyal to the GNA and the other to the LNA. The issue of Western support for Hafter and the LNA, who continued to sabotage the Western-backed GNA, remained a puzzle. On 14 September 2016, Hafter was promoted from the rank of general to field marshal by the President of the House of Representatives, on the back of celebrations to mark the LNA's seizure of the oil installations in the Libyan Crescent. The Hafter-led LNA's oversight in the Libyan Crescent constituted a significant power shift over Libya, and prompted the Prime Minister of the Tripoli-based government to announce a potential dialogue with Hafter. This, coupled with the 15 October 2016 seizure of some GNA offices by the National Salvation Congress militias, destabilized the GNA somewhat.

Reflecting the unpredictability of the Libyan security space, on 23 December 2016, two Libyan nationals hijacked an Afriqiyah Airliner airbus 320 domestic flight with 118 passengers on board, heading from Sabha to Tripoli, and diverted the flight to Malta. On arrival, they announced themselves as Gaddafi loyalists belonging to the Al-Fatah Al-Gadida group that should be allowed to set itself up as a political party in Libya without opposition from Prime Minister Fayez al-Sarraj of the GNA.[90] All passengers on board the flight were freed in Malta unharmed, and the so-called hand grenades reportedly brandished by the two hijackers turned out to be replicas. Whether or not this successful hijacking was a mere hoax, it said something about the Libyan political and security space and how unsafe it had become.

On 2 January 2017, Musa al-Koni, a deputy leader of the GNA, resigned, citing the GNA's incapacity to govern. The timing of al-Koni's resignation, at a time when ISIL had been defeated in Sirte, aroused suspicion and rang alarm bells. There appeared to be not just a nominal lack of unity among the GNA cabinet, but instead, overt opposition within the group, including procedural boycotts, issuing of contradictory statements, and the undermining of the prime minister's authority writ large. For example, it was reported that Fathi al-Majbari, an eastern member of the GNA's Supreme Council, announced a series of appointments while Fayez al-Sarraj was away on New Year's Eve, only for those appointments to be repudiated almost immediately by a colleague.[91] Certainty about the political situation had been in a constant state of flux; for example, an attempt by gunmen allied to Khalia Ghweil and the National Salvation Congress to seize three government ministries on 12 January 2017 failed as forces loyal to the GNA clashed with Ghweil's militia and forced them to retreat.

On 20 February 2017, there was an attempt on the life of GNA prime minister Fayez al-Sarraj in Tripoli: unidentified gunmen opened fire on his armour-plated motorcade which included Abdurrahman Swehli, the head of the state council, as well as Najmi Nakua, the commander of the presidential guard.[92] This was followed a few days later by violent clashes in Tripoli that resulted in at least six people being killed. Then on 3 March 2017, Hafter's LNA lost control of the Al Sidra and Ras Lanuf major oil terminals in the 'oil crescent' to the Benghazi Defence Brigades (BDB); at least nine people were killed during the fighting. Insecurity and instability had brought oil production almost to a halt; however, production returned to 700,000 barrels per day (bpd) under LNA control. This, though, is still much less than the 1.6 million bpd when Gaddafi was Libyan leader.[93]

A truce was reached between Hafter and Prime Minister al-Sarraj in Abu Dhabi on 2 May 2017, but then broken on 18 May, when Third Force militiamen loyal to the GNA launched an assault on the Brak al-Shat airbase and killed 141 LNA soldiers. Jamal al-Treiki, the head of GNA's Third Force militia, was suspended, together with the GNA's defence minister Mahdi al-Barghathi.[94] Meanwhile the self-announced dissolution by the Ansar al-Sharia group, which operated against the LNA from two Benghazi bases,[95] brought some measure of relief to Hafter and his LNA forces.

A significant factor in the continual massing of rival factions in the Libyan conflict is the contribution of mercenary fighters from northern Chad and Sudan's Darfur who align to the GNA and LNA respectively, but also participate in the people-smuggling and arms trafficking trades.

The Chadian contribution stems largely from the Teda or Tebu people in the Tibesti mountains bordering Libya and Niger.[96] It appears that this localized (sub-Saharan) and ready supply of armed banditry, which was generated from longstanding conflicts in Chad and Sudan, offset any efforts by Western intelligence operatives. According to a report by the Small Arms Survey group based in Geneva:

> Similarly, the Libyan crisis and the issue of a jihadist presence in the Sahara will not be resolved by a military intervention in southern Libya or by placing Western soldiers along porous and virtually non-existent borders. The solution, which depends largely on the Libyans themselves, is to re-establish a government in Tripoli that controls the whole of Libya.[97]

On 5 July 2017, Haftar announced total victory and full control over Bengazi, after a three-year intensive campaign.[98] This result left an indelible question mark over the aim of the Tripoli-based UN-backed GNA to govern Libya, as Haftar now controlled most of eastern and southern Libya, and had rejected the GNA's validity regardless of its UN support. Both Haftar and Fayez al-Sarraj have independently been courting and seeking strategic international mediation for the stalemate: al-Sarraj wining with France and Hafter dining with Russia, with the Arabs serving desserts in between. On 2 May 2017, the UAE hosted talks in Abu Dhabi between Haftar and al-Sarraj which ended in a stalemate and no official statement.[99] Subsequently on 25 July, President Macron hosted UN-sponsored talks with the two outside Paris, chaired by Ghassan Salamé, the new UN Envoy to Libya, which resulted in agreement to a conditional ceasefire and commitment to negotiating a mutual way forward for Libya including elections.[100] On 14 August, Haftar held secret talks in Moscow with the Russia Contact Group on Libya chaired by Sergei Lavrov. Haftar had previously visited Moscow in 2016 and in January 2017.[101]

Hafter's unconcealed and ambitious intention to become head of state of all of Libya went further than just military manouevres. Among other things, he sponsored political rallies to stake his claim that the UN-backed GNA was illegitimate, as was the case with the mass demonstrations on 17 December 2017, when he called for the GNA to be no longer recognized as a government, in a televised report:

> 17th of December has arrived and has brought with it the end of what is the so-called secure agreement (or accord). Therefore all institutions created by this agreement are void. These institutions have not obtained the full legitimacy since the first day they started working, and as of today Libyans feel that they have lost patience and that the promised period of peace and stability have become a far away dream.[102]

On 27 January 2017, the AU had held a high-level meeting of African heads of state in Congo-Brazzavile to discuss Libya and take steps toward resolving the crises. The meeting was hosted and opened by President Sassou Nguesso (who became chair of subsequent meetings), and attended by Fayez al-Sarraj, as well as former Tanzanian president Jakaya Kikwete (who became the AU High Representative for Libya). This meeting followed the commitment made at the 27th Ordinary Session of the AU Assembly in Kigali in July 2016 and the agreement reached between the AU High-Level Committee on Libya and African heads of government at the November 2016 AU Summit in Addis-Ababa.[103] A Quartet on Libya comprising the AU, the League of Arab States (LAS), the EU and UN was also formed, and agreed at their 18 March 2017 meeting to enhance and coordinate their respective border security initiatives and develop a holistic approach towards addressing the needs of affected communities.[104] Typical of such international bodies with wide geographical, conflicting and hidden agendas, the further rhetoric from the Quartet meeting on 21 September 2017 along the margins of the UN General Assembly 'resolved to continue to work together to strengthen collaboration between the four organisations and to ensure a common and complementary approach to addressing the challenges facing Libya.'[105]

The fourth meeting of the AU High Level Committee on Libya held in Brazzaville on 9 September 2017 relied on the AU Commission to take responsibility for implementing the road map outlined by the original Brazzaville Meeting, but then preferred to rely on the Quartet to mobilize international support.[106] However, more noncommittal rhetoric arose from the Quartet meeting on 11 December 2017 in

Addis Ababa, which was unfortunate, given the recent CNN, IOM and HRW revelations of slave markets and the heightened international awareness of the international refugee crisis in Libya in November 2017, for which reason some serious action was expected. However, the Quartet scheduled the next meeting for January 2018. Just how resonant was the AU's voice among the Quartet remained unclear at this stage.

Meanwhile, Hafter had been under pressure from the ICC warrant to release Saiqa special forces major Mahmoud Warfali to face war crimes charges at The Hague, including responsibility for the gruesome murders of 36 men who were handcuffed, shot in the head and buried outside Al-Abyar.[107] Civil rights lawyers from the UK-based Guernica 37 International Justice Chambers also piled extra pressure on Hafter, with representations to the ICC on behalf of alleged victims in Libya.[108]

The lack of a coherent and stable government over Libya's political space continued to loom large as the obvious elephant in the room of ideas, and overshadowed the existence of the Brazzaville consensus, the Quartet, or whatever else appeared to be a resolution movement. What emerged was another initiative (from France) that brought together prime minister Farez al-Sarraj, General Khalifa Hafter, house of representatives president Aguila Saleh and Khaled al-Mishri the new chair of the State Council, to work towards a constitution and a calendar for parliamentary and presidential elections in December 2018. Against the concurrent context of rowing among EU nations along the Mediterranean and the G5 Sahelian nations over migration handling, plus the lack of policy leadership and coherence from the IOM, the summit at the Élysée Palace on 29 May 2018 garnered the interest of at least 24 international organizations. Yet a statement released at the end of the summit was not signed by any of the four eminent Libyan representatives in attendance, let alone the other rival factions not represented, and made clear just how unrealistic the potential aims and outcomes of the conference were perceived.[109] The security over the Libyan political space remained unresolved.

On 2 September 2018, the GNA declared a state of emergency in Tripoli after 39 people were killed and 100 others were injured as a result of clashes between rival armed groups: the Seventh Brigade or Kaniyat from the town of Tarhouna against the Tripoli Revolutionaries' Brigades and the Nawasi. On 4 September 2018, UNSMIL brokered a ceasefire deal with the rival factions and hosted a consolidation meeting on

9 September in Zawiyah to agree a monitoring verification mechanism and begin talks on security arrangements in the Greater Tripoli area. On 10 September, four people died and ten were wounded when gunmen stormed the headquarters of Libya's National Oil Company in Tripoli. Meanwhile, a new US drone base in Dirkou, northeastern Niger, had assumed the role of an additional launchpad to the existing drone facilities in Agadez and Niamey, for increased surveillance and bombings against ISIS and other terrorist targets in the Saharan region. The row over stemming migration continued with an interview granted by Tripoli's foreign minister Mohamed al-Taher Siala to the Austrian newspaper Die Presse on 19 October 2018, that Libya and its North African neighbours (Tunisia, Algeria and Morocco) were opposed to the EU plans for disembarkation platforms.

CHAPTER 7

MALI

The chief peculiarity about the Malian case is not so much that the country is landlocked, or that pre-independence political arrangements plus the one-party state of the first president Modibo Keita sowed and watered the seeds of discord by concentrating development in southern Mali and alienating the northern Tuaregs, who then took advantage of subsequent political sentiments and led a series of insurgencies from January 2012 against the military and the government; Tuareg and allied insurgency is nothing new in Mali. Rather, it is that Mali has been awash with arms, resulting from the proliferation and transfer into Mali of sophisticated and heavy weaponry from the 2011 Libyan uprising, along with forces and affiliates of Al Qaeda in the Islamic Maghreb (AQIM) who began to populate the unmonitored and sparsely populated northern Mali. The Libyan uprising was itself a key consequence of the Arab Spring that began on 17 December 2010 in Tunisia and rippled to Algeria, Egypt, Libya, Morocco and Mauritania.

The arms proliferation as well as the battle-tested experience of the Arab Spring contributed to the formation of the secularist Tuareg National Movement for the Liberation of Azawad (MNLA) which wanted a northern Mali secession or autonomy for Azawad, and further boosted the capabilities of Islamist and other rebel groups in northern Mali including Ansar Dine, the Movement for Oneness and Jihad in West Africa (MUJWA/MUJAO), which was a splinter group from AQIM, and of course AQIM. All the Islamist or jihadist insurgent groups principally wanted the imposition of sharia law, first in Azawad, and then for the whole of Mali.

Mali is a landlocked country in the middle of the Sahara Desert, with some eight political divisions or regions, and most heavily populated in its southern parts which are less arid, and where the Niger and Senegal rivers contribute to environmental appeasement. Unfortunately, the southern political base of central government has not made the necessary appeasement towards northern Mali which has been consistently close to the zero end of the little development the broader country could show. It is generally not easy for Mali to thrive, even by diversifying an economy that has few natural resources, although it is the third-largest gold producer on the African continent, and has been producing historically over many centuries. Mali is the site for the Old Ghana Empire that was famous for being bountiful with gold. In 2011 when the conflict was imminent, Mali's gold revenues had surged by more than 20 per cent to 240 billion CFA francs ($475 million), principally because of the rise in gold prices and other economic prospects, for which reason more mines were opening in the country.[1]

Map 7   Map of Mali.

What Resulted from Modibo Keita

The extensive and essentialist role of France in the affairs of Mali stems from the colonial relationship, which has translated economically and politically into a large number of French citizens living in Bamako. France scrambled for the Malian territory, which was part of French Sudan that eventually became the Republic of Mali at independence on 22 September 1960. Modibo Keita, who became the first elected president, governed by a one-party state system, just like his contemporaries on the African continent, such as Kwame Nkrumah of Ghana, Sekou-Toure of Guinea, Maurice Yaméogo of Upper Volta (now Burkina Faso), Omar Bongo of Gabon, Jomo Kenyatta of Kenya and Julius Nyerere of Tanzania. He also practised African socialism, and was at the Organization of African Unity (OAU) conference in Addis Ababa in 1966.

Perhaps from the very onset, the one-party system of governance became the key modus operandi for ostracizing northern Mali. The northerners had not featured much in the anti-colonial struggle for independence which was organized from Bamako and southern Mali more generally, and for that reason the historical connections or post-colonial links with central government did not exist sufficiently to advance the cause of northern Mali. Hence one-party rule effectively set the scene for the relative discrimination and underdevelopment of northern Mali, and perpetuated it.

The principal insurgent groups are the MNLA, Ansar Dine, AQIM, MUJWA/MUJAO and the Front de Libération du Macina (FLM). Also existent is the sedentarized Ganda Iso based in the Gao district – a Black African paramilitary group of Songhai origin, and natural rivals to the olive-skinned Arabic MNLA Tuaregs. The northern territory or Azawad had always complained of relative neglect and underdevelopment at the hands of central government since the 1960s. Ongoing acute food crises had exacerbated this anti-government sentiment, particularly with the unsightly upswell of starvation camps for indigenous women and children, and refugee camps for displaced persons from neighbouring Arab Spring countries. Against the backdrop of the Arab Spring, AQIM forces had then moved into the relatively sparse and unprotected northern Mali to populate Azawad. The combination of these factors plus the potential support of both Tuareg and AQIM fighters, as well as the proliferation of weaponry from Libya and other neighbouring sources in the course of the Arab Spring, all led towards 16 January 2012, when armed conflict broke out between the insurgent groups of northern Mali led by the MNLA on the one hand, and the Malian government military in the south on the other hand. In the political history of Mali, insurgencies by the nomadic Tuaregs have dated back as far as 1916.

The Emergence of Amadou Sanogo

The northern rebel groups, now in possession of more potent and sophisticated weaponry from the Libyan Arab Spring, rendered the government military relatively incapable. Government military campaigns attempted to quell the northern insurgencies, but were defeated with severe casualties, and the regular army complained that they were ill-equipped. Even the so-called Red Berets or presidential guard, with superior kit, did not want to risk their lives to mount a challenge against the northern insurgent groups, unless the government upgraded their weaponry and tactical training. It was the government's inadequate response to this mutiny, while at the same time expecting their military to face the northern rebellions, which led to the coup of 21 March 2012 that was completed the next day, led by Captain Amadou Sanogo.

Faced with an insurgent attempt to seize the key northern town of Kidal, some Malian government soldiers fled into Algeria on 8 February 2012, prompting the MNLA to seize the Mali–Algeria border town of Tinzaouaten. There were weeks of protests against the government's handling of the northern rebellions, and complaints from government soldiers over their inadequate equipment and food supplies triggered the coup of 22 March. On 21 March, the defence minister Brigadier General Sadio Gassama visited the Kati camp to defuse a planned protest, but instead, when he talked down to the soldiers, they stormed the ammunition depot and ran riot, ending up at the presidential palace to announce a military takeover. The next day featured announcements by the military junta known as the National Committee for the Restoration of Democracy and State (CNRDR) led by Amadou Sanogo.

The northern insurgent groups took advantage of the coup in southern Mali, and made further incursions: the MNLA captured Kidal and a major military base on 30 March 2012; Ansar Dine and the MNLA jointly captured Gao on 31 March; and Timbuktu was captured on 1 April. After capturing the frontier town of Douentza, between northern and southern Mali, the MNLA went on to declare independence for Azawad on 6 April 2012. The MNLA had initial support from Ansar Dine, MUJWA/MUJAO and other Islamist groups who began imposing strict sharia law after the Malian military were driven from Azawad. Subsequently, however, the MNLA and Islamists struggled to agree on their conflicting agendas for the autonomous Azawad. The MNLA therefore had to fight the Islamists (Ansar Dine, MUJWA, AQIM) who, as we know, also had superior weaponry from the Arab Spring. For example, the MUJWA, allied with Ansar Dine, clashed with the MNLA in the battle of Gao on 26–27 June 2012. The next day, all three key Azawad cities (Gao, Timbuktu, Kidal) came under the control of Islamist allies. The fall of Timbuktu led to the destruction of parts of the United Nations Educational, Scientific and Cultural Organization (UNESCO) World Heritage Site. By 17 July 2012, the MNLA had effectively lost all the major cities of northern Mali to the Islamists.

As the onslaught continued, Douentza, the frontier town originally controlled by the Ganda Iso in the Gao region and strategically located between southern and northern Mali, was taken by MUJWA on 1 September 2012. Also, Ansar Dine cleared the MNLA from Léré in the Timbuktu region. The Malian Government had already sought foreign military support for taking back the north; control of Azawad by Islamists was considered a more serious threat than control by the secularist MNLA who were quietly considering their weakened status during the course of the following months. Ironically, on 14 February 2013, the MNLA renounced their independence claim over Azawad (which was practically no longer valid at this stage because of interference by the Islamist groups) and approached the Malian Government to renegotiate for favourable terms such as self-rule within Mali. The timing of this Tuareg surrender to central government of their hard-won secession is quite curious and could be interpreted as the MNLA having calculated that the French intervention on 10/11 January 2013, which was to last for as long as foreseeable (at least one year in the first instance), spelled defeat in advance for any party that was opposed to Bamako.

The New Pan-Africanism and French Intervention

Presidential elections were due to take place on 29 April 2012 (with a provisional second round scheduled for 13 May 2012). President Amadou Toumani Toure had already declared on 12 June 2011 that he would not stand for a third term in office. A change of government was therefore definitive and imminent. Over a period of many decades since independence, official Malian politics centralized in the south had done nothing to change the game for the northerners, who had already decided that no new government, however composed, would attempt to fight their cause, let alone redress the imbalances they had accrued over four decades since independence, and who were therefore determined to pursue their conflict. The country was therefore gearing up for elections at the same time as the northern agitations and conflict began.

The AU took the line that the coup of 22 March 2012 had disrupted the course of democracy, and called for an immediate return to constitutional order, while Mali was immediately suspended from the AU. The AU had no regard whatsoever for the CNRDR military junta, never mind the government's inability to redress the developmental imbalance that had led to the conflict in the first place. The AU had traditionally turned a blind eye to ongoing bad governance, yet at the same time condemned coups that overthrew the bad governance in countries where the status quo would not give room to redress the governance deficit. Incidentally, ECOWAS took a similar stance to the AU's.

Subsequently, on 23 March 2012, the AU and ECOWAS jointly sent diplomatic emissaries to meet with junta representatives and establish rapport. This paid off because, two days later, a second joint AU–ECOWAS delegation began negotiations with the junta towards an elected government, although the next talks with the junta on 29 March took place in Abidjan instead of Bamako, because junta supporters occupied the runway of Bamako airport and prevented the sole ECOWAS delegation from landing. In any case, the junta had made it public and clear, right from the onset, that national security (including restoring the now lost northern territories to central government control) was their priority, and would seek to return the country to constitutional order and prepare for elections as soon as the priority issues were fixed. The junta had also promised that CNRDR members would not stand in the elections.

The AU played the toothless bulldog as usual, with a suspension which the junta saw as an empty threat. Even the ECOWAS threat of 29 March 2012 with a 72-hour ultimatum, failing which Mali would face an assets freeze in the West African Monetary Zone (WAMZ), the closure of neighbouring borders and military action from regional troops on standby, was seen as half-empty, judging from the sub-region's unimpressive record in previous circumstances. Border closures had more potency, seeing that Malian oil supplies came by road from Côte d'Ivoire, and the Ivorian president at the time, Allassane Ouattara, was also chair of ECOWAS.

More importantly, the junta needed military support from neighbours to surmount the rebel insurgencies and restore territorial integrity, as the rebels had taken advantage of the coup situation in the south to begin taking over key northern cities in rapid succession: Kidal and a major military base on 30 March 2012; Gao the northern capital on 31 March; Timbuktu on 1 April; and ultimately the MNLA declaration of Azawad's independence on 6 April. Other sanctions issued by ECOWAS, the AU and the US, such as a travel ban against the junta leaders, seemed rather far-fetched within the context, and unstrategic to say the least, especially as the junta was very committed to dealing with the northern chaos and restoring constitutional order to the whole country; this CNRDR junta was of a different kind from other aimless ones Africa had seen in the past.

Hence on 6 April 2012, Captain Sanogo (and by implication the CNRDR) agreed a resignation from power with ECOWAS (which automatically guaranteed the lifting of sanctions), and handed over to a transitional government, with the Speaker of Parliament Dioncounda Traore as interim president; this prompted incumbent President Amani Toure to also submit his resignation to ECOWAS mediators on 8 April. The next day the Malian Constitutional Court gave the interim president 40 days to organize elections. The announcement of Cheick Modibo Diarra as prime minister followed about a week later.

That said, Amadou Sanogo and his men went on running the show and effectively ruling from behind the scenes. For example, an ECOWAS announcement on 29 April, of a proposed 12-month transition until presidential and parliamentary elections with ECOWAS troops in charge, was flatly rejected by Captain Sanogo and his men, who had made it clear they would stick around to supervise the transition; indeed five ministers designated by the junta joined the transitional unity government formed on 20 August 2012. As if that message was not clear enough, Prime Minister Cheick Diarra, who appeared not to be playing ball with the transitional agenda, was bundled out of his office by the junta on 10 December 2012 and ordered to announce the resignation of not just himself but his entire government. This act received a chorus of condemnation from the entire international community, amidst fears that matters were back to square one. France especially became very alarmed.

It must be noted that the March 2012 coup had already muddied the political waters in Mali and complicated the concerns of France, which had over 1,000 citizens in Bamako, and economic interests in Mali's mineral resources. France therefore kept a keen eye on proceedings from the onset of the coup. On 5 April 2012 France offered logistical support to the much-touted ECOWAS military intervention. But as this intervention never seemed to take place, and the Islamist threat increased, France decided to move in and took decisive action on 10 January 2013 to interrupt an Islamist advance on Bamako. Operation Serval, as it was named, sought first to stop the Islamist advance towards Bamako and later get rid of Islamist militants in northern Mali, in response to an urgent request for help from the interim Malian administration, supported by UNSC Resolution 2085 passed on 20 December 2012 to authorize the deployment of an African-led International Support Mission in Mali (AFISMA) for an initial period of one year.

But for the timely intervention of France, the Islamists would have made their way to Bamako, and the sheer fright that would have caused to the government forces might have caused the latter to capitulate to the Islamists. On 10 January 2013, the Islamists first captured Konna, 600 km from Bamako and just 60 km north of the French military airport Sevare. They subsequently advanced to within 20 km of Mopti, which had a military garrison. The French operation regained Konna by the night of 11 January 2013, as French air strikes were concentrated on Konna, Léré and Douentza. However, the Islamists avoided further air strikes by fleeing to Mauritania and re-routing a return advancement via the Mauritanian border to attack government areas of the city of Diabaly 400 km north of Bamako.

What followed from 11 January 2013 onwards was a northward advance by French forces as they embarked on the second phase of the intervention to get rid of Islamist militants in northern Mali. The much-awaited AFISMA also began to deploy itself gradually from 17 January 2013, while the European Union Training Mission (EUTM) in Mali launched itself on 20 February in Bamako. The French forces, however, pursued a series of intensive guerrilla battles and asymmetrical warfare from January through to April and June, assisted by Chadian forces (FATIM), during which top AQIM men Abdelhamid Abou Zeid and Mokhtar Belmokhtar, the founder of Al Mourabitoun, were reportedly killed. It is understood that Al Mourabitoun in Mali is a coalition of fighters loyal to Belmokhtar and Al Tilemsi, a founding member of MUJWA.[2] Along the way the UNSC passed Resolution 2100 on 25 April 2013 to establish the United Nations Multidimensional Integrated Stabilization Mission in Mali (MINUSMA). An initial peace deal between the Tuareg rebels and government was also signed on 18 June 2013. MINUSMA was officially deployed on 1 July 2013 with 6,000 of the total of 12,600 peacekeeping troops.

With a relatively peaceful terrain in place, the elections eventually went ahead on 28 July 2013, being concluded by a run-off on 11 August 2013, in which Ibrahim Boubacar Keita of the Rally for Mali (RPM) defeated Soumaïla Cissé of the Union for the Republic and Democracy (URD) party. The parliamentary elections on 24 November 2013 generated inconclusive results and also entered a second round on 12 December 2013, in which Ibrahim Boubacar Keita's RPM won 115 out of the 147 seats in the National Assembly; Soumaïla Cissé's party won just 17 seats and formed the Opposition. As soon as the new government got its feet under the table at the start of 2014, the most crucial agenda for Mali – peace talks between Azawad and the central government in the south, this time sponsored by MINUSMA – assumed top priority once more. However, general unrest did not cease totally in Mali, especially in the northern conflict zone, as sporadic attacks continued across the country:

- On 17 July 2014, two UN peacekeepers were reportedly killed in suicide attacks near Timbuktu;[3]

- On 3 October 2014, nine Nigerienne UN peacekeepers were killed in northern Mali;[4]
- On 7 March 2015, a gun and grenade attack took place in the La Terrase restaurant in Bamako, in which a French citizen, a Belgian security officer and three Malians were killed, with nine others injured including two international experts with the UN Mine Action Service (UNMAS). This led to an agreement between President Keita and President François Hollande of France to immediately agree new 'common measures' to reinforce security in a country that already had the benefit of 3,000 French troops stationed in the West African sub-region as a counter-insurgency force against Al Qaeda-linked militants operating in and out of the porous borders of the sub-region;[5]
- The above was followed on 8 March 2015 by a rocket attack on the UN base in Kidal, killing three people;[6] this was the third successive attack that weekend;
- On 12 May 2015, as if to wreck the ongoing peace process, just three days before the signing of an initial draft on 15 May, the Coordination of Movements for Azawad (CMA) – a rebel umbrella group – ambushed an army resupply convoy between Timbuktu and Goundam, killing nine people and wounding several others.[7] Accordingly, when the moment arrived on 15 and 16 May, the separatist militants and Tuaregs backed out of signing the deal, claming they wanted nothing short of a separate Azawad;
- On 3 August 2015, a unit of the National Guard based in Gourma-Rharous was attacked, in which 11 soldiers were killed, four vehicles destroyed and significant loot taken. AQIM claimed responsibility;[8]
- On 7 August 2015, at least five people were killed and three Russian pilots kidnapped when gunmen attacked the Byblos Hotel in Sevare which frequently hosts UN staff.[9] The hostages were freed after government troops stormed the building the next day;[10]
- On 9 August 2015, gunmen on motorbikes invaded the village of Gaberi and killed ten civilians;[11]
- On 20 November 2015, heavily armed gunmen besieged the Radisson Blu luxury hotel in Bamako, during which at least 21 people were killed.[12] A state of emergency was declared. Three groups separately claimed responsibility for the attack.[13] The hotel reopened on 15 December 2015;

- On 5 February 2016, it was reported that a car bomb exploded at a UN mission police station in Timbuktu. Defence Minister Tieman Hubert Coulibaly stated that the Malian military commander was killed in the military's response to this attack;[14]
- On 12 February 2016, a Mauritanian suicide bomber with a truck bomb blew himself up at the UN base in northern Kidal, killing six Guinean peacekeepers. Ansar Dine claimed responsibility for this attack. Also on this day, three Malian soldiers were killed when their military convoy was ambushed in Timbuktu;[15]
- On 21 March 2016, gunmen attacked the EU military mission headquarters based in Bamako's Nord-Sud Hotel which hosted some 600 EU personnel deployed to train Malian security forces. One attacker was killed and two were arrested and interrogated;[16]
- On 12 April 2016, three soldiers from the 511th Regiment serving among French special forces were killed in a land mine blast as they led a convoy of military vehicles heading from Gao to Tessalit. This brought to 17 the number of French peacekeepers killed since France began to intervene in Mali from 2013;[17]
- On 29 May 2016, five UN peacekeepers from Togo were killed and one other seriously injured in an ambush in central Mali. The convoy was attacked 30 km west of Sevare. No group claimed responsibility for this attack at the time;[18]
- On 31 May 2016, there were two explosions and rocket fire at the UN security forces base in Gao.[19]

The first post-election round of talks opened in Algiers on 1 September 2014. After five rounds of talks, the new Malian administration signed an agreement on 19 February 2015 with six armed groups – a rebel coalition including the MNLA, Azawad Arab Movement (MAA) groups and a pro-Bamako alliance[20] – to cease hostilities and provocations in northern Mali. Key representatives were President Keita on behalf of the government, Algerian foreign minister Ramtane Lamamra, MINUSMA chief Mongi Hamdi and MNLA leader Bilal Ag Acherif. This agreement was by no means a done deal, despite the MINUSMA chief's wish that it should be the precursor to a final agreement. The communiqué called for an immediate ceasefire and an end of all provocations in Azawad, to which all fighting parties should adhere, in order to allow space to tackle the causes of prolonged tensions in northern Mali. Whereas the rebel coalition mooted issues of identity plus a form of limited self-rule and more rights for Azawad, which had faced perennial neglect from central government, the government rejected outright autonomy, but indicated a willingness to consider devolved local powers. This prompted Bilal Ag Acherif, the leader of the rebel coalition, to say that he hoped the communiqué document could facilitate talks in 'good faith'.[21]

It appears that with the welcome respite provided by the relative peace attained by the timely intervention of French forces and subsequent support from AFISMA, FATIM, EUTM and now MINUSMA, the new government had soon forgotten or was not taking into full account the fundamental causes of the conflict with Azawad (the perennial neglect of Tuareg Azawad) and soon began sidelining the Tuaregs in the negotiating process. An accord that was signed on 1 March 2015 seemed almost to exclude the Tuaregs altogether as if they did not matter to any peace deal; the government described this tactic as preliminary, and said that a deal would be finalized later. Quite clearly, the government was determined right from the beginning to have control over a Mali that was to be governed from Bamako. On 2 March 2015, the vice president of the MNLA announced in an interview on France24 that they wanted federation if autonomy would not be granted.[22]

On 16 May 2015, some 22 African heads of state including the chair of the AU, President Robert Mugabe, gathered in Algeria for the signing of the Algiers Accord, which included the creation of regional assemblies but fell short of federalism. It was signed by the Malian foreign minister Abdoulaye Diop, three representatives of pro-Bamako militias, two minor members of the CMA and the Algerian-led mediation team, minus the Tuareg-dominated MNLA, the High Council for the Unity of Azawad, the MAA and the all-important principal factions of the CMA.[23] It should be noted that the Tuaregs had seized and were in control of as much as two-thirds of northern Mali, and would not be easily persuaded to relinquish it without concessions. The deal as it stood was rubbished by experts and analysts, and of course the Azawads.

Finally, on 20 June 2015, the long-drawn-out deal was able to be signed, as the process had fully incorporated all relevant northern Mali partners, and more importantly contained the concessions pertinent to them, such as:

- dropping the arrest warrants against rebel leaders;
- new security plans including Azawad assuming security responsibility for itself instead of having it exercised by Bamako;
- an Azawad economic development programme to be financed by 40 per cent of the Malian central budget; and
- a pseudo or partial autonomy with more devolved authority but short of full autonomy within a federal Mali, so that Azawad could create or form its own local institutions as well as have more parliamentary representation in central government.[24]

Unlike other deals in the post-independence history of Mali, this was to be monitored by the international community in the form of an independent commission chaired by Algeria, and with MINUSMA supporting its implementation. This time also, the deal was signed by a representative of the whole CMA, even though the CMA had its own ongoing internal struggle regarding a clearly identifiable leadership. The issue of Azawad's national identity was, however, left to be debated among Malian political parties; it should be noted that the light-skinned Arabic Tuaregs and other northerners claimed they had been marginalized or short-changed by the Bamako-based central government dominated by Black Africans.[25]

Buoyed by the signing of the peace deal, President Keita embarked on a three-day working and friendship tour of Algeria on 31 August 2015, against the background, however, of a spike of hostilities in the Anefis region between the CMA, on the one hand, and the Platform (a coalition of pro-government groups) and the pro-government GATIA local group, on the other hand. There appeared to be a CMA presence and operations in Anefis that were now under the control of the Platform and GATIA. Bilal Ag Acherif, the CMA's president, alleged that the Platform was a fabrication of the Malian Government led by Malian Army officials with state weapons, whereas Fahad ag Almahoud, GATIA's secretary-general, held that GATIA had the support of the local population.[26] On 15 October 2015, the rival sides signed a 'pact of honour' brokered by MINUSMA through a series of talks held from 4 to 14 October,[27] though this pact was loosely honoured and the two sides continued to lock horns over Anefis after signing the pact.[28] On 18 February 2016, French foreign minister Manual Valls and his defence minister Jean-Yves Le Drian visited French troops stationed in Gao.

On 2 May 2016, French foreign minister Jean-Marc Ayrault and German foreign minister Frank-Walter Steinmeier began their West African tour in Mali, in support of security operations. France had already deployed more than 3,500 soldiers across five nations in the West African sub-region. The foreign ministers encountered the short-lived optimism of the May 2015 Algiers Accord, in the form of the Azawadi claiming to have a mission to protect people and visitors in the north-east against Al Qaeda attacks. The foreign ministers' tour of the ECOWAS sub-region was also intended to support a fresh policy drive that had seen French forces expand operations against Al Qaeda to Burkina Faso, Chad, Mali, Mauritania and Niger, in direct response to recent ISIL strategic and territorial gains in Libya and their spillover effects in the form of armed and network support for Al Qaeda affiliates in the Sahelian areas of West Africa.

On 13–14 January 2017, Mali hosted the 27th Africa–France Summit, at which security, trade and climate change were high on the agenda, although it was the ECOWAS handling of Gambia's disputed presidential election results that took centre stage at the summit.

On 1 March 2017, interim political leaders of Azawad were sworn in at a ceremony held in a public square in Kidal. This occurrence was a key ingredient of the hard-won peace deal. The ceremony was symbolic but nevertheless significant, as it took some 18 months after signing the peace deal for this to occur. The event recognized Belco Maiga as the president of the Interim Authority, and Mohammed Ag Erlaf as minister for decentralization and territorial reform. The swearing-in of this interim authority became a positive sign that the region could now be governed one way or another. All the relevant groups (the Platform, the Azawad Coalition and the Government of Mali) were represented in this interim authority. National reconciliation was still yet to be achieved, and Belco Maiga said they had to work towards social cohesion so that all of Kidal's children could speak together. Ag Erlaf said to newsmen that basic social services had to be put in place and brought to the people, and subsequently, elections had to be organized, so that the interim authority could be replaced by united and democratically elected candidates and institutions. One of the first key tasks was to establish joint security patrols between the Malian Army and former rebel groups; the first of such joint patrols took place in Gao.[29]

International Political Economy

Mali is one of the poorest countries in the world, and has featured among the bottom 13 countries on the Human Development Index in the last eight years from 2010 to 2018. The recent conflict has not helped, and it will take at least a decade of sustainable development under peaceful conditions to bring real change, mainly because Mali is not too naturally resourced, and its real GDP growth rates of 6.0 per cent in 2015, 5.8 per cent in 2016, 5.3 per cent estimated for 2017, and 5.0 per cent, 4.7 per cent and another 4.7 per cent forercasted for 2018, 2019 and 2020 respectively[30] do not translate into much economic substance. The country has to rely on a few commodities such as gold, cotton and livestock as its chief exports, all of which suffer from high-risk price and environmental fluctuations. Over 60 per cent of its land area is not arable, hence the majority of the population congregate around the capital Bamako for urban and foreign pickings, and along the course of the River Niger where farming, fishing and livestock rearing can be most productive. The country tries to process most of its cereals and livestock in order to cut down on food imports; however, Mali is not yet in a position to wean itself off foreign aid.

Mali's peace ranking deteriorated after 2012 with the northern rebellions, improving slightly after the signing of the comprehensive peace deal in June 2015; corruption levels seem to have improved remarkably too. However, the development indicators remain very weak, and it will take a lot more than just peace, political stability and less corruption for development to take place, and for impact to register sustainably. Adherence to the peace deal signed between the government and Azawad would be a good starting point. The economic cost of violence in 2016 alone, which amounted to $5,025,000,000 in purchase power parity (PPP) terms,[31] reduced to $4,484,500,000 in 2017.[32]

Mali's performance on the Ibrahim Index on African Governance (IIAG) has been as follows:

- In the 2010 index, Mali ranked 17th overall, with a score of 53.4 per cent;
- In the 2011 index,[33] Mali ranked 22nd overall, with a score of 54 per cent;

- In the 2012 index, Mali ranked 20th overall, with a score of 55 per cent;
- In the 2013 index, Mali ranked 27th overall, with a score of 50.7 per cent;
- In the 2014 index, Mali ranked 28th overall, with a score of 49.5 per cent;
- In the 2015 index, Mali ranked 30th overall, with a score of 48.7 per cent.[34]
- In the 2016 index, Mali ranked 25th overall, with a score of 50.6 per cent, which constituted a −4.7-per cent comparative deterioration in performance over the decade trend index of 2006–15;
  - ✔ 32nd in Safety and Rule of Law with a score of 52.7 per cent, which signified a −8.6-per cent comparative downward spiral in the decade trend index of 2006–15, and 25th in the personal safety sub-category, which constituted a −5.9-per cent comparative downward spiral in the decade index; 40th in the national security sub-category or a −10.3-per cent comparative downward spiral in the decade index; 20th in the accountability sub-category which constituted a −12.3-per cent comparative deterioration in the decade trend index; and 24th in the rule of law sub-category or a −6.1-per cent comparative downward change in the decade trend index;
  - ✔ 27th in Participation and Human Rights with a score of 52.5 per cent, which constituted a 12.4-per cent comparative deterioration in the decade trend index 2006–15; 24th in the participation sub-category, which constituted a −17.3-per cent comparative deterioration in the decade trend index; 15th in the rights sub-category, which constituted a −13.9-per cent comparative downward change in the decade index; and 46th in the gender sub-category, which constituted a −6-per cent comparative downward change in the decade trend index;
  - ✔ 22nd in Sustainable Economic Opportunity with a score of 46.3 per cent, which constituted a 1.3-per cent rise in the comparative trend index 2006–15; 27th in the infrastructure sub-category, which constituted a 9.4-per cent comparative positive change in the decade trend index; a 2.4-per cent improvement in electricity supply over the decade; 24th in the public management sub-category, which constituted a

− 8.8-per cent comparative deterioration over the decade; 19th in the business environment sub-category which constituted a 0.5-per cent improvement in the comparative decade index; a − 4.4 indicator drop in employment creation over the decade; and 19th in the rural sector sub-category which constituted a comparative positive change of 4.4-per cent in the decade index;

✔ 37th in Human Development with a score of 50.8 per cent, which constituted a 0.6-per cent positive change in the comparative decade trend index; 45th in the education sub-category, which constituted a 5.2-per cent comparative improvement in the decade trend index; 26th in the health sub-category, which constituted a − 3.3-per cent comparative deterioration over the decade; 28th in the welfare sub-category, which constituted a mere 1-per cent improvement in the comparative index over the decade; and an 8.2 indicator improvement in poverty reduction pertaining to the living standards of the poor, comparatively over the decade 2006–15;[35]

- In the 2017 index[36] Mali ranked 25th overall with a score of 51.9 per cent, which signified a − 2.4-per cent comparative aggregate deterioration over the ten-year period from 2007 to 2016 but a 0.1-per cent improvement over the five-year period from 2012 to 2016; improved slightly from 32nd to 28th in Safety and Rule of Law over the 2007–16 decade; dropped from 27th to 28th in Participation and Human Rights; improved from 22nd to 18th in Sustainable Economic Opportunity; and deteriorated from 37th to 39th in Human Development;[37]
- In the 2018 index, Mali ranked 28th overall with a score of 50.1 per cent, which signified a − 4.0 per cent comparative aggregate deterioration over the ten-year period from 2008 to 2017; worsened significantly from 28th to 35th in Safety and Rule of Law; maintained position at 28th in Participation and Human Rights; maintained position at 18th in Sustainable Economic Opportunity; and improved from 39th to 32nd in Human Development.[38]

Mali's performance on the Global Peace Index (GPI) has been as follows:

- In the 2010 GPI, Mali ranked 109th out of 149 countries – scoring 2.242;
- In the 2011 GPI, Mali ranked 100th out of 153 countries – scoring 2.188;
- In the 2012 GPI, Mali ranked 102nd out of 159 countries – scoring 2.132;
- In the 2013 GPI, Mali ranked 125th out of 162 countries – scoring 2.346;
- In the 2014 GPI, Mali ranked 135th out of 162 countries – scoring 2.465;
- In the 2015 GPI, Mali ranked 128th out of 162 countries – scoring 2.310;[39]
- In the 2016 GPI, Mali ranked 137th out of 163 countries – scoring 2.489;[40]
- In the 2017 GPI, Mali ranked 140th out of 163 countries – scoring 2.596,[41] although from a regional perspective this amounted to placing 38th among the 44 sub-Saharan African countries listed in the index. Mali was captured as among the few countries in the sub-region with the largest deteriorations in peace;[42]
- In the related Positive Peace Index of 2017, Mali ranked 120th among 163 independent states and territories, with a score of 3.59;[43]
- In the 2018 GPI, Mali had deteriorated and ranked 144th out of 163 independent states and territories globally – scoring 2.686, and became 39th among the 44 Sub-Saharan African countries featured in the index.[44]

Below is Mali's performance on the UNDP's Human Development Index (HDI) in the Human Development Report (HDR):

- In the 2010 HDI, it ranked 160th out of 169 countries in the 2010 HDR;
- In the 2011 HDI, it ranked 175th out of 187 countries in the 2011 HDR;
- In the 2012 HDI, it ranked 176th out of 187 countries in the 2012 HDR;
- In the 2013 Index, it ranked 182nd out of 186 countries in the 2013 HDR;

- In the 2014 HDI, it ranked 176th out of 187 countries in the 2014 HDR;
- In the 2015 HDI, it ranked 179th out of 188 countries in the 2015 HDR;[45]
- In the 2016 HDI, it ranked 175th out of 188 countries in the 2016 HDR;[46]
- In the 2018 Human Development Indices and Indicators (HDII) Statistical Update, it ranked 182nd out of 189 countries.[47]

Below is Mali's performance on the Corruption Perceptions Index (CPI):

- In 2010, Mali ranked 116th out of 178 positions, with a score of 1.7 (together with Ethiopia, Guyana, Mongolia, Mozambique, Tanzania and Vietnam);
- In 2011, Mali ranked 118th out of 182 positions, scoring 2.8 (with Bolivia);
- In 2012, Mali ranked 105th out of 174 positions, scoring 34 (with Algeria, Armenia, Bolivia, Gambia, Kosovo, Mexico and the Philippines);
- In 2013, Mali ranked 127th out of 175 positions, scoring 28 (with Azerbaijan, Comoros, Gambia, Lebanon, Madagascar, Nicaragua, Pakistan and Russia);
- In 2014, Mali ranked 115th out of 174 positions, scoring 32 (with Côte d'Ivoire, Dominican Republic and Guatemala);
- In 2015, Mali ranked 85th out of 167 country positions, scoring 35 (with Armenia, Mexico and the Philippines);[48]
- In 2016, Mali ranked 116th out of 176 countries and territories, scoring 32 (with Pakistan, Tanzania and Togo).[49]
- In 2017, Mali ranked 122nd out of 180 countries and territories globally, scoring 31 (with Djibouti, Liberia, Malawi, Azerbaijan, Kazakhstan, Nepal and Moldova),[50] and also 25th (with Djibouti, Liberia and Malawi) among 49 Sub-Saharan African countries featured in the index.[51]

The impact of climate change has become a cause for concern, with reports of encroaching sands on Timbuktu amidst creeping desertification[52] by 6 m annually.[53]

Security Challenges

In the 2016 Verisk Maplecroft Political Risk Index, Mali was rated among the 'high'-risk countries.[54] How to deal with IS and other Islamist militias would remain a top security challenge for the foreseeable future, especially as IS tried to consolidate their presence in the Sahelian and West African sub-regions. Failure to adhere to the Algiers Accord would obviously generate another northern rebellion. Since 2013, French and MINUSMA troops have continued to battle jihadist fighters. Despite having been driven out of key towns, the Islamist fighters continued to attack security forces from desert hideouts, undermining national efforts to rebuild the nation, and threatening regional stability. Security forces continue to patrol the vast nomadic territory which has also become bandit territory for terrorists. The maintenance of cross-border security, heavily assisted by aerial drone monitoring, constitutes the multi-pronged strategy to handle the continual string of deadly ambushes even after the signing of the peace deal in mid-2015.

In the 2015 Global Terrorism Index (GTI), which lists rankings in reverse order, in contrast to other performance indexes, so that the worst-performing (in this case, Iraq) is at the top, Mali ranked 26th among 162 countries that featured on the index, with a score of 5.871.[55] In the 2016 GTI, Mali deteriorated to 25th among 163 countries that featured on the index, with a score of 6.03.[56]

In the 2017 GTI, Mali maintained position at 25th among 163 countries that featured on the index, with a score of 5.88,[57] and was 10th among the sub-Saharan African countries within the index.[58] According to this index, 'the Front de Libération du Macina (FLM) [...] which formed in 2015, has similar stated goals and methods to al Qaeda in the Islamic Maghreb (AQIM). The FLM was responsible for approximately 12 per cent of terror attacks in Mali in 2015 and 2016. These attacks were responsible for ten per cent of deaths from terrorism in Mali during these two years.'[59]

Terrorist attacks, as well as riots, continued unabated in Mali. On 12 July 2016, there were anti-government protests by hundreds of youths in Gao despite the ban on protests; several people were killed. The protesters had several demands, chiefly that they wanted to be integrated into the army, and would refuse to be ruled by the Tuareg armed groups who signed the 2015 peace deal with the government.[60]

Also, on 19 July 2016, gunmen attacked an army base in Nampala, killing at least 12 soldiers and wounding at least 38 others. The Deputy Mayor reported that the attackers arrived on motorbikes and trucks, seized control of the army base, made assaults and later departed; a militia linked to the Peul ethnic group said it carried out this attack. Quite clearly, fighters had kept up attacks on security forces in Mali and across West Africa, despite 11,000 UN peacekeepers bolstering local troops,[61] and this would continue unabated unless drastic measures were taken to stem the tide. On 20 July 2016, the government imposed a three-month state of emergency across the whole country. This appeared to be based on a correct assessment, because the next day, renewed fighting broke out in northern Mali near Kidal, between pro-government fighters and Tuareg separatists, resulting in at least 15 deaths.[62]

On 22 August 2016, the trial of Ahmad Al-Faqi Al-Madi of Ansar Dine began at the ICC in The Hague. He pleaded guilty to directing the destruction of religious and ancient artefacts in Timbuktu, including nine mausoleums and the door of a mosque,[63] plus other UN Heritage sites, because the attackers followed a strict interpretation of Islamic law, whereby girls were prevented from attending school and music was banned during the ten-month occupation of Ansar Dine in Timbuktu. The guilty plea could reduce the potential prison term of 30 years. This was the first time that the ICC had charged someone with war crimes against culture.[64] Al-Madi was sentenced to nine years in prison on 27 September 2016. In the week prior to his sentencing (on 19 September 2016), the 'secret door' of the Sidi Yahia fifteenth-century mosque in Timbuktu that was vandalized by Ansar Dine in 2012 was unveiled and opened to the public, after it had been restored to its full glory by UNESCO.[65]

Clashes have continued between rival Tuareg armed groups battling for control of Kidal, undermining the peace deal signed in June 2015. As long as the peace and security problem remains unresolved, aid and planned new security measures are placed on hold because any attempt to roll out the aid would benefit the brazen militants. Tensions continued between the pro-government GATIA militia and the separatist group CMA that seized Kidal in August 2016. The prices of goods nearly doubled, as goods were not circulating. MINUSMA and French troops still have to patrol the streets to stem attacks from rebel militias, as there is no government presence in the Kidal region; state services, the Malian Army and any form of state apparatus have been absent since May 2014, when a visit by former prime minister Moussa Mara ended badly, and he was chased from the town by rebel groups while several government soldiers were killed in clashes with former rebels.[66]

On 31 October 2016, Iyad Ag Gali, the head of Ansar Dine, agreed (with Mahmoud Dicko, the president of the Islamic High Council) to cease attacks throughout Mali.[67] Mali had declared a state of emergency in November 2015 after fighters stormed the Radisson Blu in Bamako. Another state of emergency was declared on 20 July 2016 to last for a three-month period. It can be argued that the impact of the July 2016 state of emergency restricted the activities of Ansar Dine, hence the group's ceasefire announcement in October 2016 should be seen as a tactical withdrawal in the face of government resistance, with a view to resuming hostilities once the state of emergency was lifted.

There was a very low turnout on 20 November 2016 when Mali held its first municipal vote since 2013 to elect 12,000 councillors. Heightened security measures were in place, despite the presence of the 13,000-strong MINUSMA. The municipal elections had been postponed four times already, and the constitution barred further delays. There were serious issues underpinning the low turnout aside from the polls being cancelled in at least seven districts for security reasons; the majority of northern Mali or Azawad populations were scattered in several refugee camps across Mali and could not participate in the voting exercise. Whereas voting might have been orderly in well-protected zones such as Bamako, the situation was very different in the northern districts of Kidal, Gao and Timbuktu. A PRVM-PASAKO party candidate for Mopti was kidnapped, and ballot boxes were burned in Timbuktu, where Mali's military intelligence had reported the ambushing of a military convoy and citizens en route to polling stations by unidentified armed men.[68]

On 23 December 2016, Operation Garikou, a ten-day mission that involved 500 soldiers from Mali, Niger and France, was completed. Its purpose was to stamp out insurgents, jihadist militants and terrorists. The operation focused on a series of border towns between Mali and Niger, and was aimed at flushing out terrorist cells with links to AQIM. This counter-terrorism operation also acted as a training exercise for the

Malian military, and flushed out arms caches, bomb-making equipment and ingredients stashed in several places by jihadist elements.[69]

On 17 May 2017, a few days after assuming office as French president, Emmanuel Macron jetted off to Mali to make a declaration that France would be uncompromising in the fight against terrorists.[70] Clearly, France's contribution in January 2013 to save the Bamako government from the northern jihadist onslaught had become an iconic achievement, making Mali a good choice of venue for issuing French foreign policy statements, and a good choice for Macron's first foreign trip. As if to test France's resolve, several French soldiers were killed on 1 June 2017 when the Nusrat al-Islam wal Muslimeen militia, an Al Qaeda local affiliate group, launched a mortar attack on the MINUSMA peacekeeping base in Timbuktu, close to a French unit operating a separate counter-terrorism mission. In retaliation, French troops killed 20 Islamic combatants in northern Mali. France has deployed at least 4,500 troops, known as the Barkhane force, to hunt down Islamists and destroy terrorist bases and equipment.[71] It was also reported on 19 June 2017 that a new alliance of Islamist militant groups linked to Al Qaeda claimed responsibility for an attack that killed at least five people in the Le Campement resort near Bamako that was popular with expatriates.[72]

Meanwhile, Malians protested in large numbers on the streets of Bamako on 15 July 2017, against a planned referendum on pro-federalism constitutional changes that form part of the 2015 peace deal to allow the creation of new regions and the official recognition of Azawad as the Tuareg homeland, amidst worsening insecurity. The mixed bag of protesters disagreed with granting any form of autonomy to Azawad if that could lead to a potential Islamic republic in the future. More pertinently, some protesters were of the view that the president was using the constitutional changes as an opportunity to grant himself extra powers (ahead of the scheduled 2018 presidential elections) to nominate a quarter of the Senate and be able to remove the prime minister at will.[73]

On 6 June 2017, France circulated a UNSC draft resolution to approve a West African/AU force from five Sahel countries known as the G5 (Mali, Burkina Faso, Chad, Niger and Mauritania), with a Chapter VII mandate to use all necessary means to combat terrorism and trafficking in the Sahel region. However, the US preferred to deny the force a resolution that mandated financial commitment from the world body, as the US bemoaned UN underfunding from the P5, among other issues. The French-drafted resolution was supported by the UN Secretary-General and the AU. The EU committed $56 million to this Sahel force,[74] International support for the force would include the funding of infrastructure, information and communications technology (ICT), improvised explosive device (IED) technology, medical training, medical capacity, land and air transport.

Despite the initial financial hiccups, the US also pledged $60 million for the start-up. By the time of the Sahel G5 summit held in Paris on 13 December 2017, the initiative had gained more than half of the $500 million it needed for its first year of operations, as extra support of $100 million came from Saudi Arabia, and the UAE also promised $30 million to fund the G5 'war school' to be located in Mauritania.[75] The Emirati and Saudi involvement here is similar to the Emirati and Egyptian involvement in the Libyan conundrum of fighting Islamist terrorism.

The francophone line-up of the G5 reflected in its Sahelian locations but was also strategic, in that France showed overt interest in the formation of the G5, whereas anglophone Nigeria that was under the onslaught of Al Qaeda-affiliated Boko Haram, was discouraged from joining. However, francophone Burkina Faso became a firm member, not least because it was on the receiving end of a jihadist retaliatory onslaught for its part in hosting the drone base at Quagadougou airport to combat Sahelian jihadist terrorism, but also because of the new threat from the Ansarul Islam (Defenders of Islam) movement in northern Burkina Faso. Moreover, maintaining a sole francophone membership of the Sahel G5 facilitated its management by France, whose principal agenda was no longer to prevent the Sahel from being the free grounds for jihadist nurturing and training, but rather a long-term exit strategy for the over 4,500 French forces that had been locked up in the region since the 2013 French intervention in Mali.[76] On 29 June 2018, the G5 headquarters in Sevare was attacked by suicide bombers. The attackers exchanged gunfire with Malian troops, fought their way into the compound and fired rockets. Photographs taken at the scene showed the charred remains of vehicles, battered walls and a crater. Al Qaeda's branch in Mali reportedly claimed responsibility for the attack in which two soldiers and four assailants were killed.[77]

With this background, the 2018 presidential election took place on 29 July amidst fear of insecurity and potential impact on voter turnout.

Over 700 polling stations could not operate on the day because of security concerns,[78] and the voting at 4,632 other sites was disrupted despite over 30,000 security personnel being deployed across the country just for the elections. An Al Qaeda-affiliated group had also fired ten mortar shells at a village in the Kidal region.[79] Regardless of the numerous candidates, the race was mainly between the incumbent and Somaila Cissé. Exit polls and pronouncements from the main rivals suggested a possible run-off to determine who would be president. President Keita failed to reach the 50 per cent threshold as he won 41.4 per cent of the vote, and Cissé came second with 17.8 per cent, which automatically ushered the two main contestants into the second round that was scheduled for 12 August. Keita won in the run-off with 67.17 per cent against Cissé who obtained 32.83 per cent, and with that, all what remains to be done or overcome in order for Mali to achieve its local and international aspirations.

CHAPTER 8

RWANDA

Current Rwandan nationalism is simply the life of President Paul Kagame, who believed he had to be president long enough for Rwandans to fully cohere as a nation, to the point where Rwandans would perceive each other as simply Rwandans and not Hutu or Tutsi, with a single national identity whereby the ethnic heterogeneity or ethnonational heterogeneity has been transformed into national homogeneity within a single state jurisdiction with the state acting as the incubator for the gestation of a homogenized nationhood of simply Rwandans,[1] where the ethnonational and political units or expressions have become one or congruent,[2] or where ethnonationalism equates with political nationalism. Paul Kagame believed he was best placed to govern the country to achieve this purpose, and that he was there to ensure that a Tutsi (himself, that is) remained president of Rwanda until the potential for a Hutu–Tutsi rivalry that could lead to hostilities was no more – a belief with a strong sense of rationalized ethnonationalism.[3]

The politics of Rwanda and Burundi have been intertwined ever since the Belgian colonial masters pitched the two identity groups of Hutu and Tutsi against each other in a single geographical area, until the unbearable rivalry split into the independence of Burundi and Rwanda at the same time. Yet each country is populated by Hutus and Tutsis in equal measure: 84 per cent Hutu, 14 per cent Tutsi and 1 per cent Twa/Pygmies, whether in Rwanda or Burundi.

Subsequently, the tussle between the two identity groups has continued in each country, with a different see-saw effect in each, with Hutus dominating the leadership of Rwanda until a Tutsi assumed

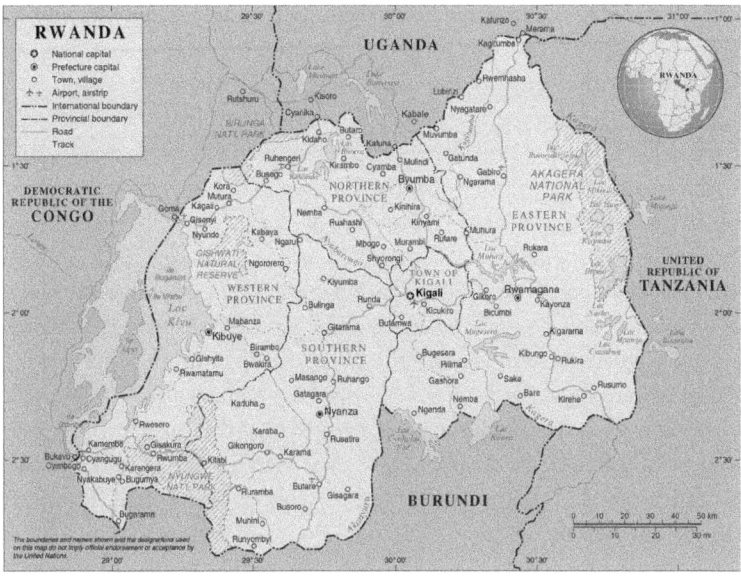

Map 8 Map of Rwanda.

the top job in the form of President Paul Kagame, and Tutsis dominating the leadership of Burundi until Hutus emerged supreme, led by President Pierre Nkurunziza. Kagame believed that he should be president for long enough to redress completely the past Hutu supremacy in Burundi; and there was no way of gauging when enough would be enough for him.

Clearly, Kagame had unfinished business, and he needed a lot of time to complete it, just like Pierre Nkurunziza, as well as Yoweri Museveni of Uganda who said that it took 20 years to get the LRA and Joseph Kony out of Uganda, so that based on his argument, the maximum limits to presidential terms could not have allowed him to deal with the LRA.[4] The LRA are still operating in central Africa; it was reported on 3 March 2016 that they had abducted 217 people in the Central African Republic (CAR) in 2016 alone, of whom 54 were children.[5] Obviously, someone else could complete the job of annihilating the LRA presence in Uganda, but Museveni deemed himself as the one destined to undertake that particular role.

Unlike Nkurunziza of Burundi, Kagame found a well-organized way of legitimizing his extended presidency, through a petition that was signed by over 3.7 million Rwandans, not least because the fear of Kagame was sufficient to disallow an opposite petition or sentiment in Rwanda. In this way, a form of rationalized ethnonationalism[6] was visited on the Rwandan electorate. Both Nkurunziza and Kagame personally suffered from the previous genocides in each country, and harboured pertinent reasons for their intense aspirations and entrenched positions. Nkurunziza's father, Eustache Ngabisha, who was previously a Burundian parliamentarian, was killed in the Tutsi-led (Micombero) Burundian Genocide of 1972 when Ngabisha was a governor. Likewise, Kagame led the Rwandan Patriotic Front (RPF) from 1991, which waged a guerrilla war against the Rwandan Army until the Arusha Accords were signed in August 1993, and has remained the RPF's leader since the accords. Kagame is therefore regarded as the one who successfully fought the Hutu government-backed militias, notably the Interahamwe and Impuzamugambi, to end the Hutu-led Rwandan Genocide of 1994.

What Existed before Paul Kagame

Rwanda is a very small landlocked country in the Great Lakes Region of Africa, bordered clockwise by Uganda to the north, Tanzania to the east, Burundi to the south and the DRC to the west. Rwandans are mainly Hutus (84 per cent) and Tutsis (14 per cent) and up to 1 per cent Twa/ Pygmies.

Rwanda and Burundi share the same origins. Their historical narrative evolves from a land of original Twa hunter-gatherers, with a subsequent influx of Bantus, consequently coalescing into clans and then kingdoms. The Tutsi kingdom emerged as a feudal monarchy that ruled over the rest from about the tenth century, until German colonialists came on the scene in the Scramble for Africa and the Partition in 1884–5, which made Rwanda part of German East Africa which also included Burundi. Hence, both Rwanda and Burundi share similar Hutu–Tutsi–Twa ethnic statistics of 84 per cent–14 per cent–1 per cent.

The Belgian intrusion in the middle of World War I and the defeat of Germany at the end of the war made the area a League of Nations territory under Belgian mandate after the war. It became a United Nations Trust Territory under Belgian administration after World War II. Together with Rwanda, this specific territory became known as

Ruanda-Urundi, under the broader Belgian colonial empire which was very good at playing the Hutu against the Tutsi as a divide-and-rule tactic.[7] In the case of Rwanda, the colonialists (both German and Belgian) governed with the status quo of Tutsi kings over everyone else, especially the Hutu.

The Rwandan Revolution of 1959 to 1961, which precipitated a move by Burundians to separate from Rwanda, was a Hutu-led revolt that led to the mass killing of Tutsis, plus the temporary subjugation of the Tutsi hegemony in Rwandan territory, and eventually independence from the Belgian colonialists on 1 July 1962, with a Hutu-dominated state. The result of the 25 September 1961 referendum in favour of abolishing the monarchy, and the parliamentary elections of the same date, had already determined a post-colonial road map at a point of no return, so independence was a natural consequence which was automatically granted on the same date as the Burundian territory gained independence. But the Hutu-versus-Tutsi rivalries raged on viciously until temporarily abated by the 5 July 1973 coup of Army Chief of Staff Juvénal Habyarimana, whose junta or pseudo party – Mouvement Révolutionaire National pour le Développement (MRND) – governed until 1993. During this period, a constitutional referendum of 17 December 1978 introduced a five-year presidential term, renewable once, which Habyarimana won both times, to last until 1993.

The Tutsis were not deceived by Habyarimana's moderate ethnic policies in Rwanda, while the pot of rebellion brewed in neighbouring Uganda, where previously displaced Tutsis had become battle-hardened in guerrilla fighting alongside Yoweri Museveni's Northern Resistance Army (NRA) and eventually in the Ugandan Army itself. The RPF rebel group originating from Uganda invaded northern Rwanda in 1990. From January 1991 when the RPF was led by Paul Kagame, it appears that even military support for the Rwandan Government from French and Zairean forces proved insufficient against the seasoned RPF fighters, so that a power-sharing treaty had to be agreed by the 4 August 1993 Arusha Accords. However, on 6 April 1994, Habyarimana's plane was shot down, allegedly on the orders of Paul Kagame, killing him and the Burundian president Cyprien Ntaryamira (both Hutus) among others. This outraged Hutus and sparked the Rwandan genocide in which an estimated 800,000 to

1,000,000 Tutsis and moderate Hutus were killed by hardline Hutus within 100 days. Under Kagame, the RPF has fought proxy wars against displaced Hutu populations in the Great Lakes area, notably the First Congo War of 1996–7, the Second Congo War of 1998–2003 and the M23 rebellion of 2003–13.

What Emerged with Paul Kagame

Paul Kagame is seen as very important to current Rwandan nationalism, having led the RPF from January 1991 to the 1994 signing of the Arusha Peace Agreement, and being the strongest man in the government as vice president and minister of defence from 1994 until 2000 when President Pasteur Bizimungu resigned and Kagame became president. He has raised Rwanda from the ashes of the genocide to an average 7–8-per cent annual GDP growth rate since 2003. Kagame believed that he must remain as Tutsi president of Rwanda sufficiently long enough to beat to ashes the embers of the Hutu-led genocide.

Paul Kagame has been president since 2000 when he was elected by government ministers and the National Assembly to replace Pasteur Bizimungu who resigned in March 2000. Winning the 25 August 2003 multiple-candidate elections with 95.1 per cent of the vote, he embarked on the first seven-year term of his presidency, which was renewable just once, according to Article 101 of the 2010 constitution amended from the 2003 original constitutional document. Subsequently, he won the 2010 multi-party elections with 93.08 per cent of the popular vote. He was supposed to hand over in 2017; however, he instituted parliamentary procedures that set in motion a constitutional amendment to allow him to continue beyond 2017. Following the 28–29 October 2015 debates in parliament, both the lower and upper houses voted massively in support of a constitutional draft that would potentially keep him in the presidency until 2034. The revised constitution granted a further one-term extension exclusively to Kagame's current term, after which the constitutional clock resets to two maximum five-year terms for whoever else takes over from that point, with Kagame entitled to compete. As the exclusive extension for Kagame's third term would take him to 2024, a further two five-year terms could proceed to 2034.

The 26 May 2003 referendum revised the transitional version of the 1991 constitution. From when the new 2003 Rwandan Constitution came into effect on 4 June 2003, it took on a variety of ad-hoc amendments through to 2010. The process of major revisions to the 2010 Rwandan constitution kicked off with a petition for constitutional changes based on Article 2 of the constitution, plus Article 193 that was wrongfully invoked by the government. The petition generated 3,784,686 signatures from Rwandans. What was in dispute is whether the petition could ask for changes to accommodate further presidential terms over and above the two maximum terms stipulated in Article 101 of the constitution, in other words whether Article 193 could be invoked in this instance. This was challenged in court by the Democratic Green Party of Rwanda (DGPR) on the basis that Article 193 only allows the duration of the presidential term (and not the number of terms) to be amended by a referendum, hence the term could be shortened or lengthened but not multiplied. Article 193 of the 2003 Rwandan constitution states:

> The power to initiate amendment of the Constitution shall be vested concurrently in the President of the Republic upon the proposal of the Cabinet and each Chamber of Parliament upon a resolution passed by a two thirds (2/3) majority vote of its members. The passage of a constitutional amendment requires a three quarters (3/4) majority vote of the members of each chamber of Parliament. However, if the constitutional amendment concerns the **term** of the President of the Republic or the system of democratic government based on political pluralism, or the constitutional regime established by this Constitution especially the republican form of the government or national sovereignty, the amendment must be passed by referendum, after adoption by each Chamber of Parliament. No amendment to this Article shall be permitted.[8]

The Rwandan Supreme Court dismissed the DGPR application on 8 October 2015 and

> held that there was nothing in the Constitution that prohibited the amendment of Article 101. Although Article 193 provides a complex procedure for amending Article 101, it does not prohibit amendment of any of its parts, meaning that if that procedure is

properly followed both the duration of presidential term and the numbers of terms are amenable to amendment [...] The Court questioned the wisdom of a people binding themselves and future generations in perpetuity without the flexibility to bring the law or the constitution in line with changed beliefs and circumstances.[9]

The court however did not set out what were the changed beliefs and circumstances at this stage of Rwanda's progress that should warrant an amendment to Article 193 when such an amendment was forbidden by the 2010 constitution. It is interesting to note that when Article 193 of the 2010 constitution reappeared in the 2015 constitution as Article 175, the word 'term' was replaced by the phrase 'term of office', which means the latter could now be multiplied whereas the former could only be shortened or lengthened. This should be seen as an attempt to address the wrongful invocation of Article 193 of the 2010 constitution in the first place, and cover up for the past. Subsequently, both chambers of parliament debated on 28–29 October 2015 and voted massively in support of the constitutional draft that could potentially keep Kagame in the presidency until 2034. The new draft granted a further one-term extension exclusively to Kagame's current seven-year term, after which the constitutional clock resets to two maximum five-year terms for whoever else takes over from that point, with Kagame again not disqualified from competing. As the exclusive extension of Kagame's third term would take him to 2024, a further two five-year terms could proceed to 2034.

Consequently, the result of the constitutional referendum to amend the presidential term that took place on 18 December 2015 was a resounding 98.3 per cent in favour, with the same figure for voter turnout. Quite clearly, rationalized ethnonationalism had been crafted for the electorate to indulge in. As defined:

Rationalized ethnonationalism is an observed electoral behaviour whereby ethnonationalism synchronizes with patriotism; whereby citizens demonstrate ethnonationalism as the most rational way of rendering their civic loyalties to the state; with the firm conviction that, for their own purposes, voting along the lines of ethnonational identity is in the best interests of the state, given the realities of the overall political context.[10]

Subsequently on 1 January 2016, Paul Kagame announced that he would seek re-election for a third term in 2017.[11] Most definitely, the behaviour of rationalized ethnonationalism that was demonstrated in the 2015 constitutional referendum was set to repeat itself in the 2017 presidential elections.

We should examine why the Supreme Court judges and parliamentarians so unflinchingly supported this constitutional referendum. Quite apart from the reverence for Paul Kagame (or the fear of him as the case may be), among the constitutional revisions voted for by this referendum, the term of service for senators, the president and vice president of the Supreme Court also changed from eight years non-renewable to a five-year term, renewable once. Furthermore, the senators, president and vice president of the Supreme Court 'in office at the time of commencement of the revised constitution shall continue the term of office for which they have been elected or appointed'.[12] Quite clearly, there was a lot in it for the senators and the Supreme Court judges, because the revised constitution would commence from 2024 or seven years from 2017, and these public servants knew which side their bread was buttered. They would surely behave themselves because whoever survived to 2024 or came in from 2024, could retain their position(s) until 2034. It also becomes clear that President Kagame would have a conniving judicial and legislative infrastructure in place that might allow him to rule for life. We are talking about a titanic government machinery in place to rule comfortably unchallenged for a considerable period of time without opposition – a sure recipe for corruption and whatever else. We know that on 4 August 2017, Kagame was elected by 98.79 per cent of votes cast in the presidential elections.

There is some strange nationalism demonstrating itself in Rwanda, and Kagame's profile is at the centre of it. At one point, he was head of military intelligence in the Ugandan Army while working for Museveni, the seasoned guerrilla specialist. He subsequently worked his way up to become Rwanda's vice president and minister of defence. A spymaster who is now the chief executive is hard to get the better of. After all, this is the man who made sure that even his old enemies under security protection in foreign countries did not escape his vengeance,[13] as happened to Rwanda's former head of external intelligence, Colonel Patrick Karegeya, who was assassinated in Johannesburg in January 2014.[14] From mid-2013, Karageya was known to be advising South

African and Tanzanian intelligence as they prepared to send troops to the DRC to fight the Rwandan-backed rebel group M23.[15] It is true that Kagame holds sway and is very much revered in Rwanda, yet to scheme in advance or galvanize 3.7 million signatures for a petition that was to become the foundation for launching the most impossible constitutional revisions suggests that friends, Rwandans and countrymen were behind him. He had both the backing and the determination to complete his unfinished business.

The New Pan-Africanism

Kagame has been so clever at his game that one has to know what specific charge to lay against him, although nothing can cover up for overriding the impossible Article 193 of the Rwandan constitution of 2004 through 2010. In the fear-ridden political space of Rwanda, citizens are not given to being flippant with negative rhetoric against Kagame.

As to external affairs, it is an open secret that Kagame and his previous boss Museveni have had some involvement in almost every conflict in the Great Lakes region of Africa. As Africa sought for a solution to the perennial conflicts in the DRC, in February 2013, Tanzania took the initiative, providing the force commander for a New Intervention Force created under the control of the Southern Africa Development Community (SADC) to deal with the M23 and other rebel groups in the eastern DRC, despite the existence of the large MONUSCO contingent charged with peacekeeping. The push for the intervention force to consist of at least 4,000 troops was led by Tanzania and supported by South Africa. This was not palatable news for Rwanda and Uganda, who have historical and continuing involvement in this conflict in the DRC.[16] We know how the First Congo War of 1996–7 began with the Rwandan Genocide of 1994 and the resumption of a Kagame (Tutsi-led) administration that resulted in mass migrations of Hutus into Congolese territory, and the Hutu pursuit of anti-Rwandan operations by the Hutu resistance, Interahamwe, from their new bases in Eastern Congo. Since then,

> clashes in North and South Kivu between the Hutu rebels of the
> Democratic Forces for the Liberation of Rwanda (FDLR), allied

with smaller groups, including the Mayi-Mayi, as well as the FARDC, left hundreds dead and forced thousands to leave their homes. One estimate put the number displaced in South Kivu during the first six months of 2012 at more than 200,000 according to the 2014 Global Peace Index.[17]

It took Burundi to gather systematic evidence and make a case against Rwandan Government interference in using the Burundian opposition to destabilize peace and aggravate the Burundian political crisis. For example, it was reported on 4 February 2016[18] that a confidential UN report had levelled allegations against the Rwandan military for recruiting and training Burundian refugees so that they could join an insurgency against Burundian president Pierre Nkurunziza. At least 400 recruits were being trained by Rwandan military personnel for this task.[19] The confidential report also revealed attempts to get arms to Burundian rebels by smuggling weapons from the DRC through Rwanda. Congolese authorities reportedly arrested Rwandan and Congolese civilians and two Congolese officers on smuggling charges at the end of 2015. The Burundian authorities also sent out agents and militias to hunt down these trained refugees sheltering in the Ndutu displaced camp in Tanzania, and abduct or kill them. Over 200,000 Burundians have been displaced since Nkurunziza's attempt at a third term, and about half of them are sheltering in refugee camps in neighbouring Tanzania.[20]

International Political Economy

The 2017 Ibrahim Index on African Governance (IIAG) states that 'since the start of the IIAG time series (2000), Rwanda is the only country in Africa to show year-on-year improvement of their overall Governance score.'[21] But at the same time, Rwanda has consistently been among the weak-performing countries on the UNDP's Human Development Index (HDI) for eight consecutive years from the 2010 Human Development Report (HDR). Underdevelopment is being systematically addressed, although the country is handicapped by being landlocked and dependent on the existing export/import infrastructure of surrounding poor countries. The country specializes in low-return export commodities such as tea and coffee for its chief exports, but with consistent and impressive real GDP growth rates of 8.8 per cent in 2015, 6.0 per cent in 2016, 6.1 per cent estimated for 2017 and 6.8 per cent, 7.1 per cent and 7.5 per cent forecasted for 2018, 2019 and 2020 respectively.[22] The economy had recovered significantly from the ashes of the genocide, and the economic cost of violence, which was $2,258,000,000 in 2016,[23] reduced to $2,004,700,000 in 2017.[24]

Here is a snapshot of Rwanda's performance on the IIAG:

- In the 2010 index, it ranked 31st overall, with a score of 47.92 per cent;
- In the 2011 index,[25] it ranked 31st overall, with a score of 48 per cent;
- In the 2012 index, it ranked 23rd overall, with a score of 53 per cent;
- In the 2013 index, it ranked 15th overall, with a score of 57.8 per cent;
- In the 2014 index, it ranked 11th overall, with a score of 60.4 per cent;
- In the 2015 index, it ranked 11th overall, with a score of 60.7 per cent;[26]
- In the 2016 index, Rwanda ranked 9th overall, with a score of 62.3 per cent, which constituted an impressive 8.4-per cent comparative improvement over the decade, in the trend index of 2006–15;
  - ✔ 15th in Safety and Rule of Law with a score of 61.5 per cent, which constituted a 1.1-per cent comparative improvement in the decade trend index of 2006–15; 4th in the personal safety sub-category, which constituted a − 0.8-per cent comparative downward spiral in the decade index; 46th in the national security sub-category which constituted a − 11.4-per cent comparative deterioration in the decade index; an impressive 2nd in the accountability sub-category which also constituted an impressive 16.4-per cent comparative improvement in the decade trend index, and; 21st in the rule of law sub-category which constituted a 0.8-per cent comparative improvement in the decade trend index;
  - ✔ 28th in Participation and Human Rights, with a score of 51.6 per cent which constituted an 8.8-per cent positive change in the comparative decade trend index 2006–15; 38th in the participation sub-category which constituted a 0.8-per cent

comparative improvement in the decade trend index; 36th in the rights sub-category which constituted a comparative positive change of 0.9 per cent in the decade index; and an impressive 1st in the gender sub-category, which constituted a significant comparative positive change of 24.6 per cent in the decade trend index;

✔ 5th in Sustainable Economic Opportunity with a score of 65.1 per cent which constituted a 9.4-per cent rise in the comparative trend index 2006–15; 18th in the infrastructure sub-category, which constituted a 3.6-per cent comparative positive change in the decade trend index; a −2.4-per cent deterioration in electricity supply over the decade; 7th in the public management sub-category, which constituted a 7.9-per cent comparative improvement over the decade; an impressive 2nd in the business environment sub-category, which constituted a significant comparative positive change of 18.4 per cent in the decade trend index; an impressive 1st in the rural sector sub-category, which constituted a positive change of 7.5 per cent on the comparative decade index;

✔ 5th in Human Development with a score of 71.2 per cent, which constituted a 14.4-per cent positive change in the comparative decade trend index; 21st in the education sub-category, which constituted a 14-per cent comparative improvement in the decade trend index; 7th in the health sub-category, which represented an 8.3-per cent comparative improvement over the decade, and; an impressive 1st in the welfare sub-category, which constituted an equally impressive comparative improvement of 20.7 per cent in the trend index over the decade.[27]

- In the 2017 index,[28] Rwanda maintained rank at 9th overall but with an improved score of 63.9 per cent, which signified an 8.9-per cent comparative aggregate improvement over the ten-year period from 2007 to 2016 and a 3-per cent improvement over the five-year period from 2012 to 2016; improved from 15th to 12th in Safety and Rule of Law over the 2007–16 decade; improved slightly from 28th to 27th in Participation and Human Rights; rose from 5th to 3rd in Sustainable Economic Opportunity; and maintained position at 5th in Human Development:[29]

- In the 2018 index, Rwanda improved rank at 8th overall with a score of 64.3 per cent, which signified a 5.9 per cent comparative aggregate improvement over the ten-year period from 2008 to 2017; but dropped from 12th to 13th in Safety and Rule of Law; improved from 27th to 26th in Participation and Human Rights; improved from 3rd to 2nd in Sustainable Economic Opportunity; and maintained rank at 5th in Human Development. The index identified Rwanda as among the top countries with the largest percentage increases in GDP, among the top two in largest improvements in Business Environment, and among the top seven showing absence of restrictions on foreign investment, over the decade.[30]

Here is the performance of Rwanda on the Global Peace Index (GPI):

- In the 2010 GPI, Rwanda ranked 75th out of 149 countries – scoring 2.012;
- In the 2011 GPI, Rwanda ranked 99th out of 153 countries – scoring 2.185;
- In the 2012 GPI, Rwanda ranked 119th out of 159 countries – scoring 2.250;
- In the 2013 GPI, Rwanda ranked 135th out of 162 countries – scoring 2.444;
- In the 2014 GPI, Rwanda ranked 137th out of 162 countries – scoring 2.494;
- In the 2015 GPI, Rwanda ranked 139th out of 162 countries – scoring 2.420;[31]
- In the 2016 GPI, Rwanda ranked 128th out of 163 countries – scoring 2.323;[32]
- In the 2017 GPI, Rwanda ranked 113th out of 163 countries – scoring 2.227.[33] The country was noted as having well-entrenched democratic institutions that have influenced sustained economic growth;[34]
- In the related Positive Peace Index (PPI) of 2017, Rwanda ranked 89th among 163 independent states and territories, with a score of 3.27,[35] and was captured among the countries that experienced the largest improvements in PPI between 2005 and 2016.[36] In Rwanda, 'significant investment was placed on education and health following the civil war which ended in 1994.';[37]

- In the 2018 GPI, Rwanda improved further and ranked 103rd out of 163 independent states and territories globally, scoring 2.14, and also became 22nd among the 44 Sub-Saharan countries featured in the index.[38]

Rwanda's performance on the UNDP's Human Development Index (HDI) has been as follows:

- In the 2010 HDI, it ranked 152nd out of 169 countries in the 2010 HDR;
- In the 2011 HDI, it ranked 166th out of 187 countries in the 2011 HDR;
- In the 2012 HDI, it ranked 166th out of 187 countries in the 2011 HDR;
- In the 2013 HDI, it ranked 167th out of 187 countries in the 2013 HDR;
- In the 2014 HDI, it ranked 151st out of 187 countries in the 2014 HDR;
- In the 2015 HDI, it ranked 163rd out of 188 countries in the 2015 HDR;[39]
- In the 2016 HDI, it ranked 159th out of 188 countries in the 2016 HDR;[40]
- In the 2018 Human Development Indices and Indicators (HDII) Statistical Update, it ranked 158th out of 189 countries.[41]

Below, we find Rwanda's rankings on the Corruption Perceptions Index (CPI):

- In 2010, it ranked 55th out of 178 positions, scoring 4.0;
- In 2011, it ranked 49th out of 182 countries, scoring 5.0;
- In 2012, it ranked 50th out of 174 positions, scoring 53;
- In 2013, it ranked 49th out of 174 positions, scoring 53 (with Costa Rica and Latvia);
- In 2014, it ranked 55th out of 174 positions, scoring 49 (with Bahrain, Jordan, Lesotho, Namibia and Saudi Arabia);
- In 2015, Rwanda ranked 44th out of 167 country positions, scoring 54;[42]

- In 2016, Rwanda ranked 50th out of 176 countries and territories, scoring 54 (with Mauritius).[43]
- In 2017, Rwanda ranked 48th out of 180 countries and territories globally, scoring 55 (with Cape Verde and St Lucia),[44] and 4th (with Cape Verde) among 49 Sub-Saharan African countries featured in the index.[45]

Security Challenges

The billion-dollar question is whether the Kagame project will arrive at its goal, when all Rwandans would perceive each other as simply Rwandans and not Hutu or Tutsi, a situation whereby the political and ethnic units are coterminus or congruent, in other words, when the potential for a Hutu–Tutsi rivalry leading to hostilities would be ultimately diminished. Within Rwanda itself, the economic climate seems progressive and congenial enough to assist ethnic homogeneity or coherence over the long term, or at least avoid endemic heterogeneity. But it cannot be said that there was absolutely no potential for internal problems to disrupt the Kagame project.

However, external factors such as Rwandan interference in neighbouring DRC and Burundi pose potential problems, especially as the Kagame establishment (together with the Museveni establishment) have gained the reputation of mischief-causing regimes, having fingers in almost every pie of conflict in the African Great Lakes sub-region. Judging from the over 200,000 displaced persons in the eastern DRC,[46] who are mostly Hutu and Tutsi refugees, the number of Rwandans just outside of Rwanda's borders and who wish to return to Rwandan soil is substantial, and their influx into Rwanda could upset the Kagame project. Also, judging from the recent Rwandan interference in the Burundian political crisis, plus other proven or unproven Rwandan involvement in the sub-region, strategic retaliations against the Kagame regime could come from any neighbouring direction, for a vast number of reasons.

It must be stated that internal Rwanda under the watchful eye of the no-nonsense Kagame is not a place for terrorism to thrive. If anything, the country is becoming safer from terrorism. In the 2015 Global Terrorism Index (GTI), which lists rankings in reverse order, in contrast to other performance indexes, so that the worst-performing (in this case, Iraq) is at the top, Rwanda ranked 56th among 162 countries on the index, with a score of 3.334.[47] In the 2016 GTI, Rwanda ranked 65th among 163 countries, with a score of 2.589.[48] In the 2017 GTI, Rwanda ranked 81st among 163 countries, with a score of 7.256,[49] and was 21st among the sub-Saharan African countries featured on the index.[50]

On 4 July 2016, the Rwandan leadership participated in the special summit between Israel and the EAC countries, at which sub-regional security concerns and new security challenges, particularly in agriculture, were top of the agenda, as part of Israeli prime minister Benjamin Netanyahu's foreign policy trip to the EAC bloc at a time when Israel was launching a £13-million aid package with Africa.[51] Obviously, Rwanda sought to gain from the package, as well as the developing security architecture that was on the table, judging that Rwanda's participation in this special summit came just a couple of days ahead of Netanyahu's visit to Rwanda on 6 July. Whatever the developing security architecture was, Netanyahu's visit to Rwanda could be considered to be the most interesting among the four countries (Uganda, Kenya, Ethiopia and Rwanda), as Rwanda seems to be the most 'security-sensitive' of all the countries in the sub-region, and especially as Rwanda was not facing the same security pressures as the other three, in terms of fighting Al-Shabaab or Islamist forces. Given that about 25 per cent of Israeli arms exports go to African countries, and furthermore, that Israel is probably the largest diamond refinery in the world,[52] against the backdrop that large quantities of Congolese diamonds make their way abroad through Rwanda, this China-styled Israeli Government trip to Africa, with as many as 80 businessmen who were predominantly arms dealers and magnates with interests in minerals from central Africa, raised very curious eyebrows.

Rwanda remains a kind of a police state, and people generally have to watch what they say, especially about President Kagame, who has eyes and ears everywhere. Several personalities who cared to opine on President Kagame's alleged involvement in the demise of former president Juvenal Yabyarimana live in forced exile, fearing for their lives. For example, Fustan Kayomba Yamwasa, the former Rwandan general who alleged that Kagame was involved in the assassination of the former president, fled to South Africa in 2010. The assassination of Yabyarimana triggered the ethnic tensions that led to the 1994 genocide and its aftermath. Meanwhile a French inquiry into the events that sparked the 1994 genocide continued as the judges sought to interview Yamwasa.[53]

Rwanda also opened a formal probe into 20 French officials suspected of playing a role in the 1994 genocide, and expects Paris to cooperate ahead of the potential charges. The re-igniting of tensions between Rwanda and France over what caused the downing of Habyarimana's plane and the subsequent slaughter of some 800,000 ethnic Tutsis by Hutus is not a surprise. As an ally of the previous Hutu government, France stood accused of ignoring the warning signs of the violence to come, of training the militia that participated in the slaughter and of failing to intervene fast enough once the killings were underway. However, Paris maintained that it eventually managed to deploy troops who saved thousands of lives, hence the guilt for failing to prevent the genocide should be shared by the entire international community.[54] Further French complicity was alleged by three Rwandan NGOs (Sherpa, Ibuka France and the Collective of Civil Parties for Rwanda – CPCR) who accused the French bank BNP Paribas of transferring $1.3 million from the Rwandan central bank to an arms dealer's Swiss account during the Rwandan genocide of 1994.[55]

On 12 October 2018, Rwandan foreign minister Louise Mush-ikiwabo was elected as Secretary-General of the Francophonie at the 17th summit held in Yerevan, Armenia. French prosecutors handling the probe into the downing of Juvénal Habyarimana's plane also said that the charges against the former RPF members should be dropped. Critics of Kagame opined that dropping the charges coincided with the Rwandan foreign minister's appointment to head the Francophonie, against the background that Kigali had always pointed the finger at Paris for supporting the Hutu perpetrators of the Rwandan genocide. That said, Kagame and his foreign minister have earned the positive reputation of strong leaders who championed the cause of reshaping the African Union (AU) into efficiency from 2016 to 2019, the period which saw to the successful 'Retreat on Financing of the Union' at the 27th AU Summit held in Kigali in July 2016, followed by Kagame taking forward this reform and financing agenda to finance the AU which had introduced a 0.2 per cent levy on eligible non-African imports for all AU member states, followed by Kagame becoming the AU Chair from January 2018 to January 2019.

CHAPTER 9

SOUTH SUDAN

The nationalism particular to South Sudan is one surrounding the personality of Salva Kiir Mayardit, who has led the Sudanese People's Liberation Movement/Army (SPLM/A) from the demise of its first leader John Garang de Mabior in 2005, through to the successful UN-sponsored secession that led to South Sudan's independence in July 2011, and to date. There is an overriding aim of building a Black African Sudanese nation separated from Arabic (North) Sudan, undermined by an undercurrent of ethnic divisions in the form of Dinka versus Nuer, or President Kiir versus vice president Riek Machar respectively, which further degenerated into Nuer rebel formations and a civil war. For the background on South Sudan prior to the secession and independence on 9 July 2011, see the discussion of Sudan in my previous book.[1]

The Intergovernmental Authority on Development (IGAD) and the New Pan-Africanism

The IGAD Monitoring and Verification Mechanism (MVM) for South Sudan was 'set up shortly after the signing of the Cessation of Hostilities Agreement (COHA) between the Government of the Republic of South Sudan (GRSS) and the SPLM/A-In Opposition (SPLM/A–IO) on 23 January 2014'.[2] It was a tactical mistake (or handicap) for the MVM not to have been firmly in place and in action before the first signing of a peace agreement on 23 January 2014, in that the signed agreement could not hold or be adhered to. With nothing on the ground to prevent or

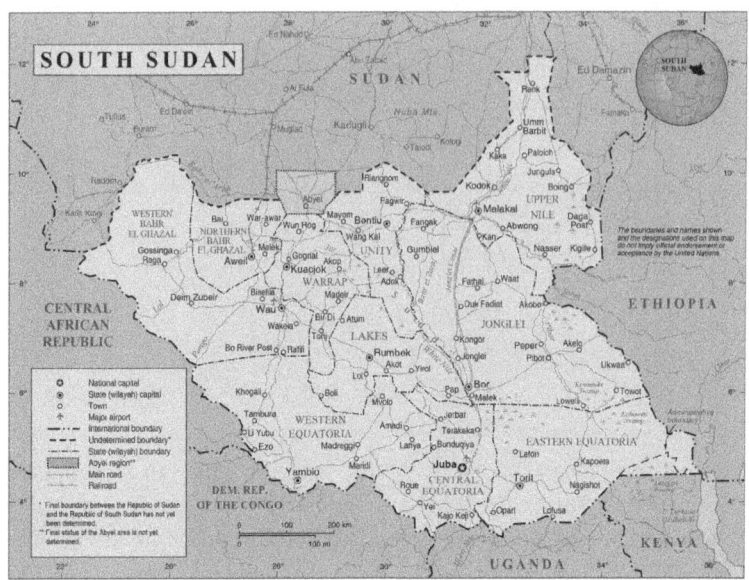

Map 9   Map of South Sudan.

monitor subsequent activity or incursions from either side, the ceasefire could not be guaranteed, as one could see from the desperate skirmishes on each side to amass as much territorial and strategic advantage as possible before the imminent signing date, particularly in the period from December 2013 to the signing in January 2014. The signing event was just paperwork; in reality, there was no ceasefire. Hostilities continued as if that were the norm, hence it became necessary to hold a second ceasefire signing event on 9 May 2014, and even at this time the MVM – officially set up in February 2014 – was not that visible or potent.

One has to wonder just when, 'shortly after' the first signing on 23 January 2014, the MVM actually materialized. The earliest official date offered so far is 2 February 2014, according to the timeline of events published by IGAD.[3] Even so, that was too little, too late. Moreover, it was quite obvious, even on the face of the signed document, that the MVM was not in place; paragraph 5.1 of the COHA that was signed on 23 January 2014 between the GRSS and the SPLM/A-IO stated that 'The Parties shall commit to the immediate formation of a Monitoring and Verification Mechanism under the leadership of IGAD.'[4]

Judging from the aftermath (of the first signing of the COHA) it was also quite obvious that the composition of the MVM did not really take place, because the yet-to-materialize Joint Technical Committee (JTC) had to form before they could fulfil their responsibility of 'setting up a Monitoring and Verification Team (MVT) and drawing up the modalities for the implementation mechanism', as stated in paragraph 5.2 of the COHA document. Hence the MVM merely existed on paper for a long time until perhaps the fourth or fifth signing of the COHA. The absence of the MVM before the first signing, and the absence of a potent MVM even afterwards, both contributed to undermining the history and efficacy of the ceasefire arrangements, a situation which benefited both sides, especially the rebel side that did not really wish to cease fire.

It is ridiculous that paragraph 8.1 of the first signed COHA stated that 'The Parties shall declare the positions of their forces to the JTC and commit to remain at the declared positions at the signing of this agreement which shall be certified by the MVT'[5] when indeed the JTC and MVT did not exist. The next paragraph (8.2), which states that 'The declared positions of the forces of the Parties shall be monitored by the MVT,'[6] is ridiculous in equal measure. The MVM was never in place. Furthermore, 'a COHA Implementation Workshop was held with Parties in November 2014 in Addis Ababa,'[7] which just goes to show the MVM's continual lack of potency on the ground even up until November 2014, although they kept negotiating and facilitating further ceasefire agreements (the one on 2 February 2015 was the fourth).

As already mentioned, the warring rebels benefited from the lack of monitoring and the practical failures of the ceasefire agreements, and revelled in making sporadic hostile advances,[8] especially in Jonglei, Unity and Upper Nile states, which had seen most of the fighting, hence the COHA Implementation Workshop in November 2014.[9] On the face of it, the MVM for the successful implementation of the COHA was also to be supported by local communities, and to monitor compliance and evaluate progress over the following broad commitments under the leadership of IGAD:

- cessation of hostilities;
- cessation of hostile propaganda;

- protection of civilians;
- humanitarian access (including the movement of MVM observers).[10]

However, each side kept violating the very Status of Mission Agreement (SOMA) that was already in place, having been signed as far back as 8 August 2011, as the UN Mission in South Sudan (UNMISS) complained.[11] At best, the most realistic monitoring mechanism – a Joint Monitoring and Evaluation Commission (JMEC) – emerged with the Proposed Compromise (Ceasefire) Agreement on the Resolution of the Conflict in the Republic of South Sudan (ARCSS). Nevertheless, this JMEC was to be initiated by the IGAD-led Mediation within 15 days of the signing of the ARCSS, as stated in Chapter VII of the ARCSS; needless to reiterate the point that the JMEC was not in place before the ARCSS. The ARCSS, which was also to establish the Transitional Government of National Unity (TGONU), was first drafted in 2015, signed by Riek Machar on 17 August 2015 and later by Salva Kiir on 26 August 2015, to take effect at midnight 30 August 2015.

The ARCSS allowed for a transitional government over a 30-month period preceded by a 90-day pre-transition period. The ARCSS was to deliver an agenda of comprehensive reform to reconfigure the political space and, among other things, amend the existing constitution to make it agreeable to all parties, and have it ready for the next elections. Even though the incumbent President Salva Kiir Mayardit would remain on paper as the top man, Article 6.3.1 of the ARCSS stated that the first vice president should, among other things, 'Coordinate the implementation of this Agreement and initiate institutional reforms as prescribed in this Agreement.'[12] This position was for Riek Machar, leader of the SPLM/A-IO. In other words, Riek Machar could run the show right under the nose of Salva Kiir who could possibly become a lame duck because the president would have to seek the consent of the first vice president before raising any suggestions or objections, if he did not appreciate whatever might be going on. The ARCSS gave Riek Machar a free hand to transform the political space to his advantage before the next election, in which he would be duty bound to stand as a candidate. Salva Kiir obviously did not like the taste of this arrangement, but kept his counsel to himself at this stage.

Entrusting the roles depicted in the ARCSS to any first vice president is the norm in situations where the candidates (for president and vice president) run for office on the same party ticket, and where the vice president effectively works for the president. That was not the case in this scenario, where Kiir and Machar belonged to two bitterly opposed and irreconcilable sides. Machar was certain not to operate in the interest of Kiir or the ruling GRSS. At best, you would have Machar trying to implement the reform agenda, and Kiir doing everything within his power to undermine that effort. No doubt the citizens would be the losers, and it is obvious right from the start that this ARCSS had been cooked up to appease personalities, rather than work towards national development. This was often the case when a mediating body (in this case IGAD) had to factor in the wishes and interests of opposing and entrenched parties, without which the parties would not even dialogue to agree a draft document for negotiation. It should be noted, however, that this broad principle featured at every stage of the mediation process.

Salva Kiir was not the only one with concerns. On the opposite side, some of Riek Machar's own generals in charge of rebel factions were fundamentally in disagreement with any form of a unity government; they wanted governance over South Sudan for themselves and nothing less, to the extent that on 11 August 2015 two of Machar's commanders, Gathoth Gatkuoth and Peter Gadget Dak, split from Machar's SPLM/A-IO and made it public that whatever Machar signed did not represent the full SPLM/A-IO.[13] This goes to show that the rebels did not want to cease fire, had no appetite for the peace recipe on the table that was being brokered by IGAD (with input from various interest groups among the international community) and were prepared to undermine the whole peace process, hence their regular provocations and military incursions that were starkly contrary to a ceasefire.

The question that loomed in the background was whether Machar's signature would be legitimate at all. The SPLM/A-IO official spokesperson Peter Gadget Dak made it clear on 14 August 2015 that Machar's signature would mean nothing to the rebel movement. Nevertheless, Machar signed on 17 August 2015, whereas Kiir announced on 18 August that he needed at least two more weeks to consider the document before signing, which prompted the US to issue threats of UN sanctions against the GRSS if Kiir did not sign. While the foot-dragging and threats of sanctions went on, two aid workers with Médecins Sans Frontières (MSF) were killed in Unity State.

On 26 August 2015, Kiir finally signed the ARCSS, to take effect at midnight on 30 August 2015, but with an appendix listing his concerns, chief of which was the demilitarization of Juba. It should be noted that military support from Juba's allies, such as the Ugandan People's Defence Forces (UPDF) stationed in Juba, had literally prevented Juba from being overrun by the rebels during the conflict, hence the UPDF's departure within the duration of the ARCSS worried Kiir. The comprehensive ARCSS included plans for newly composed forces to replace Kiir's defences when Juba became designated as a Special Arrangement Area (SAA). Yet at this stage, having Machar as part of that architecture of replacement raised both concern and suspicion for both Kiir and IGAD monitors, especially when Machar's own commanders were in open rebellion against the ARCSS itself, its implementation and the TGONU. The concerns and suspicions that arose included:

- if the rebels should attack Juba in the early part of the transition prior to Juba successfully assuming SAA status, how would Machar respond or deal with that situation, as the rebels would be his own rebels?
  - ✔ would Machar defend Juba?
  - ✔ if so, how exactly?;
- whether the last-minute rebel split and withdrawal from the ARCSS was a tactical ploy for Machar to resume hostilities from within the TGONU should he encounter future problems:
  - ✔ was this a backroom deal or fail-safe strategy?

In retrospect, the above two hypothetical scenarios did indeed soon surface, a few days prior to the weekend of 9 July 2016, to interrupt the fifth independence anniversary.

The ace card that Salva Kiir had kept close to his chest, to neutralize the powers of the first vice president, reared its ugly head soon after the ARCSS was signed into effect, in the form of the presidential decree issued by Kiir for the creation of 28 states across South Sudan, instead of the existing ten states. This plan was an open secret, yet it was proposed by Kiir at a strategic stage well before the end of the IGAD process for signing the ARCSS, and late enough for it not to feature in the ARCSS, although both IGAD and Machar had identified the proposition as a significant challenge for the future. Kiir used his executive powers as the sitting president or incumbent to establish this executive order, so as to neutralize or dismount the overall power base of the SPLM/A-IO and effectively undermine First Vice President Riek Machar even before he took office.

As the drama unfolded, Kiir's spokesperson and government spin doctor, Ateny Wek Ateny, preached devolution, and explained that the aim of the establishment order was to take services and government close to the people so as to reduce congestion in the urban centres. Members of the SPLM-IO were not convinced, and began converging in their Pagak headquarters from 16 January 2016, prior to holding two days of formal consultative deliberations over the issue of the 28 states, on 21–22 January 2016. The SPLM-IO resolved to stick to the ten existing states as a matter of policy for the colossal effort of amendments towards the new constitution, which was required for the formation of the TGONU.[14] This divisive issue caused the 22 January 2016 deadline for the formation of the TGONU to slip, not least because Machar's SPLM-IO said they would not recognize the new states.[15] The Jieng (Dinka) Council of Elders (in support of Kiir) also held an emergency meeting on 23 January 2016, and resolved to issue a warning that reversing or attempting to reverse the 28 states order could instigate a new war.[16]

Seeing red, Machar travelled to Uganda on 24 January 2016 to solicit the help of President Museveni to resolve the issue, only for Museveni to turn his back on him quite despicably. This was Machar's first trip to Uganda since the conflict began in mid-December 2013, and it appeared that he had miscalculated the consternation of Salva Kiir's friends. But besides the SPLM/A-IO, Machar had the backing of a section of the international community, in particular the Troika (US, UK and Norway) who had issued press statements.[17]

Alongside this development came a seemingly innocuous statement from the Sudanese news agency on 27 January 2016 that President Omar al-Bashir of Sudan had ordered Sudan's land border with South Sudan to be opened, and that the Sudanese authorities had been ordered to undertake all measures required to implement this decision. This would be the first time that the land border had been opened since the secession of 2011 that led to the independence of South Sudan.[18] Judging that

Sudan had in the past been accused of supporting Machar's rebellion against the GRSS, this announcement could easily be misconstrued (or could be read) as opening the gates for Sudanese support for another potential Riek Machar rebellion at the failure of South Sudan to form the TGONU, especially as Machar left South Sudan (from the rejection by Museveni) with no return date and his whereabouts on the planet were not clear. It should be noted that the disputes over the border between the two countries remain unresolved, not least because of the Heglig oilfield that straddles the border.[19]

Ironically, soon after Machar's departure for Uganda, Kiir appointed him *in absentia* as first vice president of South Sudan, in accordance with the ARCSS and the road map to forming the TGONU. Machar informed the UN that he would only return to Juba in March 2016, soon after his 1,370 soldiers were airlifted to Juba.[20] It was impossible what role existed for these Machar forces to play within the ARCSS whereby special demilitarization arrangements would designate Juba with SAA status. On the face of the signed ARCSS, Machar was at the very least required to have his own bodyguard unit 'consisting of three platoons of 65 soldiers each.'[21] On 26 March 2016, there were intelligence reports of forces loyal to Machar advancing on government bases uninvited.[22] On 28 March, an advance party of 39 rebels representing Machar officially arrived in Juba as part of a process that prepared the ground for Machar's return in April to participate in the TGONU.[23]

On 25 February 2016, UN Secretary-General Ban Ki-moon paid an official visit to South Sudan as part of an African tour.[24] Ban held a closed-door meeting with Salva Kiir, and discussed issues including the practicalities of forming the TGONU with or without the creation of 28 states, the fate of Riek Machar going forward, and the regular breaching of UN premises in the country, in particular the 18 February 2016 breach of the UNMISS Protection of Civilians (POC) site in Malakal that hosted some 48,000 civilians from three different ethnic groups.[25] This was not the first time that a UNMISS base or safe haven had been breached in the course of the conflict in South Sudan; on 18 April 2014, at least 20 people were killed and 70 others injured when gunmen posing as protesters stormed a UNMISS base;[26] and on 17 March 2015, SPLA soldiers carried out a breach in the vicinity of the UNMISS compound in Bentiu, Unity State, where some 53,000 civilians were being protected.[27] One has to wonder whether the impunity to breach was because UNMISS peacekeepers were limited by their remit to protect civilians and not to wage war against aggressors. The summary of Ban Ki-moon's message during his February 2016 visit was that South Sudan should place peace above politics, form the TGONU and carry on to implement the signed ARCSS.

Subsequently, the UN commissioned an independent high-level Board of Inquiry to conduct a special in-depth investigation into the deadly violence at the Malakal POC site on 17–18 February 2016, and to examine the external factors that led to the incident. A report completed on 21 June 2016 cited the external factors as deep-rooted historical land disputes, the '28 States Order' and the Eastern Nile Administrative Order of 1 February 2016 which dismissed all Shilluk and Nuer civil servants. The immediate trigger point was an attempt by two SPLA soldiers to smuggle ammunition into the site on 16 February 2016, followed by more armed elements in SPLA uniforms who entered the POC site and carried out the violence and destruction.[28] It appeared that the armed elements in SPLA uniforms took part in the destruction of Shilluk and Nuer accommodations on the POC site, and that the fight pitted Shilluk and Nuer against Dinka and Darfuri people.[29] The UN investigation team requested the TGONU to hold accountable the armed elements and all individuals responsible for the violence. The report noted that there was confusion with respect to command and control and rules of engagement, and a lack of coordination among civilian and uniformed peacekeepers.[30]

The UN peacekeeping chief, Herve Ladsous, made clear at a press conference the following day that action would be taken against some peacekeeping units and individuals who would be repatriated from the UN force; word had already leaked that those affected were troops from India, Ethiopa and Rwanda.[31] As at 20 June 2016, the UNMISS estimate of civilians seeking protection at POC sites across South Sudan amounted to 158,727, of whom 95,126 were at the Bentiu site, 32,719 in Malakal, 27,959 in Juba, 2,004 in Bor, 700 in Melut and 219 in Wau.[32]

Furthermore, MSF had made public that these IDPs were too frightened to go home or return to their original locations regardless of the ARCSS and the TGONU. Some were traumatized as a result of being attacked even at the POC sites of refuge, particularly Malakal. Others needed reorientation, having been at the sites for a considerable length of time, and were unsure of or unready for the political situation despite official assurances. Their scepticism was well founded because sporadic outbreaks of fighting continued to occur between armed groups allied to the TGONU and rebel groups, as well as between the rebel groups themselves. Hence the lack of security, which generated their displacement in the first place, continued to be an unresolved issue, and it appeared that IDP and POC camps had almost assumed permanent form on the South Sudanese landscape.[33]

International Political Economy

Underdevelopment is a key characteristic of the new state of South Sudan, and the country is further handicapped by being landlocked, and depends on the existing export/import infrastructure of other developing countries. Being a war-torn nation over decades, it had developed much less infrastructure of its own. Although the country has enviable natural resources such as crude oil, gold, diamonds, copper and timber, it would take sustainable peace and systematic good governance over a long period to derive significant economic development. Adherence to the signed ARCSS and progressing with the TGONU would be a good starting point.

South Sudan has 3.5 billion barrels of oil and 3 trillion cubic feet of natural gas in proven reserves.[34] Oil accounts for 98 per cent of the country's budget, but production plummeted during the civil war from the pre-war levels of 450,000 bpd to as low as 130,000 bpd in October 2017. With the fall in global oil prices during the decade, oil revenues reduced drastically, but South Sudan was making a net loss from oil production because of transit fees payable to Sudan for channelling their oil exports. At independence, South Sudan inherited the majority of the oilfields in its territory. However, a Transitional Financial Agreement signed between South Sudan and Sudan as part of the move towards independence stipulated that South Sudan pay $3 million to Sudan over a three-and-a-half-year period, composed of about $10 for transporting every barrel of oil through Sudan's pipelines, plus a $15 transaction fee for each barrel of oil transported. The *Financial Times* reported in December 2014 that South Sudan was receiving 'the lowest oil price in the world, $20-$25 a barrell, because of falling prices and unfavourable pipeline contracts';[35] the overall loss-making was clear. An attempt had been made by South Sudan to renegotiate, and began with a threat to shut down production altogether.[36] Stephen Dieu Dau, the minister for petroleum and mining, indicated that Sudan had shown willingness to review the contract.[37]

Meanwhile, the cost of living and of basic commodities such as sugar and water reportedly tripled in January 2016,[38] skyrocketing to astronomical proportions. The National Bureau of Statistics had to face the Trading Economics chart where the inflation rate had surged to 661.3 per cent in July 2016 and further to 729.7 per cent in August 2016.[39] No doubt the resurgence of fighting at the beginning of July, prior to the fifth anniversary of independence and its aftermath, had taken a severe toll. House prices had also shot up owing to the displacement of some two million people by the civil war, even though the clashes diminished in August. Data limitations have prevented the forecasting of GDP components.[40] The economic cost of violence in 2016 alone, which amounted to $11,605,000,000 in purchase power parity (PPP) terms,[41] reduced only slightly to $11,255,200,000 in 2017,[42] hence South Sudan placed itself as fifth among the ten most affected countries in the world with respect to the economic costs of violence.[43] The country has to rely on commodities imported from neigbouring countries, and the only way out of food shortage is to develop its own agriculture. On 20 February 2017, the UN declared famine in South Sudan, with an estimated 5.5 million people at risk, citing under-performance from mortality and malnutrition data indicators, with Unity Province featuring among the most affected areas. The UN resolved to publish on 21 February 2017 an urgent funding appeal for $1.6 billion (a 25-per cent increase on 2016) in further aid,[44] and another appeal for $3.2 billion a year later in 2018, of which $1.5 billion would be towards refugees fleeing the country and $1.7 billion would be towards IDPs and others in need within the country.[45]

Efforts to diversify the mineral resource base of the economy have involved both the formal and informal sectors, corporate and otherwise, especially in gold mining. Artisanal gold panners could make about $2 for every speck of gold, or $20 for a full day's digging and panning. It was estimated that some $20 million of gold left the country each year, some illegally.[46] Government regulation and licensing could bring order to the mining industry, and increase productivity, despite the widespread internal displacement of persons, and the absence of a geological database.

On 11 October 2017, South Sudan hosted its first international oil conference to revive the oil industry. Representatives from over 100 energy companies were in attendance and the country was keen to attract new investors; however, only the smaller oil companies showed serious interest. Exxon Mobil ditched exploration plans. Its closest rival, Total, placed its plans on hold and did not send a representative to the conference despite showing previous interest in two of the biggest oil blocks. Tullow Oil expressed interest in a lesser-known untapped block. The petroleum minister Ezekiel Lol Gatkuoth made a blanket announcement that the state-owned Nilepet would have a greater stake in all partnerships. A key issue was the lack of security which had dissuaded the larger firms, even if that also posed a lucrative opportunity for private security firms to which government was willing to allow operating rights.[47]

South Sudan relies on the big oil companies to provide the necessary infrastructure, in exchange for part of total oil output. Regardless of the level of production (circa 130,000 bpd in 2017), 40 per cent of output went to the large oil companies; 20 per cent to oil company shareholders; 28,000 bpd to Sudan in honour of an existing deal; and South Sudan is left with just 34,000 bpd. Investors deemed the production levels too low an incentive for the security risks involved. Furthermore, the low production had caused inflation of petrol prices, and several oil workers were not being paid as government struggled to meet its own budget; those being paid complained the salary was too low. Overall dividends to the Exchequer were insufficient to fund public services. Only 500 km of roads were paved, schools lacked basic amenities and hospitals tended to run out of medicines.[48]

In the Ibrahim Index on African Governance (IIAG) 2011 (containing data for the 2000–10 period),[49] Sudan was ranked 48th, with a score of 33 per cent. Sudan split into Sudan and South Sudan in 2011; however, neither country was included in the IIAG assessments for the 2012, 2013 and 2014 indexes due to insufficient data.

- In the 2015 index, South Sudan was 53rd out of 54 countries,[50] with a score of just 19.9 per cent;[51]
- In the 2016 index, South Sudan ranked 53rd overall, with a score of 18.6 per cent;

- ✔ 53rd in Safety and Rule of Law with a score of 11.5 per cent; 53rd in the personal safety sub-category; 53rd in the national security sub-category; 52nd in the accountability sub-category; and 50th in the rule of law sub-category;
- ✔ 49th in Participation and Human Rights with a score of 24.4 per cent; 48th in the participation sub-category; 50th in the rights sub-category; and 47th in the gender sub-category;
- ✔ 53rd in Sustainable Economic Opportunity with a score of 14.1 per cent; 52nd in the infrastructure sub-category; 52nd in the public management sub-category; 51st in the business environment sub-category; and 52nd in the rural sector sub-category;
- ✔ 53rd in Human Development with a score of 24.4 per cent; 53rd in the education sub-category; 52nd in the health sub-category; and 53rd in the welfare sub-category;[52]
- In the 2017 index,[53] South Sudan maintained position at 53rd overall, yet with an improved score of 20.2 per cent, which signified a −8.5-per cent comparative deterioration over the last five-year period (2012−16) of the 2007−16 decade of comparison;[54] maintained position at 53rd in Safety and Rule of Law; deteriorated from 49th to 52nd in Participation and Human Rights; maintained position at 53rd in Sustainable Economic Opportunity; and also in Human Development;[55]
- In the 2018 index, South Sudan maintained rank at 53rd overall with a score of 19.3 per cent; maintained position at 53rd in Safety and Rule of Law; maintained position at 52nd in participation and Human Rights; maintained position at 53rd in Sustainable Economic Opportunity; and moved up slightly from 53rd to 52nd in Human Development. The index identified South Sudan as among previous bad apples showing improvement in transparency and accountability over the past five years.[56]

The Global Peace Index (GPI) itemized the performance of Sudan and South Sudan as follows:

- In the 2010 GPI, Sudan ranked 146th out of 149 countries − scoring 3.125;

- In the 2011 GPI, Sudan ranked 151st out of 153 countries – scoring 3.223;
- In the 2012 GPI, Sudan ranked 156th out of 159 countries – scoring 3.193;
- In the 2013 GPI, South Sudan ranked 143rd out of 162 countries – scoring 2.576;
- In the 2014 GPI, South Sudan ranked 160th out of 162 countries – scoring 3.397;
- In the 2015 GPI, South Sudan ranked 159th out of 162 countries – scoring 3.383;[57]
- In the 2016 GPI, South Sudan ranked 162nd out of 163 countries – scoring 3.593.[58] Furthermore, South Sudan was recorded as having more than 20 per cent of its population displaced in some form, and suffering from an ongoing conflict;[59]
- In the 2017 GPI, South Sudan ranked 160th out of 163 independent states and territories – scoring 3.524,[60] which also translated in regional terms to the bottom on the list of 44 sub-Saharan African countries featured in the index,[61] as well as registering the worst scores across a wide range of indicators in the 2017 GPI report;
- In the related Positive Peace Index of 2017, South Sudan ranked 156th among 163 independent states and territories, with a score of 4.2;[62]
- In the 2018 GPI, South Sudan had deteriorated and ranked 161st out of 163 independent states and territories globally – scoring 3.508, and also ranked last among the 44 Sub-Saharan African countries featured in the index.[63] It had also ranked third among the five least-peaceful countries in the domains of ongoing conflict, safety and security.[64]

The UNDP's Human Development Index (HDI) did not assess South Sudan until 2015, and the assessments of Sudan prior to the independence of South Sudan from Sudan were 'often based on information collected from the northern part of the country only'.[65]

- In the 2015 HDI, South Sudan ranked 169th out of 188 countries in the 2015 Human Development Report (HDR);[66]
- In the 2016 HDI, it ranked 181st out of 188 countries in the 2016 HDR;[67]

- In the 2018 Human Development Indices and Indicators (HDII) Statistical Update, it ranked 187th out of 189 countries.[68]

The Corruption Perceptions Index (CPI) itemized South Sudan's performance from 2013, when the country first featured in the index, as follows:

- In 2013, it ranked 173rd out of 175 country positions, scoring just 14;
- In 2014, it ranked 171st out of 174 country positions, scoring just 15;
- In 2015, it ranked 163rd out of 167 country positions, scoring just 15 (with Angola);[69]
- In 2016, it ranked 175th out of 176 countries and territories, scoring 11.[70]
- In 2016, it ranked 179th out of 180 countries and territories globally, scoring 12,[71] and 48th among 49 Sub-Saharan African countries featured in the index.[72]

Security Challenges

Although South Sudan gained independence in July 2011, it soon appeared in the 2011 Maplecroft Terrorism Risk Index (for the 2010 period) even though it had not made it to the other more mundane indexes such as the Global Peace Index until 2013, the Corruption Perceptions Index until 2013, or even the Human Development Index until 2015.

- In the 2011 Terrorism Index (for the 2010 period), South Sudan ranked 5th among the top ten countries on the index and rated in the 'extreme' category;
  - ✔ In the 2012 terrorism index (for the 2011 period) Sudan (not South Sudan) was 10th, with an 'extreme' rating;
- In the 2012 Global Risks Index (for the 2012 period), South Sudan ranked 3rd and was rated 'extreme';
  - ✔ In the 2014 index (for the 2013 period) Sudan (not South Sudan) was 3rd with an 'extreme' rating;

- In the 2015 Political Violence Index (for 2014) Sudan (not South Sudan) ranked 8th among the top ten countries rated 'extreme';
- In the 2016 Political Risk Index, South Sudan was placed in the 'extreme' risk category;[73]
- In the 2015 Global Terrorism Index (GTI), which lists rankings in reverse order, in contrast to other performance indexes, so that the worst-performing (in this case, Iraq) is at the top, South Sudan ranked 15th among 162 countries that featured on the index, with a score of 6.712[74] and had already been captured among the new or emerging countries with over 500 deaths within the index;[75]
- In the 2016 GTI, South Sudan ranked 21st among 163 countries that featured on the index, with a score of 6.497;[76]
- In the 2017 GTI, South Sudan ranked 14th among 163 countries that featured on the index, with a score of 6.821,[77] and was 4th among the sub-Saharan African countries listed within the index.[78] It was also tenth globally among countries with the highest number of deaths from terrorism.[79]

The OHCHR's assessment of the situation since the civil war began lists horrendous human rights violations, war crimes and crimes against humanity, including homes and humans being burned alive.[80] The US and Russia disagreed on an arms embargo against South Sudan being part of the UNSC list of sanctions.[81]

As has been discussed at length in this book, it is obvious that the situation will remain insecure until the TGONU (with or without Riek Machar) was firmly in place and the transitional arrangements were being followed, in particular the security of Juba before and after SAA status. From the IIAG record, governance in the Sudan had never been great, and it was asking a lot to expect the TGONU to work. The territory had always been one of the very bottom countries on the peace index, and had not known peace since Darfur, plus the subsequent crises that led to the secession. In the recent civil war in South Sudan alone, 'tens of thousands have been killed, and over two million South Sudanese have been displaced from their homes, more than 1.5 million of them within the country',[82] with direct impact on human development, as reflected in South Sudan's ranking on the 2015 HDI.

Furthermore, perceptions of corruption deriving from the Sudanese leadership of Omar al-Bashir have continued to rub off on the new country of South Sudan, as it has found itself among the bottom five countries in the Corruption Perceptions Index since its first appearance in it in 2013; this is one more reason why the TGONU must be made to work, if the international image of the new country is to improve.

HIV is now on the rise in South Sudan[83] even though it was once regarded as a forbidden disease in Sudan. The latest development is a far cry from the previous situation, as Sudan (before the secession of South Sudan) required an HIV status declaration for entry or stay, and foreign residents faced deportation once HIV status was discovered.[84] This is perhaps a result of assessments and data collection by agencies having historically been more efficient or concentrated in the north (currently Sudan), where the Khartoum government had proper control and also held a stronger influence on culture, social attitudes and politics. The UN High Commissioner for Human Rights' report on the situation in South Sudan since the civil war began found over 50 reported cases of rape in September to October 2015 in southern and central Unity State alone, and over 1,300 reported cases from April 2015 and September 2015,[85] and furthermore that government forces were being allowed to rape women as a type of payment.[86]

In the long term, the establishment of a lasting peace on the landscape of South Sudan remains a key challenge despite the signed ARCSS and the progress of the TGONU. Sporadic outbreaks of fighting continued to occur between armed groups allied to the TGONU and rebel groups and between rebel groups. Furthermore, the reluctance of IDPs to return to their original locations also has implications for the future, in terms of the 'peacetime' continuation of the POC sites vis-à-vis the UN's own position set out by the UN Peacekeeping Chief that the refugees could not be forced to leave the IDP/POC camps.

The South Sudan leadership participated in the 4 July 2016 special summit between Israel and the EAC countries, at which sub-regional security concerns and new security challenges particularly in agriculture were top of the agenda, as part of Israeli prime minister Benjamin Netanyahu's foreign policy trip to the EAC bloc at a time when Israel was launching a £13-million aid package with Africa.[87] Surely South Sudan sought to gain from the package, as well as the developing security architecture that was on the table, bearing in mind the strategic role that summit host Yoweri Museveni played in resolving the South Sudan conflict, the implications of the conflict on the EAC as a whole, the fact that about 25 per cent of Israeli arms exports go to African countries, and most notably Israel's alleged involvement in the South Sudan civil war. Netanyahu's entourage consisted of some 80 businessmen, mostly arms dealers and magnates with interests in minerals from central Africa.[88]

Broadly, the lack of security, which in many ways generated the internal displacement of persons, continued to be an unresolved issue, and justified the continual presence of IDPs and POC sites that had now almost assumed permanent form on the South Sudanese landscape.[89] On 6 July 2016, MSF doctors estimated that up to 150,000 people had either escaped or been displaced and were hiding in the bush, fearing more attacks after the outbreak of renewed fighting from the end of June 2016 between forces loyal to the peace deal and rebel soldiers claiming to be loyal to Riek Machar but who had been disenfranchised from the peace deal that had been negotiated. Government soldiers reported that at least 40 people were killed when the armed rebel groups fired on civilians in Wau which already hosted a POC camp under UN protection. Some displaced persons that had taken to the bush were now averse to remaining there, and risked attempting to return to their homes.[90]

The government spokesperson Lieutenant General Babriel Jok Riak announced that protecting civilians and repelling armed groups at the same time was a challenge; however, they were doing their part as government soldiers in support of the existing peace deal to quell hostilities, and therefore appealed to the international community to talk to the rebel soldiers loyal to Riek Machar to persuade them to also do their part. It appeared that the armed rebel groups wanted to set up bases in the Wau area, hence the renewed conflict. There seemed to be a fundamental point of disagreement about the disenfranchisement of these particular armed rebels in the post-independence disposition of armed forces, as the rebels claimed that they fought together for South Sudan's independence. This rather far-fetched disagreement (at this stage long after the signed peace deal) is what generated the controversy as to which military factions had official rights to operate in the Wau area.[91] It will be recalled that on 11 August 2015, two of Machar's commanders, Gathoth Gatkuoth and Peter Gadget Dak, split from Machar's SPLM/A-IO and made it public that whatever Machar signed did not represent the full SPLM/A-IO.[92] Major General Ashhab Fahal Ukanda who spoke for the so-called Riek Machar loyalists complained that they also had territorial military rights in Wau. The IDPs created by the renewed fighting sought refuge in the Wau POC site, churches, schools or in the bush.[93]

The SPLM/A-IO made some glaring tactical errors, thereby displaying an absolute lack of commitment to, and in fact a deliberate effort to undermine, the process of executing the ARCSS. For example, Peter Gadget Dak, one of Machar's main commanders, who alongside another commander, Gathoth Gatkuoth, openly rebelled against the ARCSS and split from the SPLM/A-IO on 11 August 2015, became the official spokesperson and chief press contact for the SPLM/A-IO, and was spinning and spewing off statements and policy positions quite antithetical to the progress of the ARCSS. Judging that Peter Gadget had announced on 14 August 2015 that the ARCSS which Machar signed up to did not represent the full SPLM/A-IO,[94] it was unthinkable for him to resume such a central role for Machar or the SPLM/A-IO in Juba at any point afterwards.

It became obvious that the SPLM/A-IO was conducting business to derail the ARCSS, and this became even more obvious with SPLM/A-IO activity against security procedures set in place to protect Salva Kir and Riek Machar himself. As both the president and first vice president were now working very closely at the presidential palace complex to get on with the TGONU and the ARCSS, it appeared that the SPLM/A-IO were using Riek Machar as bait to invade the confines of Salva Kiir and assassinate the president in the process. While Machar pretended not to be in control of whoever directed the mischief from his camp, it also appeared that Kiir was not in control of his army chief of staff, Paul Malong Awan, who was bent on facing off with Peter Gadget Dak and his mischievous others. The tit for tat carried on. General Malong was later sacked by a routine presidential decree announced on 9 May 2017 for conducting an ethnic war against non-Dinkas and allegedly ruling with an unqualified clique of friends.[95] Malong was replaced by General James Ajongo Mawut, the former deputy chief of general staff for administration and finance, who then became the new head of the armed forces.

The renewed fighting that began at the end of June was a campaign that built up strategically towards the fifth independence anniversary on 9 July 2016. On the night of 7 July 2016, five government soldiers were killed when forces loyal to the SPLM/A-IO and to Riek Machar opened fire at a checkpoint inside Juba that was manned by troops loyal to the peace deal and to Salva Kiir.[96] Related daylight skirmishes on 8 July 2016 involved heavy mortar, tank and machine gun fire in parts of Juba. The resident Director of UNESCO was injured and a US embassy convoy was also hit. As to the heavy battle that erupted at the presidential palace complex where both President Salva Kiir and First Vice President Riek Machar were to attend a press conference with journalists waiting inside the state house building, it appears that this was brought under control.[97] However, congestion at the Juba hospital morgue, which became full to capacity, confirmed the circulated reports that at least 150 soldiers had died in the heavy fighting on 8 July, in what appeared to be an attempted coup by SPLM/A-IO forces or troops loyal to Machar, who was all the time seen to be 'performing' his official duties in the presence of Kiir, so that he was absolved of suspicion that he ordered the attack. The president literally ordered his personal bodyguards to escort Machar to his quarters on the night of 8 July 2016.[98]

Nevertheless, the independence anniversary on Saturday 9 July was overshadowed by the hostilities leading up to it, and what followed, because by the next day a total of 272 people were reportedly killed by the close of that weekend alone,[99] and this is just the reported figure. Some of the skirmishes in the lead-up to this independence anniversary had affected UN refugee facilities, particularly in Wau and Juba.

What remains poignant is that the signed ARCSS as it stood did not make room, or had no built-in mechanism or caveat, for a third party to intervene if there was a hiccup; the two principal signatories to the ARCSS (the SPLM/A and the SPLM/A-IO) were the main parties tasked with ensuring its implementation, and forming the TGONU. When the UNSC held an emergency closed-door meeting on 10 July, it therefore became problematic to follow any particular procedure to resolve the situation, other than demand a de-escalation of hostilities from both sides, and explore ways of making it easy for peacekeeping operations to continue, while looking at ways of limiting the future arms capability of the warring factions; hence the issue of an arms embargo, which was previously vetoed by the US, reappeared on the table.

The officially worded positions set out by Ban Ki-moon were 'to impose an immediate arms embargo, enact additional targeted sanctions on leaders and commanders blocking implementation of the peace deal, and to fortify the UN mission in the country'.[100] Quite frankly, an arms embargo might not bite, and the hot air of sanctions against force commanders carrying out the escalating orders (with or without directions from Salva Kiir or Riek Machar) meant nothing unless, for example, arrest warrants were issued by the ICC to show potency, as in the instances that led to the prosecution of similar war criminals such as Jean-Pierre Bemba Gombo, Germain Katanga and Bosco Ntaganda in relation to the DRC.

As to addressing the renewed fighting directly, the UNSC appealed further to neighbouring countries to contribute or compose a neutral force to step into the situation until the two principal opposing sides de-escalated fighting and returned to civil ways. By implication, this appeal was directed in practical terms at IGAD and the AU's Peace and Security Council (AU-PSC), to oversee the formation of this intervention brigade, as even the regional bodies did not have the exclusive mandate to offer direct assistance, even if they wished to or could. Furthermore, the precise role of this intervention brigade vis-à-vis all the warring factions (including government forces, opposition forces and renegade rebels, as well as UNMISS), plus the direct lines of control over its purse-strings and capability, needed to be firmly established by IGAD and the AU-PSC prior to its formation and deployment.

This therefore dominated the agenda at the 27th AU Summit which commenced in Kigali, Rwanda, on 16 July 2016, during which African leaders agreed to a rapid intervention brigade, to stop any further resurgence of violence after the latest resurgence that occurred around the fifth independence anniversary, of which at least 300 people had been killed. How rapidly this intervention force was to materialize was another matter, as the proposal was to be ratified by the AU-PSC and then escalated to the UNSC that would finance it. However, Salva Kiir's government (or the TGONU) had made clear in advance its disapproval of this intervention force, or any more foreign/regional troops for that matter.

The 2015 ARCSS for the formation of the TGONU and other political milestones going forward stipulated a presence of SPLM/A and SPLM/A-IO forces and police to operate a stalemate to facilitate a neutral political space so that the processes set out in the ARCSS could evolve; however, with the renewed disappearance (or disaffection) of Riek Machar from the TGONU and of course the SPLM/A-IO forces away from Juba, Salva Kiir's government deemed it to their strategic advantage that the SPLM/A forces had 'consolidated' control of Juba, hence the logical government opposition to the proposed intervention force. On 20 July 2016, there were government-sponsored demonstrations, with protesters sending their petition to the UN and the IGAD authorities in Juba, to express their avowed disapproval of the proposed intervention force.

Meanwhile UNMISS investigated allegations of potential war crimes of sexual violence, rape as a weapon of war, and rape by uniformed soldiers against a number of civilians around the UNMISS camp for the displaced based in Juba, as well as concerns about harassment of UNMISS personnel, and increased levels of obstruction of UNMISS operations, such as denial of flight clearances and restrictions on UNMISS patrols outside of Bor town and market. UNMISS further reported that more than 5,000 people had fled to Uganda since the latest insurgences around the fifth independence anniversary period alone.[101] UNMISS had documented some 120 cases of rape and sexual violence in Juba since the latest fighting began around the period of the fifth independence anniversary, and it appeared that UNMISS staff failed to render assistance to civilians in distress, and just looked on.[102]

On a more sensitive and embarrassing note, the content of a leaked internal UN headquarters memo revealed that Germany, Sweden and the United Kingdom unilaterally pulled out their 12 police forces from South Sudan without prior consultation with UNMISS amid the deteriorating security situation that arose with the resurgence of clashes between SPLM/A and SPLM/A-IO forces in the days leading up to the fifth independence anniversary, thereby undermining the operational capacity of UNMISS and further deflating the morale of other UNMISS staff and troops, particularly from non-P5 countries without permanent seats or veto powers on the UNSC. The memo stressed that Germany, Sweden and the UK would not be invited to rejoin UNMISS when the situation improved in South Sudan, especially as their forces abandoned their posts in the challenging situation.[103]

On 22 July 2016, President Salva Kiir issued an ultimatum to the absconded Riek Machar to return to duties within 48 hours or face the consequences. On expiry of the ultimatum and Machar not showing up, the SPLM/A-IO appointed the TGONU's minister of mining, General Taban Deng Gai, to act for them temporarily as first vice president of South Sudan in the absence of Riek Machar. Taban Deng Gai was the SPLM/A-IO's chief negotiator during the peace talks that led to the signed ARCSS. This appointment by the SPLM/A-IO was very revealing, in that it brought out the issue of Machar's loss of broad support among the SPLM/A-IO, perhaps because he had undermined his own authority by, among other things, harbouring the likes of Peter Gadget Dak to discredit the SPLM/A-IO and undermine the transitional process with continual mischief. For example, the Northern Bahr el Ghazal SPLM/A-IO forces defected to the government side during the insurgency and fighting of July 2016.

On 27 July 2016, Machar granted an interview to Al Jazeera, in which he claimed that General Deng Gai's installation was illegal, and called for the international community to intervene. Machar said he was waiting for the regional (AU/IGAD) body to deploy the intervention brigade so that he could return to Juba to take his position as first vice president. He claimed he was around Juba, but could not discharge his duties because he was sacked by the president.[104] On 2 August, Lam Makol, the TGONU agriculture and food security minister (from the SPLM/A-IO), resigned, saying that the ARCSS was dead and that there was no free political space in South Sudan. He claimed that the ARCSS could not be implemented while Salva Kiir remained in Juba, hence the SPLM/A-IO had no option but to organize outside Juba.[105] All SPLM/A-IO absences or resignations on the TGONU were replaced officially by the SPLM/A-IO.

On 29 July 2016, East African chiefs of defence staff met and agreed a Rapid Protection Force as the basis for subsequent UNSC discussion on authorizing its formation under an UNMISS command. This was reaffirmed by the IGAD-PLUS Extra-Ordinary Summit convened on 5 August 2016, at which meeting the TGONU agreed in principle, in paragraph 13 of the summit's communiqué, to allow in the Rapid Protection Force if its mandate was principally to protect IDPs, humanitarian agencies and the JMEC, and so long as its composition, mandate, armament, deployment, timing and funding should be agreed by the TGONU and the Troop Contributing Countries (TCCs).[106] The South Sudanese Government became jittery about the proposed Rapid Protection Force, not least because it was to: control Juba airport and the overall security entry and exit from Juba; disarm all forces (including government forces) who became a threat to civilians, protected persons and UN sites; and assume military control of Juba in case of an emergency. Riek Machar was to rejoin the peace process, but whether prior to deployment of the Rapid Protection Force or afterwards was open to question. It looked like the Troika and their allies within the UN were pushing buttons behind the scenes to bring Machar back into the fray from his self-imposed exile and disenfranchisement from the ARCSS and TGONU process. No wonder Juba had become jittery about the Rapid Protection Force, despite the legitimate concerns already outlined.

On 11 August 2016, the UNSC deliberated on the IGAD Plus recommendations for setting up the Rapid Protection Force, and on 12 August adopted Resolution 2304 (2016) to extend until 15 December 2016 the UNMISS mandate that had been rolled over until 12 August 2016 through UNSC Resolution 2302 of 29 July 2016, as well as authorize the formation of a Rapid Protection Force to consist of 4,000 troops, to augment the the 12,000-strong UNMISS force. Annex 1 of Resolution 2304 (2016) carried a UN Charter Chapter VII arms embargo against all principal operators (the SPLM/A and SPLM/A-IO minus UNMISS) if the situation continued to pose a threat to peace and security in the region.[107]

It is an open secret that the intense rivalry and competition among key international partners, including the P5 or veto-holding members of the UNSC, as well as sub-regional African power brokers, had contributed to the political debacle, as they each have their fingers in the South Sudan pie. This translated itself into the membership of IGAD-PLUS that is supposed to assist the peace process (AU, UN, China, US, UK, EU, Norway and the IGAD Partners Forum – an interesting concoction of (un)diplomatic partnerships). Despite the Rapid Protection Force's authorization tag from the UNSC, it was a non-starter from the minute Uganda announced its decision to be a non-TCC hours before the 12 August 2016 adoption of UNSC Resolution 2304. Furthermore, Uganda's position highlighted the futility or fragility of any IGAD-PLUS proposals going forward. It appeared that the US and its allies wanted a group of neighbouring African countries to form a Rapid Protection Force to destabilize South Sudan or oust Salva Kiir, and were prepared to throw money at it – as the case would soon reveal.

Meanwhile, the South Sudanese Government disputed claims in the UNHCR report that government soldiers had committed acts of rape and other human rights violations in Juba during the July 2016 fighting, and announced a probe of its own. While that ensued, the government executed by firing squad Sergeant-Major Atian Deng and Lance Corporal Matem Ariic Mayom who were convicted by a military court of murdering a couple in a residential area in Wau earlier in 2016. This was the first instance of capital punishment since the new country seceded from Sudan on 9 July 2011. Some 19 others were arrested in Juba and detained on assorted charges including murder, random shooting and looting.[108] UNICEF also reported on 19 August 2016 that up to 16,000 children had been recruited by armed groups and forces since the civil war began in December 2013; UNICEF had overseen the release of 1,775 former child soldiers in 2015.[109]

On 18 August 2016, UN spokesperson Farhan Haq announced at a press conference that Riek Machar had escaped to the DRC, where MONUSCO had taken responsibility for escorting him to the DRC authorities, although the latter publicly denied this, whether to avoid any overtures from South Sudan and interested third parties, or for Machar's own safety, as would later be discovered. The overall picture was beginning to look awkward and unhelpful for the UN as they appeared to be on the side of Machar. It will be recalled that Kiir had complained all along (in the period between December 2013 and the signing of the ARCSS in 2015) that the US and UN were supporting Machar against him, especially as Machar was originally dismissed from the government because of insurrection, and it appeared therefore that the US and UN were favouring Machar's cause against the democratic incumbent, Kiir, by coercing the latter to sit and deliberate or negotiate with someone who was more or less a coup plotter.[110]

The potential formation and deployment of the Rapid Protection Force to South Sudan remained a thorny issue, and had to feature on the agenda when US Secretary of State John Kerry visited Kenya on 22 August 2016 to discuss regional security with President Uhuru Kenyatta and some foreign ministers from the EAC sub-region. At this meeting Kerry announced $138 million of direct funding towards the deployment of the Rapid Protection Force and the provision of basic needs. His position that the Rapid Protection Force was not an intervention force but a protection force to 'protect access and the freedom of movement to and from Juba, and the ability of recognized forces and personnel to remain free from attack and ambush'[111] was not convincing, and came across as an insult to the intelligence of his African counterparts.

The audit trail for the Rapid Protection Force showed the exact opposite of Kerry's position. The genesis of the Rapid Protection Force consisted of: (a) the rhetoric of Ban Ki-moon asking for an intervention brigade to be constituted from among neighbouring countries to respond to the post-ARCSS stalemate generated between SPLM/A and SPLM/A-IO forces as a result of the July 2016 resurgence of violence prior to the 2016 independence day celebrations, followed by: (b) the recommendation by AU leaders on 19 July 2016 at the AU summit in Kigali that this intervention brigade be constituted from Ethiopia, Kenya, Rwanda, Sudan and Uganda,[112] which was (c) affirmed at the IGAD-PLUS Extra-Ordinary Summit on 5 August 2016,[113] which then (d) formed the basis for the subsequent process at the UNSC to authorize the Rapid Protection Force by UNSC Resolution 2304 (2016) that was adopted on 12 August 2016. Therefore, in a press conference on 22 August 2016, the acting first vice president of the TGONU, General Taban Deng Gai, reiterated South Sudan's strong reservations against the proposed mandate of the Rapid Protection Force, especially the management and control of Juba airport, saying that it would usurp the sovereignty of South Sudan.

While Ban Ki-moon appointed Major General (retired) Patrick Cammaert of the Netherlands on 23 August 2016 to lead an independent special investigation into the July 2016 violence in Juba and the UNMISS response,[114] it was also reported that Riek Machar had escaped the DRC to Sudan where he was reportedly receiving medical treatment. Just why this so-called urgent medical treatment could not take place in the DRC, where MONUSCO had ferried him to safety (even if his presence in the DRC was denied by the DRC Government), but should rather be taken care of in Sudan, is not difficult to surmise. Machar has a long history of obtaining the SPLM/A-IO's military support from Khartoum. Hence the acting first vice president of the TGONU, General Taban Deng Gai, visited Khartoum during the week to seek assurances that Sudan was not siding with Machar.[115]

From 2 to 5 September 2016, a UNSC delegation visited South Sudan to urge the protection of civilians by a Rapid Protection Force, armed with deadly force, and to try to persuade government leaders in South Sudan to accept UNSC Resolution 2304 (2016) for the Rapid

Protection Force, amidst a political context of Juba accusing the world body (UN) of neo-colonialism, and, more pertinently, the reasons for the Rapid Protection Force no longer existing, to wit, Riek Machar was no longer a factor in South Sudanese politics and the country was no longer at war. Humanitarian and civil society organizations made observations that although UNMISS peacekeepers already had a Chapter VII mandate to use deadly force to protect civilians and POC sites, they hardly exercised this mandate, and were generally not minded to risk their lives in the use of deadly force for any country deemed as not their own, but preferred to return safely to their origins, having earned their wages wearing the blue helmet. Although the government of South Sudan agreed with the UNSC delegation to accept extra troops, they were adamant that the size, make-up, armaments, mandate, command and control of the Rapid Protection Force should be agreed first with the TGONU, before any foreign troops would be allowed in, which was the exact government position prior to the three-day visit of the UNSC delegation. The South Sudanese authorities were anxious (and rightly so) about the potential for elite foreign troops operating under UN cover to topple the government, as happened in Libya with Gaddafi, and wanted to prevent that at all costs.

Hot on the heels of the UNSC delegation to Juba, the UK hosted the annual UN Peacekeeping Defence Ministerial in London on 8 September 2016, at which sexual abuse allegations against UN troops were top of the agenda. The British defence secretary Michael Fallon used the opportunity to announce that the UK was expanding its total contribution to the UN effort in South Sudan, by raising its next planned contribution from 300 to 400 peacekeeping troops, of which the additional 100 were to build a hospital unit to assist with future peacekeeping operations. The London event was attended by defence ministers from some 80 countries; the discussions brought out a concern that the UN was too stretched to manage the scale of conflict across the globe, and alongside the trend that most boots on the ground came from the South (8,000 from Ethiopia, 7,000 each from India and Pakistan etc.) whereas the North funded the wages of blue helmets. Hence it was not clear if peacekeepers on the ground were that committed to their jobs in countries irrelevant to their background, or if it took too long to muster troops even where TCCs could relate to the cause, as in the case of the Rapid Protection Force for South Sudan that was voted for by UNSC Resolution 2304 on 12 August 2016.

Following his arrival in Sudan from the DRC (with the help of MONUSCO), Machar (who had voluntarily absconded from the ARCSS/TGONU) declared war from Khartoum by announcing the ridiculous, that the South Sudan peace deal he signed with Salva Kiir was dead. There had since been sporadic clashes as Machar's forces continued to fight in Eastern Nile State which borders Sudan and South Sudan, and in former Greater Equatoria which borders the DRC, Uganda, Kenya and South Sudan. SLPM/A spokesman Lul Ruai stated that, in former Greater Equatoria, Machar's rebel forces ambushed a number of commercial vehicles transporting civilians and intensified operations against government positions.[116]

Meanwhile, the report of the UN-commissioned investigation into the July 2016 clashes between the SPLM/A and SPLM/A-IO, made damning indictments of UNMISS, particularly that UNMISS troops refused to respond to an attack on a Juba hotel or when SPLM/A forces invaded the international aid compound in Juba, and furthermore that the clashes allegedly derailed the smooth progress of the TGONU to end the civil war. As a result, the UN Secretary-General sacked Lieutenant General Johnson Ondieku, the Kenyan UNMISS commander, on 31 October 2016. In response, Kenya announced an immediate pull-out of its 1,000-troop contribution to UNMISS, commencing with a first batch of at least 100 soldiers on 9 November 2016.[117] After this, it was difficult to see what inducement could be given to the Kenyan troops to continue with UNMISS, seeing that their commander had been sacked.

On 18 November 2016, the US circulated a draft resolution to the UNSC to impose the much-touted arms embargo on South Sudan, plus targeted sanctions against some individual personalities including rebel leader Riek Machar, army chief Paul Malong and information minister Michael Makuei. However, China and Russia were opposed to this draft, with China staking the claim that an arms embargo would make no difference as it could not be robustly enforced, and Russia jibing that 'introducing targeted sanctions against South Sudanese leaders woud be the height of irresponsibility now.'[118]

On 21 November 2016, a contingent of 350 Japanese Self Defence Forces licensed for combat arrived in Juba to replace a previous contingent that joined UNMISS without a combat mandate because of pacifism enshrined in the Japanese military. It was just as well that the replacement contingent was licensed for battle, because in all practicality they were assigned to respond to urgent calls for help from UN staff and aid workers at or near UN bases that had previously been attacked with reference to the fiasco that saw the exit of the Kenyan troops, even if this new Japanese contingent was officially responsible for engineering and construction work in Juba.[119]

Following Machar's exit from the scene, and the lack of consensus at the UNSC to make the case for sending in the proposed extra 4,000 members of the Rapid Protection Force, the whole idea had now assumed a semblance of propaganda, and did not seem to gather strength going forward. A view also arose regarding alleged ethnic cleansing and genocide, which had no empirical basis. Certainly the situation in the country was far from peaceful, but genocide was a rather far-fetched allegation or propaganda claim for the UN and Western allies to pursue. At an emergency session of the UN Human Rights Council in Geneva on 14 December 2016, Yasmin Sooka (chair of the UN Commission on Human Rights in South Sudan) attempted to amplify the propaganda by suggesting that the 4,000 Rapid Protection Force reinforcement was the only means to rescue South Sudan from the brink of catastrophe due to a reportedly unprecedented level of violence, ethnic tension, sexual slavery and sexual assault on women and children, with complicity from both government and opposition.[120] However, all this was nothing new, and certainly did not amount to genocide. Clearly, either Sooka was naïve about the politics of the Rapid Protection Force up to that point, or was spinning very wildly.

The propaganda war against the state (or TGONU) instigated an address to parliament and the nation from President Salva Kiir, in which he said:

> we are grateful for the continued humanitarian support to our request for the resumption of development assistance. I likewise urge the international community, in the spirit of national dialogue, to also cease any negative propaganda against the people and the government of the Republic of South Sudan.[121]

Furthermore, the propaganda war may have led to the crackdown on journalists, activists and humanitarian workers. It was reported on

7 December 2016 that Justin Lynch, an American freelance journalist, was deported without explanation,[122] followed by two senior employees of the Norwegian Refugee Council (NRC).[123] The UNSC's lack of consensus raged on, as they could not even reach the nine votes needed for a resolution on the arms embargo, sanctions and/or the Rapid Protection Force.[124] On 23 December 2016, the UNSC formally rejected a US resolution for a one-year weapons sales embargo on South Sudan and targeted sanctions of an asset freeze and global travel ban against identified individuals, including Riek Machar. Only seven members voted in favour, five including the African members of the UNSC (Angola, Egypt and Senegal) voted against,[125] while China, Russia and Japan abstained.[126]

The existing fundamental challenges to state capability to protect or secure citizens were compounded by the 2017 famine which generated further security challenges, in that the state could not guarantee the safe passage of aid deliveries and the security of aid workers. On 13 March 2017, rebel militias kidnapped in Mayendit village eight locals working for Samaritan's Purse, a US charity, and demanded aid deliveries as ransom.[127]

President Kiir used his 14 December 2016 speech to the Transitional National Legislative Assembly to launch a national dialogue and a call for national unity, which Riek Machar, who was exiled in neighbouring Sudan, and whose rebels continued to pose a threat, rejected and dismissed. Kiir's call for national reconciliation generated a variety of interesting responses, including a coalition of organizations known as The Voluntary Civil Society Taskforce on Implementation of the Peace Agreement. The Organization for Nonviolence and Development (ONAD), which trades as the South Sudan branch of the International Fellowship for Reconciliation (IFOR), also joined the coalition of organizations which held three consultative meetings in Juba on 15, 22 and 24 February 2017.[128] A notable olive branch following President Kiir's national unity charm offensive was the sacking of the notorious army chief of staff General Paul Malong on 9 May 2017. However, skirmishes by rebel factions continued, and the potential for new rebel factions to spring up remained undiminished. In February 2017, several high-ranking officers resigned from the army in frustration at Malong's power tactic. Lieutenant-General Thomas Cirillo who was one of the quitters has since announced plans to launch his own rebellion.[129]

In the course of events, the JMEC, which failed to form in time (within 15 days of the signing of the ARCSS), and for which reason the key players and signatories to ARCSS could not be effectively monitored for violations and subsequent spiralling incursions, managed to publish a report in September 2017 saying that the parties to the conflict had failed to implement substantive elements of the ARCSS. The JMEC failure to form in time is no surprise at all, as this was typical of IGAD structures, especially the JMEC's predecessors such as the MVM, JTC and MVT, which were not in place after the signing of the COHA, allowing for the continuation of hostilities. Quite plainly, there had been no effective monitoring capability on the ground to stop hostilities, and it is ridiculous for the JMEC (or IGAD for that matter) to point fingers at the parties to the conflict. One wonders whether the UNSC took this context into account when it took note of the JMEC's September 2017 report on the situation. Perhaps the JMEC also needed sufficient protection to do its work, which at one point was to come from the Rapid Protection Force mooted in 2016, but which did not materialize.

On 1 November 2017, Kiir paid a two-day visit to President al-Bashir of Sudan to discuss oil pipeline fees, border disputes and other security issues, including signing an agreement to avoid hosting each other's rebels, and approaching consensus on the 60 per cent of undemarcated border between Sudan and South Sudan. Fresh talks or a High-Level Revitalization Forum for all key players of the South Sudan peace process were to follow on 15–17 December 2017 in Addis Ababa under the auspices of the very IGAD that failed to form the JMEC. By now, a lot of water had passed under the bridge, leading to the disappearace of Riek Machar from South Sudan, and signalling the strategic weakening of the SPLM/A-IO in the long game of chess.

However, in the geopolitique that was to emerge, two factions pitched against each other at the revitalization talks: Salva Kiir was backed by Uganda and Egypt whereas the SPLM/A-IO were backed by Sudan, Ethiopia and the Troika. The overall threat against Salva Kiir amounted to the imposition of an external solution (regime change) and an arms embargo if he did not play ball in reopening the already signed ARCSS of 2015 and returning South Sudan to the original ten states instead of the 32 newly created by Kiir to assuage ethnic divisions. It appeared that Egypt was siding with South Sudan against the Ethiopian River Nile Project, while Uganda remained the unabashed supporter of President Kiir in all matters. The TGONU made clear it was unwilling to go back to the ARCSS drawing board in detail, and had long accused the US, as one of the Troika, of a regime-change agenda, and the IGAD chair from Ethiopia of sidelining Juba at the 28 November 2017 Council of Ministers meeting held in Abidjan.

A series of events in 2018 reshuffled the future path. Perhaps fearful of, or intimdated by, the sound of war drums and external intervention beating from international quarters, together with the imminent threat of arms embargo and further sanctons from the UNSC, plus an ultimatum from IGAD, Salva Kiir cooperated positively with a series of events towards resolving the conflict, commencing with: (a) a permanent ceasefire agreement signed on 28 June 2018 to allow for a 'new' TGONU to run the country for three years; (b) a power-sharing proposal brokered in Entebbe by Presidents Museveni and Omar al-Bashir on 7 July 2018 for the TGONU; (c) a vote in South Sudan's parliament on 12 July 2018 to extend Salva Kiir's mandate for three years to cover the period of the TGONU; and (d) a gentlemen's handshake on 25 July 2018 between Salva Kiir and Riek Machar to complete drafting the power-sharing agreement within a month, and commence in earnest the TGONU within three months.[130] Riek Machar was to be one of four vice presidents in the power share over a South Sudanese political landscape significantly revised from when he was the sole vice president in 2005, 2011 or 2016. Under the terms of the 'new' transitional power share, Machar would be free to form his own political party, as the SPLM-IO was now in dissolution, and present himself as a presidential candidate in multiparty elections to occur at the end of the transition.

It is important to note that the principal players on the South Sudanese political landscape, whether from the GRSS side or the SPLM-IO side, had begun demonstrating signs of conflict fatigue, wanted to implement the ARCSS/TGONU, and had therefore become tired of Riek Machar's periodic absconding from the political scene, and by implication Machar's support from neighbouring Sudan which at this point also had its own geopolitical needs to be met in relation to oil dealings with South Sudan and Nile water issues with neighbours. Hence that all-important power sharing proposal was brokered in Entebbe by Presidents Museveni and Omar al-Bashir - the two heavyweights behind Kiir and Machar respectively, at which meeting al-Bashir would have been told categorically to cease all support for Machar if he knew what was good for him. Subsequently, on 5 August 2018, the warring sides signed a preliminary power-sharing deal in Khartoum that saw Machar installed as first vice president among other vice presidents representing the other political groups on the landscape. There were to be 35 ministers in the TGONU, 20 for Kiir, 9 for Machar and six for the other groups. The parliament would also consist of 550 legislators, 332 for Kiir, 128 for Machar, and the remainder for the other groups. An independent commission was to be formed to work out the number and demarcation of provinces in the country. A final deal that was to be signed should hope to steer the warring factions on a path towards an uninterrupted three-year TGONU period, which would hopefully evolve into multiparty democracy and peaceful elections for the future.

CHAPTER 10

CONCLUSIONS

The sheer number, breadth and intensity of conflicts in Africa make the African Union (AU) almost synonymous with conflicts. The original African Peace and Security Architecture (APSA) was conceived at the birth of the AU in 2001. Subsequent APSA documents have always been underpinned by two fundamental AU documents: the 2000 Constitutive Act and the 2002 Protocol Relating to the Establishment of the Peace and Security Council. Judging from the increasing conflicts on the continent, the Panel of the Wise to adjudicate and execute peace and security, the Continental Early Warning System (CEWS), the Peace Fund and the African Standby Force became obvious by-products or pillars of the APSA. Hence the 2011–13 APSA had almost all of its constituent parts operational, even if not to full capacity. As a result, the AU developed confidence in touting the deployment of troops in crisis situations, as happened for Mali in 2012, the CAR in 2013, the DRC in 2013 and Burkina Faso and Burundi in 2015, despite the fact that in all of these cases, APSA could not achieve concrete military goals on the ground. ECOWAS demonstrated some ability to resolve a sub-regional conflict by putting military pressure on former president Jammeh to leave Banjul in January 2017, even if that action also usurped Jammeh's constitutional rights to challenge the spurious election results announced, regardless of him being an unpopular head of state.

The operational capacity of the African Standby Force (ASF) was always going to be subject to funding, as well as the political will and capability of member states to contribute towards its Rapid Deployment Capability (RDC). Progress on ASF action plans had included policy coordination and training, development of the ASF's Civilian and Police Components, harmonizing ASF with the African Capacity for Immediate Response to Crises (ACIRC) and incorporating ACIRC into the Amani Africa II Field Training Exercise that should validate the ASF's operational readiness.

As astute as the APSA's CEWS might be, it is a lofty aspiration only, because the very nature and culture of African politics constitutes the stumbling block to the aims of the CEWS. As discussed in Chapter 1, the chief cause of conflict in Africa has been, and continues to be, extensions to presidential term limits and the concomitant electoral and ethnic conflicts. What could cause these conflicts to cease on the continent would be a stark troubleshooting agenda for the CEWS, at continental and sub-regional levels, that would address the ticking time bombs and require those heads of state who exceed or plan to exceed their maximum term limits to either leave office or be suspended from the AU. The fundamental standpoint from which the EWS could operate was the very thing which the African heads of state did not want to provide, in that, it would be impossible for conflicts to cease in Africa if extensions to presidential term limits continued.

Out of the 19 country cases listed in Chapter 1 regarding the removal or extension of limits to presidential terms, at least 12 had produced heads of state that once chaired the AU or its OAU, and therefore could not be relied upon to take decisions to undermine extended presidential rule. A practical example of how this political deficit at the presidential level undermined the CEWS occurred at the January 2016 AU Summit, where heads of state voted on the draft proposal to send AU peacekeepers to Burundi to handle the political crises arsing from Nkurunziza's third presidential term. This vote required at least a two-thirds majority from heads of state to pass, but this was not attained, not because of absenteeism, but rather because the voters were themselves long-term presidents. At the summit were at least 20 countries' leaders who had exceeded their terms of office or had abolished constitutional limits to presidential terms in their respective countries. Even the AU chair at the time of the summit, Idriss Deby, abolished presidential limits in 2005 and had already been in power for 26 consecutive years in Chad; his predecessor as AU chair, Robert Mugabe, had then been in power for 29 years in Zimbabwe; and among Mugabe's predecessor AU chairs was

Teodoro Obiang, who had then been in power for 37 years in Equatorial Guinea, and so on.

The political will does not exist to tackle the fundamental causes of conflict, and even if this bridge were crossed, the capability of the ASF to respond to so many large-scale conflicts on a single continent would be very stretched, which is why the continent should cut down on conflicts or the potential for conflict. The solution lies with the heads of government. It was therefore useful to see a revised 2016–2020 APSA Roadmap which has the following five Strategic Priorities (embedded with detailed performance indicators):

- Conflict Prevention;
- Crisis/Conflict Management;
- Post-conflict Reconstruction and Peacebuilding;
- Strategic Security Issues;
- Coordination and Partnerships.

However, measures to troubleshoot the ticking time bombs must be potent. The indicators set out in Priority 1 on conflict prevention are relevant, but without stringent measures in place to practically prevent politics from abusing governance, everything else within the APSA will remain a joke.

As it stands, the AU-PSC, which manages the APSA, reports to the heads of government, most of whom by their actions do not want to prevent conflict, but are actively contributing to it. As suggested in the conclusion to Chapter 1 of this book, the AU would need to restructure itself and erect a superstructure body over and above the heads of government, with mandatory powers to address the CEWS and deal with presidential terms of office, simply because presidential peers would not referee, repudiate or sanction one another, even from the position of the AU chair, as the case has proved to be. The AU chain of command needs to be revised to have a technocratic body to which heads of government must answer for their actions related to the CEWS, so that, in practical terms, the October 2015 referendum that paved the way for Nguesso of Congo-Brazzaville to remain as president should not have been allowed; Teodoro Obiang of Equatorial Guinea who had already been in power for 39 years should not have been allowed to remain beyond 2018 when his newly introduced first term expired; Yoweri Museveni of Uganda who was 74 years old in 2018 should not have been allowed in December 2017 to repeal the presidential age limit of 75 and pave way for him to run in the 2021 elections; Paul Biya of Cameroon should not have been allowed to stand as president in the 2018 elections; Faurre Gnassingbe of Togo should step down immediately; and so forth.

An opportunity presented itself in July 2016, when Paul Kagame was assigned to oversee a review of the AU and propose institutional reforms. The January 2017 Kagame Report suggested a fundamental restructuring of the AU's institutions. Unfortunately, paragraph 17 of the report placed the responsibility for delivering the much-needed restructuring back in the court of the very heads of state who do not want the right change to occur. As already argued, unless the heads of state consent to a technocratic superstructure to manage their politics and sanction them in response to the CEWS, the AU will be wasting its time, simply because the presidents will not sanction themselves.

The sub-regional equivalents of rapid deployment so far have lacked teeth, whether it be the North African Regional Capacity, the Southern African Development Community (SADC) Standby Brigade, the Eastern Africa Standby Force, the Economic Community of Central African States (ECCAS) Standby Force or the Economic Community of West African States (ECOWAS) Standby Force. In the ECOWAS sub-region, for example, there have been too many cases of threats to send troops to deal with insurrections against democratic norms, all of which amounted to nothing, the most recent examples being Mali in 2012, Burkina Faso in 2015 and Burundi and South Sudan in 2016. Gambia in 2017 was a little different, in that the target (Yahya Jammeh) bowed to international pressure and escaped into political exile in Equatorial Guinea, hence there was not much left to be done by the military force that had convened to tackle the conflict.

Potential coup plotters across the continent already know in advance that the only opposition they will be likely to meet is a mere temporary suspension from the AU, and even that can be avoided if the coup is staged to appear to be not a coup, as happened with Operation Restore Legacy in Zimbabwe that removed Robert Mugabe from office.

While the superstructure antidote for handling unlimited presidencies and governance abuse is being considered, one other political imperative which gathered steam from the Kagame report was the African Continental Free Trade Area (AfCFTA) with the objective to cut

90 per cent of tariffs from their current average of 6.1 per cent to eventually zero and address the multiplicity of non-tariff barriers, such as poor infrastructure and inefficient border posts, which are often the dominant barrier and cost to trading on the continent. The agreement establishing the AfCFTA was signed by 53 heads of state on 21 March 2018.

The evolution of the New Pan-Africanism has been, and continues to be, ad hoc. For example, as regards:

- Burundi in 2015–16, where the AU thought that Nkurunziza was going to be an easy ride and got a rude shock when he called the AU's (as well as the UN's) bluff by disallowing the imposition of a UN police force into Burundi that was authorized by UNSC Resolution 2303 (2016). Burundi subsequently exited the ICC in October 2017 after it came under the threat of ICC prosecution; or
- South Sudan, where the Intergovernmental Authority on Development (IGAD) had to plod its way through negotiating the ARCSS when there was no monitoring capability on the ground, and where the UN equally got a rude shock when the South Sudanese authorities rejected the imposition of a Rapid Intervention Force or Rapid Protection Force in Juba that was authorized by UNSC Resolution 2304 (2016); or
- Burkina Faso, where the AU and ECOWAS became toothless bulldogs but the Burkinabe regular army proved their worth in dismantling and ousting the presidential guard (RSP); or
- The Central African Republic (CAR), where the challenge is to navigate the thick unmonitored and unlegislated forests within which Joseph Kony and the Lord's Resistance Army (LRA) have sought refuge for decades and have abducted 217 people in the CAR in 2016 alone, of whom 54 were children.[1] Other armed groups in the CAR such as the UPF are still in operation because it is practically difficult to get around them, let alone disarm them; or
- Rwandan politics, which the AU generally does not even dare to interfere with. At the July 2016 AU Summit held in Kigali, the untouchable Kagame was assigned to carry out a review of AU institutions and propose reforms to improve efficiency. He subsequently submitted his report at the 28th AU Summit held in Addis Ababa in January 2017; or

- The Democratic Republic of the Congo (DRC) in 2016, where the AU took steps to facilitate a national dialogue between government and whatever was represented of the opposition, at least to navigate, and, if possible, to arrive at, a solution prior to midnight on 20 December 2016 when Kabila's second term of office was to end. Even though the AU attempt failed, it ploughed the ground for the Catholic National Episcopal Conference of Congo (CENCO) to facilitate a process of dialogues that at least managed to broker some temporary amicability. Kabila therefore remained in office until his replacement was ready; or

- Gabon in 2016, where the AU sent a mission to the Constitutional Court's review of the disputed presidential election of 27 August 2016. It remained unclear what influence this particular AU mission exerted on the crucial aspects of rectifying the anomalies in the vote recount, when their EU election monitoring counterparts made clear that they were restricted in observing the crucial aspects of rectifying the anomalies and that the Gabonese Constitutional Court 'had been unable to satisfactorily rectify anomalies observed during the count'.[2] It should be noted that the AU chair at this point was Idriss Deby of Chad who had been head of state for 26 years since 1990, and had abolished the limits to the presidential term in 2005; or

- Gambia in late 2016 to early 2017, when the AU refused to recognize Yahya Jammeh as head of state after he refused to accept the result of the December 2016 presidential election that was ironically rigged against him by the Independent Electoral Commission, and ECOWAS forced him to flee into exile.

On the whole, the New Pan-Africanism seems to be working somewhat, even if Libya in 2011 was a missed opportunity and is now work in progress. Apart from Libya, the AU is now better advised to respond more quickly on African issues rather than leave it totally in the hands of Western political and economic interests. Among other things, the AU should have a progressive policy towards dealing with North Africa and not treat this territory of Africa as the Middle East just because it bears an Arabic semblance and has oil. From this trajectory, it should be characterized as work in progress that the AU forged back to assume responsibility for Libya through the High-Level Committee on Libya, and adjunctly through the Quartet (the AU, the League of Arab States (LAS), the EU and UN), notwithstanding the scale and level of operations by NATO secret service agents and special forces that are required to continually deal with the presence of ISIL and affiliates on Libyan soil, and related parts of the Sahel. It remains to be seen how the G5 Sahel initiative progresses.

There have been some obvious successes, such as the African Union Mission in Somalia (AMISOM) that was formed to support the Federal Government of Somalia in dealing with Al-Shabaab, even if Kenya has had to pay a heavy price for its troop contributions. AMISOM consists principally of Ugandan and Kenyan forces, with minimal further troop contributions from Burundi, Ethiopia and Djibouti. On 22 August 2016, US Secretary of State John Kerry met with President Uhuru Kenyatta to discuss AMISOM and regional security, as Kenya sought military support for its campaign against Al-Shabaab. It will be recalled that on 21 September 2013, unidentified gunmen suspected to be Islamists from Al-Shabaab attacked the Westgate shopping mall in Nairobi, resulting in 67 deaths and some 175 wounded. Also on 2 April 2015, gunmen attacked the Garissa University College campus in eastern Kenya, massacring 148 people and injuring at least 79 others. Al-Shabaab had been taking advantage of the security vacuum across the vast and relatively unprotected stretch of eastern Kenya that shares a long border with Somalia.

In another example of success, the SADC took the initiative to form the New Intervention Force to deal with the M23 and other rebel groups in the eastern DRC, where MONUSCO could not go beyond their job of merely defending and peacekeeping. The AU-led Regional Task Force (RTF) was also established to deal with the LRA. At least ECOWAS stayed on top of the issues and worked with the United Nations Office for West Africa (UNOWA) and the AU-PSC to sort out the Burkinabe crisis.

Money is still a big issue for Africa, and sometimes funding issues (rather than political will) were behind the lackadaisical attitudes to massing forces for emergencies and proving the ASF's operational readiness. It appears that AU member states have been quicker at releasing their troops for assignments when they would wear blue helmets, as for example in AMISOM for Somalia, MINUSCA for the CAR, MONUSCO for the DRC and MINUSMA for Mali. The AU-PSC would certainly need a well-stocked Peace Fund for the future. Meanwhile the Kigali Decision on Financing the AU, taken by African finance and foreign ministers on 16 July 2016 to introduce a 0.2-per cent levy on eligible non-African imports to finance AU programmes, peace and security operations, gained traction as 14 member states were already collecting the levy as at the 31st AU summit in Nouakchott, Mauritania in July 2018.[3] The Kigali Financing Decision was reiterated in the 2017 Kagame report which highlighted the point that 97 per cent of the AU's programmes were funded by donors, and which advocated for sustainable financial independence from external donors. It became both consequential and auspicious for the AU financing and reform agendas to receive impetus under the leadership of Kagame who became Chair of the AU in January 2018, immediately after his report on the AU's reform.

There appears to be no specific formula on whether the AU-PSC wades into any particular matter, and how it should be done. Some of the strategic geopolitical reasons underlying peculiar extensions to presidential term limits could be understood (but not necessarily excused) for the peculiarity of their circumstances, such as the Burundian versus Rwandan Hutu–Tutsi complex. A vast number of other cases were outrightly inexcusable, whether in Equatorial Guinea, Congo-Brazzaville, Cameroon, Togo, Uganda or any others. It behoves the AU leadership (including the heads of state) to decide, above their parochial interests, that presidential extensions beyond term limits should not be condoned and that whoever attempts it must be stopped.

At the July 2016 summit in Kigali, members of the AUC failed to elect a replacement for AUC chair Nkosazana Dlamini-Zuma. Members had to wait until January 2017 for a new AUC chair to take over, as a vote to replace the incumbent did not deliver the required two-thirds majority for any of the candidates:

- Dr Specioza Kasibwe Wandira, former vice president of Uganda, whose candidacy was supported by nine EAC neighbours;
- Pelonomi Venson Moitoi, foreign minister of Botswana; and
- Agapito Nba Mokuy, foreign minister of Equatorial Guinea.

After subsequent and unsuccessful procedural attempts, further contestants emerged in the persons of:

- Abdoulai Bathily of Senegal, who is the UN Special Representative for Central Africa;
- Amina Mohamed, who is the Kenyan Government's cabinet secretary for foreign affairs; and
- Moussa Faki Mahamat, the Chadian foreign minister.

The new AU chairperson was chosen after seven rounds of voting on 29 January 2017 at the 28th Ordinary Session of the AU Assembly in Addis Ababa. Moussa Faki Mahamat became the new appointee and was formally announced at the summit on 30 January 2017.

Also at the July 2016 Kigali summit, Morocco tabled a request to rejoin the AU, and sent an envoy to lobby at the summit. Morocco left the antecedent OAU in 1984 when the organization recognized the independence of Western Sahara and as a result sidelined Morocco for annexing Western Sahara. The issue is not fully resolved, in that Morocco would like to grant autonomy to Western Sahara, albeit under Morocco's sovereignty. Morocco's protracted negotiations to re-enter the AU proved fruitful, and it was readmitted on 30 January 2017 at the 28th AU Summit.

The AU passport was also launched at the July 2016 Kigali summit, with no formal timetable yet for rolling out. The AU passport was carried only by heads of state and other senior African dignitaries, hence the initiative was to make it available to the general African citizenry in order to facilitate visa-free travel across the continent.

An important new item that appeared on the agenda at the 28th AU Summit was Africa's response to the anti-immigration executive orders of the new US administration under Donald Trump. Libya, Sudan and Somalia are on the list of countries facing a ban on immigration into the US.

The 2018 AfCFTA continues to be the flagship cutting edge continental economic policy which takes interregional trade and economic cooperation to another level, to forge the continental trade protocol in goods and services, address non-tariff barriers, and evolve as a base from which to negotiate economic relations with the rest of the world. Meanwhile, the APSA portends alongside the AfCFTA, to assure the much needed security space for trade and development to transact with the least hindrance. A good leadership is needed to carry the agenda through.

LIST OF ACRONYMS

ABAKO	Alliance des Bakongo
ACC	Anti-Corruption Commission
ACIRC	African Capacity for Immediate Response to Crises
ADF	Allied Democratic Forces
AfCFTA	African Continental Free Trade Area
AfDB	African Development Bank
AFDL (ADFLC)	Alliance of Democratic Forces for the Liberation of Congo-Zaire
AFISMA	African-led International Support Mission in Mali
AFRICOM	US Africa Command
AJMCC	Area Joint Military Ceasefire Committees
AMISOM	African Union Mission in Somalia
APRM	African Peer Review Mechanism
APRODH	Association for the Protection of Human Rights and Detained Persons
APSA	African Peace and Security Architecture
AQIM	Al Qaeda in the Islamic Maghreb
ARCSS	Proposed Compromise (Ceasefire) Agreement on the Resolution of the Conflict in the Republic of South Sudan
ASF	African Standby Force
AU	African Union
AUC	African Union Commission
AUCOI	African Union Commission of Inquiry
AUEOM	AU Electoral Observation Mission

AUHLAHC	African Union High-level Ad Hoc Committee
AU-PSC	African Union Peace and Security Commission
AUSF	Amalgamated Units of the Security Forces of South Sudan
AUSTO	AU Short-Term Observer
BDB	Benghazi Defence Brigades
BRSC	Benghazi Revolutionaries Shura Council
CAR	Central African Republic
CDD	Forces for the Defense of Democracy
CDP	Congress for Democracy and Progress
CDPM	Cameroon People's Democratic Movement
CDPS	Convergencia para la Democracia Social de Guinea Ecuatorial
CDR	Committee for the Defense of the Revolution
CENCO	Roman Catholic National Episcopal Conference of Congo
CENI	National Independent Electoral Commission of the DRC
CEN-SAD	Committee of Sahel-Saharan States
CIA	Central Intelligence Agency
CMA	Coordination of Movements for Azawad
CNARED	National Council for Compliance with the Arusha Agreement for Peace and Reconciliation in Burundi and the Rule of Law
CNDD	Conseil National pour la Défense de la Démocratie or National Council for the Defense of Democracy
CNDD-FDD	National Council for the Defense of Democracy-Forces for the Defense of Democracy
CNR	National Council for the Revolution
CNRDR	National Committee for the Restoration of Democracy and State
CoH	cessation of hostilities
CoHA	Cessation of Hostilities Agreement (23 January 2014)
CPCR	Collective of Civil Parties for Rwanda
CPI	Corruption Perceptions Index
CPJP	Convention of Patriots for Justice and Peace
CPSK	Patriotic Convention for Saving the Country

CSO	civil society organization
CSP	Council of Popular Salvation
DGPR	Democratic Green Party of Rwanda
DRC	Democratic Republic of Congo
EAC	East African Community
ECCAS	Economic Community of Central African States
ECOWAS	Economic Community of West African States
ELECAM	Elections Cameroon
EUTM	European Union Training Mission
FACA	Central African Armed Forces
FAZ	Zairean Armed Forces
FDPC	Democratic Front of the Central African Republic
FLM	Front de Libération du Macina
FOMAC	Multinational Force of Central Africa
GATIA	Imghad Tuareg Self-Defense Group and Allies
GNA	Interim Government of National Accord
GNC	General National Congress
GRSS	Government of the Republic of South Sudan (Pre-Transition Period)
HDI	Human Development Index
HDR	Human Development Report
HRW	Human Rights Watch
HSGOC	Heads of State and Government Orientation Committee of NEPAD
IBD	Inter-Burundi Dialogue
ICC	International Criminal Court
ICGLR	International Conference on the Great Lakes Region
IDPs	internally displaced persons
IFOR	International Fellowship for Reconciliation
IGAD	Intergovernmental Authority on Development
IGAD PLUS	An extended form of the IGAD-led Mediation
IIAG	Ibrahim Index on African Governance
IMF	International Monetary Fund
IPF	IGAD Partners' Forum
JMEC	Joint Monitoring and Evaluation Commission
JTC	Joint Technical Committee of IGAD MVM
LNA	Libyan National Army
LRA	Lord's Resistance Army

MAA	Azawad Arab Movement
MEDAC	Mouvement d'évolution démocratique de l'Afrique centrale
MESAN	Movement for the Social Evolution of Black Africa
MICOPAX	Mission for the Consolidation of Peace in CAR
MINURCA	United Nations Mission in the Central African Republic
MINUSCA	UN Multidimensional Integrated Stabilization Mission in the CAR
MINUSMA	UN Multidimensional Integrated Stabilization Mission in Mali
MISCA	International Support Mission to CAR
MLC	Mouvement de Liberation du Congo
MLPC	Mouvement pour la Libération du Peuple Centrafricain
MNC	Mouvement National Congolais
MNLA	National Movement for the Liberation of Azawad
MONUC	United Nations Organization Mission in the DRC
MONUSCO	United Nations Organization Stabilization Mission in the DRC
MPLA	People's Movement for the Liberation of Angola
MPP	People's Movement for Progress
MRND	Mouvement Révolutionaire National pour le Développement
MSF	Médecins Sans Frontières / Doctors Without Borders
MUJWA/ MUJAO	Movement for Oneness and Jihad in West Africa
MVM IGAD	Monitoring and Verification Mechanism
MVT IGAD	Monitoring and Verification Team
NATO	North Atlantic Treaty Organization
NCAC	National Constitutional Amendment Committee
NCD	National Council for Democracy
NDC	National Defence Council
NEPAD	New Partnership for African Development
NGO	non-governmental organization
NRC	Norwegian Refugee Council
NRM	National Resistance Movement
NTC	National Transitional Council

OAU	Organization of African Unity
OCHA	UN Office for the Coordination of Humanitarian Affairs
OHCHR	Office of the Commissioner for Human Rights (UN Human Rights Council)
OIC	Organisation of the Islamic Conference
ONAD	Organization for Nonviolence and Development
OPEC	Organization of Petroleum Exporting Countries
PCA	permanent ceasefire arrangements
PCT	Congolese Labour Party
PDG	Democratic Party of Guinea
PDG	Gabonese Democratic Party
PDGE	Democratic Party of Equatorial Guinea
PFG	Petroleum Facilities Guard
PFMA	Public Financial Management and Accountability Act, 2011
POC	Protection of Civilians Site
QRF	Quick-Reaction Force
RCD	Rally for Congolese Democracy
RCI-LRA	Regional Cooperation Initiative for the elimination of the LRA
RDC	Rassemblement Démocratique Centrafricain
RECs	regional economic communities
ROE	Rationalization of Ethnonanationalism
RPF	Rapid Protection Force for South Sudan
RPF	Rwandan Patriotic Front
RPM	Rally for Mali
RSP	Regiment of Presidential Security
RTF	Regional Task Force
RTNB	Radio-Télévision Nationale du Burundi
SAA	Special Arrangement Area
SADC	Southern Africa Development Community
SDSR	Strategic Defence and Security Review
SOMA	Status of Mission Agreement
SPLA	Sudan People's Liberation Army
SPLM	Sudan People's Liberation Movement
SPLM/A	Sudanese People's Liberation Movement/Army

SPLM Leaders (FDs)	Sudan People's Liberation Movement Leaders (Former Detainees)
SPLM/A-IO	Sudan People's Liberation Movement/Army (In Opposition)
STOs	AU Short-Term Observer(s)
TCC	Troop Contributing Countries
TGoNU	Transitional Government of National Unity (Transition Period)
UAE	United Arab Emirates
UDPS	Union for Democracy and Social Progress
UDV	Voltaic Democratic Union
UFDR	Union of Democratic Forces for Unity
UK	United Kingdom
UN	United Nations
UNDP	United Nations Development Programme
UNESCO	United Nations Educational, Scientific and Cultural Organization
UNHRC	UN Human Rights Council
UNICEF	United Nations Children's Fund
UNIIB	United Nations Independent Investigation on Burundi
UNITA	National Union for the Total Integration of Angola
UNMAS	UN Mine Action Service
UNMISS	United Nations Mission in South Sudan
UNOCHA	UN Office for the Coordination of Humanitarian Affairs
UNOWA	United Nations Office for West Africa
UNSC	United Nations Security Council
UNSMIL	United Nations Support Mission in Libya
UPC	Union for Progress and Reform
UPDF	Ugandan People's Defence Forces
UPRONA	Union for National Progress
US	United States of America
WAMZ	West African Monetary Zone
WFP	United Nations World Food Programme
WHO	World Health Organization
ZANU-PF	Zimbabwe African National Union – Patriotic Front

NOTES

Chapter 1   Introduction

1. Michael Amoah, *Reconstructing the Nation in Africa* (London: I.B.Tauris, 2007).
2. Ibid., vii.
3. Michael Amoah, *Nationalism, Globalization, and Africa* (New York: Palgrave Macmillan, 2011), pp. 1–16.
4. Yoon Se Young, 'The Presidential System in Korea: Is It a Little Too Old?' *The Granite Tower*, 5 September 2014, www.thegranitetower.com/news/articleView.html?idxno=942 (accessed 21 December 2015).
5. Government of Algeria, *Constitution of the People's Democratic Republic of Algeria 1989 (amended by the constitutional revision of 1996)* (Algiers, Algeria: Government of Algeria, 1996), 9.
6. IFES Election Guide, 'Algeria', www.electionguide.org/elections/id/2456/ (accessed 19 December 2015).
7. IFES Election Guide, 'Angola', www.electionguide.org/elections/id/1509/ (accessed 16 December 2015).
8. Reuters, 'Angola's Dos Santos not up for re-election in 2017: party document', Reuters, 2 December 2016, www.reuters.com/article/us-angola-dossantos-idUSKBN13R2EZ?il=0 (accessed 9 December 2016).
9. Comparative Constitutions Project, 'Burkina Faso's Constitution of 1991 with Amendments through 2012', Comparative Constitutions Project, www.constituteproject.org (accessed 1 February 2016).
10. IRIN, 'BURKINA FASO: Compaore gets green light to run for third mandate', IRIN, www.irinnews.org/report/56742/burkina-faso-compaore-gets-green-light-to-run-for-third-mandate (accessed 21 December 2015).
11. IFES Election Guide, 'Burkina Faso', www.electionguide.org/elections/id/2169/ (accessed 21 December 2015).

12. Al Jazeera, 'Trial of Burkina Faso's ex-leader Blaise Compaore adjourned', 16 May 2017, www.aljazeera.com/video/news/2017/05/trial-burkina-fasos-ex-leader-blaise-compaore-adjourned-170516062245570.html (accessed 31 May 2017).
13. Comparative Constitutions Project, 'Burundi's Constitution of 2005', www.constituteproject.org (accessed 1 February 2015).
14. Government of Burundi, *Arusha Peace and Reconciliation Agreement for Burundi* (Arusha, Tanzania: Government of Burundi, 2000), 33.
15. Ibid., 32.
16. Ibid., 49.
17. Ibid., 8.
18. African Union, Constitutive Act of the African Union (Addis Ababa: African Union, 2001), 7.
19. Government of Cameroon, *Constitution of the Republic of Cameroon* (Yaounde: Groupe Mauger, 1996), 7.
20. Amoah, *Nationalism, Globalization, and Africa*, 154.
21. Ibid.
22. IFES Election Guide, 'Cameroon', www.electionguide.org/elections/id/2205/ (accessed 19 December 2015).
23. Comparative Constitutions Project, 'Chad's Constitution of 1996 with Amendments through 2005', www.constituteproject.org (accessed 1 February 2015).
24. IFES Election Guide, 'Congo-Brazzaville', www.electionguide.org/elections/id/2111/ (accessed 16 December 2015).
25. Amoah, *Nationalism, Globalization, and Africa*, 147.
26. VOA, 'DRC Political Dialogue Stalls Over Opposition Demands', 3 September 2016, www.voanews.com/a/congo-national-dialogue/3492400.html (accessed 10 September 2016).
27. *Eye on Africa*, France24 English, 8 September 2016.
28. Reuters, 'Congo's election head says presidential vote unlikely this year', Reuters, 9 July 2017, www.reuters.com/article/us-congo-politics-idUSKBN19U0ZA (accessed 17 July 2017).
29. Amoah, *Nationalism, Globalization, and Africa*, 162–6.
30. Vanguard, 'After 36 years in office, EGuinea president wants new term', 11 November 2015, www.vanguardngr.com/2015/11/after-36-years-in-office-eguinea-president-wants-new-term/ (accessed 21 December 2015).
31. Amanpour, CNN, Sky Channel 506, 5 October 2012.
32. EGJustice, 'Constitutional Reform', www.egjustice.org/post/constitutional-reform (accessed 21 December 2015).
33. Ibid.
34. Ibid.
35. Amoah, *Nationalism, Globalization, and Africa*, 141–3.
36. ENCA, 'Gabon's court failed to rectify "anomalies" in presidential poll: EU', 26 September 2016, www.enca.com/africa/gabons-court-failed-to-rectify-anomalies-in-presidential-poll-eu (accessed 17 July 2017).

37. Amoah, *Nationalism, Globalization, and Africa*, 133–6.
38. BBC, 'No third term for Nigerian leader', http://news.bbc.co.uk/1/hi/world/africa/4986904.stm (accessed 17 December 2015).
39. Comparative Constitutions Project, 'Rwanda's Constitution of 2003 with Amendments through 2010', www.constituteproject.org (accessed 1 February 2015).
40. IGIHE, 'Supreme Court rules against Green Party constitutional amendment petition', 8 October 2015, http://en.igihe.com/justice/supreme-court-rules-against-green-party.html (accessed 17 December 2015).
41. Government of Rwanda, 'The Constitution of the Republic of Rwanda of 2003 Revised in 2015' (Kigali: Government of Rwanda, 2015), 154.
42. *The Observer*, 'NRM doesn't believe in term limits theatre – Museveni', www.observer.ug/news-headlines/41196-nrm-doesn-t-believe-in-term-limits-theatre-museveni (accessed 19 December 2015).
43. IFES Election Guide, 'Senegal', IFES Election Guide, www.electionguide.org/elections/id/2230/ (accessed 21 December 2015).
44. Comparative Constitutions Project, 'Togo's Constitution on 1992 with Amendments through 2007', Comparative Constitutions Project, www.constituteproject.org (accessed 19 December 2015).
45. IFES Election Guide, 'Togo', IFES Election Guide, www.electionguide.org/elections/id/2111/ (accessed 19 December 2015).
46. Comparative Constitutions Project, 'Togo's Constitution on 1992 with Amendments through 2007', Comparative Constitutions Project, www.constituteproject.org (accessed 19 December 2015).
47. Government of Tunisia, *Constitution of The Republic of Tunisia* (Tunis: Government of Tunisia, 2010), 23.
48. IFES Election Guide, 'Tunisia', www.electionguide.org/elections/id/2122/ (accessed 21 December 2015).
49. Amoah, *Nationalism, Globalization, and Africa*, 74.
50. *The Observer*, 'NRM doesn't believe in term limits theatre – Museveni'.
51. Amoah, *Nationalism, Globalization, and Africa*, 116–18.
52. Louis Odion, 'Cameron: Fantastically un-Nigerian', *Sahara Reporters*, 30 June 2016, http://saharareporters.com/2016/06/30/cameron-fantastically-un-nigerian-louis-odion (accessed 3 July 2016).

Chapter 2   Burkina Faso

1. Comparative Constitutions Project, 'Constitution of Burkina Faso 1991 with Amendments through 2012', www.constituteproject.org (accessed 1 February 2015).
2. IRIN, 'BURKINA FASO: Compaore gets green light to run for third mandate', www.irinnews.org/report/56742/burkina-faso-compaore-gets-green-light-to-run-for-third-mandate (accessed 21 December 2015).

3. IFES Election Guide, 'Burkina Faso', IFES Election Guide, www.election guide.org/elections/id/2169/ (accessed 21 December 2015).

4. *Newshour*, Al Jazeera English, Sky Channel 514, 4 November 2015.

5. Comparative Constitutions Project, 'Constitution of Burkina Faso', 10.

6. *News & Magazines*, France24 English, 8 November 2014.

7. *Newshour*, Al Jazeera English, 11 November 2014.

8. Comparative Constitutions Project, 'Constitution of Burkina Faso', 21.

9. Faith Karimi and Sandra Betsis, 'Burkina Faso attack: At least 29 dead, scores freed after hotel siege', CNN online, 18 January 2016, http://edition.cnn.com/2016/01/16/africa/burkina-faso-hotel-terrorist-attack/ (accessed 15 February 2016).

10. *Newshour*, Al Jazeera English, 17 January 2016; *News & Magazines*, France 24 English, 17 January 2016.

11. World Bank Group, *Global Economic Prospects, June 2018: The Turning of the Tide?* (Washington, DC: World Bank Group, 2018).

12. Institute for Economics and Peace, 'Global Peace Index 2017', http://visionofhumanity.org/reports/ (accessed 23 December 2017), 129.

13. *Global Peace Index 2018*, 95.

14. Data quoted in the 2011 Ibrahim Index are from 2010. The dataset used to calculate the 2011 Ibrahim Index contains data from 2000 to 2010.

15. Mo Ibrahim Foundation, '2015 Ibrahim Index of African Governance', www.moibrahimfoundation.org/iiag/launch/ (accessed 9 March 2015).

16. Data from this index ran from 2006 to 2015 – a decade of African governance.

17. Mo Ibrahim Foundation, '2016 Ibrahim Index of African Governance: Index Report', http://mo.ibrahim.foundation/iiag/downloads/ (accessed 24 November 2016).

18. Data from this index ran from 2007 to 2016 – a ten-year period.

19. Mo Ibrahim Foundation, '2017 Ibrahim Index of African Governance: Index Report', http://mo.ibrahim.foundation/iiag/2017-key-findings/ (accessed 20 December 2017).

20. Data from this index ran from 2008 to 2017 covering 54 countries.

21. Mo Ibrahim Foundation, '2018 Ibrahim Index of African Governance: Index Report', http://mo.ibrahim.foundation/iiag/ (accessed 29 October 2018).

22. Institute for Economics and Peace, 'Global Peace Index', Institute for Economics and Peace, www.visionofhumanity.org/#/page/indexes/global-peace-index/2015 (accessed 9 March 2015).

23. Institute for Economics and Peace, 'Global Peace Index 2016', www.visionofhumanity.org/ (accessed 8 December 2016).

24. *Global Peace Index 2016*, 15.

25. *Global Peace Index 2017*.

26. Ibid., 18.

27. Institute for Economics and Peace, 'Positive Peace Report 2017: Tracking Peace Transitions Through a Systems Thinking Approach', October 2017, http://visionofhumanity.org/reports/ (accessed 23 December 2017).

28. *Positive Peace Report 2017*, 4.
29. *Global Peace Index 2018*.
30. UNDP, '2015 Human Development Report', http://hdr.undp.org/en/2015-report/download (accessed 9 March 2016).
31. UNDP, '2016 Human Development Report', http://hdr.undp.org/en/2016-report (accessed 22 December 2017).
32. UNDP, 'Human Development Indices and Indicators: 2018 Statistical Update', http://hdr.undp.org/en/2018-update (accessed 20 October 2018).
33. Transparency International, 'Corruption Perceptions Index 2015', www.transparency.org/ (accessed 9 March 2016).
34. Transparency International, 'Corruption Perceptions Index 2016', Transparency International, www.transparency.org/news/feature/corruption_perceptions_index_2016 (accessed 23 December 2017).
35. Transparency International, 'Corruption Perceptions Index 2017', Transparency International, https://www.transparency.org/news/feature/corruption_perceptions_index_2017 (accessed 24 July 2018).
36. Transparency International, 'CPI Results Brochure 2017', https://www.transparency.org/news/feature/corruption_perceptions_index_2017 (accessed 24 July 2018).
37. Institute for Economics and Peace, *Global Peace Index 2013*, 1.
38. Karimi and Betsis, 'Burkina Faso attack'.
39. Reuters, 'Twelve soldiers killed in attack on Burkina Faso army post', 16 December 2016, www.reuters.com/article/us-burkina-attack-idUSKBN1451MP (accessed 26 December 2016).
40. *Newshour*, Al Jazeera English, 16 December 2016.
41. BBC, 'Burkina Faso gun attack kills 18 people at café', 14 August 2017, www.bbc.co.uk/news/world-africa-40920338 (accessed 14 August 2017).
42. Institute for Economics and Peace, 'Global Terrorism Index 2015', http://visionofhumanity.org/reports/ (accessed 23 December 2017).
43. *Global Terrorism Index 2016*.
44. *Global Terrorism Index 2017*, 75.
45. *Global Terrorism Index 2017*.
46. Ibid., 73.
47. BBC, 'Burkina Faso's war against militant Islamists', BBC, 14 August 2017, www.bbc.co.uk/news/world-africa-39279050 (accessed 14 August 2017).
48. The Defense Post, 'Eight Burkina Faso soldiers killed roadside bomb blast near Baraboulé', 26 September 2018, https://thedefensepost.com/2018/09/26/burkina-faso-soldiers-killed-roadside-bomb-baraboule/ (accessed 23 October 2018).
49. World Health Organization (WHO), 'Dengue Fever – Burkina Faso', 18 November 2016, www.who.int/csr/don/18-november-2016-dengue-burkina-faso/en/ (accessed 5 January 2017).
50. BBC, 'Dengue fever kills 20 in Burkina Faso', 23 November 2016, www.bbc.co.uk/news/world-africa-38078754 (accessed 5 January 2017).

51. *Eye on Africa*, France24 English, 3 January 2017.
52. Reuters, 'Court delays trial of Burkina Faso ex-leader for protest killings', 27 April 2017, www.reuters.com/article/uk-burkina-trial-idUKKBN17T1MH (accessed 31 May 2017).
53. *Across Africa*, France24 English, Sky Channel 513, 21 May 2017.
54. Al Jazeera, 'Trial of Burkina Faso's ex-leader Blaise Compaore adjourned', 16 May 2017, www.aljazeera.com/video/news/2017/05/trial-burkina-fasos-ex-leader-blaise-compaore-adjourned-170516062245570.html (accessed 31 May 2017).

Chapter 3   Burundi

1. Michael Amoah, *Reconstructing the Nation in Africa* (London: I.B.Tauris, 2007), 114, 116–19.
2. *The Observer*, 'NRM doesn't believe in term limits theatre – Museveni', www. observer.ug/news-headlines/41196-nrm-doesn-t-believe-in-term-limits-theatre-museveni (accessed 19 December 2015).
3. *Newshour*, Al Jazeera English, Sky Channel 514, 3 March 2016.
4. Government of Burundi, *Arusha Peace and Reconciliation Agreement for Burundi* (Arusha, Tanzania: Government of Burundi, 2000), 15.
5. It is interesting to note that the Tutsi-led UPRONA party is very much diminished in current Burundian politics. In the July 2015 presidential election, Gerard Nduwayo, the UPRONA candidate, managed to gain only 2.14 per cent of the ballot, or just 60,380 votes.
6. Government of Burundi, *Arusha Agreement*, 38 and 64.
7. Ibid., 65.
8. Comparative Constitutions Project, 'Burundi's Constitution of 2005', www. constituteproject.org (accessed 1 February 2016).
9. Government of Burundi, *Arusha Agreement*, 33.
10. Ibid., 25.
11. Ibid., 18–19.
12. Comparative Constitutions Project, 'Burundi's Constitution of 2005', 19, 20 and 24.
13. Government of Burundi, *Arusha Agreement*, 8.
14. Amoah, *Reconstructing the Nation*, 114.
15. Comparative Constitutions Project, 'Burundi's Constitution of 2005', 14.
16. Government of Burundi, *Arusha Agreement*, 33.
17. Ibid., 32.
18. Ibid., 49.
19. France24, 'Grenade blast follows string of attacks on Burundi capital', www. france24.com/en/20160215-grenade-attack-bujumbura-burundi-unrest-injured (accessed 15 February 2016).
20. Government of Burundi, *Arusha Agreement*, 2–3.

21. Al Jazeera, 'Election official flees crisis-hit Burundi', www.aljazeera.com/news/2015/05/election-official-flees-crisis-hit-burundi-150530124830312.html (accessed 15 February 2016).

22. BBC, 'Burundi Vice-President Gervais Rufyikiri flees', www.bbc.co.uk/news/world-africa-33267428 (accessed 16 February 2016).

23. Reuters, 'African Union says Burundi election not free or fair, Speaker flees', www.reuters.com/article/us-burundi-politics-africanunion-idUSKCN0P80YD20150628.

24. Newshour, Al Jazeera English, 10 November 2015.

25. News & Magazines, France24 English, 10 November 2015.

26. Paragraph 8 of UNSC Resolution 2248 (2015).

27. BBC, 'Burundi grenade attack kills four, including boy', 7 February 2016, www.bbc.co.uk/news/world-africa-35516968 (accessed 15 February 2016).

28. Reuters, 'Grenade attack kills child, wounds his father in Burundi's capital', www.reuters.com/article/us-burundi-attacks-idUSKCN0VN0EO (accessed 15 February 2016).

29. France24, 'Grenade blast follows string of attacks on Burundi capital', 15 February 2016, www.france24.com/en/20160215-grenade-attack-bujumbura-burundi-unrest-injured (accessed 15 February 2016).

30. BBC, 'Burundi general shot dead dropping child off at school', BBC, 25 April 2016, www.bbc.co.uk/news/world-africa-36129899 (accessed 7 June 2016).

31. Ibid.

32. Reuters, 'Burundi school sends home 230 students for defacing president's photo', http://uk.reuters.com/article/uk-burundi-politics-idUKKCN0Z02D6 (accessed 14 June 2016).

33. Eye on Africa, France24 English, 14 June 2016.

34. BBC, 'Burundi crisis: MP Hasfa Mossi gunned down', 13 July 2016, www.portland-communications.com/2016/07/what-happened-at-last-weeks-african-union-summit/ (accessed 22 August 2016).

35. Newshour, Al Jazeera English, 15 December 2015.

36. African Union, Constitutive Act of the African Union (Addis Ababa, Ethiopia: African Union 2001), 7.

37. Amnesty International, My Children Are Scared: Burundi's Deepening Human Rights Crisis (London: Amnesty International, 2015), 6.

38. Newshour, Al Jazeera English, 28 January 2016; News & Magazines, France24 English, 29 January 2016.

39. Amnesty International, My Children Are Scared, 7.

40. Eye on Africa, France24 English, 4 February 2016.

41. Jeffrey Gettleman, U.N. Report Accuses Rwanda of Training Rebels to Oust Burundian Leader', New York Times, 4 February 2016. www.nytimes.com/2016/02/05/world/africa/un-report-accuses-rwanda-of-training-rebels-to-oust-burundian-leader.html?_r=0# (accessed 12 March 2016).

42. *Newshour*, Al Jazeera English, 5 February 2016.
43. UN News Centre, 'Ban arrives in Burundi in support of UN efforts to resolve political crisis', www.un.org/apps/news/story.asp?newsID=53287 (accessed 23 February 2016).
44. *Eye on Africa*, France24 English, 23 February 2016.
45. ENCA, 'High Level AU delegation in second day of Burundi talks', www.enca.com/africa/high-level-au-delegation-second-day-burundi-talks (accessed 26 February 2016).
46. UN Women, 'Women mediators promote peace in Burundi', 25 January 2016, www.unwomen.org/en/news/stories/2016/1/women-mediators-promote-peace-in-burundi (accessed 7 June 2016).
47. *Eye on Africa*, France24 English, 12 July 2016.
48. France24, 'Burundi wants to quit ICC to avoid possible charges', 7 October 2016, www.france24.com/en/20161007-burundi-wants-quit-icc-avoid-possible-charges (accessed 1 November 2016).
49. *Eye on Africa*, France24 English, 8 December 2016.
50. Reuters, 'U.N. identifies 41 Burundi, Gabon troops accused of abuse in Central Africa', Reuters, 5 December 2016, www.reuters.com/article/us-centralafrica-un-crime-idUSKBN13U28H (accessed 9 December 2016).
51. *Eye on Africa*, France24 English, 16 February 2017.
52. AMISOM, 'New Burundi battle group arrives in Somalia', 14 February 2017, http://amisom-au.org/2017/02/new-burundi-battle-group-arrives-in-somalia/ (accessed 7 March 2017).
53. World Bank Group, *Global Economic Prospects, June 2018: The Turning of the Tide?* (Washington, DC: World Bank Group, 2018).
54. Institute for Economics and Peace, 'Global Peace Index 2017', http://visionofhumanity.org/reports/ (accessed 23 December 2017), p. 129.
55. *Global Peace Index 2018*, p. 93.
56. Thomson Reuters, 'Burundi expects econ growth, spending to pick up in 2018', 13 December 2017, https://uk.reuters.com/article/burundi-budget/burundi-expects-econ-growth-spending-to-pick-up-in-2018-idUKL8-N1OD4C1 (accessed 19 December 2017).
57. Reuters, 'Burundi paralyzed by fuel shortages as leaders blame lack of dollars', 30 May 2017, www.reuters.com/article/us-burundi-oil-idUSKBN18Q1RN (accessed 6 July 2017).
58. Data quoted in the 2011 Ibrahim Index are from 2010. The dataset used to calculate the 2011 Ibrahim Index contains data from 2000 to 2010.
59. Mo Ibrahim Foundation, '2015 Ibrahim Index of African Governance', www.moibrahimfoundation.org/iiag/launch/ (accessed 9 March 2015).
60. Mo Ibrahim Foundation, '2016 Ibrahim Index of African Governance: Index Report', http://mo.ibrahim.foundation/iiag/downloads/ (accessed 24 November 2016).
61. Data from this index ran from 2007 to 2016 – a ten-year period.

62. Mo Ibrahim Foundation, '2017 Ibrahim Index of African Governance: Index Report', http://mo.ibrahim.foundation/iiag/2017-key-findings/ (accessed 20 December 2017).

63. Mo Ibrahim Foundation, '2018 Ibrahim Index of African Governance: Index Report', http://mo.ibrahim.foundation/iiag/ (accessed 29 October 2018).

64. Institute for Economics and Peace, 'Global Peace Index', www.visionofhumanity.org/#/page/indexes/global-peace-index/2015 (accessed 9 March 2015).

65. Institute for Economics and Peace, 'Global Peace Index 2016', www.visionofhumanity.org/ (accessed 8 December 2016).

66. *Global Peace Index 2016*, 2.

67. *Global Peace Index 2017*.

68. Ibid., 14, 18.

69. Ibid., 19.

70. Institute for Economics and Peace, 'Positive Peace Report 2017: Tracking Peace Transitions Through a Systems Thinking Approach', October 2017, http://visionofhumanity.org/reports/ (accessed 23 December 2017).

71. *Global Peace Index 2018*.

72. UNDP, '2015 Human Development Report', http://hdr.undp.org/en/2015-report/download (accessed 9 March 2016).

73. UNDP, '2016 Human Development Report', http://hdr.undp.org/en/2016-report (accessed 22 December 2017).

74. UNDP, 'Human Development Indices and Indicators: 2018 Statistical Update', http://hdr.undp.org/en/2018-update (accessed 20 October 2018).

75. Transparency International, 'Corruption Perceptions Index 2015', www.transparency.org/ (accessed 9 March 2016).

76. Transparency International, 'Corruption Perceptions Index 2016', www.transparency.org/news/feature/corruption_perceptions_index_2016 (accessed 23 December 2017).

77. Transparency International, 'Corruption Perceptions Index 2017', Transparency International, https://www.transparency.org/news/feature/corruption_perceptions_index_2017 (accessed 24 July 2018).

78. Transparency International, 'CPI Results Brochure 2017', https://www.transparency.org/news/feature/corruption_perceptions_index_2017 (accessed 24 July 2018).

79. Page 40 of the 2017 Ibrahim Index on African governance.

80. Ibid., 55.

81. Institute for Economics and Peace, *Global Peace Index 2014*, 13.

82. Ibid.

83. Institute for Economics and Peace. 'Global Terrorism Index 2015', http://visionofhumanity.org/reports/ (accessed 23 December 2017).

84. *Global Terrorism Index 2016*.

85. Ibid., p. 21.

86. *Global Terrorism Index 2017*.

87. Al Jazeera, 'Israeli PM Netanyahu in historic East Africa trip', www.aljazeera.com/news/2016/07/israel-pm-netanyahu-historic-east-africa-trip-16070408 4656635.html (accessed 4 July 2016).
88. *Newshour*, Al Jazeera English, 4 July 2016.
89. UN Security Council Resolution 2303 (2016).
90. UNOHCHR, *Report of the United Nations Independent Investigation on Burundi (UNIIB) established pursuant to Human Rights Council resolution S-24/1* (Geneva: OHCHR, 2016, 7).
91. Al Jazeera, 'UN probe finds "gross human rights abuses" in Burundi', 21 September 2016, www.aljazeera.com/news/2016/09/probe-finds-gross-human-rights-abuses-burundi-160920193304827.html (accessed 1 October 2016).
92. *Eye on Africa*, France24 English, Sky Channel 513, 24 October 2016.
93. Reuters, 'Burundi president's aide survives attack, guard killed – officials', 29 November 2016, http://uk.reuters.com/article/uk-burundi-violence-idUKKBN13O0V1 (accessed 4 December 2016).
94. *Eye on Africa*, France24 English, Sky Channel 513, 29 November 2016.
95. Reuters, 'Burundi says will not co-operate with UN investigation into violence', Reuters, 24 November 2016, http://af.reuters.com/article/burundiNews/idAFL4N1DP3PA?sp=true (accessed 4 December 2016).
96. Reuters, 'Burundi minister shot dead in capital – police', 2 January 2017, http://af.reuters.com/article/topNews/idAFKBN14L0VK?sp=true (accessed 5 January 2017).
97. Reuters, 'Grenade attack kills three members of Burundi ruling party', 18 May 2017, www.reuters.com/article/us-burundi-violence-idUSKCN18E1SL (accessed 6 July 2017).
98. Reuters, 'Burundi authorities purging army on ethnic lines: rights group', 4 July 2017, www.reuters.com/article/us-burundi-politics-idUSKBN19P1MA (accessed 6 July 2017).
99. UN Human Rights Council, *Report of the Commission of Inquiry on Burundi* (Geneva: UNHRC, 2017), p. 1.
100. Ibid.

Chapter 4   Central African Republic

1. ICC, 'ICC Trial Chamber III sentences Jean-Pierre Bemba Gombo to 18 years' imprisonment for war crimes and crimes against humanity committed in the Central African Republic in 2002–2003', www.icc-cpi.int//Pages/item.aspx?name=PR1223 (accessed 23 June 2016).
2. ICC, 'ICC Appeals Chamber Acquits Mr Bemba from charges of war crimes and crimes against humanity', https://www.icc-cpi.int/Pages/item.aspx?name = PR1390 (accessed 26 July 2018).
3. Al Jazeera, 'Looting and gunfire in captured CAR capital', www.aljazeera.com/news/africa/2013/03/201332481729584103.html (accessed 31 December 2017).

4. Ibid., for the recording of my interview on the breaking news; *Newshour*, Al Jazeera English, Sky Channel 514, 24 March 2013.
5. *Newshour*, Al Jazeera English, 18 December 2015.
6. Ibid.
7. Ibid.
8. *Newshour*, Al Jazeera English, 29 January 2016.
9. Ibid.; at the televised press conference on 29 January 2016.
10. *Newshour*, Al Jazeera English, 29 January 2016.
11. *Eye on Africa*, France24 English, 4 February 2016.
12. Ibid.
13. *Newshour*, Al Jazeera English, 31 March 2016.
14. Human Rights Watch, 'Central African Republic: Moslems Trapped in Enclave', www.hrw.org/news/2014/12/22/central-african-republic-muslims-trapped-enclaves (accessed 16 March 2016).
15. *News & Magazines*, France24 English, 29 September 2015.
16. *Newshour*, Al Jazeera English, 29 September 2015.
17. MSF, 'CAR: MSF Condemns Violent Attack and Killing of Staff Member', www.doctorswithoutborders.org/article/car-msf-condemns-violent-attack-and-killing-staff-member (accessed 18 June 2016).
18. Kieran Guilbert, 'Fresh Violence in Central African Republic kills several, forces thousands to flee – U.N.', Thomson Reuters Foundation News, 17 June 2016, http://news.trust.org/item/20160617133151-3mpa5 (accessed 18 June 2016).
19. *Newshour*, Al Jazeera English, 10 July 2016.
20. *News & Magazines*, France24 English, 1 October 2015.
21. *Newshour*, Al Jazeera English, 14 February 2016.
22. *Newshour*, Al Jazeera English, 3 March 2016.
23. *Eye on Africa*, France24 English, 8 June 2016.
24. Reuters, 'Donors pledge 2 billion euros for Central African Republic', 17 November 2016, www.reuters.com/article/us-centralafrica-conference-idUSKBN13C282 (accessed 19 November 2016).
25. World Bank Group, *Global Economic Prospects, June 2018: The Turning of the Tide?* (Washington, DC: World Bank Group, 2018).
26. Reuters, 'Central African Republic's economy to grow by 4.7pct in 2017 – IMF', 1 June 2017, http://af.reuters.com/article/centralAfricanRepublicNews/idAFL8N1IY6IC (accessed 6 June 2017).
27. Institute for Economics and Peace, 'Global Peace Index 2017', http://visionofhumanity.org/reports/ (accessed 23 December 2017), p. 128.
28. *Global Peace Index 2018*, 93.
29. *Global Peace Index 2018*, 48.
30. Data quoted in the 2011 Ibrahim Index are from 2010. The dataset used to calculate the 2011 Ibrahim Index contains data from 2000 to 2010.
31. Mo Ibrahim Foundation, '2015 Ibrahim Index of African Governance', www.moibrahimfoundation.org/iiag/launch/ (accessed 9 March 2015).

32. Mo Ibrahim Foundation, '2016 Ibrahim Index of African Governance: Index Report', http://mo.ibrahim.foundation/iiag/downloads/ (accessed 24 November 2016).
33. Data from this index ran from 2007 to 2016 – a ten-year period.
34. Mo Ibrahim Foundation, '2017 Ibrahim Index of African Governance: Index Report', http://mo.ibrahim.foundation/iiag/2017-key-findings/ (accessed 20 December 2017).
35. Mo Ibrahim Foundation, '2018 Ibrahim Index of African Governance: Index Report', http://mo.ibrahim.foundation/iiag/ (accessed 29 October 2018).
36. Institute for Economics and Peace, 'Global Peace Index', www.visionofhumanity. org/#/page/indexes/global-peace-index/2015 (accessed 9 March 2015).
37. Institute for Economics and Peace, 'Global Peace Index', www.visionofhumanity. org/ (accessed 8 December 2016).
38. *Global Peace Index 2016*, 9 and 16.
39. *Global Peace Index 2017*.
40. Ibid., p. 19.
41. Institute for Economics and Peace, 'Positive Peace Report 2017: Tracking Peace Transitions Through a Systems Thinking Approach', October 2017, http://visionofhumanity.org/reports/ (accessed 23 December 2017).
42. *Global Peace Index 2018*, 11 and 48.
43. UNDP, '2015 Human Development Report', http://hdr.undp.org/en/2015-report/download (accessed 9 March 2016).
44. UNDP, '2016 Human Development Report', http://hdr.undp.org/en/2016-report (accessed 22 December 2017).
45. UNDP, 'Human Development Indices and Indicators: 2018 Statistical Update', http://hdr.undp.org/en/2018-update (accessed 20 October 2018).
46. Transparency International, 'Corruption Perceptions Index 2015', www. transparency.org/ (accessed 9 March 2016).
47. Transparency International, 'Corruption Perceptions Index 2016', www. transparency.org/news/feature/corruption_perceptions_index_2016 (accessed 23 December 2017).
48. Transparency International, 'Corruption Perceptions Index 2017', Transparency International, https://www.transparency.org/news/feature/corruption_ perceptions_index_2017 (accessed 24 July 2018).
49. Transparency International, 'CPI Results Brochure 2017', https://www. transparency.org/news/feature/corruption_perceptions_index_2017 (accessed 24 July 2018).
50. Verisk Maplecroft, 'Political Risk Index 2016', www.maplecroft.com/accounts/ dashboard/ (accessed 9 March 2016).
51. Institute for Economics and Peace, 'Global Terrorism Index 2015', http:// visionofhumanity.org/reports/ (accessed 23 December 2017).
52. *Global Terrorism Index 2016*.
53. Ibid., 20.
54. Ibid., 3.

55. *Global Terrorism Index 2017*.
56. Ibid., 46.
57. UN.Org, 'Half of the population of Central African Republic faces hunger, UN warns', www.un.org/sustainabledevelopment/blog/2016/01/half-the-population-of-central-african-republic-faces-hunger-un-warns/ (accessed 28 June 2016).
58. UN News Centre, 'UN rights chief warns of violence re-escalating in Central African Republic', www.un.org/apps/news/story.asp?NewsID=54396 (accessed 5 July 2016).
59. *Newshour*, Al Jazeera English, 5 July 2016.
60. Reuters, 'At least 12 killed in fighting in Central African Republic town', http://af.reuters.com/article/centralAfricanRepublicNews/idAFL8N19R4JE (accessed 11 July 2016).
61. *Newshour*, Al Jazeera English, 5 July 2016.
62. *Eye on Africa*, France24 English, Sky Channel 513, 24 October 2016.
63. BBC, 'France ends Sangaris military operation in CAR', BBC, 31 October 2016, www.bbc.co.uk/news/world-africa-37823047 (accessed 1 November 2016).
64. *Focus on France*, France24 English, Sky Channel 513, 24 October 2016.
65. BBC, 'France ends Sangaris military operation in CAR', 31 October 2016, www.bbc.co.uk/news/world-africa-37823047 (accessed 1 November 2016).
66. Reuters, 'At least 22 dead in clashes in central African Republic town – UN', 20 May 2017, http://af.reuters.com/article/topNews/idAFKCN18G0HW-OZATP (accessed 6 June 2017), 64 VOA, 'Spiralling Violence in Central African Republic Isolates Neediest', 22 June 2017, www.voanews.com/a/spiraling-violence-in-central-african-republic-isolates-neediest/3912673.html (accessed 23 June 2017).
67. BBC, 'Central African Republic: UN peacekeeper killed in attack', 24 July 2017, www.bbc.co.uk/news/world-africa-40701128 (accessed 27 September 2017).
68. Reuters, 'Red Cross says six volunteers killed in Central African Republic', 9 August 2017, www.reuters.com/article/us-centralafrica-violence/red-cross-says-six-volunteers-killed-in-central-african-republic-idUSKBN1AP195 (accessed 27 September 2017).

Chapter 5   Democratic Republic of the Congo

1. BBC, 'DR Congo senate amends census law to allow 2016 election', 23 January 2015, www.bbc.co.uk/news/world-africa-30947880 (accessed 17 March 2016).
2. PGI Intelligence, 'Congo, DRC: Decentralisation to increase transport and taxation costs in Katanga', https://pgi-intelligence.com/news/getNewsItem/Congo-DRC-Decentralisation-to-increase-transport-and-taxation-costs-in-Katanga/562 (accessed 17 March 2016).

3. Reuters, 'Bishops urge Congolese to reject third term for Kabila', www. reuters.com/article/congodemocratic-politics-idUSL8N13L2C320151126 (accessed 26 November 2015).

4. UN News Centre, 'Ban arrives in Burundi in support of UN efforts to resolve political crisis', UN News Centre, www.un.org/apps/news/story.asp?news ID=53287 (accessed 23 February 2016).

5. *Eye on Africa*, France24 English, Sky Channel 513, 23 February 2016.

6. Michael Amoah, *Reconstructing the Nation in Africa* (London: I.B.Tauris, 2007), 114, 116–19.

7. *Across Africa*, France24 English, Sky Channel 513, 19 June 2016.

8. Al Jazeera, 'Deadly clashes hit DR Congo camp for M23 Fighters', www. aljazeera.com/news/2016/06/deadly-clashes-hit-dr-congo-camp-m23-fighters-160617083231682.html (accessed 18 June 2016).

9. AU-PSC, 'Inaugural Meeting of the Support Group for the Facilitation of the National Dialogue in the Democratic Republic of Congo', AU-PSC, 4 July 2016, www.peaceau.org/en/article/inaugural-meeting-of-the-support-group-for-the-facilitation-of-the-national-dialogue-in-the-democratic-republic-of-congo (accessed 10 September 2016).

10. *Eye on Africa*, France24 English, 27 July 2016.

11. VOA, 'DRC Political Dialogue Stalls Over Opposition Demands', 3 September 2016, www.voanews.com/a/congo-national-dialogue/3492400.html (accessed 10 September 2016).

12. *Eye on Africa*, France24 English, 8 September 2016.

13. Ibid., France24 English, 20 September 2016.

14. *Newshour*, Al Jazeera English, Sky Channel 514, 29 September 2016.

15. Reuters, 'Congo's top court approves postponement of presidential election', 18 October 2016, http://af.reuters.com/article/topNews/idAFKCN12I0HC (accessed 19 October 2016).

16. *Newshour*, Al Jazeera English, 19 October 2016.

17. Al Jazeera, 'DR Congo: Opposition figure Samy badibanga named PM', 19 October 2016, www.aljazeera.com/news/2016/11/dr-congo-opposition-figure-samy-badibanga-named-pm-161117175108538.html (accessed 19 November 2016).

18. Comparative Constitutions Project, 'Congo (Democratic Republic of the)'s Constitution of 2005 with Amendments through 2011', www.constitute project.org (accessed 19 October 2016), 19.

19. Ibid., 20.

20. *Eye on Africa*, France24 English, 22 December 2016.

21. *Newshour*, Al Jazeera English, 22 December 2016.

22. Comparative Constitutions Project, 'Congo (Democratic Republic of the)'s Constitution of 2005 with Amendments through 2011', 17.

23. Al Jazeera, 'Kabila names Bruno Tshibala new DRC prime minister', 7 April 2017, www.aljazeera.com/news/2017/04/kabila-names-bruno-tshibala-drc-prime-minister-170407201215507.html (accessed 6 June 2017).

24. *The Telegraph*, 'US warns against travel to the Democratic Republic of Congo after UN investigators murdered', 30 March 2017, www.telegraph.co.uk/news/2017/03/29/us-warns-against-travel-democratic-republic-congo-un-investigators/ (accessed 6 June 2017).

25. *Eye on Africa*, France24 English, Sky Channel 513, 29 May 2017.

26. Reuters, 'Congo's election head says presidential vote unlikely this year', 9 July 2017, www.reuters.com/article/us-congo-politics-idUSKBN19U0ZA (accessed 17 July 2017).

27. ENCA, 'No DRC presidential poll before 2019: electoral commission', 12 October 2017, www.enca.com/africa/no-drc-presidential-poll-before-2019-electoral-commission (accessed 11 December 2017).

28. Human Rights Watch, 'Special Mission', 4 December 2017, www.hrw.org/report/2017/12/04/special-mission/recruitment-m23-rebels-suppress-protests-democratic-republic-congo (accessed 11 December 2017).

29. AU-PSC, 'Congo hands over 500 strong contingent to the African Union-led Regional Task Force for the elimination of Lord's Resistance Army', www.peaceau.org/en/article/democratic-republic-of-congo-hands-over-500-strong-contingent-to-the-african-union-led-regional-task-force-for-the-elimination-of-the-lord-s-resistance-army (accessed 17 March 2016).

30. Stephanie Wolters, 'Tanzanian-led anti rebel force in DRC given teeth', *Mail & Guardian*, 15 February 2013, http://mg.co.za/article/2013-02-15-00-tanzanian-led-anti-rebel-force-in-drc-given-teeth (accessed 17 March 2016).

31. *Newshour*, Al Jazeera English, Sky Channel 514, 17 June 2016.

32. ICC, 'ICC Trial Chamber III sentences Jean-Pierre Bemba Gombo to 18 years' imprisonment for war crimes and crimes against humanity committed in the Central African Republic in 200202003', ICC, www.icc-cpi.int//Pages/item.aspx?name=PR1223 (accessed 23 June 2016).

33. *Newshour*, Al Jazeera English, 21 June 2016.

34. Ibid., 31 March 2016.

35. ICC, 'ICC Appeals Chamber Acquits Mr Bemba from charges of war crimes and crimes against humanity', https://www.icc-cpi.int/Pages/item.aspx?name = PR1390 (accessed 26 July 2018).

36. Al Jazeera, 'Jean-Pierre Bamba named as DRC presidential candidate', 14 July 2018, https://www.aljazeera.com/news/2018/07/jean-pierre-bemba-named-drc-presidential-candidate-180714141750891.html (accessed 26 July 2018).

37. The Independent, 'CR Congo's tainted ex-police chief made national hero', 6 June 2017, www.independent.co.ug/dr-congos-tainted-ex-police-chief-numbi-made-national-hero/ (accessed 9 June 2017).

38. World Bank Group, *Global Economic Prospects, June 2018: The Turning of the Tide?* (Washington, DC: World Bank Group, 2018).

39. *Global Peace Index 2017*, 128.

40. *Global Peace Index 2018*, 93.

41. PGI Intelligence, 'Congo, DRC: Decentralisation to increase transport and taxation costs in Katanga'.

42. France24, 'People of Kinshasa welcome bask their postmen', 8 December 2016, www.france24.com/en/20161208-people-kinshasa-welcome-back-postmen (accessed 9 December 2016).

43. *Eye on Africa*, France24 English, 8 December 2016.

44. Data quoted in the 2011 Ibrahim Index are from 2010. The dataset used to calculate the 2011 Ibrahim Index contains data from 2000 to 2010.

45. Mo Ibrahim Foundation, '2015 Ibrahim Index of African Governance', www.moibrahimfoundation.org/iiag/launch/ (accessed 9 March 2015).

46. Mo Ibrahim Foundation, '2016 Ibrahim Index of African Governance: Index Report', http://mo.ibrahim.foundation/iiag/downloads/ (accessed 24 November 2016).

47. Data from this index ran from 2007 to 2016 – a ten-year period.

48. Mo Ibrahim Foundation, '2017 Ibrahim Index of African Governance: Index Report', http://mo.ibrahim.foundation/iiag/2017-key-findings/ (accessed 20 December 2017).

49. Mo Ibrahim Foundation, '2018 Ibrahim Index of African Governance: Index Report', http://mo.ibrahim.foundation/iiag/ (accessed 29 October 2018).

50. Institute for Economics and Peace, 'Global Peace Index', www.visionofhumanity.org/#/page/indexes/global-peace-index/2015 (accessed 9 March 2015).

51. Institute for Economics and Peace, 'Global Peace Index', www.visionofhumanity.org/ (accessed 8 December 2016).

52. *Global Peace Index 2016*, 30.

53. *Global Peace Index 2017*, 19.

54. Institute for Economics and Peace, 'Positive Peace Report 2017: Tracking Peace Transitions Through a Systems Thinking Approach', October 2017, http://visionofhumanity.org/reports/ (accessed 23 December 2017).

55. *Global Peace Index 2018*.

56. UNDP, '2015 Human Development Report', UNDP, http://hdr.undp.org/en/2015-report/download (accessed 9 March 2016).

57. UNDP, '2016 Human Development Report', UNDP, http://hdr.undp.org/en/2016-report (accessed 22 December 2017).

58. UNDP, 'Human Development Indices and Indicators: 2018 Statistical Update', http://hdr.undp.org/en/2018-update (accessed 20 October 2018).

59. Transparency International, 'Corruption Perceptions Index 2015', www.transparency.org/ (accessed 9 March 2016).

60. Transparency International, 'Corruption Perceptions Index 2016', www.transparency.org/news/feature/corruption_perceptions_index_2016 (accessed 23 December 2017).

61. Transparency International, 'Corruption Perceptions Index 2017', Transparency International, https://www.transparency.org/news/feature/corruption_perceptions_index_2017 (accessed 24 July 2018).

62. Transparency International, 'CPI Results Brochure 2017', https://www. transparency.org/news/feature/corruption_perceptions_index_2017 (accessed 24 July 2018).

63. Verisk Maplecroft, 'Political Risk Index 2016', www.maplecroft.com/ accounts/dashboard/ (accessed 9 March 2016).

64. Institute for Economics and Peace, 'Global Terrorism Index 2015', http:// visionofhumanity.org/reports/ (accessed 23 December 2017).

65. *Global Terrorism Index 2016*.

66. *Global Terrorism Index 2017*.

67. Ibid., 16.

68. *Global Terrorism Index 2017*, 46.

69. *Eye on Africa*, France24 English, 8 June 2016.

70. *Across Africa*, France24 English, 19 July 2016.

71. The Guardian, 'Thirty-six people are killed in DRC in "revenge" attack by ADF rebels', 14 August 2016, www.theguardian.com/world/2016/aug/14/ thirty-six-people-are-killed-in-drc-in-revenge-attack-by-adf-rebels (accessed 14 August 2016).

72. Al Jazeera, "Scores hacked to death" in machete attack in DRC', 14 August 2016, www.aljazeera.com/news/2016/08/scores-hacked-death-machete-attack-dr-congo-160814133550565.html (accessed 14 August 2016).

73. Reuters, 'Bomb attack kills child, wounds 32 Indian peacekeepers in east Congo: UN', Reuters, 8 November 2016, www.reuters.com/article/us-congo-un-idUSKBN1330NV (accessed 8 November 2016).

74. *Eye on Africa*, France24 English, 16 February 2017.

75. UN News Centre, 'UN Security Council calls for immediate investigation into recent violence in DR Congo's Kasai region', 25 February 2017, www.un.org/ apps/news/story.asp?NewsID=56243 (accessed 7 March 2017).

76. Al Jazeera, 'DR Congo floods leave 10,000 homeless', 4 January 2017, www.aljazeera.com/news/2017/01/dr-congo-floods-170104042037452.html (accessed 5 January 2017).

77. UN News Centre, 'UN opens international probe into alleged abuses in DR Congo's Kasai provinces', UN News Centre, 23 June 2017, www.un.org/apps/ news/story.asp?NewsID=57046#.WU1MJGetM98 (accessed 23 June 2017).

78. Human Rights Watch, 'DR Congo: UN Experts to investigate Kasai Region Violence', 23 June 2017, www.hrw.org/news/2017/06/23/dr-congo-un-experts-investigate-kasai-region-violence (accessed 23 June 2017).

79. The Independent, 'Congo: 250 people killed in ethnic based massacres in the DRC, says UN', *The Independent*, 4 August 2017, www.independent. co.uk/news/world/africa/congo-massacres-ethnic-conflict-250-people-killed-m-united-nations-crimes-humanity-civil-war-a7876266.html (accessed 29 September 2017).

80. Africa News, 'U.S. security alert for DRC city as govt, rebels clash in South Kivu', 29 September 2017, www.africanews.com/2017/09/29/us-security-

alert-for-drc-city-as-govt-rebels-clash-in-south-kivu/ (accessed 9 October 2017).

81. Reuters, 'UPDATE2: Militants attack Congo bases in northeast, killing U.N. peacekeeper', 9 October 2017, http://af.reuters.com/article/commodities News/idAFL8N1MK1VU (accessed 9 October 2017).

82. Monusco, 'North Kivu – Attacks on MONUSCO troops at Semuliki, at least 14 peacekeepers and 5 FARDC soldiers killed', 8 December 2017, https:// monusco.unmissions.org/en/north-kivu-%E2%80%93-attack-monusco-troops-semuliki-least-14-peacekeepers-and-5-fardc-soldiers-killed (accessed 11 December 2017).

83. News & Magazines, France24 English, Sky Channel 513, 8 December 2017.

Chapter 6   Libya

1. UNSC, Resolution 1973 (2011) (New York: UNSC, 2011), 1.

2. Vanguard, 'Libya: Nigeria votes in favour of no-fly resolution', www.vanguardngr.com/2011/03/libya-nigeria-votes-in-favour-of-no-fly-resolution/ (accessed 10 October 2011).

3. UNSC, Resolution 1973 (2011), 2.

4. Ibid., 3.

5. YALIBNAN, 'Syria Voted against Libya no fly zone', http://yalibnan.com/2011/03/12/20757/ (accessed 4 February 2011).

6. New Zimbabwe, 'Libya: Mugabe slams "naïve" Nigeria, South Africa and Gabon', www.newzimbabwe.com/news-5166-Libya+Mugabe+slams+Africas+naive+UN+vote/news.aspx (accessed 10 October 2011).

7. Simon Rogers, 'Nato operations in Libya: data journalism breaks down which country does what', Guardian, 31 October 2011, www.theguardian.com/news/datablog/2011/may/22/nato-libya-data-journalism-operations-country (accessed 5 February 2016).

8. BBC, 'Divide Nigeria into two, says Muammar Gaddafi', http://news.bbc.co.uk/1/hi/8570350.stm (accessed 4 February 2016).

9. The Citizen, 'Mugabe blasts SA and Nigeria at AU Summit', http://citizen.co.za/403464/mugabe-blasts-sa-and-nigeria-at-au-summit/ (accessed 12 December 2015).

10. The White House, 'Statement by President Donald J Trump on the Apprehension of Mustafa al-Imam for His Alleged Role in the September 11, 2012 Attacks in Benghazi, Libya, Resulting in the deaths of Four Americans', 30 October, 2017, www.whitehouse.gov/briefings-statements/statement-president-donald-j-trump-apprehension-mustafa-al-imam-alleged-role-september-11-2012-attacks-benghazi-libya-resulting-deaths-four-americans/ (accessed 17 December 2017).

11. Al Jazeera English, 'Libya Police Chief Assassinated', Al Jazeera English, www.aljazeera.com/news/middleeast/2014/08/libyan-police-chief-assassinated-2014812153923868906.html (accessed 6 February 2014).

12. Alastair Beach and Hassan Morajea, 'Egypt and UAE "launched air strikes against Libyan Islamists"', *Telegraph*, 25 August 2014, www.telegraph.co.uk/news/worldnews/africaandindianocean/libya/11055436/Egypt-and-UAE-launched-air-strikes-against-Libyan-Islamists.html (accessed 6 February 2016).

13. Al Jazeera, 'African leaders urge West to act on Libya', www.aljazeera.com/news/middleeast/2014/12/african-leaders-urge-west-act-libya-20141217130 6708936.html (accessed 6 February 2016).

14. Jared Malsin and Chris Stephen, 'Egypt air strikes in Libya kill dozens of Isis militants', *Guardian*, 17 February 2015, www.theguardian.com/world/2015/feb/16/egypt-air-strikes-target-isis-weapons-stockpiles-libya (accessed 6 February 2016).

15. BBC, 'Mediterranean migrants: Deadly "capsize" captain in court', www.bbc.co.uk/news/world-europe-32448591 (accessed 6 February 2015).

16. *News & Magazines*, France24 English, Sky Channel 513, 24 April, 2015.

17. RT, 'At least 65 killed in bomb attack on Libya police training centre', www.rt.com/news/328154-libya-police-bomb-killed/ (accessed 6 February 2016).

18. *Eye on Africa*, France24 English, Sky Channel 513, 27 January 2016; Georja Calvin-Smith presenting.

19. *Newshour*, Al Jazeera English, Sky Channel 514, 7 February 2016.

20. France24, 'Deadly air strike hits hospital in east Libya: medic', www.france24.com/en/20160207-deadly-air-strike-hits-hospital-east-libya-medic (accessed 7 February 2016).

21. *Newshour*, Al Jazeera English, 14 February 2016.

22. Reuters, 'UPDATE 2: Two car bombs explode in Tripoli, no casualties', 8 September 2016, http://af.reuters.com/article/libyaNews/idAFL8N1BK1OG (accessed 10 September 2016).

23. Libyan Express, 'Death toll of Benghazi car bombing hits 7', 21 November 2016, www.libyanexpress.com/death-toll-of-benghazi-car-bombing-hits-7/ (accessed 24 November 2016).

24. Reuters, 'Blast in Libya's Benghazi kills three children: hospital official', 21 November 2016, www.reuters.com/article/us-libya-security-benghazi-idUSKBN13G1BZ (accessed 24 November 2016).

25. *Newshour*, Al Jazeera English, 24 February 2016.

26. *News & Magazines*, France24 English, 24 February 2016.

27. UN, *Charter of the United Nations* (San Francisco: UN, 1945), 11–12.

28. Ibid., 12.

29. *Newshour*, Al Jazeera English, 2 March 2016.

30. Ibid., 31 March 2016.

31. Al Jazeera, 'Libya's UN-backed government sails into Tripoli', www.aljazeera.com/news/2016/03/libya-backed-unity-government-arrives-tripoli-16033012 5804929.html (accessed 31 March 2016).

32. Reuters, 'Libyan government of national accord seeks arms', http://uk.reuters.com/article/libya-security-talks-arms-idUKZ8N156281 (accessed 18 May 2016).

33. *Newshour*, Al Jazeera English, 22 June 2016.
34. *News & Magazines*, France24 English, 16 August 2016.
35. Karim El-Bar, 'REVEALED: Leaked tapes expose Western support for renegade Libyan general', Middle East Eye, www.middleeasteye.net/news/revealed-leaked-tapes-expose-western-support-renegade-libyan-general-185825787 (accessed 9 July 2016).
36. Karim El-Bar, 'UK troops "operating from French-led Libyan base aiding renegade general"', Middle East Eye, www.middleeasteye.net/news/french-led-secret-operations-room-backing-renegade-general-libya-81826394 (accessed 9 July 2016).
37. *Newshour*, Al Jazeera English, 8 July 2016.
38. *News & Magazines*, France24 English, Sky Channel 513, 20 July 2016.
39. *Newshour*, Al Jazeera English, 21 July 2016.
40. *Newshour*, Al Jazeera English, 24 July 2016.
41. *Inside Story*, Al Jazeera English, 23 July 2016.
42. The Guardian, 'UAE and Egypt behind bombing raids against Libyan militias, says US officials', *Guardian*, 26 August 2014, www.theguardian.com/world/2014/aug/26/united-arab-emirates-bombing-raids-libyan-militias (accessed 2 August 2016).
43. The Guardian, 'Egyptian air strikes in Libya kill dozens of Isis militants', *Guardian*, 17 February 2015, www.theguardian.com/world/2015/feb/16/egypt-air-strikes-target-isis-weapons-stockpiles-libya (accessed 2 August 2016).
44. The Guardian, 'Egypt hits Libyan terror camps again after attackers kill 29 Copts', 27 May 2017, www.theguardian.com/world/2017/may/27/egypt-hits-libyan-terror-camps-again-after-attack-kills-29-copts (accessed 6 June 2017).
45. *Newshour*, Al Jazeera English, 2 August 2016.
46. *Eye on Africa*, France24 English, 22 August 2016.
47. *News & Magazines*, France24 English, 28 August 2016.
48. France24, 'Libyan forces launch "final battle" to oust IS group from Sirte', 28 August 2016, www.france24.com/en/20160828-libyan-forces-final-battle-islamic-state-group-sirte (accessed 29 August 2016).
49. Al Jazeera, 'Libya: Government forces block ISIL at Sirte coastline', 6 September 2016, http://video.aljazeera.com/channels/eng/videos/libya%3A-government-forces-block-isil-at-sirte-coastline/5113689037001 (accessed 10 September 2016).
50. Al Jazeera, 'Rival group seizes UN-backed government offices', 16 October 2016, www.aljazeera.com/news/2016/10/libya-rival-group-seizes-backed-government-offices-161015131821294.html (accessed 1 November 2016).
51. APS (Algeria Press Service), 'Libya's neighbouring countries meeting in Niamey: Deepening consultation, supporting political process', 17 October 2016, www.aps.dz/en/world/14711-libya-s-neighbouring-countries-meeting-in-niamey-deepening-consultation,-supporting-political-process (accessed 24 November 2016).

52. Al Jazeera, 'Libyan forces claim control of ISIL stronghold of Sirte', Al Jazeera, 6 December 2016, www.aljazeera.com/news/2016/12/libyan-forces-claim-control-isil-stronghold-sirte-161205140941343.html (accessed 26 December 2016).

53. World Bank Group, *Global Economic Prospects, June 2018: The Turning of the Tide?* (Washington, DC: World Bank Group, 2018).

54. Institute for Economics and Peace, 'Global Peace Index 2017', www.visionofhumanity.org/ (accessed 23 December 2017).

55. *Global Peace Index 2018*, 93.

56. Data quoted in the 2011 Ibrahim Index are from 2010. The dataset used to calculate the 2011 Ibrahim Index contains data from 2000 to 2010.

57. Mo Ibrahim Foundation, '2015 Ibrahim Index of African Governance', www.moibrahimfoundation.org/iiag/launch/ (accessed 9 March 2015).

58. Mo Ibrahim Foundation, '2016 Ibrahim Index of African Governance: Index Report', http://mo.ibrahim.foundation/iiag/downloads/ (accessed 24 November 2016).

59. Data from this index ran from 2007 to 2016 – a ten-year period.

60. Mo Ibrahim Foundation, '2017 Ibrahim Index of African Governance: Index Report', http://mo.ibrahim.foundation/iiag/2017-key-findings/ (accessed 20 December 2017).

61. Mo Ibrahim Foundation, '2018 Ibrahim Index of African Governance: Index Report', http://mo.ibrahim.foundation/iiag/ (accessed 29 October 2018).

62. Institute for Economics and Peace, 'Global Peace Index', www.visionofhumanity.org/#/page/indexes/global-peace-index/2015 (accessed 9 March 2015).

63. Institute for Economics and Peace, 'Global Peace Index', www.visionofhumanity.org/ (accessed 8 December 2016).

64. *Global Peace Index 2016*, 9, 21, 30.

65. Institute for Economics and Peace, 'Global Peace Index 2017', http://visionofhumanity.org/reports/ (accessed 23 December 2017).

66. *Global Peace Index 2017*, 20.

67. Institute for Economics and Peace, 'Positive Peace Report 2017: Tracking Peace Transitions Through a Systems Thinking Approach', October 2017, http://visionofhumanity.org/reports/ (accessed 23 December 2017).

68. *Global Peace Index 2018*.

69. *Global Peace Index 2018*, 68.

70. Institute for Economics and Peace, *Global Peace Index 2015* (New York: IEP, 2015), 19.

71. UNDP, '2015 Human Development Report', UNDP, http://hdr.undp.org/en/2015-report/download (accessed 9 March 2016).

72. UNDP, '2016 Human Development Report', UNDP, http://hdr.undp.org/en/2016-report (accessed 22 December 2017).

73. UNDP, 'Human Development Indices and Indicators: 2018 Statistical Update', http://hdr.undp.org/en/2018-update (accessed 20 October 2018).

74. Transparency International, 'Corruption Perceptions Index 2015', www.transparency.org/ (accessed 9 March 2016).

75. Transparency International, 'Corruption Perceptions Index 2016', www.transparency.org/news/feature/corruption_perceptions_index_2016 (accessed 23 December 2017).

76. Transparency International, 'Corruption Perceptions Index 2017', Transparency International, https://www.transparency.org/news/feature/corruption_perceptions_index_2017 (accessed 24 July 2018).

77. Transparency International, 'CPI Results Brochure 2017', https://www.transparency.org/news/feature/corruption_perceptions_index_2017 (accessed 24 July 2018).

78. Reuters, 'Libyan commander's seizure of oil ports risks new conflict', 12 September 2016, http://uk.reuters.com/article/libya-security-idUKL8N1BO33Y (accessed 13 September 2016).

79. Institute for Economics and Peace, *Global Peace Index 2015*, 19.

80. Verisk Maplecroft, 'Political Risk Index 2016', www.maplecroft.com/accounts/dashboard/ (accessed 9 March 2016).

81. Ibid.

82. Institute for Economics and Peace, 'Global Terrorism Index 2015', http://visionofhumanity.org/reports/ (accessed 23 December 2017).

83. *Global Terrorism Index 2016*.

84. Ibid., 85.

85. Ibid.

86. *Global Terrorism Index 2017*.

87. Ibid., 45.

88. *Newshour*, Al Jazeera English, 9 June 2016.

89. Joey Ayoub, 'How the EU is responsible for slavery in Libya', Al Jazeera, 29 November 2017, www.aljazeera.com/indepth/opinion/slavery-walls-fortress-europe-171128094218944.html (accessed 16 December 2017).

90. BBC, 'Libya Malta hijack: Hijackers arrested as drama ends peacefully', 23 December 2016, www.bbc.co.uk/news/world-europe-38416112 (accessed 26 December 2016).

91. Reuters. 'Deputy leader of Libya's U.N.-backed government resigns', 2 January 2017, www.reuters.com/article/us-libya-security-politics-idUSKBN14M13A?il=0 (accessed 5 January 2017).

92. Al Jazeera, 'Fayez al-Sarraj not hurt after convoy comes under fire', Al Jazeera, 20 February 2017, www.aljazeera.com/news/2017/02/fayez-al-sarraj-hurt-convoy-fire-170220130904166.html (accessed 7 March 2017).

93. *Newshour*, Al Jazeera English Television, Sky Channel 514, 4 March 2017.

94. Al Jazeera, 'Libya: 141 killed in Brak al-Shat airbase attack', 20 May 2017, www.aljazeera.com/news/2017/05/libya-141-people-killed-brak-al-shat-airbase-attack-170520082052419.html (accessed 6 June 2017).

95. Al Jazeera, 'Libya's Ansar al-Sharia announces dissolution', 28 May 2017, www.aljazeera.com/news/2017/05/libya-ansar-al-sharia-announces-dissolution-170528045219409.html (accessed 6 June 2017).

96. Reuters, 'Hundreds of Fighters from Chad, Darfur feeding off Libya's turmoil – report', 27 June 2017, http://uk.reuters.com/article/uk-libya-security-report-idUKKBN19I2H9 (accessed 29 June 2017).

97. Jérôme Tubiana and Claudio Gramizzi, *Tubu Trouble: State and Statelessness in the Chad–Libya–Sudan Triangle* (Geneva: Graduate Institute of International and Development Studies, Small Arms Survey, June 2017), 153.

98. Reuters, 'Libya's eastern commander declares victory in battle for Benghazi', 5 July 2017, www.reuters.com/article/us-libya-security-benghazi-idUSKBN19Q2SK (accessed 7 July 2017).

99. Al Jazeera, 'Fayez al-Sarraj meets Khalifa Haftar in UAE for talks', 2 May 2017, www.aljazeera.com/news/2017/05/fayez-al-sarraj-meets-khalifa-haftar-uae-talks-170502140623464.html (accessed 9 October 2017).

100. The Guardian, 'Libyan rival leaders agree to ceasefire after Macron-hosted talks', 25 July 2017, www.theguardian.com/world/2017/jul/25/france-raises-hopes-of-deal-between-libyan-rival-factions (accessed 9 October 2017).

101. Reuters, 'Libyan military commander Haftar visiting Russia: RIA', 12 August 2017, www.reuters.com/article/us-libya-security-russia/libyan-military-commander-haftar-visiting-russia-ria-idUSKBN1AS0LD (accessed 9 October 2017).

102. *Newshour*, Al Jazeera English Television, Sky Channel 514, 17 December 2017.

103. African Union. *Communiqué of the Meeting of the AU High Level Committee on Libya* (Addis Ababa: African Union, 2016).

104. Reliefweb, 'Joint Communiqué of the Quartet meeting on Libya', 18 March 2017, https://reliefweb.int/report/libya/joint-communique-quartet-meeting-libya (accessed 16 December 2017).

105. Reliefweb, 'Joint Communiqué of the Quartet meeting on Libya', 21 September 2017, https://reliefweb.int/report/libya/joint-communique-quartet-meeting-libya-21-september-2017 (accessed 16 December 2017).

106. AU-PSC, '719th PSC meeting on the situation in Libya and the outcomes of the 4th meeting of the AU High Level committee on Libya, held on 9 September 2017', 22 September 2017, www.peaceau.org/en/article/719th-psc-meeting-on-the-situation-in-libya-and-the-outcomes-of-the-4th-meeting-of-the-au-high-level-committee-on-libya-held-on-9-september-2017 (accessed 16 December 2017).

107. Libya Herald, 'ICC tells UN Hafter should hand over Warfali out of respect for justice', 8 November 2017, www.libyaherald.com/2017/11/08/icc-tells-un-hafter-should-hand-over-warfali-out-of-respect-for-justice/ (accessed 17 December 2017).

108. Libya Herald, 'Civil rights lawyers to press ICC to probe Khalifa Hafter over war crimes', 13 November 2017, www.libyaherald.com/2017/11/13/civil-rights-lawyers-to-press-icc-to-charge-khalifa-hafter-with-war-crimes/ (accessed 17 December 2017)

109. The Guardian, 'Libyan factions agree to hold elections on 10 December', 29 May 2018, https://www.theguardian.com/world/2018/may/29/macron-hosts-libyan-factions-in-paris-in-push-to-secure-elections (accessed 26 July 2018).

Chapter 7   Mali

1. Reuters, 'Mali gold reserves rise in 2011 alongside price', Reuters, www.sabc.co.za/news/a/65656d0049a2edb0a589ef9f13675c4c/Mali-gold-reserves-rise-in-2011-alongside-price-20120101 (accessed 22 February 2016).
2. Adama Diarra and John Irish, 'Islamist militants kill 5 in restaurant attack in Mali capital', Reuters, 7 March 2015, www.reuters.com/article/us-mali-attacks-idUSKBN0M305G20150307 (accessed 8 February 2016).
3. Newshour, Al Jazeera English, Sky Channel 514, 17 July 2014; News & Magazines, France24 English, Sky Channel 513, 17 July 2014.
4. Newshour, Al Jazeera English, 3 October 2014.
5. Adama Diarra and John Irish, 'Islamist militants kill 5 in restaurant attack in Mali capital'.
6. BBC, 'Rocket attack hits Kidal UN base in northern Mali', www.bbc.co.uk/news/world-africa-31788395 (accessed 8 February 2016).
7. DW, 'Separatist rebels kill nine soldiers in Mali days ahead of peace deal', www.dw.com/en/separatist-rebels-kill-nine-soldiers-in-mali-days-ahead-of-peace-deal/a-18445002 (accessed 8 February 2016).
8. Yahoo News, '11 soldiers killed in attack on Mali camp: government', http://news.yahoo.com/10-soldiers-killed-attack-mali-camp-military-112548040.html (accessed 8 February 2016).
9. Al Jazeera, 'UN employee among those killed in Mali hotel attack', www.aljazeera.com/news/2015/08/gunmen-attack-hotel-mali-hostages-150807161908433.html (accessed 8 February 2015).
10. BBC, 'Mali hotel siege: Several killed in Sevare, four UN workers saved', BBC, www.bbc.co.uk/news/world-africa-33833363 (accessed 8 February 2016).
11. Adama Diarra, 'UPDATE 3 – Gunmen kill 10 in attack on village in Mali – army spokesman', Reuters, 9 August 2015, http://af.reuters.com/article/mali News/idAFL5N10K0CU20150809?sp=true (accessed 8 February 2016).
12. Jason Hanna, Ed Payne and Steve Almasy, 'Deadly Mali hotel attack: "They were shooting at anything that moved"', CNN, 20 November 2015, http://edition.cnn.com/2015/11/20/africa/mali-shooting/ (accessed 8 February 2016).
13. BBC, 'Mali attack: Bamako's Radisson Blu hotel re-opens', www.bbc.co.uk/news/world-africa-35101130 (accessed 8 February 2015).
14. Eye on Africa, France24 English, 5 February 2016.
15. Reuters, 'Mali Islamist group Ansar Dine claims attack on UN base', http://uk.reuters.com/places/mali (accessed 22 February 2016).
16. Reuters, 'Gunmen attack EU military mission HQ in Mali: one attacker killed', www.reuters.com/article/us-mali-attack-idUSKCN0WN234 (accessed 22 March 2016).

17. *Eye on Africa*, France24 English, 13 April 2016.
18. BBC, 'Mali: United Nations peacekeepers killed in attack', www.bbc.co.uk/news/world-africa-36408943 (accessed 30 May 2016).
19. *News & Magazines*, France24 English, 31 May 2016.
20. Patrick Markey, 'Mali, Tuareg-led rebels agree to cease hostilities for peace talks', Reuters, www.reuters.com/article/2015/02/19/us-mali-talks-idUSKB N0LN1UJ20150219 (accessed 14 September 2015).
21. Ibid.
22. *Eye on Africa*, France24 English, 5 February 2016.
23. AFP, 'Mali peace accord signed without main rebel groups', http://news.yahoo.com/mali-peace-accord-signed-without-main-rebel-groups-180906184.html (accessed 8 February 2016).
24. *Newshour*, Al Jazeera English, Sky Channel 514, 20 June 2015; BBC, 'Mali's Tuareg rebels sign peace deal', www.bbc.co.uk/news/world-africa-33213931 (accessed 8 February 2016).
25. Reuters, 'Malian rebel alliance signs peace deal with government', www.reuters.com/article/us-mali-rebels-deal-idUSKBN0P00PI20150621 (accessed 8 February 2016).
26. *Eye on Africa*, France24 English, 31 August 2015.
27. Reliefweb, 'Malian armed groups sign peace deal', http://reliefweb.int/report/mali/mali-armed-groups-sign-peace-deal (accessed 8 February 2016).
28. Reuters, 'Tuareg separatists seize north Mali town in battle', 12 July 2017, https://uk.reuters.com/article/uk-mali-security-idUKKBN19X2CG (accessed 17 July 2017).
29. *Eye on Africa*, France24 English, 1 March 2017.
30. World Bank Group, *Global Economic Prospects, June 2018: The Turning of the Tide?* (Washington, DC: World Bank Group, 2018).
31. Institute for Economics and Peace, 'Global Peace Index 2017', www.visionofhumanity.org/ (accessed 23 December 2017), 128.
32. *Global Peace Index 2018*, 93.
33. Data quoted in the 2011 Ibrahim Index are from 2010. The dataset used to calculate the 2011 Ibrahim Index contains data from 2000 to 2010.
34. Mo Ibrahim Foundation, '2015 Ibrahim Index of African Governance', www.moibrahimfoundation.org/iiag/launch/ (accessed 9 March 2015).
35. Mo Ibrahim Foundation, '2016 Ibrahim Index of African Governance: Index Report', http://mo.ibrahim.foundation/iiag/downloads/ (accessed 24 November 2016).
36. Data from this index ran from 2007 to 2016 – a ten-year period.
37. Mo Ibrahim Foundation, '2017 Ibrahim Index of African Governance: Index Report', http://mo.ibrahim.foundation/iiag/2017-key-findings/ (accessed 20 December 2017).
38. Mo Ibrahim Foundation, '2018 Ibrahim Index of African Governance: Index Report', http://mo.ibrahim.foundation/iiag/ (accessed 29 October 2018).

39. Institute for Economics and Peace, 'Global Peace Index', www.visionofhumanity. org/#/page/indexes/global-peace-index/2015 (accessed 9 March 2015).
40. Institute for Economics and Peace, 'Global Peace Index', www.visionofhumanity. org/ (accessed 8 December 2016).
41. Institute for Economics and Peace, 'Global Peace Index 2017', www.vision ofhumanity.org/ (accessed 23 December 2017).
42. Ibid., 14.
43. Institute for Economics and Peace, 'Positive Peace Report 2017: Tracking Peace Transitions Through a Systems Thinking Approach', October 2017, http://visionofhumanity.org/reports/ (accessed 23 December 2017).
44. *Global Peace Index 2018*.
45. UNDP, '2015 Human Development Report', UNDP, http://hdr.undp.org/en/ 2015-report/download (accessed 9 March 2016).
46. UNDP, '2016 Human Development Report', http://hdr.undp.org/en/2016- report (accessed 22 December 2017).
47. UNDP, 'Human Development Indices and Indicators: 2018 Statistical Update', http://hdr.undp.org/en/2018-update (accessed 20 October 2018).
48. Transparency International, 'Corruption Perceptions Index 2015', www. transparency.org/ (accessed 9 March 2016).
49. Transparency International, 'Corruption Perceptions Index 2016', www. transparency.org/news/feature/corruption_perceptions_index_2016 (accessed 23 December 2017).
50. Transparency International, 'Corruption Perceptions Index 2017', Transparency International, https://www.transparency.org/news/feature/corruption_ perceptions_index_2017 (accessed 24 July 2018).
51. Transparency International, 'CPI Results Brochure 2017', https://www. transparency.org/news/feature/corruption_perceptions_index_2017 (accessed 24 July 2018).
52. *Across Africa*, France24 English, Sky Channel 513, 30 October 2017.
53. *Eye on Africa*, France24 English, Sky Channel 513, 4 November 2017.
54. Verisk Maplecroft, 'Political Risk Index 2016', www.maplecroft.com/ accounts/dashboard/ (accessed 9 March 2016).
55. Institute for Economics and Peace, 'Global Terrorism Index 2015', http:// visionofhumanity.org/reports/ (accessed 23 December 2017).
56. *Global Terrorism Index 2016*.
57. *Global Terrorism Index 2017*.
58. Ibid., 46.
59. Ibid., 76.
60. *Eye on Africa*, France24 English, 12 July 2016.
61. *Newshour*, Al Jazeera English, 19 July 2016.
62. Ibid., 21 July 2016
63. ICC, 'Al Mahdi Case: trial to open on 22 August 2016', www.icc-cpi.int/ Pages/item.aspx?name=pr1217 (accessed 22 August 2016).

64. *Newshour*, Al Jazeera English, 22 August 2016.
65. *News & Magazines*, France24 English, Sky Channel 513, 20 September, 2016.
66. *Eye on Africa*, France24 English, 18 October 2016.
67. Reuters, 'UPDATE 1: Mali Islamist militant leader announces unilateral ceasefire', 31 October 2016, http://af.reuters.com/article/commoditiesNews/idAFL8N1D13II?sp=true (accessed 1 November 2016).
68. Reuters, 'Mali's local elections marred by boycotts, kidnapping', 21 November 2016, http://in.reuters.com/article/mali-elections-idINKBN13G09E (accessed 24 November 2016).
69. *Eye on Africa*, France24 English, 23 December 2016.
70. BBC, 'Macron in Mali: France will be "uncompromising" in fight against Terrorism', 19 May 2017, www.bbc.co.uk/news/world-europe-39968319 (accessed 6 June 2017).
71. Reuters, 'France says soldiers killed 20 Islamists in Mali', 2 June 2017, http://af.reuters.com/article/maliNews/idAFL8N1IZ5M0 (accessed 6 June 2017).
72. Reuters, 'Al Qaeda-linked group claims deadly attack at Malsi resort', 19 June 2017, www.reuters.com/article/us-mali-security-idUSKBN1990TY (accessed 6 July 2017).
73. Reuters, 'Thousands march against referendum, extra powers for Mali president', 15 July 2017, www.reuters.com/article/us-mali-politics-idUSKBN1A00LH (accessed 17 July 2017).
74. Reuters, 'U.S. wary of French push for U.N. to back Sahel force: diplomats', 8 June 2017, www.reuters.com/article/us-africa-security-sahel-un-idUSKBN18Z2R7?il=0 (accessed 9 June 2017).
75. Al Jazeera, 'UAE, Saudi Arabia join G5 Sahel force summit in Paris', 13 December 2017, www.aljazeera.com/news/2017/12/g5-sahel-force-leaders-arrive-summit-paris-171213063153149.html (accessed 16 December 2017).
76. Al Jazeera, 'UAE, Saudi Arabia join G5 Sahel force summit in Paris'.
77. Reuters, 'Islamist militants attack African military base in Mali, at least six dead', 29 June 2018, https://uk.reuters.com/article/uk-mali-violence/islamist-militants-attack-african-military-base-in-mali-at-least-six-dead-idUKKBN1JP243 (accessed 30 July 2018).
78. *Eye on Africa*, France24 English, Sky Channel 513, 31 July 2018.
79. A Jazeera, 'Vote counting under way in Mali's tense elections', 30 July 2018, https://www.aljazeera.com/news/2018/07/vote-counting-mali-tense-elections-180730133330607.html (accessed 1 August 2018).

Chapter 8   Rwanda

1. Michael Amoah, Reconstructing the Nation in Africa (London: I.B.Tauris, 2007), p. 108.
2. Ernest Gellner, Nations and Nationalism, (Oxford: Basil Blackwell, 1983), p. 1.

3. Michael Amoah, *Reconstructing the Nation in Africa* (London: I.B.Tauris, 2007), 114, 116–19.

4. *The Observer*, 'NRM doesn't believe in term limits theatre – Museveni', www.observer.ug/news-headlines/41196-nrm-doesn-t-believe-in-term-limits-theatre-museveni (accessed 19 December 2015).

5. *Newshour*, Al Jazeera English, Sky Channel 514, 3 March 2016.

6. Amoah, *Reconstructing the Nation*, 114, 116–19.

7. Government of Burundi, *Arusha Peace and Reconciliation Agreement for Burundi* (Arusha, Tanzania: Government of Burundi 2000), 15.

8. Comparative Constitutions Project, 'Rwanda's Constitution of 2003 with Amendments through 2010', www.constituteproject.org (accessed 1 February 2015).

9. IGIHE, 'Supreme Court rules against Green Party constitutional amendment petition', 8 October 2015, http://en.igihe.com/justice/supreme-court-rules-against-green-party.html (accessed 17 December 2015).

10. Amoah, *Reconstructing the Nation*, p. 114.

11. BBC, 'Rwanda's Paul Kagame to run for third presidential term', www.bbc.co.uk/news/world-africa-35209186 (accessed 11 June 2016).

12. Government of Rwanda, *The Constitution of the Republic of Rwanda of 2003 Revised in 2015* (Kigali: Government of Rwanda, 2015), p. 154.

13. *Upfront*, Al Jazeera English, 10 June 2016.

14. *The Telegraph*, 'Rwanda ex-spy chief "murdered" in South Africa', *The Telegraph*, www.telegraph.co.uk/news/worldnews/africaandindianocean/rwanda/10546528/Rwanda-ex-spy-chief-murdered-in-South-Africa.html (accessed 11 June 2016).

15. BBC, 'Patrick Karageya: Mysterious death of a Rwandan exile', www.bbc.co.uk/news/world-africa-26752838 (accessed 11 June 2016).

16. Stephanie Wolters, 'Tanzanian-led anti rebel force in DRC given teeth', *Mail & Guardian*, 15 February 2013, http://mg.co.za/article/2013-02-15-00-tanzanian-led-anti-rebel-force-in-drc-given-teeth (accessed 17 March 2016).

17. Institute for Economics and Peace, *Global Peace Index 2014* (New York: IEP, 2014), 23.

18. *Eye on Africa*, France24 English, Sky Channel 513, 4 February 2016.

19. Jeffrey Gettleman, 'U.N. Report Accuses Rwanda of Training Rebels to Oust Burundian Leader', *New York Times*, 4 February 2016, www.nytimes.com/2016/02/05/world/africa/un-report-accuses-rwanda-of-training-rebels-to-oust-burundian-leader.html?_r=0# (accessed 12 March 2016).

   17 *Newshour*, Al Jazeera English, 5 February 2016.

20. Ibid.

21. Page 13 of the 2017 Ibrahim Index on African Governance.

22. World Bank Group, *Global Economic Prospects, June 2018: The Turning of the Tide?* (Washington, DC: World Bank Group, 2018).

23. Institute for Economics and Peace, 'Global Peace Index 2017', www.visionof humanity.org/ (accessed 23 December 2017), p. 128.

24. *Global Peace Index 2018*, p. 94.
25. Data quoted in the 2011 Ibrahim Index are from 2010. The dataset used to calculate the 2011 Ibrahim Index contains data from 2000 to 2010.
26. Mo Ibrahim Foundation, '2015 Ibrahim Index of African Governance', www.moibrahimfoundation.org/iiag/launch/ (accessed 9 March 2015).
27. Mo Ibrahim Foundation, '2016 Ibrahim Index of African Governance: Index Report', http://mo.ibrahim.foundation/iiag/downloads/ (accessed 24 November 2016).
28. Data from this index ran from 2007 to 2016 – a ten-year period.
29. Mo Ibrahim Foundation, '2017 Ibrahim Index of African Governance: Index Report', http://mo.ibrahim.foundation/iiag/2017-key-findings/ (accessed 20 December 2017).
30. Mo Ibrahim Foundation, '2018 Ibrahim Index of African Governance: Index Report', http://mo.ibrahim.foundation/iiag/ (accessed 29 October 2018).
31. Institute for Economics and Peace, 'Global Peace Index', www.visionofhumanity.org/#/page/indexes/global-peace-index/2015 (accessed 9 March 2015).
32. Institute for Economics and Peace, 'Global Peace Index 2016', www.visionofhumanity.org/ (accessed 8 December 2016).
33. Institute for Economics and Peace, 'Global Peace Index 2017', Institute for Economics and Peace, www.visionofhumanity.org/ (accessed 23 December 2017).
34. *Global Peace Index 2017*, 18.
35. Institute for Economics and Peace, 'Positive Peace Report 2017: Tracking Peace Transitions Through a Systems Thinking Approach', October 2017, http://visionofhumanity.org/reports/ (accessed 23 December 2017).
36. *Positive Peace Report 2017*, 18.
37. Ibid., 89.
38. *Global Peace Index 2018*, 8 and 18.
39. UNDP, '2015 Human Development Report', http://hdr.undp.org/en/2015-report/download (accessed 9 March 2016).
40. UNDP, '2016 Human Development Report', http://hdr.undp.org/en/2016-report (accessed 22 December 2017).
41. UNDP, 'Human Development Indices and Indicators: 2018 Statistical Update', http://hdr.undp.org/en/2018-update (accessed 20 October 2018).
42. Transparency International, 'Corruption Perceptions Index 2015', www.transparency.org/ (accessed 9 March 2016).
43. Transparency International, 'Corruption Perceptions Index 2016', www.transparency.org/news/feature/corruption_perceptions_index_2016 (accessed 23 December 2017).
44. Transparency International, 'Corruption Perceptions Index 2017', Transparency International, https://www.transparency.org/news/feature/corruption_perceptions_index_2017 (accessed 24 July 2018).
45. Transparency International, 'CPI Results Brochure 2017', https://www.transparency.org/news/feature/corruption_perceptions_index_2017 (accessed 24 July 2018).

46. Institute for Economics and Peace, *Global Peace Index 2014*, 23.
47. Institute for Economics and Peace, 'Global Terrorism Index 2015', http://visionofhumanity.org/reports/ (accessed 23 December 2017).
48. *Global Terrorism Index 2016*.
49. *Global Terrorism Index 2017*.
50. Ibid., 45.
51. Al Jazeera, 'Israeli PM Netanyahu in historic East Africa trip', www.aljazeera.com/news/2016/07/israel-pm-netanyahu-historic-east-africa-trip-16070408465 6635.html (accessed 4 July 2016).
52. *Newshour*, Al Jazeera English, 4 July 2016.
53. *Eye on Africa*, France24 English, Sky Channel 513, 7 October 2016.
54. Ibid., 29 November 2016.
55. Reuters, 'NGOs file suit alleging BNP Paribas complicity in Rwandan-genocide', 29 June 2017, http://uk.reuters.com/article/uk-rwanda-bnp-paribas-lawsuit-idUKKBN19K1IP?il=0 (accessed 29 June 2017).

Chapter 9   South Sudan

1. Michael Amoah, *Nationalism, Globalization, and Africa* (New York: Palgrave Macmillan, 2011), 47–61.
2. IGAD, 'Monitoring and Verification Mechanism', http://southsudan.igadhost.com/index.php/about-us/timeline-of-events (accessed 9 February 2016).
3. IGAD, 'Time line of major events – IGAD-led Mediation Process for South Sudan', http://southsudan.igadhost.com/index.php/about-us/timeline-of-events (accessed 9 February 2016).
4. IGAD, *Agreement on Cessation of Hostilities Between the Government of the Republic of Sudan (GRSS) and the Sudan People's Liberation Movement/Army In Opposition (SPLM/A-IO)* (Addis Ababa: IGAD 2014), 4.
5. Ibid.
6. Ibid.
7. IGAD, *Factsheet: A Summary of the Cessation of Hostilities Agreement (COHA), Signed 23 January 2014* (Addis Ababa: IGAD, 2014), 1.
8. Reuters, 'Fighting erupts in two South Sudan states after latest truce', www.reuters.com/article/us-southsudan-unrest-idUSKBN0LE2FQ20150210 (accessed 9 February 2016).
9. Ibid.
10. IGAD, *Factsheet: A Summary of the Cessation of Hostilities Agreement (COHA), Signed 23 January 2014*, 2.
11. Sudan Tribune, 'UN calls on South Sudan to respect status agreement', www.sudantribune.com/spip.php?article51036 (accessed 9 February 2016).
12. IGAD, *Proposed Compromise Agreement on the Resolution of the Conflict in the Republic of South Sudan* (Addis Ababa: IGAD, 2015), 8.

13. Yahoo News, 'South Sudan rebels split, reject peace efforts', http://news.yahoo.com/south-sudan-rebels-split-reject-peace-efforts-145538680.html (accessed 19 March 2016).

14. Tesfa-Alem Tekle, 'South Sudan's Machar heads to Uganda to ask for help from Museveni', *Sudan Tribune*, 25 January 2016, Online edition www.sudantribune.com/spip.php?article57795 (accessed 9 February 2016).

15. Sudan Tribune, 'President Kiir's 28 states are obstacle to peace in South Sudan: Troika', www.sudantribune.com/spip.php?article57794 (accessed 9 February 2016).

16. Tesfa-Alem Tekle, 'South Sudan's Machar heads to Uganda to ask for help from Museveni'.

17. Foreign and Commonwealth Office, 'South Sudan: Troika Statement', www.gov.uk/government/news/south-sudan-troika-statement (accessed 9 February 2016).

18. BBC, 'Sudan's Bashir orders border with South Sudan to reopen', www.bbc.co.uk/news/world-africa-35425558 (accessed 9 February 2016).

19. Ibid.

20. Peter Clottey, 'South Sudan's Machar Tells UN Chief He'll Return to Juba in March', *VOA News*, 25 February 2016. www.voanews.com/content/south-sudan-machar-return-juba-march/3208351.html (accessed 17 March 2016).

21. IGAD, *Proposed Compromise Agreement*, 23.

22. Claver Ndushabandi, 'Machar Rebels Advancing on SPLA Base', *Chimp Reports*, 26 March 2016, www.chimpreports.com/machar-rebels-advancing-on-spla-base/ (accessed 29 March 2016).

23. Mail & Guardian, 'South Sudan rebels arrive in Juba to clear way for their chief Machar to share power', *Mail & Guardian*, http://mgafrica.com/article/2016-03-29-ssudan-rebels-arrive-in-juba-to-clear-way-for-their-leader-machar-to-share-power (accessed 29 March 2016).

24. UN News Centre, 'Ban arrives in Burundi in support of UN efforts to resolve political crisis', www.un.org/apps/news/story.asp?NewsID=53287 (accessed 23 February 2016).

25. The Daily Beast, 'Exclusive: UN Camp in South Sudan burned to the ground', www.thedailybeast.com/articles/2016/02/18/nowhere-to-run-to-in-south-sudan-nowhere-to-hide-not-even-with-un.html (accessed 25 February 2016).

26. The East African, 'Gunmen kill 20 in attack on South Sudan UN base', www.theeastafrican.co.ke/news/Gunmen-kill-20-in-attack-on-South-Sudan-UN-base/-/2558/2284652/-/8p0ejj/-/index.html (accessed 25 February 2016).

27. Radio Tamazuj, 'Soldiers breach UN base perimeter in Bentiu during fighting', https://radiotamazuj.org/en/article/soldiers-breach-un-base-perimeter-bentiu-during-fighting (accessed 25 February 2016).

28. UN News Centre, 'South Sudan: Special investigation into Malakal vilence completed, says UN', www.un.org/apps/news/story.asp?NewsID=54289 (accessed 23 June 2016).

29. Reuters, 'U.N. to send peacekeepers home over reaction to South Sudan violence', http://uk.reuters.com/article/uk-southsudan-unrest-un-idUKKCN 0Z900J (accessed 23 June 2016).

30. UN News Centre, 'South Sudan: Special investigation into Malakal'.

31. *Newshour*, Al Jazeera English Television, Sky Channel 514, 23 June 2016.

32. UN News Centre, 'South Sudan: UN peacekeeping chief says action will be taken on probe into Malakal violence', www.un.org/apps/news/story.asp?News ID=54300 (accessed 23 June 2016).

33. *Newshour*, Al Jazeera English Television, Sky Channel 514, 26 June 2016.

34. Reuters, 'South Sudan oil conference fails to draw biggest energy firms', 11 October 2017, https://af.reuters.com/article/africaTech/idAFL8N1MM43F (accessed 15 October 2017).

35. Financial Times, 'War-torn South Sudan under economic attack from fall in oil price', 21 December 2014, https://www.ft.com/content/6ba9f528-869c-11e4-8a51-00144feabdc0 (accessed 21 July 2018).

36. *Newshour*, Al Jazeera English Television, Sky Channel 514, 30 January 2016.

37. Ibid.

38. Ibid.

39. Trading Economics, 'South Sudan Inflation Rate 2008–2016', www.tradi ngeconomics.com/south-sudan/inflation-cpi (accessed 10 September 2016).

40. World Bank Group, *Global Economic Prospects, June 2018: The Turning of the Tide?* (Washington, DC: World Bank Group, 2018).

41. Institute for Economics and Peace, 'Global Peace Index 2017', www.vision ofhumanity.org/ (accessed 23 December 2017), 128.

42. *Global Peace Index 2018*, 93.

43. *Global Peace Index 2018*, 48.

44. *Eye on Africa*, France24 English, 21 February 2017.

45. UNHCR, 'Aid appeals seek over US$3 billion as South Sudan set to become Africa's refugee and humanitarian crisis', 1 February 2018, http://www.unhcr.org/news/press/2018/2/5a7222da4/aid-appeals-seek-us3-billion-south-sudan-set-become-africas-largest-refugee.html (accessed 27 July 2018).

46. *Newshour*, Al Jazeera English Television, Sky Channel 514, 15 August 2016.

47. Reuters, 'South Sudan oil conference fails to draw biggest energy firms', 11 October 2017, https://af.reuters.com/article/africaTech/idAFL8N1MM43F (accessed 15 October 2017).

48. *Newshour*, Al Jazeera English Television, Sky Channel 514, 12 October 2017.

49. Data used in the 2011 Ibrahim Index are from 2010, prior to South Sudan's secession from Sudan. The dataset used to calculate the 2011 Ibrahim index contains data from 2000 to 2010.

50. Including Sudan.

51. Mo Ibrahim Foundation, '2015 Ibrahim Index of African Governance', www.moibrahimfoundation.org/iiag/launch/ (accessed 9 March 2015).

52. Mo Ibrahim Foundation, '2016 Ibrahim Index of African Governance: Index Report', http://mo.ibrahim.foundation/iiag/downloads/ (accessed 24 November 2016).

53. Data from this index ran from 2007 to 2016 – a ten-year period.

54. South Sudan was part of Sudan when the index began in 2000, and did not participate in the index in 2012, 2013 and 2014 because of insufficient data.

55. Mo Ibrahim Foundation, '2017 Ibrahim Index of African Governance: Index Report', http://mo.ibrahim.foundation/iiag/2017-key-findings/ (accessed 20 December 2017).

56. Mo Ibrahim Foundation, '2018 Ibrahim Index of African Governance: Index Report', http://mo.ibrahim.foundation/iiag/ (accessed 29 October 2018).

57. Institute for Economics and Peace, 'Global Peace Index', www.visionofhumanity.org/#/page/indexes/global-peace-index/2015 (accessed 9 March 2015).

58. Institute for Economics and Peace, 'Global Peace Index', www.visionofhumanity.org/ (accessed 8 December 2016).

59. *Global Peace Index 2016*, 2, 30.

60. *Global Peace Index 2017*.

61. Ibid., 19.

62. Institute for Economics and Peace, 'Positive Peace Report 2017: Tracking Peace Transitions Through a Systems Thinking Approach', October 2017, http://visionofhumanity.org/reports/ (accessed 23 December 2017).

63. *Global Peace Index 2018*, 9 and 18.

64. *Global Peace Index 2018*, 2 and 11.

65. UNDP, Human Development Report 2011 (New York: UNDP, 2011), 124.

66. UNDP, '2015 Human Development Report', http://hdr.undp.org/en/2015-report/download (accessed 9 March 2016).

67. UNDP, '2016 Human Development Report', http://hdr.undp.org/en/2016-report (accessed 22 December 2017).

68. UNDP, 'Human Development Indices and Indicators: 2018 Statistical Update', http://hdr.undp.org/en/2018-update (accessed 20 October 2018).

69. Transparency International, 'Corruption Perceptions Index 2015', www.transparency.org/ (accessed 9 March 2016).

70. Transparency International, 'Corruption Perceptions Index 2016', www.transparency.org/news/feature/corruption_perceptions_index_2016 (accessed 23 December 2017).

71. Transparency International, 'Corruption Perceptions Index 2017', Transparency International, https://www.transparency.org/news/feature/corruption_perceptions_index_2017 (accessed 24 July 2018).

72. Transparency International, 'CPI Results Brochure 2017', https://www.transparency.org/news/feature/corruption_perceptions_index_2017 (accessed 24 July 2018).

73. Verisk Maplecroft, 'Political Risk Index 2016', www.maplecroft.com/accounts/dashboard/ (accessed 9 March 2016).

74. Institute for Economics and Peace, 'Global Terrorism Index 2015', http://visionofhumanity.org/reports/ (accessed 23 December 2017).

75. *Global Terrorism Index 2015*, 2.

76. *Global Terrorism Index 2016*.

77. *Global Terrorism Index 2017*.

78. Ibid., 46.

79. Ibid., 16.

80. UNOHCHR, Assessment Mission by the Office of the UNHCHR to improve human rights, accountability, reconciliation and capacity in South Sudan: detailed findings (Geneva: OHCHR, 2016), 44, 73.

81. *Newshour*, Al Jazeera English, 11 March 2016.

82. UNOHCHR, Assessment Mission by the Office of the UNHCHR to improve human rights, accountability, reconciliation and capacity in South Sudan: detailed findings (Geneva, Switzerland: OHCHR, 2016), 34.

83. *Eye on Africa*, France24 English, Sky Channel 513, 3 March 2016.

84. Amoah, *Nationalism, Globalization, and Africa*, 61.

85. UNOHCHR, Assessment Mission by the Office of the UNHCHR to improve human rights, accountability, reconciliation and capacity in South Sudan: detailed findings (Geneva: OHCHR, 2016), 47.

86. *Newshour*, Al Jazeera English, 11 March 2016.

87. Al Jazeera, Israeli PM Netanyahu in historic East Africa trip', www.aljazeera.com/news/2016/07/israel-pm-netanyahu-historic-east-africa-trip-160704084656635.html (accessed 4 July 2016).

88. *Newshour*, Al Jazeera English, 4 July 2016.

89. Ibid., 26 June 2016.

90. Ibid., 6 July 2016.

91. Ibid.

92. Yahoo News, 'South Sudan rebels split, reject peace efforts', http://news.yahoo.com/south-sudan-rebels-split-reject-peace-efforts-145538680.html (accessed 19 March 2016).

93. *Newshour*, Al Jazeera English, 6 July 2016.

94. Yahoo News, 'South Sudan rebels split, reject peace efforts', http://news.yahoo.com/south-sudan-rebels-split-reject-peace-efforts-145538680.html (accessed 19 March 2016).

95. Al Jazeera, 'South Sudan's Kiir replaces army chief Paul Malong', 9 May 2017, www.aljazeera.com/news/2017/05/south-sudan-kiir-replaces-army-chief-paul-malong-170509211057369.html (accessed 31 May 2017).

96. BBC, 'South Sudan: Five soldiers killed in Juba clashes', www.bbc.co.uk/news/world-africa-36744636 (accessed 8 July 2016).

97. *Newshour*, Al Jazeera English, 8 July 2016.

98. Ibid., 9 July 2016.

99. Denis Dumo and Michelle Nichols, 'Renewed Fighting erupts in South Sudan as fears of civil war mount', Reuters, 10 July 2016, www.reuters.com/article/us-south-sudan-security-casualties-idUSKCN0ZQ08J (accessed 11 July 2016).

100. UN News Centre, '"Time to massively reinforce UN action" on South Sudan, ban says ahead of Security Council meeting', UN News Centre, www.un.org/apps/news/story.asp?NewsID=54434 (accessed 12 July 2016).

101. *Newshour*, Al Jazeera English, 19 July 2016.

102. Ibid., 27 July 2016.

103. Ibid., 21 July 2016.

104. Ibid., 27 July 2016.

105. Ibid., 2 August 2016.

106. IGAD, *Communiqué of the Second IGAD Plus Extra-Ordinary Summit on the Situation in the Republic of South Sudan* (Addis Ababa: IGAD 2016).

107. UN News Centre, 'Vote on Resolution Strengthening UN Mission in South Sudan Mandate', 12 August 2016, www.whatsinblue.org/2016/08/renewal-of-un-mission-in-south-sudan-mandate.php (accessed 13 August 2016).

108. Reuters, 'South Sudan says probes any army abuses, executes two soldiers', 17 August 2016, www.reuters.com/article/us-southsudan-security-idUSKCN10S1R8?il=0 (accessed 20 August 2016).

109. UN News Centre, 'South Sudan: Hundreds of children recruited into armed groups, reports UNICEF', 19 August 2016, www.un.org/apps/news/story.asp?NewsID=54712 (accessed 20 August 2016).

110. Al Jazeera, 'The real reasons behind South Sudan crisis', 27 December 2013, www.aljazeera.com/indepth/opinion/2013/12/real-reasons-behind-south-sudan-crisis-2013122784119779562.html (accessed 24 August 2016).

111. *Eye on Africa*, France24 English, 8 June 2016.

112. BBC, 'South Sudan conflict: African Union approves regional force', 19 July 2016, www.bbc.co.uk/news/world-africa-36833875 (accessed 24 August 2016).

113. IGAD, *Communiqué of the Second IGAD Plus Extra-Ordinary Summit.*

114. UN News Centre, 'Ban names retired Dutch general to lead probe into South Sudan violence', 23 August 2016, http://www.un.org/apps/news/story.asp?NewsID=54742&&Cr=southsudan&&Cr1= (accessed 24 August 2016).

115. BBC, 'South Sudan conflict: Riek Machar in Khartoum for "medical treatment"', 23 August 2016, www.bbc.co.uk/news/world-africa-37166536 (accessed 24 August 2016).

116. *Newshour*, Al Jazeera English, 17 October 2016.

117. Reuters, 'Kenya withdraws first batch of troops from U.N. South Sudan mission', 9 November 2016, http://uk.reuters.com/article/uk-southsudan-un-idUKKBN13426Q?il=0 (accessed 11 November 2016).

118. Reuters, 'U.S. proposes U.N. arms embargo on South Sudan, sanctions', 18 November 2016, www.reuters.com/article/us-southsudan-security-un-idUSKBN13C2P6 (accessed 19 November 2016).

119. Al Jazeera, 'Japanese peacekeepers arrive in South Sudan', 21 November 2016, www.aljazeera.com/amp/news/2016/11/japanese-peacekeepers-arrive-south-sudan-161121134251492.html (accessed 24 November 2016).

120. Reuters, 'Troops and court needed fast to avert South Sudan genocide', 14 December 2016, http://uk.reuters.com/article/uk-southsudan-un-idUKK BN1430ZW (accessed 23 December 2016).
121. *Newshour*, Al Jazeera English, 17 October 2016.
122. ENCA, 'American freelance journalist kicked out of South Sudan', 7 December 2016, www.enca.com/africa/american-freelance-journalist-deported-from-south-sudan (accessed 26 December 2016).
123. ENCA, 'South Sudan expels second aid worker in a week', 14 December 2016, www.enca.com/africa/south-sudan-expels-second-aid-worker-in-a-week (accessed 23 December 2016).
124. *Newshour*, Al Jazeera English, 14 December 2016.
125. Al Jazeera, 'Outrage after UN blocks South Sudan arms embargo', 23 December 2016, www.aljazeera.com/news/2016/12/outrage-blocks-south-sudan-arms-embargo-161223153844996.html (accessed 26 December 2016).
126. *Eye on Africa*, France24 English, 23 December 2016.
127. Reuters, 'South Sudan rebels kidnap eight local aid workers – military', 13 March 2017, http://af.reuters.com/article/southSudanNews/idAFL5N1GQ27O (accessed 13 March 2017).
128. IFOR, 'ONAD Responds to Call for National Dialogue in South Sudan', 10 March 2017, www.ifor.org/news/2017/3/10/onad-responds-to-call-for-national-dialogue-in-south-sudan (accessed 31 May 2017).
129. Al Jazeera, 'South Sudan's Kiir replaces army chief Paul Malong', 9 May 2017.
130. Al Jazeera, 'What next for South Sudan's Peace Agreement', 28 June 2018.

Chapter 10   Conclusions

1. *Newshour*, Al Jazeera English, 3 March 2016.
2. ENCA, 'Gabon's court failed to rectify "anomalies" in presidential poll: EU', 26 September 2016, www.enca.com/africa/gabons-court-failed-to-rectify-anomalies-in-presidential-poll-eu (accessed 17 July 2017).
3. African Union, 'Key decisions of the 31st African Union Summit in Nouakchott', 17 July 2018, https://www.africa-eu-partnership.org/en/stay-informed/news/key-decisions-31st-african-union-summit-nouakchott (accessed 29 July 2018).

BIBLIOGRAPHY

Across Africa. France24 English, Sky Channel 513, 19 June 2016.

Across Africa. France24 English, Sky Channel 513, 21 May 2017.

Across Africa. France24 English, Sky Channel 513, 30 October 2017.

Africa News. 'U.S. security alert for DRC city as govt, rebels clash in South Kivu', 29 September 2017, www.africanews.com/2017/09/29/us-security-alert-for-drc-city-as-govt-rebels-clash-in-south-kivu// (accessed 9 October 2017).

African Union. *Constitutive Act of the African Union.* Addis Ababa: African Union, 2001.

African Union. *Communiqué of the Meeting of the AU High Level Committee on Libya.* Addis Ababa: African Union, 2016.

African Union. 'Key decisions of the 31st African Union Summit in Nouakchott', 17 July 2018, https://www.africa-eu-partnership.org/en/stay-informed/news/key-decisions-31st-african-union-summit-nouakchott (accessed 29 July 2018).

African Union Commission. *African Peace and Security Architecture (APSA) Roadmap 2016–2020.* Addis Ababa: African Union Commission, 2015.

Al Jazeera. 'Looting and gunfire in captured CAR capital', www.aljazeera.com/news/africa/2013/03/201332481729584103.html (accessed 31 December 2017).

Al Jazeera. 'Election official flees crisis-hit Burundi', www.aljazeera.com/news/2015/05/election-official-flees-crisis-hit-burundi-150530124830312.html.

Al Jazeera. 'UN employee among those killed in Mali hotel attack', www.aljazeera.com/news/2015/08/gunmen-attack-hotel-mali-hostages-150807161908433.html (accessed 8 February 2015).

Al Jazeera. 'Libya Police Chief Assassinated', Al Jazeera English, www.aljazeera.com/news/middleeast/2014/08/libyan-police-chief-assassinated-2014812153923868906.html (accessed 6 February 2014).

Al Jazeera. 'African leaders urge West to act on Libya', www.aljazeera.com/news/middleeast/2014/12/african-leaders-urge-west-act-libya-201412171306708936.html (accessed 6 February 2016).

Al Jazeera. 'Libya's UN-backed government sails into Tripoli', Al Jazeera News, www.aljazeera.com/news/2016/03/libya-backed-unity-government-arrives-tripoli-160330125804929.html (accessed 31 March 2016).

Al Jazeera. 'Deadly clashes hit DR Congo camp for M23 Fighters', www.aljazeera. com/news/2016/06/deadly-clashes-hit-dr-congo-camp-m23-fighters-160617 083231682.html (accessed 18 June 2016).

Al Jazeera. 'Israeli PM Netanyahu in historic East Africa trip', www.aljazeera.com/ news/2016/07/israel-pm-netanyahu-historic-east-africa-trip-16070408465 6635.html (accessed 4 July 2016).

Al Jazeera. '"Scores hacked to death" in machete attack in DRC', 14 August 2016, www.aljazeera.com/news/2016/08/scores-hacked-death-machete-attack-dr-congo-160814133550565.html (accessed 14 August 2016).

Al Jazeera. 'The real reasons behind South Sudan crisis', 27 December 2013, www. aljazeera.com/indepth/opinion/2013/12/real-reasons-behind-south-sudan-crisis-2013122784119779562.html (accessed 24 August 2016).

Al Jazeera. 'Libya: Government forces block ISIL at Sirte coastline', 6 September 2016, http://video.aljazeera.com/channels/eng/videos/libya%3A-government-forces-block-isil-at-sirte-coastline/5113689037001 (accessed 10 September 2016).

Al Jazeera. 'UN probe finds "gross human rights abuses" in Burindi', 21 September 2016, www.aljazeera.com/news/2016/09/probe-finds-gross-human-rights-abuses-burundi-160920193304827.html (accessed 1 October 2016).

Al Jazeera. 'Rival group seizes UN-backed government offices', 16 October 2016, www.aljazeera.com/news/2016/10/libya-rival-group-seizes-backed-government-offices-161015131821294.html (accessed 1 November 2016).

Al Jazeera. 'DR Congo: Opposition figure Samy Badibanga named PM', 19 October 2016, www.aljazeera.com/news/2016/11/dr-congo-opposition-figure-samy-badibanga-named-pm-161117175108538.html (accessed 19 November 2016).

Al Jazeera. 'Japanese peacekeepers arrive in South Sudan', 21 November 2016, www. aljazeera.com/amp/news/2016/11/japanese-peacekeepers-arrive-south-sudan-161121134251492.html (accessed 24 November 2016).

Al Jazeera. 'Libyan forces claim control of ISIL stronghold of Sirte', 6 December 2016, www.aljazeera.com/news/2016/12/libyan-forces-claim-control-isil-stronghold-sirte-161205140941343.html (accessed 26 December 2016).

Al Jazeera. 'Outrage after UN blocks South Sudan arms embargo', 23 December 2016, www.aljazeera.com/news/2016/12/outrage-blocks-south-sudan-arms-embargo-161223153844996.html (accessed 26 December 2016).

Al Jazeera. 'DR Congo floods leave 10,000 homeless', 4 January 2017, www.aljazeera. com/news/2017/01/dr-congo-floods-170104042037452.html (accessed 5 January 2017).

Al Jazeera. 'Fayez al-Sarraj not hurt after convoy comes under fire', 20 February 2017, www.aljazeera.com/news/2017/02/fayez-al-sarraj-hurt-convoy-fire-170220130904166.html (accessed 7 March 2017).

Al Jazeera. 'Kabila names Bruno Tshibala new DRC prime minister', 7 April 2017, www.aljazeera.com/news/2017/04/kabila-names-bruno-tshibala-drc-prime-minister-170407201215507.html (accessed 6 June 2017).

Al Jazeera. 'South Sudan's Kiir replaces army chief Paul Malong', 9 May 2017, www. aljazeera.com/news/2017/05/south-sudan-kiir-replaces-army-chief-paul-malong-170509211057369.html (accessed 31 May 2017).

Al Jazeera. 'Trial of Burkina Faso's ex-leader Blaise Compaore adjourned', 16 May 2017, www.aljazeera.com/video/news/2017/05/trial-burkina-fasos-ex-leader-blaise-compaore-adjourned-170516062245570.html (accessed 31 May 2017).

Al Jazeera. 'Libya: 141 killed in Brak al-Shat airbase attack', 20 May 2017, www.aljazeera.com/news/2017/05/libya-141-people-killed-brak-al-shat-airbase-attack-170520082052419.html (accessed 6 June 2017).

Al Jazeera. 'Libya's Ansar al-Sharia announces dissolution', 28 May 2017, www.aljazeera.com/news/2017/05/libya-ansar-al-sharia-announces-dissolution-170528045219409.html (accessed 6 June 2017).

Al Jazeera. 'Fayez al-Sarraj meets Khalifa Haftar in UAE for talks', 2 May 2017, www.aljazeera.com/news/2017/05/fayez-al-sarraj-meets-khalifa-haftar-uae-talks-170502140623464.html (accessed 9 October 2017).

Al Jazeera. 'UAE, Saudi Arabia join G5 Sahel force summit in Paris', 13 December 2017, www.aljazeera.com/news/2017/12/g5-sahel-force-leaders-arrive-summit-paris-171213063153149.html (accessed 16 December 2017).

Al Jazeera. 'Jean-Pierre Bamba named as DRC presidential candidate', 14 July 2018, https://www.aljazeera.com/news/2018/07/jean-pierre-bemba-named-drc-presidential-candidate-180714141750891.html (accessed 26 July 2018).

Al Jazeera. 'What next for South Sudan's Peace Agreement', 28 June 2018, https://www.aljazeera.com/news/2018/06/south-sudan-peace-agreement-180627194714644.html (accessed 27 July 2018).

Al Jazeera. 'Vote counting under way in Mali's tense elections', 30 July 2018, https://www.aljazeera.com/news/2018/07/vote-counting-mali-tense-elections-180730133330607.html (accessed 1 August 2018).

Amanpour. CNN, Sky Channel 506, 5 October 2012.

AMISOM. 'New Burundi battle group arrives in Somalia', 14 February 2017, http://amisom-au.org/2017/02/new-burundi-battle-group-arrives-in-somalia/ (accessed 7 March 2017).

Amnesty International. *My Children Are Scared: Burundi's Deepening Human Rights Crisis* (London: Amnesty International, 2015).

Amoah, Michael. *Reconstructing the Nation in Africa* (London: Tauris Academic Studies, 2007).

Amoah, Michael. *Nationalism, Globalization, and Africa* (New York: Palgrave Macmillan, 2011).

Angola. IFES Election Guide (2012), *Presidential Election Results* [Online]. Available from www.electionguide.org/elections/id/1509/ (accessed 16 December 2015).

APS (Algeria Press Service). 'Libya's neighbouring countries meeting in Niamey: Deepening consultation, supporting political process', 17 October 2016, www.aps.dz/en/world/14711-libya-s-neighbouring-countries-meeting-in-niamey-deepening-consultation,-supporting-political-process (accessed 24 November 2016).

AU-PSC. 'Congo hands over 500 strong contingent to the African Union-led Regional Task Force for the elimination of Lord's Resistance Army', www.peaceau.org/en/article/democratic-republic-of-congo-hands-over-500-strong-contingent-to-the-african-union-led-regional-task-force-for-the-elimination-of-the-lord-s-resistance-army (accessed 17 March 2016).

AU-PSC. 'Inaugural Meeting of the Support Group for the Facilitation of the National Dialogue in the Democratic Republic of Congo', 4 July 2016, www.peaceau.org/en/article/inaugural-meeting-of-the-support-group-for-the-facilitation-of-the-national-dialogue-in-the-democratic-republic-of-congo (accessed 10 September 2016).

AU-PSC. '719th PSC meeting on the situation in Libya and the outcomes of the 4th meeting of the AU High Level committee on Libya, held on 9 September 2017', 22 September 2017, www.peaceau.org/en/article/719th-psc-meeting-on-the-situation-in-libya-and-the-outcomes-of-the-4th-meeting-of-the-au-high-level-committee-on-libya-held-on-9-september-2017 (accessed 16 December 2017).

Ayoub, Joey. 'How the EU is responsible for slavery in Libya', Al Jazeera, 29 November 2017. www.aljazeera.com/indepth/opinion/slavery-walls-fortress-europe-171128094218944.html (accessed 16 December 2017).

BBC. 'Burundi grenade attack kills four, including boy', 7 February 2016, www.bbc.co.uk/news/world-africa-35516968 (accessed 15 February 2016).

BBC. 'Burundi Vice-President Gervais Rufyikiri flees', www.bbc.co.uk/news/world-africa-33267428 (accessed 16 February 2016).

BBC. 'Mediterranean migrants: Deadly "capsize" captain in court', www.bbc.co.uk/news/world-europe-32448591 (accessed 6 February 2016).

BBC. 'Divide Nigeria into two, says Muammar Gaddafi', http://news.bbc.co.uk/1/hi/8570350.stm (accessed 4 February 2016).

BBC. 'No third term for Nigerian leader', http://news.bbc.co.uk/1/hi/world/africa/4986904.stm (accessed 17 December 2015).

BBC. 'Mali attack: Bamako's Radisson Blu hotel re-opens', www.bbc.co.uk/news/world-africa-35101130 (accessed 8 February 2015).

BBC. 'Mali hotel siege: Several killed in Sevare, four UN workers saved', www.bbc.co.uk/news/world-africa-33833363 (accessed 8 February 2016).

BBC. 'Sudan's Bashir orders border with South Sudan to reopen', www.bbc.co.uk/news/world-africa-35425558 (accessed 9 February 2016).

BBC. 'Rocket attack hits Kidal UN base in northern Mali', www.bbc.co.uk/news/world-africa-31788395 (accessed 8 February 2016).

BBC. 'Mali's Tuareg rebels sign peace deal', www.bbc.co.uk/news/world-africa-33213931 (accessed 8 February 2016).

BBC. 'DR Congo senate amends census law to allow 2016 election', 23 January 2015, www.bbc.co.uk/news/world-africa-30947880 (accessed 17 March 2016).

BBC. 'Mali: United Nations peacekeepers killed in attack', www.bbc.co.uk/news/world-africa-36408943 (accessed 30 May 2016).

BBC. 'Burundi general shot dead dropping child off at school', 25 April 2016 www.bbc.co.uk/news/world-africa-36129899 (accessed 7 June 2016).

BBC. 'Rwanda's Paul Kagame to run for third presidential term', www.bbc.co.uk/news/world-africa-35209186 (accessed 11 June 2016).

BBC. 'Patrick Karageya: Mysterious death of a Rwandan exile', www.bbc.co.uk/news/world-africa-26752838 (accessed 11 June 2016).

BBC. 'South Sudan: Five soldiers killed in Juba clashes', www.bbc.co.uk/news/world-africa-36744636 (accessed 8 July 2016).

BBC. 'Burundi crisis: MP Hasfa Mossi gunned down', 13 July 2016, www.portland-communications.com/2016/07/what-happened-at-last-weeks-african-union-summit/ (accessed 22 August 2016).

BBC. 'South Sudan conflict: Riek Machar in Khartoum for "medical treatment"', 23 August 2016, www.bbc.co.uk/news/world-africa-37166536 (accessed 24 August 2016).

BBC. 'South Sudan conflict: African Union approves regional force', 19 July 2016, www.bbc.co.uk/news/world-africa-36833875 (accessed 24 August 2016).

BBC. 'France ends Sangaris military operation in CAR', 31 October 2016, www.bbc.co.uk/news/world-africa-37823047 (accessed 1 November 2016).

BBC. 'Libya Malta hijack: Hijackers arrested as drama ends peacefully', 23 December 2016, www.bbc.co.uk/news/world-europe-38416112 (accessed 26 December 2016).

BBC. 'Dengue fever kills 20 in Burkina Faso', 23 November 2016, www.bbc.co.uk/news/world-africa-38078754 (accessed 5 January 2017).

BBC. 'Macron in Mali: France will be "uncompromising" in fight against Terrorism', 19 May 2017, www.bbc.co.uk/news/world-europe-39968319 (accessed 6 June 2017).

BBC. 'Burkina Faso gun attack kills 18 people at café', 14 August 2017, www.bbc.co.uk/news/world-africa-40920338 (accessed 14 August 2017).

BBC. 'Burkina Faso's war against militant Islamists', 14 August 2017, www.bbc.co.uk/news/world-africa-39279050 (accessed 14 August 2017).

BBC. 'Central African Republic: UN peacekeeper killed in attack', 24 July 2017, www.bbc.co.uk/news/world-africa-40701128 (accessed 27 September 2017).

Beach, Alastair and Hassan Morajea. 'Egypt and UAE "launched air strikes against Libyan Islamists"', Telegraph, 25 August 2014, www.telegraph.co.uk/news/worldnews/africaandindianocean/libya/11055436/Egypt-and-UAE-launched-air-strikes-against-Libyan-Islamists.html.

CIA. 'World Factbook on Sudan', www.cia.gov/library/publications/the-world-factbook/geos/su.html (accessed 26 January 2016).

Clottey, Peter. 'South Sudan's Machar Tells UN Chief He'll Return to Juba in March', VOA News, 25 February 2016, www.voanews.com/content/south-sudan-machar-return-juba-march/3208351.html (accessed 17 March 2016).

Comparative Constitutions Project. 'Burkina Faso's Constitution of 1991 with Amendments through 2012', www.constituteproject.org (accessed 1 February 2016).

Comparative Constitutions Project. 'Burundi's Constitution of 2005', www.constituteproject.org (accessed 1 February 2016).

Comparative Constitutions Project. 'Constitution of Burkina Faso 1991 with Amendments through 2012', www.constituteproject.org (accessed 1 February 2016).

Comparative Constitutions Project. 'Chad's Constitution of 1996 with Amendments through 2005', www.constituteproject.org (accessed 1 February 2016).

Comparative Constitutions Project. 'Congo (Democratic Republic of the)'s Constitution of 2005 with Amendments through 2011', www.constituteproject.org (accessed 19 October 2016).

Comparative Constitutions Project. 'Rwanda's Constitution of 2003 with Amendments through 2010', www.constituteproject.org (accessed 1 February 2016).

Comparative Constitutions Project. 'Togo's Constitution of 1992 with Amendments through 2007', www.constituteproject.org (accessed 19 December 2015).

Comparative Constitutions Project. 'Uganda's Constitution of 1995 with Amendments through 2005', www.constituteproject.org (accessed 26 December 2017).

Diarra, Adama. 'UPDATE 3- Gunmen kill 10 in attack on village in Mali – army spokesman', Reuters, 9 August 2015, http://af.reuters.com/article/maliNews/idAFL5N10K0CU20150809?sp=true (accessed 8 February 2016).

Diarra, Adama and John Irish. 'Islamist militants kill 5 in restaurant attack in Mali capital', Reuters, 7 March 2015, www.reuters.com/article/us-mali-attacks-idUSKBN0M305G20150307 (accessed 8 February 2016).

Dumo, Denis and Michelle Nichols, 'Renewed Fighting erupts in South Sudan as fears of civil war mount', Reuters, 10 July 2016, www.reuters.com/article/us-south-sudan-security-casualties-idUSKCN0ZQ08J (accessed 11 July 2016).

EGJustice. 'Constitutional Reform', www.egjustice.org/post/constitutional-reform (accessed 21 December 2015).

El-Bar, Karim. 'REVEALED: Leaked tapes expose Western support for renegade Libyan general', *Middle East Eye*, 8 July 2016, www.middleeasteye.net/news/revealed-leaked-tapes-expose-western-support-renegade-libyan-general-185825787 (accessed 9 July 2016).

El-Bar, Karim. 'UK troops "operating from French-led Libyan base aiding renegade general"', *Middle East Eye*, 23 June 2016, www.middleeasteye.net/news/french-led-secret-operations-room-backing-renegade-general-libya-81826394 (accessed 9 July 2016).

ENCA. 'High Level AU delegation in second day of Burundi talks', www.enca.com/africa/high-level-au-delegation-second-day-burundi-talks (accessed 26 February 2016).

ENCA. 'Gabon's court failed to rectify "anomalies" in presidential poll: EU', 26 September 2016, www.enca.com/africa/gabons-court-failed-to-rectify-anomalies-in-presidential-poll-eu (accessed 17 July 2017).

ENCA. 'South Sudan expels second aid worker in a week', 14 December 2016, www.enca.com/africa/south-sudan-expels-second-aid-worker-in-a-week (accessed 23 December 2016).

ENCA. 'American freelance journalist kicked out of South Sudan', 7 December 2016, www.enca.com/africa/american-freelance-journalist-deported-from-south-sudan (accessed 26 December 2016).

ENCA. 'No DRC presidential poll before 2019: electoral commission', 12 October 2017, www.enca.com/africa/no-drc-presidential-poll-before-2019-electoral-commission (accessed 11 December 2017).

Eye on Africa. France24 English, Sky Channel 513, 27 January 2016.

Eye on Africa. France24 English, Sky Channel 513, 23 February 2016.

Eye on Africa. France24 English, Sky Channel 513, 13 April 2016.

Eye on Africa. France24 English, Sky Channel 513, 8 June 2016.

Eye on Africa. France24 English, Sky Channel 513, 14 June 2016.

Eye on Africa. France24 English, Sky Channel 513, 12 July 2016.

Eye on Africa. France24 English, Sky Channel 513, 27 July 2016.

Eye on Africa. France24 English, Sky Channel 513, 22 August 2016.

Eye on Africa. France24 English, Sky Channel 513, 8 September 2016.

Eye on Africa. France24 English, Sky Channel 513, 20 September 2016.

Eye on Africa. France24 English, Sky Channel 513, 7 October 2016.

Eye on Africa. France24 English, Sky Channel 513, 18 October 2016.

Eye on Africa. France24 English, Sky Channel 513, 24 October 2016.

Eye on Africa. France24 English, Sky Channel 513, 29 November 2016.

Eye on Africa. France24 English, Sky Channel 513, 8 December 2016.

Eye on Africa. France24 English, Sky Channel 513, 22 December 2016.

Eye on Africa. France24 English, Sky Channel 513, 23 December 2016.

Eye on Africa. France24 English, Sky Channel 513, 3 January 2017.

Eye on Africa. France24 English, Sky Channel 513, 16 February 2017.

Eye on Africa. France24 English, Sky Channel 513, 1 March 2017.

Eye on Africa. France24 English, Sky Channel 513, 29 May 2017.

Eye on Africa. France24 English, Sky Channel 513, 4 November 2017.

Eye on Africa. France24 English, Sky Channel 513, 31 July 2018.

Financial Times. 'War-torn South Sudan under economic attack from fall in oil price', 21 December 2014, https://www.ft.com/content/6ba9f528-869c-11e4-8a51-00144feabdc0 (accessed 21 July 2018).

Focus on France. France24 English, Sky Channel 513, 24 October 2016.

Foreign and Commonwealth Office. 'South Sudan: Troika Statement', www.gov.uk/government/news/south-sudan-troika-statement.

France24. 'Grenade blast follows string of attacks on Burundi capital', www.france24.com/en/20160215-grenade-attack-bujumbura-burundi-unrest-injured (accessed 15 February 2016).

France24. 'Deadly air strike hits hospital in east Libya: medic', www.france24.com/en/20160207-deadly-air-strike-hits-hospital-east-libya-medic (accessed 7 February 2016).

France24. 'Libyan forces launch "final battle" to oust IS group from Sirte', 28 August 2016, www.france24.com/en/20160828-libyan-forces-final-battle-islamic-state-group-sirte (accessed 29 August 2016).

France24. 'Burundi wants to quit ICC to avoid possible charges', 7 October 2016, www.france24.com/en/20161007-burundi-wants-quit-icc-avoid-possible-charges (accessed 1 November 2016).

France24. 'People of Kinshasa welcome bask their postmen', 8 December 2016, www.france24.com/en/20161208-people-kinshasa-welcome-back-postmen (accessed 9 December 2016).

Gellner, Ernest, Nations and Nationalism, (Oxford: Basil Blackwell, 1983).

Government of Algeria. *Constitution Of The People's Democratic Republic of Algeria 1989 (amended by the constitutional revision of 1996)*. Algiers: Ministry of Justice, 1996.

Government of Burundi. *Arusha Peace and Reconciliation Agreement for Burundi*. Arusha, Tanzania: Government of Burundi, 2000.

Government of Cameroon. *Constitution of the Republic of Cameroon*. Yaounde: Groupe Mauger, 1996.

Government of Rwanda. *The Constitution of the Republic of Rwanda of 2003 Revised in 2015*. Kigali: Government of Rwanda, 2015.

Government of Tunisia. *Constitution of The Republic of Tunisia*. Tunis: Government of Tunisia, 2010.

Guilbert, Kieran. 'Fresh Violence in Central African Republic kills several, forces thousands to flee – U.N.', Thomson Reuters Foundation News, 17 June 2016, http://news.trust.org/item/20160617133151-3mpa5 (accessed 18 June 2016).

Human Rights Watch. 'Central African Republic: Moslems Trapped in Enclave', www.hrw.org/news/2014/12/22/central-african-republic-muslims-trapped-enclaves (accessed 16 March 2016).

Human Rights Watch. 'DR Congo: UN Experts to investigate Kasai Region Violence', 23 June 2017, www.hrw.org/news/2017/06/23/dr-congo-un-experts-investigate-kasai-region-violence (accessed 23 June 2017).

Human Rights Watch. *'Special Mission': Recruitment of M23 Rebels to Suppress Protests in the Democratic Republic of Congo*. USA: Human Rights Watch, December 2017.

Hanna, Jason, Ed Payne and Steve Almasy. 'Deadly Mali hotel attack: "They were shooting at anything that moved"', CNN, 20 November 2015, http://edition. cnn.com/2015/11/20/africa/mali-shooting/ (accessed 8 February 2016).

ICC. 'ICC Trial Chamber III sentences Jean-Pierre Bemba Gombo to 18 years' imprisonment for war crimes and crimes against humanity committed in the Central African Republic in 2002–2003', www.icc-cpi.int//Pages/item.aspx? name=PR1223 (accessed 23 June 2016).

ICC. 'Al Mahdi Case: trial to open on 22 August 2016', www.icc-cpi.int/Pages/item. aspx?name=pr1217 (accessed 22 August 2016).

ICC. 'ICC Appeals Chamber Acquits Mr Bemba from charges of war crimes and crimes against humanity', https://www.icc-cpi.int/Pages/item.aspx?name= PR1390 (accessed 26 July 2018).

IFES Election Guide. 'Algeria', www.electionguide.org/elections/id/2456/ (accessed 19 December 2015).

IFES Election Guide. 'Angola', www.electionguide.org/elections/id/1509/ (accessed 16 December 2015).

IFES Election Guide. 'Burkina Faso', www.electionguide.org/elections/id/2169/ (accessed 21 December 2015).

IFES Election Guide. 'Cameroon', www.electionguide.org/elections/id/2205/ (accessed 19 December 2015).

IFES Election Guide. 'Congo-Brazzaville', www.electionguide.org/elections/id/ 2111/ (accessed 16 December 2015).

IFES Election Guide. 'Senegal', www.electionguide.org/elections/id/2230/ (accessed 21 December 2015).

IFES Election Guide. 'Togo', www.electionguide.org/elections/id/2111/ (accessed 19 December 2015).

IFES Election Guide. 'Tunisia', www.electionguide.org/elections/id/2122/ (accessed 21 December 2015).

IFOR (International Fellowship for Reconciliation). 'ONAD Responds to Call for National Dialogue in South Sudan', 10 March 2017, www.ifor.org/news/2017/ 3/10/onad-responds-to-call-for-national-dialogue-in-south-sudan (accessed 31 May 2017).

IGAD. *Agreement on Cessation of Hostilities Between the Government of the Republic of Sudan (GRSS) and the Sudan People's Liberation Movement/Army In Opposition (SPLM/A-IO)* (Addis Ababa: IGAD, 2014).

IGAD. *Factsheet: A Summary of the Cessation of Hostilities Agreement (COHA), Signed 23 January 2014* (Addis Ababa: IGAD, 2014).

IGAD. *Proposed Compromise Agreement on the Resolution of the Conflict in the Republic of South Sudan* (Addis Ababa: IGAD, 2015).

IGAD. 'Monitoring and Verification Mechanism', http://southsudan.igadhost.com/ index.php/about-us/timeline-of-events (accessed 9 February 2016).

IGAD. 'Time line of major events – IGAD-led Mediation Process for South Sudan', http://southsudan.igadhost.com/index.php/about-us/timeline-of-events (accessed 9 February 2016).

IGAD. *Communiqué of the Second IGAD Plus Extra-Ordinary Summit on the Situation in the Republic of South Sudan* (Addis Ababa: IGAD, 2016).

IGIHE. 'Supreme Court rules against Green Party constitutional amendment', http://en.igihe.com/justice/supreme-court-rules-against-green-party.html (accessed 17 December 2015).

Inside Story. Al Jazeera English, 23 July 2016.

Institute for Economics and Peace. *Global Peace Index 2013*. New York: IEP 2013.

Institute for Economics and Peace. *Global Peace Index 2014*. New York: IEP 2014.

Institute for Economics and Peace. *Global Peace Index 2015*. New York: IEP 2015.

Institute for Economics and Peace. *Global Peace Index 2016*. New York: IEP 2016.

Institute for Economics and Peace. *Positive Peace Report 2017: Tracking Peace Transitions Through a Systems Thinking Approach*, Report No. 54. Sydney: IEP, 2017.

Institute for Economics and Peace. 'Global Peace Index 2015', www.visionofhumanity. org/#/page/indexes/global-peace-index/2015 (accessed 9 March 2015).

Institute for Economics and Peace. 'Global Peace Index 2016', http://visionofhumanity. org/reports/ (accessed 23 December 2017).

Institute for Economics and Peace. 'Global Peace Index 2017', http://visionofhumanity. org/reports/ (accessed 23 December 2017).

Institute for Economics and Peace. 'Global Peace Index 2018', http://visionofhumanity. org/app/uploads/2018/06/Global-Peace-Index-2018-2.pdf (accessed 24 July 2018).

Institute for Economics and Peace. 'Global Terrorism Index 2015', http://vision ofhumanity.org/reports/ (accessed 23 December 2017).

Institute for Economics and Peace. 'Global Terrorism Index 2016', http://visionof humanity.org/reports/ (accessed 23 December 2017).

Institute for Economics and Peace. 'Global Terrorism Index 2017', http://visionof humanity.org/reports/ (accessed 23 December 2017).

Institute for Economics and Peace. 'Positive Peace Report 2017: Tracking Peace Transitions Through a Systems Thinking Approach', October 2017, http://vision ofhumanity.org/reports/ (accessed 23 December 2017).

IRIN. 'BURKINA FASO: Compaore gets green light to run for third mandate', IRIN, www.irinnews.org/report/56742/burkina-faso-compaore-gets-green-light-to-run-for-third-mandate (accessed 21 December 2015).

Kagame, Paul. *The Imperative To Strengthen Our Union: Report on the Proposed Recommendations for the Institutional Reform of the African Union*. Addis Ababa: African Union Commission, 2017.

Karimi, Faith and Sandra Betsis. 'Burkina Faso attack: At least 29 dead, scores freed after hotel siege', CNN, online edition, 18 January 2016, http://edition.cnn. com/2016/01/16/africa/burkina-faso-hotel-terrorist-attack/.

Libya Herald. 'ICC tells UN Hafter should hand over Warfali out of respect for justice', 8 November 2017, www.libyaherald.com/2017/11/08/icc-tells-un-hafter-should-hand-over-warfali-out-of-respect-for-justice/ (accessed 17 December 2017).

Libya Herald. 'Civil rights lawyers to press ICC to probe Khalifa Hafter over war crimes', 13 November 2017, www.libyaherald.com/2017/11/13/civil-rights-lawyers-to-press-icc-to-charge-khalifa-hafter-with-war-crimes/ (accessed 17 December 2017).

Libyan Express. 'Death toll of Benghazi car bombing hits 7', 21 November 2016, www.libyanexpress.com/death-toll-of-benghazi-car-bombing-hits-7/ (accessed 24 November 2016).

Mail & Guardian. 'South Sudan rebels arrive in Juba to clear way for their chief Machar to share power', http://mgafrica.com/article/2016-03-29-ssudan-rebels-arrive-in-juba-to-clear-way-for-their-leader-machar-to-share-power (accessed 29 March 2016).

Malsin, Jared and Chris Stephen, 'Egypt air strikes in Libya kill dozens of Isis militants', *Guardian*, 17 February 2015, www.theguardian.com/world/2015/feb/16/egypt-air-strikes-target-isis-weapons-stockpiles-libya (accessed 6 February 2016).

Markey, Patrick. 'Mali, Tuareg-led rebels agree to cease hostilities for peace talks', Reuters, www.reuters.com/article/2015/02/19/us-mali-talks-idUSKBN0LN1UJ 20150219 (accessed 14 September 2015).

Médecins Sans Frontières (MSF), 'CAR: MSF Condemns Violent Attack and Killing of Staff Member', www.doctorswithoutborders.org/article/car-msf-condemns-violent-attack-and-killing-staff-member (accessed 18 June 2016).

Mo Ibrahim Foundation. 'The Ibrahim Index of African Governance 2009', www.moibrahimfoundation.org/en/section/theibrahim-Index (accessed 26 May 2010).

Mo Ibrahim Foundation. '2010 Ibrahim Index of African Governance', www.moibrahimfoundation.org/en/section/the-ibrahim-index (accessed 13 October 2010).

Mo Ibrahim Foundation. '2015 Ibrahim Index of African Governance', www.moibrahimfoundation.org/iiag/launch/ (accessed 9 March 2015).

Mo Ibrahim Foundation. '2016 Ibrahim Index of African Governance: Index Report', http://mo.ibrahim.foundation/iiag/downloads/ (accessed 24 November 2016).

Mo Ibrahim Foundation. '2017 Ibrahim Index of African Governance: Index Report', http://mo.ibrahim.foundation/iiag/2017-key-findings/ (accessed 20 December 2017).

Mo Ibrahim Foundation. '2018 Ibrahim Index of African Governance: Index Report', http://mo.ibrahim.foundation/iiag/ (accessed 29 October 2018).

Monusco. 'North Kivu – Attacks on MONUSCO troops at Semuliki, at least 14 peacekeeprs and 5 FARDC soldiers killed', 8 December 2017, https://monusco.unmissions.org/en/north-kivu-%E2%80%93-attack-monusco-troops-semuliki-least-14-peacekeepers-and-5-fardc-soldiers-killed (accessed 11 December 2017).

Ndushabandi, Claver. 'Machar Rebels Advancing on SPLA Base', *Chimp Reports*, 26 March 2016, www.chimpreports.com/machar-rebels-advancing-on-spla-base/ (accessed 29 March 2016).

New Zimbabwe. 'Libya: Mugabe slams "naïve" Nigeria, South Africa and Gabon', www.newzimbabwe.com/news-5166-Libya+Mugabe+slams+Africas+naive+UN+vote/news.aspx (accessed 10 October 2011).

News & Magazines. France24 English, Sky Channel 513, 17 July 2014.

News & Magazines. France24 English, Sky Channel 513, 8 November 2014.

News & Magazines. France24 English, Sky Channel 513, 24 April 2015.

News & Magazines. France24 English, Sky Channel 513, 29 September 2015.

News & Magazines. France24 English, Sky Channel 513, 10 November 2015.

News & Magazines. France24 English, Sky Channel 513, 17 January 2016.

News & Magazines. France24 English, Sky Channel 513, 29 January 2016.

News & Magazines. France24 English, Sky Channel 513, 31 May 2016.

News & Magazines. France24 English, Sky Channel 513, 20 July 2016.

News & Magazines. France24 English, Sky Channel 513, 16 August 2016.

News & Magazines. France24 English, Sky Channel 513, 28 August 2016.

News & Magazines. France24 English, Sky Channel 513, 20 September 2016.

News & Magazines. France24 English, Sky Channel 513, 8 December 2017.

Newshour. Al Jazeera English, Sky Channel 514, 24 March 2013.
Newshour. Al Jazeera English, Sky Channel 514, 17 July 2014.
Newshour. Al Jazeera English, Sky Channel 514, 3 October 2014.
Newshour. Al Jazeera English, Sky Channel 514, 11 November 2014.
Newshour. Al Jazeera English, Sky Channel 514, 29 September 2015.
Newshour. Al Jazeera English, Sky Channel 514, 4 November 2015.
Newshour. Al Jazeera English, Sky Channel 514, 10 November 2015.
Newshour. Al Jazeera English, Sky Channel 514, 15 December 2015.
Newshour. Al Jazeera English, Sky Channel 514, 28 January 2016.
Newshour. Al Jazeera English, Sky Channel 514, 29 January 2016.
Newshour. Al Jazeera English, Sky Channel 514, 30 January 2016.
Newshour. Al Jazeera English, Sky Channel 514, 7 February 2016.
Newshour. Al Jazeera English, Sky Channel 514, 14 February 2016.
Newshour. Al Jazeera English, Sky Channel 514, 24 February 2016.
Newshour. Al Jazeera English, Sky Channel 514, 2 March 2016.
Newshour. Al Jazeera English, Sky Channel 514, 3 March 2016.
Newshour. Al Jazeera English, Sky Channel 514, 11 March 2016.
Newshour. Al Jazeera English, Sky Channel 514, 31 March 2016.
Newshour. Al Jazeera English, Sky Channel 514, 9 June 2016.
Newshour. Al Jazeera English, Sky Channel 514, 17 June 2016.
Newshour. Al Jazeera English, Sky Channel 514, 21 June 2016.
Newshour. Al Jazeera English Television, Sky Channel 514, 22 June 2016.
Newshour. Al Jazeera English Television, Sky Channel 514, 23 June 2016.
Newshour. Al Jazeera English Television, Sky Channel 514, 26 June 2016.
Newshour. Al Jazeera English Television, Sky Channel 514, 4 July 2016.
Newshour. Al Jazeera English Television, Sky Channel 514, 5 July 2016.
Newshour. Al Jazeera English Television, Sky Channel 514, 8 July 2016.
Newshour. Al Jazeera English Television, Sky Channel 514, 10 July 2016.
Newshour. Al Jazeera English Television, Sky Channel 514, 19 July 2016
Newshour. Al Jazeera English Television, Sky Channel 514, 21 July 2016.
Newshour. Al Jazeera English Television, Sky Channel 514, 24 July 2016.
Newshour. Al Jazeera English Television, Sky Channel 514, 2 August 2016.
Newshour. Al Jazeera English Television, Sky Channel 514, 15 August 2016.
Newshour. Al Jazeera English Television, Sky Channel 514, 22 August 2016.
Newshour. Al Jazeera English Television, Sky Channel 514, 29 September 2016.
Newshour. Al Jazeera English Television, Sky Channel 514, 17 October 2016.
Newshour. Al Jazeera English Television, Sky Channel 514, 19 October 2016.
Newshour. Al Jazeera English Television, Sky Channel 514, 14 December 2016.
Newshour. Al Jazeera English Television, Sky Channel 514, 16 December 2016.
Newshour. Al Jazeera English Television, Sky Channel 514, 22 December 2016.
Newshour. Al Jazeera English Television, Sky Channel 514, 4 March 2017.
Newshour. Al Jazeera English Television, Sky Channel 514, 12 October 2017.
Newshour. Al Jazeera English Television, Sky Channel 514, 17 December 2017.
Odion, Louis. 'Cameron: Fantastically un-Nigerian', Sahara Reporters, 30 June 2016,
     http://saharareporters.com/2016/06/30/cameron-fantastically-un-nigerian-louis-
     odion (accessed 3 July 2016).
PGI Intelligence. 'Congo, DRC: Decentralisation to increase transport and taxation
     costs in Katanga', https://pgi-intelligence.com/news/getNewsItem/Congo-DRC-

Decentralisation-to-increase-transport-and-taxation-costs-in-Katanga/562 (accessed 17 March 2016).

Radio Tamazuj. 'Soldiers breach UN base perimeter in Bentiu during fighting', https://radiotamazuj.org/en/article/soldiers-breach-un-base-perimeter-bentiu-during-fighting (accessed 25 February 2016).

Reliefweb. 'Malian armed groups sign peace deal', http://reliefweb.int/report/mali/mali-armed-groups-sign-peace-deal (accessed 8 February 2016).

Reliefweb. 'Joint Communiqué of the Quartet meeting on Libya', 18 March 2017, https://reliefweb.int/report/libya/joint-communique-quartet-meeting-libya (accessed 16 December 2017).

Reliefweb. 'Joint Communiqué of the Quartet meeting on Libya', 21 September 2017, https://reliefweb.int/report/libya/joint-communique-quartet-meeting-libya-21-september-2017 (accessed 16 December 2017).

Reuters. 'African Union says Burundi election not free or fair, Speaker flees', www.reuters.com/article/us-burundi-politics-africanunion-idUSKCN0P80YD20 150628 (accessed 16 February 2016).

Reuters. 'Bishops urge Congolese to reject third term for Kabila', www.reuters.com/article/congodemocratic-politics-idUSL8N13L2C320151126 (accessed 26 November 2015).

Reuters. 'Grenade attack kills child, wounds his father in Burundi's capital', www.reuters.com/article/us-burundi-attacks-idUSKCN0VN0EO (accessed 15 February 2016).

Reuters. 'Fighting erupts in two South Sudan states after latest truce', www.reuters.com/article/us-southsudan-unrest-idUSKBN0LE2FQ20150210 (accessed 9 February 2016).

Reuters. 'Malian rebel alliance signs peace deal with government', www.reuters.com/article/us-mali-rebels-deal-idUSKBN0P00PI20150621 (accessed 8 February 2016).

Reuters. 'Mali gold reserves rise in 2011 alongside price', www.sabc.co.za/news/a/65656d0049a2edb0a589ef9f13675c4c/Mali-gold-reserves-rise-in-2011-alongside-price-20120101 (accessed 22 February 2016).

Reuters. 'Mali Islamist group Ansar Dine claims attack on UN base', http://uk.reuters.com/places/mali (accessed 22 February 2016).

Reuters. 'Gunmen attack EU military mission HQ in Mali: one attacker killed', www.reuters.com/article/us-mali-attack-idUSKCN0WN234 (accessed 22 March 2016).

Reuters. 'Libyan government of national accord seeks arms', http://uk.reuters.com/article/libya-security-talks-arms-idUKZ8N156281 (accessed 18 May 2016).

Reuters. 'Burundi school sends home 230 students for defacing president's photo', http://uk.reuters.com/article/uk-burundi-politics-idUKKCN0Z02D6 (accessed 14 June 2016).

Reuters. 'U.N. to send peacekeepers home over reaction to South Sudan violence', http://uk.reuters.com/article/uk-southsudan-unrest-un-idUKKCN0Z900J (accessed 23 June 2016).

Reuters. 'At least 12 killed in fighting in Central African Republic town', http://af.reuters.com/article/centralAfricanRepublicNews/idAFL8N19R4JE (accessed 11 July 2016).

Reuters. 'South Sudan says probes any army abuses, executes two soldiers', 17 August 2016, www.reuters.com/article/us-southsudan-security-idUSKCN10S1R8?il=0 (accessed 20 August 2016).

Reuters. 'UPDATE 2: Two car bombs explode in Tripoli, no casualties', 8 September 2016, http://af.reuters.com/article/libyaNews/idAFL8N1BK1OG (accessed 10 September 2016).

Reuters. 'Libyan commander's seizure of oil ports risks new conflict', 12 September 2016, http://uk.reuters.com/article/libya-security-idUKL8N1BO33Y (accessed 13 September 2016).

Reuters. 'Congo's top court approves postponement of presidential election', 18 October 2016, http://af.reuters.com/article/topNews/idAFKCN12I0HC (accessed 19 October 2016).

Reuters. 'UPDATE 1: Mali Islamist militant leader announces unilateral ceasefire', 31 October 2016, http://af.reuters.com/article/commoditiesNews/idAFL8N1D1 3II?sp=true (accessed 1 November 2016).

Reuters. 'Bomb attack kills child, wounds 32 Indian peacekeepers in east Congo: UN', 8 November 2016, www.reuters.com/article/us-congo-un-idUSKBN1 330NV (accessed 8 November 2016).

Reuters. 'Kenya withdraws first batch of troops from U.N. South Sudan mission', 9 November 2016, http://uk.reuters.com/article/uk-southsudan-un-idUKKB N13426Q?il=0 (accessed 11 November 2016).

Reuters. 'U.S. proposes U.N. arms embargo on South Sudan, sanctions', 18 November 2016, www.reuters.com/article/us-southsudan-security-un-idUSKBN13C2P6 (accessed 19 November 2016).

Reuters. 'Donors pledge 2 billion euros for Central African Republic', 17 November 2016, www.reuters.com/article/us-centralafrica-conference-idUSKBN13C282 (accessed 19 November 2016).

Reuters. 'Blast in Libya's Benghazi kills three children: hospital official', 21 November 2016, www.reuters.com/article/us-libya-security-benghazi-idUSKBN13G1BZ (accessed 24 November 2016).

Reuters. 'Mali's local elections marred by boycotts, kidnapping', 21 November 2016, http://in.reuters.com/article/mali-elections-idINKBN13G09E (accessed 24 November 2016).

Reuters. 'Burundi president's aide survives attack, guard killed – officials', 29 November 2016, http://uk.reuters.com/article/uk-burundi-violence-idUKK BN13O0V1 (accessed 4 December 2016).

Reuters. 'Burundi says will not co-operate with UN investigation into violence', 24 November 2016, http://uk.reuters.com/article/burundiNews/idAFL4N1DP 3PA?sp=true (accessed 4 December 2016).

Reuters. 'U.N. identifies 41 Burundi, Gabon troops accused of abuse in Central Africa', 5 December 2016, www.reuters.com/article/us-centralafrica-un-crime-idUSKBN13U28H (accessed 9 December 2016).

Reuters. 'Angola's Dos Santos not up for re-election in 2017: party document', 2 December 2016, www.reuters.com/article/us-angola-dossantos-idUSKBN13 R2EZ?il=0 (accessed 9 December 2016).

Reuters. 'Troops and court needed fast to avert South Sudan genocide', 14 December 2016, http://uk.reuters.com/article/uk-southsudan-un-idUKKBN1430ZW (accessed 23 December 2016).

Reuters. 'Twelve soldiers killed in attack on Burkina Faso army post', 16 December 2016, www.reuters.com/article/us-burkina-attack-idUSKBN1451MP (accessed 26 December 2016).

Reuters. 'Burundi minister shot dead in capital – police', 2 January 2017, http://af.reuters.com/article/topNews/idAFKBN14L0VK?sp=true (accessed 5 January 2017).

Reuters. 'Deputy leader of Libya's U.N.-backed government resigns', 2 January 2017, www.reuters.com/article/us-libya-security-politics-idUSKBN14M13A?il=0 (accessed 5 January 2017).

Reuters. 'South Sudan rebels kidnap eight local aid workers – military', 13 March 2017, http://af.reuters.com/article/southSudanNews/idAFL5N1GQ27O (accessed 13 March 2017).

Reuters. 'Court delays trial of Burkina Faso ex-leader for protest killings', 27 April 2017, www.reuters.com/article/uk-burkina-trial-idUKKBN17T1MH (accessed 31 May 2017).

Reuters. 'France says soldiers killed 20 Islamists in Mali', 2 June 2017, http://af.reuters.com/article/maliNews/idAFL8N1IZ5M0 (accessed 6 June 2017).

Reuters. 'At least 22 dead in clashes in Central African Republic town – UN', 20 May 2017, http://af.reuters.com/article/topNews/idAFKCN18G0HW-OZATP (accessed 6 June 2017).

Reuters. 'Central African Republic's economy to grow by 4.7pct in 2017 – IMF', 1 June 2017, http://af.reuters.com/article/centralAfricanRepublicNews/idAFL8N1IY6IC (accessed 6 June 2017).

Reuters. 'U.S. wary of French push for U.N. to back Sahel force: diplomats', 8 June 2017, www.reuters.com/article/us-africa-security-sahel-un-idUSKBN18Z2R7?il=0 (accessed 9 June 2017).

Reuters. 'Hundreds of Fighters from Chad, Darfur feeding off Libya's turmoil – report', 27 June 2017, http://uk.reuters.com/article/uk-libya-security-report-idUKKBN19I2H9 (accessed 29 June 2017).

Reuters. 'NGOs file suit alleging BNP Paribas complicity in Rwandan genocide', 29 June 2017, http://uk.reuters.com/article/uk-rwanda-bnp-paribas-lawsuit-idUKKBN19K1IP?il=0 (accessed 29 June 2017).

Reuters. 'Burundi paralyzed by fuel shortages as leaders blame lack of dollars', 30 May 2017, www.reuters.com/article/us-burundi-oil-idUSKBN18Q1RN (accessed 6 July 2017).

Reuters. 'Grenade attack kills three members of Burundi ruling party', 18 May 2017, www.reuters.com/article/us-burundi-violence-idUSKCN18E1SL (accessed 6 July 2017).

Reuters. 'Burundi authorities purging army on ethnic lines: rights group', 4 July 2017, www.reuters.com/article/us-burundi-politics-idUSKBN19P1MA (accessed 6 July 2017).

Reuters. 'Al Qaeda-linked group claims deadly attack at Malsi resort', 19 June 2017, www.reuters.com/article/us-mali-security-idUSKBN1990TY (accessed 6 July 2017).

Reuters. 'Libya's eastern commander declares victory in battle for Benghazi', 5 July 2017, www.reuters.com/article/us-libya-security-benghazi-idUSKBN19Q2SK (accessed 7 July 2017).

Reuters. 'Tuareg separatists seize north Mali town in battle', 12 July 2017, https://uk.reuters.com/article/uk-mali-security-idUKKBN19X2CG (accessed 17 July 2017).

Reuters. 'Thousands march against referendum, extra powers for Mali president', 15 July 2017, www.reuters.com/article/us-mali-politics-idUSKBN1A00LH (accessed 17 July 2017).

Reuters. 'Congo's election head says presidential vote unlikely this year', 9 July 2017, www.reuters.com/article/us-congo-politics-idUSKBN19U0ZA (accessed 17 July 2017).

Reuters. 'Red Cross says six volunteers killed in Central African Republic', 9 August 2017, www.reuters.com/article/us-centralafrica-violence/red-cross-says-six-volunteers-killed-in-central-african-republic-idUSKBN1AP195 (accessed 27 September 2017).

Reuters. 'UPDATE2: Militants attack Congo basesin northeast, killing U.N. peacekeeper', 9 October 2017, http://af.reuters.com/article/commoditiesNews/idAFL8N1MK1VU (accessed 9 October 2017).

Reuters. 'Libyan military commander Haftar visiting Russia: RIA', 12 August 2017, www.reuters.com/article/us-libya-security-russia/libyan-military-commander-haftar-visiting-russia-ria-idUSKBN1AS0LD (accessed 9 October 2017).

Reuters. 'South Sudan oil conference fails to draw biggest energy firms', 11 October 2017, https://af.reuters.com/article/africaTech/idAFL8N1MM43F (accessed 15 October 2017).

Reuters. 'Islamist militants attack African military base in Mali, at least six dead', 29 June 2018, https://uk.reuters.com/article/uk-mali-violence/islamist-militants-attack-african-military-base-in-mali-at-least-six-dead-idUKKBN1JP243 (accessed 30 July 2018).

Rogers, Simon. 'Nato operations in Libya: data journalism breaks down which country does what', *Guardian*, 31 October 2011, www.theguardian.com/news/datablog/2011/may/22/nato-libya-data-journalism-operations-country.

RT. 'At least 65 killed in bomb attack on Libya police training centre', www.rt.com/news/328154-libya-police-bomb-killed/ (accessed 6 February 2016).

Se Young, Y. (2014) 'The Presidential System in Korea: Is It a Little Too Old?' *The Granite Tower*, 5 September 2014, www.thegranitetower.com/news/articleView.html?idxno=942 (accessed 21 December 2015).

Sudan Tribune. 'UN calls on South Sudan to respect status agreement', www.sudantribune.com/spip.php?article51036 (accessed 9 February 2016).

Sudan Tribune. 'President Kiir's 28 states are obstacle to peace in South Sudan: Troika', www.sudantribune.com/spip.php?article57794 (accessed 9 February 2016).

Tekle, Tesfa-Alem. 'South Sudan's Machar heads to Uganda to ask for help from Museveni', *Sudan Tribune*, 25 January 2016, www.sudantribune.com/spip.php?article57795.

The Citizen. 'Mugabe blasts SA and Nigeria at AU Summit', http://citizen.co.za/403464/mugabe-blasts-sa-and-nigeria-at-au-summit/ (accessed 12 December 2015).

The Daily Beast. 'Exclusive: UN Camp in South Sudan burned to the ground', www.thedailybeast.com/articles/2016/02/18/nowhere-to-run-to-in-south-sudan-nowhere-to-hide-not-even-with-un.html (accessed 25 February 2016).

The Defense Post. 'Eight Burkina Faso soldiers killed roadside bomb blast near Baraboulé', 26 September 2018, https://thedefensepost.com/2018/09/26/burkina-faso-soldiers-killed-roadside-bomb-baraboule/ (accessed 23 October 2018).

The East African. 'Gunmen kill 20 in attack on South Sudan UN base', www.theeas tafrican.co.ke/news/Gunmen-kill-20-in-attack-on-South-Sudan-UN-base/-/2558/2284652/-/8p0ejj/-/index.html (accessed 25 February 2016).

The Guardian. 'UAE and Egypt behind bombing raids against Libyan militias, say US officials', 26 August 2014, www.theguardian.com/world/2014/aug/26/united-arab-emirates-bombing-raids-libyan-militias (accessed 2 August 2016).

The Guardian. 'Egyptian air strikes in Libya kill dozens of Isis militants', 17 February 2015, www.theguardian.com/world/2015/feb/16/egypt-air-strikes-target-isis-weapons-stockpiles-libya (accessed 2 August 2016).

The Guardian. 'Thirty-six people are killed in DRC in "revenge" attack by ADF rebels', 14 August 2016, www.theguardian.com/world/2016/aug/14/thirty-six-people-are-killed-in-drc-in-revenge-attack-by-adf-rebels (accessed 14 August 2016).

The Guardian. 'Egypt hits Libyan terror camps again after attacks kill 29 Copts', 27 May 2017, www.theguardian.com/world/2017/may/27/egypt-hits-libyan-terror-camps-again-after-attack-kills-29-copts (accessed 6 June 2017).

The Guardian. 'Libyan rival leaders agree to ceasefire after Macron-hosted talks', 25 July 2017, www.theguardian.com/world/2017/jul/25/france-raises-hopes-of-deal-between-libyan-rival-factions (accessed 9 October 2017).

The Guardian. 'Libyan factions agree to hold elections on 10 December', 29 May 2018, https://www.theguardian.com/world/2018/may/29/macron-hosts-libyan-factions-in-paris-in-push-to-secure-elections (accessed 26 July 2018).

The Independent. 'DR Congo's tainted ex-police chief made national hero', 6 June 2017, www.independent.co.ug/dr-congos-tainted-ex-police-chief-numbi-made-national-hero/ (accessed 9 June 2017).

The Independent. 'Congo: 250 people killed in ethnic based massacres in the DRC, says UN', 4 August 2017, www.independent.co.uk/news/world/africa/congo-massacres-ethnic-conflict-250-people-killed-m-united-nations-crimes-humanity-civil-war-a7876266.html (accessed 29 September 2017).

The Observer. 'NRM doesn't believe in term limits theatre – Museveni', www.observer.ug/news-headlines/41196-nrm-doesn-t-believe-in-term-limits-theatre-museveni (accessed 19 December 2015).

The Telegraph. 'Rwanda ex-spy chief "murdered" in South Africa', www.telegraph.co.uk/news/worldnews/africaandindianocean/rwanda/10546528/Rwanda-ex-spy-chief-murdered-in-South-Africa.html (accessed 11 June 2016).

The Telegraph. 'US warns against travel to the Democratic Republic of Congo after UN investigators murdered', 30 March 2017, www.telegraph.co.uk/news/2017/03/29/us-warns-against-travel-democratic-republic-congo-un-investigators/ (accessed 6 June 2017).

The White House. 'Statement by President Donald J Trump on the Apprehension of Mustafa al-Imam for His Alleged Role in the September 11, 2012 Attacks in Benghazi, Libya Resulting in the deaths of Four Americans', 30 October, 2017, www.whitehouse.gov/briefings-statements/statement-president-donald-j-trump-apprehension-mustafa-al-imam-alleged-role-september-11-2012-attacks-benghazi-libya-resulting-deaths-four-americans/ (accessed 17 December 2017).

Thomson Reuters. 'Burundi expects econ growth, spending to pick up in 2018', 13 December 2017, https://uk.reuters.com/article/burundi-budget/burundi-expects-econ-growth-spending-to-pick-up-in-2018-idUKL8N1OD4C1 (accessed 19 December 2017).

Trading Economics. 'South Sudan Inflation Rate 2008–2016', www.tradingeconomics. com/south-sudan/inflation-cpi (accessed 10 September 2016).

Trading Economics. 'Burundi GDP', https://tradingeconomics.com/burundi/gdp (accessed 23 December 2017).

Transparency International. 'Corruption Perceptions Index 2015', www.transparency. org/ (accessed 9 March 2016).

Transparency International. 'Corruption Perceptions Index 2016', www.transparency. org/news/feature/corruption_perceptions_index_2016 (accessed 23 December 2017).

Transparency International. 'Corruption Perceptions Index 2017', Transparency International, https://www.transparency.org/news/feature/corruption_perceptions_ index_2017 (accessed 24 July 2018).

Transparency International. 'CPI Results Brochure 2017', https://www.transparency. org/news/feature/corruption_perceptions_index_2017 (accessed 24 July 2018).

Tubiana, Jérôme and Claudio Gramizzi. *Tubu Trouble: State and Statelessness in the Chad–Libya–Sudan Triangle* (Geneva: Graduate Institute of International and Development Studies, Small Arms Survey, June 2017).

UN. *Charter of the United Nations* (San Francisco: UN, 1945).

UN.Org. 'Half of the population of Central African Republic faces hunger, UN warns', www.un.org/sustainabledevelopment/blog/2016/01/half-the-population-of-central-african-republic-faces-hunger-un-warns/ (accessed 28 June 2016).

UNHCR. 'Aid appeals seek over US$3 billion as South Sudan set to become Africa's refugee and humanitarian crisis', 1 February 2018, http://www.unhcr.org/news/press/2018/2/5a7222da4/aid-appeals-seek-us3-billion-south-sudan-set-become-africas-largest-refugee.html (accessed 27 July 2018).

UN Human Rights Council. *Report of the Commission of Inquiry on Burundi* (Geneva: UNHRC 2017).

UN News Centre. 'Ban arrives in Burundi in support of UN efforts to resolve political crisis', www.un.org/apps/news/story.asp?NewsID=53287 (accessed 23 February 2016).

UN News Centre. 'South Sudan: Special investigation into Malakal vilence completed, says UN', www.un.org/apps/news/story.asp?NewsID=54289 (accessed 23 June 2016).

UN News Centre. 'South Sudan: UN peacekeeping chief says action will be taken on probe into Malakal violence', www.un.org/apps/news/story.asp?NewsID=54300 (accessed 23 June 2016).

UN News Centre. 'UN rights chief warns of violence re-escalating in Central African Republic', UN.Org, www.un.org/apps/news/story.asp?NewsID=54396 (accessed 5 July 2016).

UN News Centre. '"Time to massively reinforce UN action" on South Sudan, Ban says ahead of Security Council meeting', www.un.org/apps/news/story.asp?News ID=54434 (accessed 12 July 2016).

UN News Centre. 'South Sudan: Hundreds of children recruited into armed groups, reports UNICEF', 19 August 2016, www.un.org/apps/news/story.asp?News ID=54712 (accessed 20 August 2016).

UN News Centre. 'Ban names retired Dutch general to lead probe into South Sudan violence', 23 August 2016, http://www.un.org/apps/news/story.asp?news ID=54742&&Cr=south sudan&&Cr1= (accessed 24 August 2016).

UN News Centre. 'UN Security Council calls for immediate investigation into recent violence in DR Congo's Kasai region', 25 February 2017, www.un.org/apps/news/story.asp?NewsID=56243 (accessed 7 March 2017).

UN News Centre. 'UN opens international probe into alleged abuses in DR Congo's Kasai provinces', 23 June 2017, www.un.org/apps/news/story.asp?NewsID=57046#.WU1MJGetM98 (accessed 23 June 2017).

UN Women. 'Women mediators promote peace in Burundi', 25 January 2016, www.unwomen.org/en/news/stories/2016/1/women-mediators-promote-peace-in-burundi (accessed 7 June 2016).

UNDP. 'Human Development Report 2009'.

UNDP. 'Human Development Report 2010'.

UNDP. 'Human Development Report 2011'.

UNDP. 'Table 2: Human Development Index Trends, 1980–2013', http://hdr.undp.org/en/content/table-2-human-development-index-trends-1980-2013.

UNDP. '2015 Human Development Report', http://hdr.undp.org/en/2015-report/download (accessed 9 March 2016).

UNDP. '2016 Human Development Report', http://hdr.undp.org/en/2016-report (accessed 22 December 2017).

UNDP. 'Human Development Indices and Indicators: 2018 Statistical Update', http://hdr.undp.org/en/2018-update (accessed 20 October 2018).

UNOHCHR. *Assessment Mission by the Office of the UNHCHR to improve human rights, accountability, reconciliation and capacity in South Sudan: detailed findings* (Geneva: OHCHR, 2016).

UNOHCHR. *Report of the United Nations Independent Investigation on Burundi (UNIIB) established pursuant to Human Rights Council resolution S-24/1* (Geneva: OHCHR, 2016).

UNSC. *Resolution 1973 (2011)* (New York: UNSC, 2011).

Upfront. Al Jazeera English, Sky Channel 514, 10 June 2016.

Vanguard. 'After 36 years in office, EGuinea president wants new term', 11 November 2015, www.vanguardngr.com/2015/11/after-36-years-in-office-eguinea-president-wants-new-term/ (accessed 21 December 2015).

Vanguard. 'Libya: Nigeria votes in favour of no-fly resolution', www.vanguardngr.com/2011/03/libya-nigeria-votes-in-favour-of-no-fly-resolution/ (accessed 10 October 2011).

Verisk Maplecroft. 'Political Risk Index 2016', www.maplecroft.com/accounts/dashboard/ (accessed 9 March 2016).

VOA. 'DRC Political Dialogue Stalls Over Opposition Demands', 3 September 2016, www.voanews.com/a/congo-national-dialogue/3492400.html (accessed 10 September 2016).

VOA. 'Spiralling Violence in Central African Republic Isolates Neediest', 22 June 2017, www.voanews.com/a/spiraling-violence-in-central-african-republic-isolates-neediest/3912673.html (accessed 23 June 2017).

Wolters, Stephanie. 'Tanzanian-led anti rebel force in DRC given teeth', *Mail & Guardian*, 15 February 2013. http://mg.co.za/article/2013-02-15-00-tanzanian-led-anti-rebel-force-in-drc-given-teeth (accessed 17 March 2016).

World Bank Group. *Global Economic Prospects, June 2018: The Turning of the Tide?* (Washington, DC: World Bank Group, 2018).

World Health Organization (WHO). 'Dengue Fever – Burkina Faso', 18 November 2016, www.who.int/csr/don/18-november-2016-dengue-burkina-faso/en/ (accessed 5 January 2017).

Yahoo News. '11 soldiers killed in attack on Mali camp: government', http://news.yahoo.com/10-soldiers-killed-attack-mali-camp-military-112548040.html (accessed 8 February 2016).

Yahoo News. 'South Sudan rebels split, reject peace efforts', http://news.yahoo.com/south-sudan-rebels-split-reject-peace-efforts-145538680.html (accessed 19 March 2016).

INDEX